What Church and Denominational Leaders Are Saying

"A stunningly good work. *Participating in God's Mission* will be an instant classic. This volume offers a sweeping commentary on American church missiology . . . with a cogent analysis and synthesis of historical trends."

— REGGIE MCNEAL
Senior Fellow at Leadership Network,
City Coach at Good Cities

"For twenty years we have been hearing missiologists say, 'We need a missiology of American culture.' *Participating in God's Mission* is the best example I know of a book that provides that vision."

— DR. WILLIAM R. BURROWS
Managing Editor Emeritus,
Orbis Books

"The call to develop a new missiology beyond 'Euro-tribal faith traditions' is a hopeful and life-giving invitation for the church in the United States as we embrace a new Pentecost after Christendom. . . . This is the perfect resource to assist current and future Christian leaders to find their way forward in unknown and changing times."

— THE RT. REV. IAN T. DOUGLAS
Bishop Diocesan,
Episcopal Church in Connecticut

"I work with many congregations that are seeking a fix for their current challenges by focusing on the who, what, and how of ministry. Van Gelder and Zscheile remind us that we need to begin by exploring the why, namely the reason we even have congregations: to engage in God's mission."

— BISHOP PAUL D. ERICKSON
Greater Milwaukee Synod ELCA

"There are plenty of books about the American religious experience and a growing number of resources reviewing missional ecclesiology. *Participating in God's Mission* has given us both. . . . A rich gift to those willing to risk letting go of the structures and assumptions of today's church to respond to the call to participate in God's ongoing mission."

> — REV. DR. BETSY MILLER
> *President,*
> *Provincial Elders' Conference,*
> *Moravian Church Northern Province*

"This book challenges us to reframe the primary missiological question from 'What is the relationship between the church and culture?' to 'What is the relationship between gospel and culture?' It gives us some clear direction as well as nourishing 'bread for the journey' into the future God has for the church in America."

> — REV. DR. T. MARK VERDER
> *General Presbyter/Stated Clerk,*
> *Providence Presbytery, PCUSA*

"An ambitious book that digs deeply into the history and theological development of American churches. This is a wise guide for churches that seek to understand how we have arrived in this place. For years, I have been awaiting a book of this sort, and I am eager to share it with others who care about the health and future of God's people."

> — C. CHRISTOPHER SMITH
> *Founding Editor,*
> The Englewood Review of Books

"A highly readable and informative book that is illuminating in its explanation of the history of mission in America, challenging in its analysis of the crisis facing the church today, and hopeful in reminding the reader that the Spirit continues to be at work in the world. I recommend this book for discussion and reflection to lay and clergy, denominational and congregational leaders."

> — BISHOP ANDREW TAYLOR
> *Pacifica Synod, ELCA*

"This is a one-of-a-kind book. The historical analysis of the American church alone is worth the price of the book, but the perceptive missiological lens and the pointers for a faithful and fruitful future make *Participating in God's Mission* a must-read for any professor, pastor, or leader interested in the state of the church today."

— Dr. John Wagenveld
President,
Multiplication Network Ministries

"Throughout history, Christians have had a compelling gospel message to proclaim. In this carefully researched look at the church in America and its 21st-century mission with its 'great unraveling,' its 'dones' and 'nones,' we are challenged to listen deeply to what the Spirit of God might be speaking to this moment."

— Nancy Park Hungerford
Retired Executive Director of Natchez Children's Services

"For too long we have thought of mission as something an elite group of people do 'over there.' But mission is central to the character of God and the life of the local church. This book helps to rectify that, casting a historically informed and theologically robust vision for a faithful way forward—a way that church leaders of all stripes will benefit from enormously."

— J. R. Rozko
Missio Alliance

What Theological Educators Are Saying

"How did we get here? With appreciation for the times and a desire to be discerning, the authors provide key themes, events, demographic shifts, and theological underpinnings for helping church leaders at all levels become better equipped to bear witness to the active presence of the triune God who is still at work! If you are looking for a compass to the future, here is one to use!"

— Rev. Julius T. Medenblik
President of Calvin Theological Seminary

"There is nothing like this book on the market today. For many years, I've longed for a book that surveyed the history of congregational forms of life in the US. These authors demonstrate how urgent that need is. I will recommend this book to regional church leaders and incoming seminarians. . . . It will orient them well to the world in which they are called to lead."

— Dr. Gary Peluso-Verdend
President and Associate Professor of Practical Theology,
Phillips Theological Seminary

"The authors brilliantly provide a rare gift with their wise, gracious, and hopeful integration of missional theology and practice. With prophetic, pastoral, and practical sensitivities, they succinctly articulate a mature missional ecclesiology, astutely assess the Christian church in its American context, and boldly advocate a courageous engagement between gospel and culture."

— James H. Furr, PhD
President and Professor of Church and Culture,
Houston Graduate School of Theology

"From the day I first heard the gospel proclaimed as a college student on the sands of Daytona Beach, Florida, I have given myself to helping and urging the body of Christ to participate with the Spirit of God in witness to the world. If I had had this brilliant piece earlier, I would have done it much better. I have it now and I will put it to use! I urge every reader to join me in the same!"

— Dr. Timothy Brown
President and Henry Bast Professor of Preaching,
Western Theological Seminary

"An in-depth study and an invaluable missiological framework for responding to the profound changes and unravelings experienced by the church in the United States today. Following an insightful analysis of the various public missiologies throughout its history, the authors offer a solid theological missiology for the US church to engage its own context in the 21st century."

— Dr. Roger Schroeder
Louis J. Luzbetak, SVD,
Professor of Mission and Culture,
Catholic Theological Union

"An invaluable guide to faithful Christian witness for the contemporary American church during the 'great unraveling.' This timely publication traces the history of the church in America as it has grappled with its self-understanding and mission. The authors provide the reader with a very hopeful and helpful theological missiology for today that addresses the challenges of the church in a pluralist, post-establishment America."

— DR. BONNIE SUE LEWIS
Professor of Mission and World Christianity,
University of Dubuque Theological Seminary

"This book advances the missional church conversation in a variety of ways. To my knowledge, it is the only 'missional church book' that takes into account the Euro-American churches' interaction with Native- and African-Americans as part of their historical overview. Their proposal for a new missiology in the United States takes seriously the diversifying of the American landscape."

— DR. AL TIZON
Associate Professor of Missional and Global Leadership,
North Park Theological Seminary,
and Executive Minister of Serve Globally,
Evangelical Covenant Church

"A very thoughtful and useful volume that should be read by all Christian leaders interested in a flourishing future for Christianity in America. The authors examine the past and present of how the Christian faith has been incarnated in American culture, and provide insightful analyses and pointed suggestions for the future. This volume contributes substantially to the ongoing discussions of Christianity in America."

— DR. MARK GRANQUIST
Associate Professor of the History of Christianity,
Luther Seminary

"The authors challenge the reader to dig deep within American church history to reclaim a useable past, to use their own words. Their approach of 'abiding, listening, and accompanying' offers a needed corrective to the church's over-reliance on traditional hierarchical structures and leadership models. As a Roman Catholic theologian and scholar, I believe this offers great hope for the abundance of a Spirit-led church."

> — DR. EMILY A. DYKMAN
> *Chair and Associate Professor of Religious Studies,*
> *Viterbo University (WI)*

"A masterful study that is prophetic and hopeful. Integrating historical, theological, and cultural analyses, the authors discern how Christian communities might faithfully participate in the Spirit's movement in America today. They help the church to recontextualize the gospel by exposing the assumptions of the church's organizational forms, missiologies, and formation of leaders utilized in the past."

> — DR. DAVID RYLAARSDAM
> *Professor of the History of Christianity and Worship,*
> *Calvin Theological Seminary*

What Local Church Pastors Are Saying

"A timely addition to the missional theological conversation in America. The authors provide a historical context unlike anything I have seen in other books. They end with a hopeful prescription of what could be, suggesting a posture of a theologically sound, eminently practical missiology. This book is required reading for missional scholars and pastor-theologians alike."

> — REV. DR. TANNER SMITH
> *Lead Pastor,*
> *Harbor Life Church RCA (MI)*

"Essential reading for pastors, church leadership teams, teachers, and students. This book traces the evolution of missionary approaches in different eras of US history and frames critical questions for Christian leaders in America today. The authors invite the church to rediscover its missional identity by discerning the Spirit's agency, embracing incarnational ministry, and joining God's mission for the life of the world."

— Rev. Dr. David Carlson
Pastor,
Gloria Dei Lutheran Church ELCA (MN)

"The church's privileged place in society has frayed as it now navigates decline in the midst of significant shifts in today's world. The authors challenge the church both to consider how we got here and to engage present opportunities. These opportunities embolden the church to respond to the promise that our missional, triune God is faithful and will weave together our future."

— Rev. Dr. Sarah Cordray
Pastor,
Luther Memorial ELCA (NE)

"This is the book missional practitioners like me have been waiting for. Highly, highly recommended! It provides decisive analysis of what is going on inside and outside the church, posits why this is happening, and describes what can happen if we focus first on God's mission. The authors, missiologists from two different generations, have given hopeful direction for leading us into God's future."

— Rev. Dr. Philip J. Reed
Pastor/Head of Staff,
Grosse Ile Presbyterian Church PCUSA (MI)

"The authors have provided a tremendous service to church leaders. Their comprehensive scrutiny of American church history offers a keen analysis of underlying American cultural narratives and shifts. Their vibrant goal of helping the church in America recapture its missionary nature is invigorating. I am thankful for this book that will help leaders to better empower their churches to participate more fully in God's mission in the world."

— Dr. Steve Cloer
Preaching Minister,
Southside Church of Christ (TX)

"We're not in Kansas anymore! This book speaks directly to the most urgent issues our congregation is facing. These authors use a missiological lens to interpret and develop a framework for understanding the past of the American church and then create vital pathways for the future! We need to stop trying to fix the church—enough with technical changes! It is time for engaging in adaptive changes that align the identity of the church with God's mission."

— Rev. Dr. David Werner
Pastor,
Forest Hills United Methodist Church, Forest Lake, MN

"So much of what I was trained to do as a pastor is counterproductive in today's congregations. Rather than merely offering another negative diagnosis, this book provides a missiological lens that focuses on the heart of our call as Christians, providing new insights into our past and shining an invigorating light on a path forward as we follow Jesus into our neighborhoods and communities."

— The Very Rev. Stephen Carlsen
Dean of Christ Church Cathedral,
Episcopal, Indianapolis

THE GOSPEL AND OUR CULTURE SERIES

A series to foster the missional encounter of the gospel
with North American culture

John R. Franke
Series Editor

• •

Recently Published

Michael W. Goheen, ed., *Reading the Bible Missionally*

Stefan Paas, *Church Planting in the Secular West:
Learning from the European Experience*

Darrell L. Guder, *Called to Witness: Doing Missional Theology*

Michael J. Gorman, *Becoming the Gospel: Paul, Participation, and Mission*

George R. Hunsberger, *The Story That Chooses Us:
A Tapestry of Missional Vision*

For a complete list of published volumes in this series, see the back of the book.

Participating in God's Mission

A Theological Missiology for the Church in America

Craig Van Gelder and Dwight J. Zscheile

WILLIAM B. EERDMANS PUBLISHING COMPANY
GRAND RAPIDS, MICHIGAN

Wm. B. Eerdmans Publishing Co.
2140 Oak Industrial Drive NE, Grand Rapids, Michigan 49505
www.eerdmans.com

27 26 25 24 23 22 21 20 19 18   1 2 3 4 5 6 7 8 9 10

ISBN 978-0-8028-7498-6

Library of Congress Cataloging-in-Publication Data

Names: Van Gelder, Craig, author.
Title: Participating in God's mission : a theological missiology for the
　　church in America / Craig Van Gelder and Dwight J. Zscheile.
Description: Grand Rapids : Eerdmans Publishing Co., 2018. | Series: The
　　Gospel and our culture series | Includes bibliographical references and
　　index.
Identifiers: LCCN 2017027356 | ISBN 9780802874986 (pbk. : alk. paper)
Subjects: LCSH: Missions. | Mission of the church. | Missions—United States.
Classification: LCC BV2061.3 .V36 2018 | DDC 266—dc23
　　LC record available at https://lccn.loc.gov/2017027356

*We dedicate this book to the church in the United States,
which exists in all of its diverse complexity and has continued
over the centuries to bear witness to the active
presence of the triune God.*

Contents

List of Illustrations

Tables

Chart

Foreword

It would not be hard to argue that the church in the United States is currently facing the most difficult and perplexing challenges in its history. This is not simply the result of changing circumstances. Change has always been part of the social context that invites the church to imagine new forms of proclamation, discipleship, and organizational expression in keeping with its calling to bear witness to the gospel of Jesus Christ. It is not that fact of change that presents the church with such daunting challenges, but its nature. The intuitions and assumptions of late modernity that have shaped the entire history of the US church have unraveled at high speed, producing a generation that, more than simply not sharing those intuitions and assumptions, is increasingly unaware that they ever existed. The speed of these tectonic cultural shifts, fueled by the digital revolution in information technology and social media, presents the church with a set of challenges unprecedented in its history. In this setting technical changes forged from the outlooks of late modernity are almost certainly doomed to failure. Adaptive change is required but elusive, particularly for a generation of senior leaders shaped by traditional ways.

It is in this context that the work of Van Gelder and Zscheile provides a significant and much-needed resource for Christian communities in the United States. While their analysis and discussion naturally arise from their particular embeddedness in what they describe as "Euro-tribal Protestant denominations along with the made-in-America denominations that were offshoots from them," they highlight and develop three aspects of a missiology for the United States that are vital for all Christian communities concerned with faithful witness and that should shape ecclesial formation as well as missiological theory and practice. In the midst of diverse particularities, churches focused on the challenges of bearing witness to the gospel in the midst of changing cultural circumstances will be contextually aware, missionally alert, and theologically attentive.

One of the particularly significant elements of Van Gelder and Zscheile's work is its focus on the particular context of the United States for the development of missiology. They explore the historical development and backgrounds that have shaped American churches and continue to exert influence through deep-seated and long-standing assumptions. Their analysis and discussion remind us that missiology, like all disciplines, is inherently contextual. All forms of thought are embedded in social conditions and bear the marks and influences of the historical and cultural settings from which they emerge. As an endeavor bound up with the task of interpretation, the discipline of missiology bears the marks of the particular contexts in which it is produced.

Van Gelder and Zscheile provide us with a missiology that both reflects the historical particularities of the US context and is geared to address the unique challenges of that setting. They also realize that in an important sense the American experience is pluralistic and multifaceted, defying a one-size-fits-all approach to mission. Their work invites Christian communities of all forms, sizes, and locations to be contextually aware of the particular circumstances in which they are situated and to respond in ways that are appropriate to those settings. This means that such work is always ongoing since the situation into which the church proclaims the message of the gospel is constantly changing. Missiology assists the church in the proclamation and application of its message in the varied and shifting contexts of changing neighborhoods and communities. Van Gelder and Zscheile invite churches to a deep and appreciative awareness of their particular social and cultural contexts that is vital to the work of mission and gospel witness.

This contextual awareness will translate into missional alertness for communities that are centered on mission. In their development of a missiology for US churches, Van Gelder and Zscheile point to a mission-centeredness that is consistent with ecumenical witness and vital for the future of the church. One of the central developments in ecumenical conversation is the broad consensus that the mission of the church finds its rationale in *missio Dei*, the mission of God. While the specific connection between the mission of God and the mission of the church remains the subject of much debate, this consensus points to two important conclusions:

first, that God, by God's very nature, is a missionary God; and second, that the church of this missionary God must therefore be a missionary church.

For Van Gelder and Zscheile, this means that Christian communities are called to participate in the mission of the triune God and to cultivate a mission-centeredness that corresponds to this primary calling. Communities that find their reason for being in the mission of God will become increasingly alert to the challenges and opportunities for gospel proclamation and Christian witness as they grow in their awareness of their local settings. This is what it means to be sent into the world as the followers of Jesus who are called to participate in the mission of God as a sign, instrument, and foretaste of the kingdom of God.

This means that the agency of God is the critical lens for developing an understanding of the participation of the church in mission. The focus is not so much on the mission of the church as it is on the participation of the church in the mission of God. Framing the matter in this way moves the conversation on mission from its more common associations with practical ministry concerns, though these remain important, to a more expressly theological framework. For Van Gelder and Zscheile, this theological approach to mission means shifting the conversation away from its traditional framing of the relationship between the church and culture to the more basic relationship between the gospel and culture. They maintain that, while the former was well intentioned, it had the result of leading to endless efforts to change the church in order to engage a changing culture, often to the detriment of distinctive gospel witness.

Van Gelder and Zscheile urge a more theological approach to mission that underscores the primacy of God in the outworking of mission in the world and calls on communities to be increasingly attentive theologically as they discern what the Spirit is saying to the church. This is crucial to the future of the missional conversation that has become seemingly ubiquitous in churches and seminaries. One of the questions people frequently ask about this conversation and movement concerns its long-term significance. Is it really as significant as some claim or is it simply the latest fad for church growth? Certainly many have come to see it as the latter. From my perspective, its future depends on the sort of robust theological framings offered by Van Gelder and Zscheile. Where these theological impulses are developed and followed I believe the conversation concerning the missional turn is just beginning. Where they are not followed the discussion becomes simply another in a seemingly endless series of hopeful strategies for renewal that will be viewed by many as having "jumped the shark" more than a few years ago.

Participating in God's Mission makes an important contribution to the discipline of missiology that will be much discussed in the days ahead. It deserves to be widely read and studied in the lecture halls and seminar rooms of colleges, seminaries, and graduate schools. However, I believe its potential impact is even greater and more significant in the life of the church called to participate in the mission of God in the United States and throughout the world. I hope it will be read and discussed widely in ecclesial settings and its conclusions prayed over and implemented by those in the church who are committed to forming Christian communities that are contextually aware, missionally alert, and theologically attentive for the sake of the gospel and the sake of the world. The future of the church in the United States depends on it.

JOHN R. FRANKE
Theologian in Residence, Second
Presbyterian Church, Indianapolis
General Coordinator, Gospel and Our
Culture Network, North America

Acknowledgments

A book of this kind, which draws on so many disciplines and summarizes a long period of history, is always challenging in terms of what to include and how much to say. We were greatly served in our efforts to strengthen the argument of this book by the robust feedback we received from the many colleagues who agreed to read and critique an advance copy of the manuscript. We take full responsibility for the final version of the manuscript, but we want these early readers to know how much they aided us with their suggestions.

We want to thank, in particular, a number of missiologists who read the manuscript. Stephen Bevans offered invaluable suggestions from a Roman Catholic perspective. Gregory Leffel provided a very helpful critique for better focusing the overall argument we are making. Alan Roxburgh offered constructive ideas for keeping congregations as a primary focus. Ed Stetzer assisted in shaping the intent of the book with respect to the various audiences we hope will read it.

Mission historian Dana Robert not only offered her own invaluable suggestions, but in the fall of 2016 she invited her doctoral seminar at Boston University to read, discuss, and respond to the manuscript. These students, from diverse faith traditions, provided their own rich feedback. We're especially grateful to Anika Fast, William Green, Alex Mayfield, and Michael Rossman, SJ, who shared detailed thoughts.

Our Luther Seminary colleague and church historian Mark Granquist also offered helpful historical suggestions. In addition, the following former PhD and DMin students from Luther Seminary read the manuscript and provided numerous constructive suggestions, along with some careful editing assistance: Michael Binder, David Carlson, Steve Cloer, Scott Hagley, Harvey Kwiyani, and Tanner Smith.

The research and writing was conducted during a sabbatical leave for Dwight, for which he is grateful to Luther Seminary. As always, we thank our wives, Barbara and Blair, for their support and encouragement.

Introduction

The first decades of the twenty-first century are experiencing a period of profound change in the cultural landscape of the United States, and this is bringing a profound change and challenge to the church as well. Of course, the cultural environment of the United States has always been in flux, and the church has been forced to adapt itself accordingly. This dynamic context has regularly created opportunities for new forms of Christian witness and organizational expressions of the church to emerge. But what appears to be new today is the extent to which the underlying assumptions and basic organizing framework that gave birth to the development of the American church now appear to be unraveling. This is happening in the midst of what in our time appears to be the continued unraveling of many of the assumptions and cultural expressions of late modernity. These changes represent two great unravelings taking place in our day.

This book focuses on this question: *What might faithful and meaningful Christian witness look like within the contemporary American context amid these unravelings?* To answer it, we must take up the dynamic relationship between the gospel of Jesus Christ and local culture in different times and places, as well as how the Spirit of God brings forth new forms of church even while it reforms existing ones. We reflect on the long, complex, and contested history of Christian mission within America over the centuries with a particular eye toward local congregations and their public witness. It is not our intent to offer a new history of the church in the United States; that story has been—and continues to be—told richly by others more qualified than are we. Rather, we draw on that historical record to take a distinctly missiological read on the church's engagement with its neighbors and the broader nation.

1

We believe that understanding the contemporary church's situation in a United States that is rapidly being transformed requires us to probe deeper roots. Contemporary American Christians are inheritors of a rich, but also problematic, legacy of cultural engagement and witness over many different eras. Making sense of our present time makes it necessary for us to know where we have been and reflects critically on how those contexts differ from today's. Heretofore, scholarly work on American mission has tended to pay more attention to American missionary efforts abroad and less to missionary engagement with Americans' own surrounding neighborhoods, towns, cities, and nation. There are good reasons for this that are embedded within the discipline of missiology itself.

What Is Missiology?

In simplest terms, missiology is the study of Christian mission. The church has engaged in mission for as long as the church has existed; but the actual discipline of missiology developed fairly recently. Interpreting the story of the church in the United States through the lens of missiology may not be familiar to many who read this book—for several reasons. The actual formal study of missiology as a discipline only began to emerge in the theological academy of the Protestant churches in Europe and America in the early 1800s, as the modern missions movement from the West to the rest of the world began to take root. The initial focus was on preparing persons to serve as missionaries in foreign lands. The teaching of missiology dealt largely with understanding and developing skills associated with cross-cultural missions.

The focus and actions of the churches in the West during the time of the modern missions movement were largely shaped by the expansion of the extensive colonial systems of the Western nations around the world. By the end of the nineteenth century, significant progress had been made in establishing and growing the church in many areas. But this collusion of missions with colonialism, whether by default or by design, was deeply flawed. There were two challenges confronting the discipline of missiology because it grew up alongside the modern missions movement.

First, the discipline emerged in the theological academy as a "practical" discipline, one that focused primarily on the practice of missions. This took place long after the theological curriculum in Western schools had already been firmly established around the core confessional doctrines hammered out during the Protestant Reformation in the sixteenth and seventeenth centuries.[1] Typically, missiology was located within the curriculum under the theological locus of ecclesiology (doctrine of the church) and was taught as something the church was responsible to carry out. This resulted in a failure of the discipline of missiology to develop sufficient theological rigor relative to the other theological disciplines, such as biblical studies, church history, and systematic theology; it was thus unable to achieve a sure footing on theological grounds in the academy's curriculum.

Second, foreign missions and the discipline of missiology developed largely in relation to the domination the Western colonial powers exercised over much of the rest of the world. When these systems were dismantled in the mid-twentieth century, both were critiqued as having relied too heavily on the church's privileged position provided by colonialism. In reaction, many seminaries and theological schools in the United States simply dropped the teaching of missions and missiology from their curriculum, especially those institutions associated with mainline Protestant denominations. Many evangelical seminaries continued to teach it, but they changed the language describing their programs from "missions" to "intercultural studies."

A Missiology for the United States

The modern missions movement largely shaped the development and focus of missiology with respect to the involvement of the churches in the West in foreign missions. It has been assumed that the Western nations were already Christian.[2] It is long past time for the focus of missiology to come home and engage explicitly the United States as its own unique mission location. The primary missiological conversation in the United States for too long has been about American churches strategizing and mobilizing to extend their reach to the broader world—that is, foreign missions. This book is an effort to study and analyze the missiological engagement

---

1. A system of seven classic loci drawn from Reformation confessions was used for systematically teaching the Christian faith. These included the doctrines of: (1) God; (2) Revelation; (3) Creation/Anthropology; (4) Christ/Christology; (5) Salvation/Soteriology; (6) Church/Ecclesiology; and (7) End Times/Eschatology.

2. Some traditions made the distinction between the church engaging in *missions* toward the rest of the world, while *evangelism* was to be practiced at home where the church existed within what was assumed to be a Christian country.

of the churches within America in their own context. Today, mission is understood as being from everywhere to everywhere, with every location being a mission location.[3] The old categories of "Christendom" (Europe) and "churched culture" (United States) no longer describe the complexity of Christianity in the world, especially as the majority church in the Global South continues to grow, and as Europe and the United States both become more religiously and culturally pluralistic. There is today a great need to take the context of America seriously as a mission location and to use a missiological focus to do so.

Despite the fact that the United States has not received adequate attention in using a formal missiological approach, the churches in America have all along functionally engaged their own changing contexts missiologically. These engagements, as explored in this book, are understood to be the "public missiologies" developed by the US churches in their long and complex history of missionary activity within their own neighborhoods, towns, cities, and wider communities.[4] This history of functional missiological engagements warrants critical scrutiny because many of these legacy public missiologies remain alive and influential in continuing to shape the relationship of the churches to the culture. For missiology to come home means that the churches need to delve deeply into the ambiguous history of Christian mission within what became the United States. It requires wrestling with the diverse theological traditions, social locations, and cultural expressions of Christianity in this land. It recognizes that mission was often experienced as both oppressive *and* liberating, as both coercive *and* creative. And it invites naming the operative underlying assumptions and commitments of the various public missiologies that shaped the church's engagement with culture at various points in American history.

3. This missiological concept was first introduced in 1963 at the Mexico City conference of the Commission on World Mission and Evangelism (CWME), which had been formed in 1961, when the International Missionary Council (IMC) was merged into the World Council of Churches (WCC). See chap. 6 below.

4. The emphasis on public theology and public missiology has been a rising trend over the past decade, as illustrated by the following sources: Robert A. Danielson and William L. Selvidge, *Working Papers of the American Society of Missiology*, vol. 3: *Public Theology* (Wilmore, KY: First Fruits, 2017); Haemin Lee, *International Development and Public Religion*, American Society of Missiology Monograph (Eugene, OR: Pickwick Publications, 2016); Miroslav Volf, *A Public Faith: How Followers of Christ Should Serve the Common Good* (Grand Rapids: Brazos, 2011); Kevin Ahern et al., *Public Theology and the Global Common Good: The Contribution of David Hollenbach* (Maryknoll, NY: Orbis, 2016); and several articles featured in *Missiology* 44, no. 2 (2016).

Introduction

A Theological Missiology for the United States

It is timely for churches in the United States to use an explicit missiological lens for engaging in their work. But it is also critical to reframe the primary question used in pursuing mission in a changing context. The focus throughout the history of the church in America, but especially so in the past sixty years, has been on the relationship between church and culture. This has led to seemingly endless efforts to change the church in order to engage a changing culture. That approach, while well intended, is fundamentally misdirected. The question needs to be reframed to a more basic one: the relationship between gospel and culture.

The challenge before the church in the United States today begs for a sustained conversation about the relationship between the gospel and culture in relation to the church's missionary activity. This reframing requires us to shift from starting with the church as the initiator of mission to starting with God as the primary agent. Beginning with God's mission and reframing the question as one about the relationship of the gospel and culture introduces God's agency as the critical lens for understanding the church's engaging in mission. This requires an understanding of the Spirit of God's activity both in the world and in the midst of the diverse and complex human reality known as the church.

In this book we argue that American life and American Christianity are experiencing a moment of major transition. This moment calls for a renewed and sustained conversation about the mission of God with respect to the church's missionary witness and engagement with the cultures and peoples that make up contemporary America. Many of the narratives and structures that have framed and organized our lives and the place of the church within that context appear to be coming apart. This is a time of uncertainty and challenge, but it is also a time of great opportunity.

In the midst of the disruption now taking place, the Spirit of God is still very much at work, even though we may struggle to discern where and how. There are no quick and easy answers to reinterpreting and renewing the church's identity and its participation in God's mission amid the massive shifts now under way. A faithful future will emerge only through drawing deeply from the Bible and Christian tradition, discerning what stories and structures to keep and which ones to leave behind, and then engaging in a plethora of grass-roots experiments in relationships of mutuality with our neighbors. Ultimately, this is a moment that calls for a missiological turn toward the triune God's life and love for the world, in which the church's identity and purpose need to be grounded. This is why we chose this title for our book: *Participating in God's Mission: A Theological Missiology for the Church in America.*

This book is also unique in situating congregations as a central part of the effort to understand the growth and development of the church in the United States. Much of the literature that deals with this story has tended to focus on the growth and decline of denominations. Our study includes a denominational perspective, but it attempts also to deal with understanding what has been happening to congregations over the many years of the church's history in America. It offers an explanation, in particular, concerning how the primary organizational expressions of congregations have evolved over time—as the context and culture continued to change—from neighborhood-geographic congregations to lifestyle congregations.

The Three Parts of This Book

This book is divided into three parts. Part 1 sets up, in several ways, the story of the church in the United States. The first chapter provides an overview of two great unravelings that appear to be taking place now and makes the argument that the church is currently in the midst of both a crisis and an opportunity. Chapter 2 explores more deeply the nature of missiology and how this book uses it as a framework for taking a missiological approach to understanding the development of the church over time in the particular context of the United States.

Part 2 provides a survey of the missionary history of the church in the American context with respect to five major periods of time in which the church developed particular organizational forms to engage in ministry. Each of these periods was followed by a time of transition in which the existing forms morphed to respond to new conditions and as new expressions of the church came into existence. As with any survey, limitations are required in dealing with such a broad and complex story. This book's intent in narrating the missiological development of the church within the context of the United States is hardly to be exhaustive. Rather, this narrative version of the story seeks to identify the various public missiologies the church developed in response to the prevailing cultural themes and demographic changes of the day. We focus on identifying the public missiologies that were used by the churches with regard to the following: changes taking place in the systems of congregations; the changing patterns of denominations; the development, use, and teaching of the discipline of missiology; and changes in theological-education practices for forming leaders for the church.

The final four chapters, which make up Part 3, move the story forward to the present day and the realities confronting the church in the contemporary American context. Chapter 8 provides a deeper investigation of the unraveling now taking place within society and within the churches, especially those that came out of the Euro-tribal faith traditions. Chapter 9 first offers a critical reflection on the legacy of public missiologies that were identified within the historical survey of the American church. It then proposes the key tenets of what a theological missiology might entail in order for the church to engage the contemporary American cultural context missiologically. Chapter 10 offers insights and guidelines, in light of this theological missiology, for the church to consider as it engages today in further developing both its organizational forms and its practices of leadership formation. The concluding chapter provides perspective on what the Spirit of God might be up to as the church attempts to navigate through the changes now taking place and as it seeks to discern a new future.

Two Ways to Read This Book

We would like to suggest that there are two ways to read this book. The first approach is to read it sequentially, proceeding from chapter to chapter. This approach allows the reader (1) to understand the need for taking a missiological approach to frame the story of the church in the United States, as well as what this entails (chapters 1 and 2); (2) to review the unfolding of this story through the five periods of time in the history of the church in America as the diverse expressions of various public missiologies were developed (chapters 3–7); and (3) to engage the contemporary context with respect to understanding the culture more deeply and developing a theological missiology to engage it (chapters 8–11).

But, for some readers, that approach might seem to take too long to get to the payoff of the argument this book is making. Such readers might better be served by carefully engaging the first two chapters to establish a missiological framework, and then proceeding to chapter 7, which takes up what has been happening in the last several decades. They should then follow that by reading the final four chapters, which offer a substantive perspective on how to engage our present context. After that, this second style of reader would find it helpful to reenter the historical narrative in chapters 3 through 6/7 in order to more deeply understand what has shaped and given rise to the present situation.

About the Authors

The primary purpose of this book is to present a proposal for a theological missiology that can assist the church in the United States to better navigate the complexities of the present terrain and engage the future. We are writing this book as scholars and as practitioners of Christian mission who have dedicated our lives to wrestling with the United States as a distinct mission location. We develop this argument from our own social locations and perspectives, which both overlap with each other and diverge from one another.

Craig holds academic doctorates in both missiology and administration of urban affairs/public policy. Ordained in the Reformed tradition, he spent decades as a theological educator and church consultant focusing on North America. Craig was an early leader in the Gospel and Our Culture Network and served as a member of the writing team on the seminal book *Missional Church*. He is the author or editor of eleven books on missiology and ecclesiology, all of which have a particular focus on Western cultural contexts. He retired from full-time teaching as professor of congregational mission at Luther Seminary in 2014, after having served sixteen years there, and having previously served for ten years as professor of domestic missiology at Calvin Theological Seminary. Originally, he was ordained in the Presbyterian Church (USA), but later transferred his ordination to the Christian Reformed Church, from which he is now honorably retired.

Dwight is an adult convert to the Christian faith who grew up in a secular home in California as a member of Generation X. He holds a PhD degree from Luther Seminary, where he is an associate professor of congregational mission and leadership. Ordained in the Anglican tradition, Dwight remains rooted within local church leadership as a part-time staff member of an Episcopal congregation in St. Paul, MN. He also serves as a consultant to congregations, church systems, and other organizations. Dwight has written or edited four previous books on mission, with a focus on Western cultural contexts.

We jointly drafted Part 1 of this book; Craig took the lead on Part 2; and Dwight took the lead on Part 3. For both of us, the challenges and opportunities of engaging in meaningful, holistic Christian mission in our time are matters not only of academic concern but of personal passion and commitment. We invite you to join in this journey of exploration of God's ongoing mission in the unique, complex, and diverse setting that is America.

As is perhaps inevitable in a project such as this, our book tends to focus on the traditions with which we are most familiar and in which we are embedded. In our case, that means the Euro-tribal Protestant denominations along with the "made-in-America" denominations that were off-shoots from them. Other traditions, such as Roman Catholic, Pentecostal, and the African American churches, for instance, deserve fuller treatments than we have been able to provide. Our hope is to contribute to a much larger conversation currently emerging in many places throughout the churches of America. This conversation needs missiologists to speak to it from many locations, perspectives, and traditions. We offer this in the hope that colleagues from many locations will add their voices for the sake of the church's faithful participation in God's mission in our time and place.

PART 1

DEFINING THE CHALLENGE

The first part of this book sets up the argument that is being made throughout the whole. It does so by introducing the significant changes that now appear to be taking place within both the culture of the United States and within the church in that context, and by developing a missiological framework for engaging this new reality.

Chapter 1 discusses the changes that are taking place today in both the US context as a whole and the church within that context. While life is always dynamic, there have been certain periods of time throughout the history of the church when disruptions and the scope and pace of change in the culture have contributed to substantive and systemic shifts within church life. During these periods of time, many of the core narratives and sustaining practices of the church are challenged and fundamentally changed. These are times in which what has been can no longer hold, but what is emerging is not yet clear. The church as we have known it, the church that was built up over the past four hundred years in America, now appears to be going through such a period of change.

The changes taking place are occurring, first, in both the denominations and their congregations that came into existence in the wake of European immigration (what we refer to as the "Euro-tribal faith traditions" in this book) and, second, in the denominations and congregations that were given birth within the new nation (what we refer to as the "made-in-America" faith traditions). This chapter provides an overview of these macro-shifts and also offers examples of what is happening today to congregations on the ground by relaying some stories of what lay leaders, pastors, and denominational executives are experiencing.

Chapter 2 develops a framework for engaging these changes missiologically. Missiology offers a vital lens for understanding what is happening—and for engaging it. The missiology developed in this chapter, however, does not begin with the church; rather, it begins with understanding the mission of the triune God. The conversation is framed in terms of God's mission within all of creation, where the church that is created by the Spirit of God is missionary by nature. In light of the incarnation of Jesus Christ, the church embodies the presence of God in the world and has the ability to come to a contextualized expression in every, and any, culture. The missiology framework we present argues that God's mission, lived out in the world through a Spirit-created church, bears witness to a gospel that is multidimensional. It relates to every dimension of life and comes to expression through a variety of redemptive strains and emphases.

We all live within a world of meaning consisting of multiple narratives. This chapter explains how a Spirit-created church and the multidimensional gospel that it proclaims has the capacity to both challenge and change the deep cultural narratives that shape our world of meaning. We provide examples of some of those narratives within the United States that have shaped and continue to shape our culture and influence church life. In this chapter we also examine how the church lives with the tension of either overcontextualizing the Christian faith or undercontextualizing it. We argue that there is an inherent dynamic that the Spirit provides the church to empower it to live within this tension: it is always forming even as it is always reforming. This chapter explains how this inherent dynamic given to the church by the Spirit lives itself out in relation to seven missiological capacities that the church possesses to help it navigate the challenge of being contextual without becoming either over- or undercontextualized.

CHAPTER 1

Why a Theological Missiology for the United States?

The Great Unraveling

The seventy-five pastors gathered for an annual judicatory clergy retreat had come from urban, suburban, and rural congregations of varying sizes in a Southeastern state. On the second day of the retreat, the senior pastor of one of the larger churches spoke up: "Can we name the elephant in the room? Our church is one of the largest and seemingly most 'successful' represented here, but what we're currently doing doesn't have a future. We've tried all sorts of things, but people aren't joining, participating, volunteering, or giving like they used to." Heads nodded around the room.

Others expressed a sense of weariness about pouring energy into efforts to sustain inherited patterns and structures of church life that seemed increasingly disconnected from their neighbors. A younger pastor wondered aloud, "What does it look like when there are no longer professional jobs for clergy here?" Pastors shared stories of meaningful connections with neighbors, but most of these happened outside of—and sometimes in spite of—established church programs and activities. These congregations had existed and thrived for decades, some even for hundreds of years. But many of them now seemed rather fragile as they faced a precarious and unpredictable future.

Over the past several decades, churches have experienced an era of rapid and unsettling change. We refer to this as a "great unraveling."[1] This

---

1. We are indebted to Alan Roxburgh for the metaphor of "unraveling." See Alan J. Roxburgh, *Joining God, Remaking Church, Changing the World: The New Shape of the Church in Our Time* (New York: Morehouse Publishing, 2015).

includes both an unraveling of many of the assumptions and institutions of modernity within the broader culture and an unraveling of the church systems as they have struggled to adjust. From the 9/11 terror attacks, through the Great Recession of 2008–09, and into a decade that is being defined by random acts of terror, resurgent populism, and ever-increasing technological change, this new century has ushered in a deep sense of insecurity in American life and a new set of challenges for local church ministry.

Globalization and technology continue to disrupt established economic structures and diminish the middle class in the United States. A culture of individual autonomy that has been taken to an extreme trajectory has eroded many traditional structures, institutions, and ways of belonging. Immigration and changing demographic patterns have increased cultural, ethnic, racial, and religious diversity in American neighborhoods. And diverse voices and perspectives are increasingly being expressed within a democratized, participatory social-media culture that offers new kinds of connections. The nation increasingly finds itself splintered into cultural micro-tribes, fueled by the rise of social media. Common spaces and structures that once connected Americans are disintegrating amidst a new pluralism that celebrates and promises freedom, choice, and ease of expression but struggles to discover unity or foster communities of trust. Taking polarized positions without listening to one another is now pervasive. Cultural narratives that once provided meaning and cohesion are fraying or are being eclipsed, and it is not clear what will replace them.

A "great acceleration" of technological progress, following an exponential curve, has outpaced the capacity for people and existing human institutions to adapt.[2] People find themselves constantly caught off guard, as if the settled points by which to orient life had disappeared or were just now set in motion. Instead of occasional periods of disorientation and disruption, destabilization has become a constant state.[3] And many people experience this dizzying pace of change as overwhelming.

Churches and church systems are being caught in this unraveling alongside other structures and institutions in society. Long-established patterns and practices that worked for decades are now failing to connect internally or with the larger world. Many people, especially those in younger generations, are not joining or participating in church organizations and

2. Thomas Friedman, *Thank You for Being Late: An Optimist's Guide to Thriving in the Age of Accelerations* (New York: Farrar, Straus, and Giroux, 2016), 28–34.

3. Friedman, *Thank You for Being Late*, 35.

institutions as they used to do. Christian influence in the wider society has weakened and is contested. Questions of the church's identity and faithful engagement with a changing cultural context have become paramount. What was built up over the past several hundred years—and what churches have been trying to revision, renew, or restructure for the past fifty years—is now coming apart at the seams.

On the one hand, Christian witness within America has always been a diverse, dynamic, and complex phenomenon. The churches have always wrestled with changing social and cultural circumstances and have adapted their missionary engagements accordingly. On the other hand, the first decades of the twenty-first century appear to represent something of a turning point. The transitions now underway represent systemic challenges for many established forms of church life that were inherited from very different eras. This is especially true of the churches descended from European Christianity, which have played such a prominent role in American history—the Euro-tribal faith traditions.[4] Their legacy structures and standardized procedures, largely rooted in Christendom, increasingly are at odds with the changing and emerging cultures now present. The chapters that follow unpack these dilemmas more deeply. But before proceeding to tell this story, we find it worth noting at the outset some key shifts that frame the scope of the challenges now facing the church in the United States.

Population Trends and Demographic Shifts

Rosedale Lutheran Church was started in the early 1950s in a first-ring suburb on the edge of a large city. It was a typical suburban church of that era with lots of young families who helped give birth to the baby-boom generation. Typical of suburban churches of that period, Rosedale peaked in membership growth in the early 1980s and began a slow decline, a decline that has become increasingly precipitous in the early decades of the twenty-first century. Sociologically speaking, many families, as they experienced the "empty nest," moved out to second- and third-ring suburbs.

---

4. In this book we choose to refer to the Protestant state churches that emerged in Europe and later became denominations in the United States as the "Euro-tribal faith traditions." Their distinctive characteristics emanated as much from their particular ethnicities as they did from their distinctive doctrinal positions. These ethnicities had engaged for centuries in intertribal warfare. These faith traditions became denominations in the American context, and they also helped spawn the formation of other made-in-America denominations.

Some of these families continue to drive back to attend Rosedale, but these faithful few are becoming fewer and fewer each year. Quite a number of younger families bought the smaller starter homes that were left behind in the immediate neighborhood of the church; but the church is struggling to connect with those families. This is partially because a large number of these families are African American and Hispanic, and since Rosedale has been historically white, they just aren't connecting with each other. The congregation continues to struggle on by reducing staff and cutting programs to balance the budget; but the church council now realizes that, unless they begin to significantly change their ministry, the church will not survive.

This congregation is all too typical of what is happening today, largely the result of population changes. This book traces the patterns associated with these population shifts over time, as well as the changes occurring in the demographic composition of the American population that have also greatly impacted the church. We provide details of the history of the church in the United States in chapters 3–7 below. Here we simply identify a few of the more pronounced patterns that illustrate the unraveling of the key narratives within which the church in the United States functions.

Growing Population of the United States[5]

The population of the United States experienced substantial growth during the last half century, increasing from about 180 million in 1960 to over 320 million as of 2015. This represents a nearly 80 percent increase during that fifty-five-year period. Much of this increase resulted from changed immigration laws, beginning in 1965, that opened up increased flows of persons from Latin America, Africa, and Asia. The total population is projected to be about 400 million by 2050, which would represent another 25 percent increase, with a large portion of this anticipated increase of 80 million persons coming from continued immigration, especially from countries in the Global South. The number of foreign-born Americans between 2014 and 2060 is projected to grow from 42 million to 78 million, an increase of 85 percent. This presents a significant challenge and opportunity for many of the historic faith traditions in the United States, who built their membership primarily around white European immigrants from previous decades.

5. All population figures reported in this book come from documents published by the US Census Bureau. Its website can be accessed at: www.census.gov.

Changing Composition of the US Population[6]

As suggested above, a significant change is occurring in the composition of the population in the United States, partly as a result of increased immigration among people of color. But this is also due to lower birthrates among the non-Hispanic white portion of the existing population and higher birthrates in most communities of color. This is especially true in the Hispanic/Latino proportion of the US population, which was under 4 percent in 1960, but increased to 17 percent by 2014. It is anticipated that the Hispanic/Latino population will nearly double by 2060—to 29 percent of the US total. While the non-Hispanic white population is still projected to be the largest ethnic group in 2060, it is projected to become a numerical minority (i.e., under 50 percent) by 2044.

The growing population and the changes in its composition and life-style patterns have far-reaching implications for the churches in America. This is especially true of the predominantly white churches that have struggled to reflect the changing face of race and ethnicity in America. This becomes even more pronounced when we look at the religious makeup of the immigrants who are now coming. The majority of legal immigrants continue to be Christian, but that proportion dropped from 68 percent in 1992 to 61 percent in 2012. The religiously unaffiliated portion of immigrants has held steady at 14 percent; those affiliated with religions other than Christianity are increasing and now stand at 25 percent. The largest increases have come from Muslims (whose proportion doubled, to 10 percent, in 2012) and Hindus (7 percent in 2012 versus 3 percent in 1992).[7] America is not only becoming increasingly diverse in its racial, cultural, and ethnic makeup; it is also becoming more *religiously* diverse.

Changing Family Makeup and Shifting Economic Realities[8]

Marriage practices in the United States are continuing to change—with a smaller percentage of persons between the ages of thirty and forty-four get-

---

6. Source: Sandra Colby and Jennifer M. Ortman, "Projections of the Size and Composition of the U.S. Population: 2014–2060" (Washington, DC: US Census Bureau, 2015).

7. "The Religious Affiliation of U.S. Immigrants: Majority Christian, Rising Share of Other Faiths" (Washington, DC: Pew Research Center, May 17, 2013).

8. The source of this information is: http://www.prb.org/Publications/Articles/2010/us marriagedecline.aspx (accessed July 25, 2016); see also Pew Research Center.

ting married each year. For those in that age group, born and raised in the United States, the marriage rate has declined from 84 percent as recently as 1970 to only 60 percent as of 2007. Parallel to this shift, the proportion of children under age seventeen growing up in two-parent households (and parents in their first marriage) has declined from 73 percent in 1960 to 46 percent as of 2013. At the same time, the proportion of children under age seventeen growing up in single-parent households has increased from 9 percent in 1960 to 34 percent as of 2013. These shifts in marriage and family makeup represent a real challenge to many churches, which all too often continue to focus on the two-parent nuclear family as their primary feeder for membership growth.

Changing Church Patterns and Trends

Trinity Methodist Church is a suburban congregation located on the north side of a large metropolitan area. Recently, the committee on outreach gathered for its regular monthly meeting to continue an ongoing discussion about what might be done to attract more Millennials (those between the ages of twenty and thirty-five) to their congregation. The discussion had begun several months earlier, when it was observed that most of the young adults in that age range who were raised as children at Trinity were no longer attending. Two members of the committee who had volunteered to do some research on how other churches were dealing with this issue made the following report:

> Five area congregations that we interviewed are all experiencing the same problem with not being able to keep or reach this age group. But what we found is that there is a megachurch in the city currently attracting many young adults. It is named "Growing Edge," and has over 2,500 in attendance each week at its several services, with at least 1,500 of these persons being Millennials. We're not sure how to compete with that.

Changing Patterns in the Types of Congregations

One of the most remarkable shifts within the church in the United States relates to the various kinds of congregations that started up over the years. The basic pattern was the geographic-neighborhood congregation that served as the norm for the first 350 years of American church life, up through the 1960s: persons who lived in geographic proximity to a congregation participated in the life of that congregation. Over time, there were variations of this basic congregational type, which included ethnic-immigrant churches, village churches, city neighborhood churches, and suburban churches. But the basic logic of the denominational, geographic-neighborhood congregation was the same over many decades. Most of these churches were successful in their time largely as a result of reaching people living within geographic proximity of each other, persons who were usually either part of extended families or who shared a common ethnicity.

However, a fundamental shift in the logic of this kind of congregation occurred between the late 1960s and early 1970s, when massive disruptions took place within US society—for example, the civil rights movement, the countercultural movement, the Vietnam War and antiwar movement, the ecological movement, and the feminist movement. Congregations that had provided structures for community belonging and participation in a more conformist mid-twentieth-century America now found themselves swept up by waves of cultural change. The new reality facing the church was that relying on geographic proximity and denominational affiliation to grow the church had rapidly become obsolete.

These disruptions contributed to the rise of what we are calling the "attractional-lifestyle congregation." This type of church seeks to target and reach a niche market of the population amidst the breakdown of the geographic-neighborhood church. This soon became the norm in starting new kinds of congregations: for example, seeker-driven and seeker-sensitive churches, emerging churches, multisite churches, and social-network churches. An interesting pattern is that the life cycle of these various attractional approaches has tended to last roughly fifteen to twenty years, since each expression has become largely tied to an emerging generation.

Changes in Numbers of Adherents within Denominations

A dramatic transformation has taken place during the past fifty years in the United States in the relative membership of various denominational groups. The following chart of selected denominations indicates that a precipitous decline has taken place in the number of overall adherents in mainline Protestant denominations since 1971. It also indicates that there has been a substantial slowing of growth for evangelicals, Pentecostals, and Roman Catholics since 2000—after those groups showed significant gains between 1971 and 2000.

Table 1.1[9] Growth/Decline of Select Denominations, 1971–2000 and 2000–2010

Denomination	1971	2000	% Gain/Loss	2010	% Gain/Loss
Mainline					
Am. Baptist	1,693,423	1,767,462	+ 4.3	1,284,296	−27.3
Disciples	1,158,855	1,017,784	−12.1	785,776	−25.4
U.C.C.	2,271,432	1,698,918	−25.2	1,284,296	−24.4
PCUSA	4,694,440	3,141,566	−33.1	2,451,980	−21.9
Episcopal	3,024,724	2,314,756	−23.4	1,951,907	−15.6
U.M.C.	11,535,986	10,350,629	−10.2	9,860,653	−4.7
Evangelical					
Chs. of Christ	994,926	1,439,253	+44.6	1,453,160	+ 0.9
SBC	14,488,635	19,881,467	+37.2	19,896,279	+0.07
LCMS	2,772,996	2,521,062	−9.0	2,270,921	−9.0
CRCNA	208,965	248,938	+19.1	224,003	−10.0
Pentecostal/ Holiness					
Assemblies	678,813	2,561,998	+277.0	2,944,887	+14.9
Ch. God (CL)	368,798	974,198	+164.1	1,109,992	+13.9
Nazarene	869,831	907,331	+4.3	893,649	−1.5
Catholic					
Rom. Catholic	44,863,492	62,035,042	+38.2	58,963,835	−4.9

The denominations listed are, in order: American Baptists, Disciples of Christ, United Church of Christ, Presbyterian Church USA, The Episcopal Church, United Methodist Church, Christian Churches and Churches of Christ, Southern Baptist Convention, Lutheran Church Missouri Synod, Christian Reformed Church of North America, Assemblies of God, Church of God (Cleveland), Church of the Nazarene, and Roman Catholic Church.

These numbers reflect the increasing marginalization of the mainline Protestant churches. Those churches once played a central role in American Christianity; but now they find themselves diminished in adherents and

9. These data from the US Religion Census available at: http://www.rcms2010.org/com pare.php (accessed August 18, 2016).

overall influence as they struggle to connect with younger generations and an increasingly diverse population. Conservative-evangelical and Pentecostal churches surged in growth between 1971 and 2000, as mainline denominations began to decline in the late 1960s, due in part to a significant trend of people switching from mainline churches to evangelical ones. However, growth trends for many of these denominations have slowed recently or even begun to decline: Southern Baptists lost 4 percent of their membership between 2010 and 2014; the Assemblies of God have grown only modestly (by 5 percent) since 2010; and the Roman Catholic Church has shown a net loss since 2000 as increasing numbers of native-born adherents leave the church.

The Decline of White Christian America

It is helpful to break down this data by age and race to get a fuller picture of what is happening. Religious affiliation trends show a significant decline in white Protestantism in particular. Over the past several decades—from 1974 to 2014—Protestant numbers dropped: they have gone from constituting 63 percent of the US population to only 47 percent; however, this decline was disproportionately due to a decline in white Protestants. As recently as 1993, 51 percent of Americans identified as white Protestant; but that number had taken a steep drop—to 32 percent—by 2014.[10] Black Protestants have held steady at around 10 percent, while Hispanic Protestants have increased to 4 percent of all Americans. It is vital to note that both mainline and evangelical white Protestants are in decline as a percentage of the American population. White mainline Protestants decreased from 24 percent of the US population to 14 percent during the period from 1988 to 2014, while white evangelical Protestants dropped from 22 percent to 18 percent after a slight increase in the early 1990s.[11]

White Christians are also significantly older than other groups in the United States, as the chart below reflects:[12]

---

10. Robert P. Jones, *The End of White Christian America* (New York: Simon and Schuster, 2016), 50–51.
11. Jones, *The End of White Christian America*, 53.
12. Jones, *The End of White Christian America*, 48.

Table 1.2 US Religious Affiliation by Age, 2014

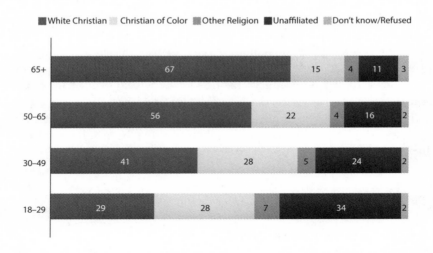

White Christian　Christian of Color　Other Religion　Unaffiliated　Don't know/Refused

Age	White Christian	Christian of Color	Other Religion	Unaffiliated	Don't know/Refused
65+	67	15	4	11	3
50–65	56	22	4	16	2
30–49	41	28	5	24	2
18–29	29	28	7	34	2

The median age of white Protestants in 2014 was fifty-three (up from forty-six in 1972), significantly higher than the median age of Americans as a whole (forty-six).[13] By 2014 there was no difference between the median ages of white evangelicals and white mainline Protestants.[14]

These snapshots of population trends and demographic shifts, as well as of church participation trends, illustrate some of the dramatic changes now taking place in the United States: the churches that long claimed centrality in American religious history—white Protestant churches—are being rapidly displaced by Christians of color (including Roman Catholics and Pentecostals), the unaffiliated, and adherents of other religions. But in order to understand the fuller implications of these trends, we must set

13. Jones, *The End of White Christian America*, 55.

14. The ten oldest religious groups in the United States by age breakdown are the following (oldest first): Presbyterian Church in America, Presbyterian Church USA, United Church of Christ, Anglican Church, United Methodist Church, Lutheran Church-Missouri Synod, Episcopal Church, Evangelical Lutheran Church in America, Southern Baptist Convention, and Church of the Nazarene. The youngest are Hindu, Muslim, Atheist, Agnostic, "Nothing in Particular," and Buddhist. Of note is the predominance of Euro-tribal denominations on the list of aging religious groups, as well as the prevalence of both mainline and conservative evangelical denominations. See Michael Lipka, "Which U.S. Religious Groups Are Oldest and Youngest?" (Washington, DC: Pew Research Center, 2016).

them in the context of an even larger transformation that is unfolding in world Christianity.

The Church in a Changing Global Context

First Christian Church had been in existence for over 150 years and is still located on its original site: downtown in a major city. First Christian has responded to many changes taking place over the years as the city has grown: for example, people moving out of the nearby streetcar neighborhoods to the suburbs in the 1940s and '50s, the dramatic shift in the role of the downtown central business districts in the 1960s and '70s, and the increased costs of maintenance, not to mention upgrades to its facilities to make them more accessible (required by law during the 1980s and '90s). But in the last twenty years, First Christian has faced a significantly different kind of change: the influx of large numbers of first-generation immigrants, many of whom are Christians. They are coming from African nations—Kenya and Nigeria—as well as an Asian country, Laos. An energetic and creative pastor at First Christian is attempting to lead the church into ministry with these new communities, but he is facing an uphill battle: many existing members do not want a change to their way of being church.

This congregation's experience illustrates well that American churches exist today in relationship to a world Christian movement that is also undergoing profound changes. These churches are reshaping many of the historical narratives within which the church in America has functioned for so long. It is helpful to review some of these patterns to appreciate the overall scope and significance of the shifts now taking place:[15]

- This past Sunday, more Anglicans attended church in each of the separate countries of Kenya, South Africa, Tanzania, and Uganda than did Anglicans in Britain and Canada and Episcopalians in the United States—combined.
- This past Sunday, more Presbyterians were at church in Ghana than in Scotland, and more in the Uniting Presbyterian Church in South Africa than in all of the United States.

15. As reported by Mark A. Noll, *The New Shape of World Christianity: How American Experience Reflects Global Faith* (Downers Grove, IL: IVP Academic, 2009), 20–21.

- This past Sunday, there were more worshipers at church in Brazil's Pentecostal Assemblies of God congregations than in the combined total of the two largest US Pentecostal denominations—Assemblies of God and Church of God in Christ.
- This past Sunday, more Roman Catholics attended Mass in the Philippines than in any single country of Europe, including the historically Catholic countries of Italy, Spain, and Poland.
- This past week in Great Britain, at least fifteen thousand Christian missionaries having foreign origins were at work evangelizing the locals; most of these missionaries were from Africa and Asia.

These examples point toward changes in the church around the world that have significant implications for the church in the United States.

The Rise of the Majority Church in the Global South[16]

The World Christian Database provides perspective on how many Christians there are in the world and where they are located.[17] These data include all persons identified in any way with Christianity, regardless of the character of their faith life; thus, these numbers also include nominal members. It is helpful to examine four decade marker points over time: 1900, 1970, 2010, and 2050. In 1900, Europe and North America had 82 percent of the estimated total of 558 million Christians in the world at that time. By 1970, that majority had declined to 57 percent, with the then slightly minority Christian church in the Southern Hemisphere just on the verge of becoming the majority. By 2010, that shift had become pronounced: Europe still had the largest total concentration, but now the North American church came in a distant fifth—following Latin America, Africa, and Asia. In one century, the Western proportion of Christians in the world declined from 82 percent to approximately 38 percent; and it is projected to decline to only 27 percent by 2050. The churches in the United States are increasingly living on the margins of the world Christian movement.

16. See Philip Jenkins, *The Next Christendom: The Coming of Global Christianity*, 3rd ed. (New York: Oxford University Press, 2011); Elijah F. Kim, *The Rise of the Church in the Global South: The Decline of Western Christianity and the Rise of Majority World Christianity* (Eugene, OR: Wipf and Stock, 2012); Sebastian Kim and Kirsteen Kim, *Christianity as a World Religion* (New York: Continuum, 2008); and Noll, *The New Shape of World Christianity*.

17. World Christian Database: http://www.worldchristiandatabase.org/wcd/ (accessed July 25, 2016); see also Jenkins, *The Next Christendom*, 3.

Changing Makeup of the Global Church as of 2010[18]

Another way to view the dramatic changes taking place is within the context of the various faith traditions. In 1910, the major Christian faith traditions in order of size based on membership were: Roman Catholic, with 47 percent of all Christians; Orthodox, with 20 percent; Protestants, with 18 percent; Anglicans, with 5 percent; followed by Independents, with 1.5 percent; and what are now referred to as the "Renewalists" (combined Pentecostals and Charismatics), with 0.1 percent of all Christians.

The changes by 2010 are palpable, especially with regard to the rapid growth of the Renewalists. As of 2010, this combined group of Pentecostal and Charismatic Christians had increased in one century from only 3 million in 1910 to over 614 million, which now represents 27 percent of all Christians worldwide. This was paralleled by the growth of Independents, from 1.5 percent in 1910 to over 16 percent in 2010—or 369 million souls. The Roman Catholic and traditional Protestant proportions remained relatively stable at roughly 50 percent and 18 percent respectively, while the Orthodox and Anglican proportions each declined somewhat. The composition of the church in the United States continues to change in reflecting these shifts.

A Changing Perspective in Light of These Global Realities

Redeemer International Church was started in a suburb of a large metropolitan area in the mid-2000s by Christian Nigerian immigrants. They brought their Pentecostal faith with them from their native country, and they are intentionally trying to evangelize their new neighbors, as they had back home in Africa. Some of those neighbors are also recent immigrants from various African countries, but most are white. Redeemer members are taking seriously their efforts to enact the biblical faith in their new home, a faith that regularly experiences manifestations of the Spirit by way of various signs and wonders. Most of the existing area churches have little contact with Redeemer International, however, and cast a wary eye on its evangelism efforts.

This congregation's life and ministry illustrate the changing shape of the world church and the rise of the majority church in the Global South,

---

18. Kim and Kim, *Christianity as a World Religion*, 5–7.

which are reframing how American Christians might imagine their participation in the mission of God in America. While many American churches
still participate in various forms of global mission, the tide of missionary
activity has turned. Increasingly, the West is being reevangelized by Global
South missionaries, many of whom are already immigrants to Western contexts for other reasons.[19] These missionaries bring expressions of Christianity that have been shaped by majority-world cultures. A dynamic encounter
is taking place between representatives of a rapidly growing world Christian movement based in the Global South and Westerners whose Christian
identity and practice has been diminished or lost. We provide a few examples of this encounter below.

Bearing Witness to the Gospel as a Minority Faith Community

The experience of many Christian communities in the majority churches
in the South is their living as a minority faith within their local contexts.
This reality stands in stark contrast to the experience of the Christian communities in the West that gave birth to the modern missions movement.
Christians in these Western countries once had significant population
majorities that led to a hegemonic worldview of being in control of the
sociocultural order—that is, creating a "churched culture." This history
of having domain deeply shaped Western Christianity, for both Catholics
and Protestants.

These Christian communities in the Western world, who have relied
on social and cultural privilege, have struggled with the issue of how to
engage their religiously diverse neighbors. Developing a genuine relationship with such neighbors invites—indeed requires—a reciprocity that involves mutual learning from one another. The long history of the American
church's assumption that it has domain and its exercise of cultural hegemony has often limited its ability to develop genuine reciprocal relationships with its neighbors who are different. Christian immigrant communities have much to teach the church in the United States about how to be in
mission with neighbors in a pluralist context.

---

19. See Harvey C. Kwiyani, *Sent Forth: African Missionary Work in the West* (Maryknoll, NY: Orbis, 2014); Jehu Hanciles, *Beyond Christendom: Globalization, African Migration, and the Transformation of the West* (Maryknoll, NY: Orbis, 2008).

Self and Community

There are deeply contrasting worldviews between the West and many of the cultures in the Global South, where the majority church is now located. The Western worldview is deeply shaped by the notion of the individual self. René Descartes's seventeenth-century maxim "I think, therefore I am" is often quoted to illustrate the fundamental logic of this concept of self. An operational individualism still lives deeply within American culture and continues to inform much of American church life, including its mission practices. In contrast, the common worldview of many cultures of the majority church in the Global South is shaped around an understanding of community and identity that would rephrase Descartes's maxim to: "We are, therefore I am." These perspectives start with a we when they view and engage the world, in contrast to beginning with an I, as demonstrated, for instance, in the African concept of ubuntu. Ubuntu is a personal identity based on togetherness in community, where the self is deeply interdependent with others.[20] Many churches in the United States are struggling today to cultivate a sense of community. They have much to learn from the immigrant faith communities.

The Bible, Spirits, and Pneumatology

There is a sharp contrast between how many of the emerging Christian communities in the majority church in the Global South read the Bible and understand the spirits and pneumatology, compared to many of the Christian communities in America. Historically, the Western emphasis, especially among Protestants, was on developing primarily an intellectual understanding of the faith that codified their biblical understanding into formal confessions accompanied by instructional catechisms. These various confessional traditions later came to organizational expression in the United States as diverse Protestant denominations.

In the midst of these developments, the influence of the Enlightenment made it increasingly difficult to read the Bible on its own cultural terms, that is, relative to a world of the Holy Spirit, spirits, and demonstrations of spiritual power. Many of those who are part of the majority church in the Global South have an inherent understanding that all of life is spir-

---

20. See Desmond Tutu, *No Future without Forgiveness* (New York: Doubleday, 1999), 31.

itual, that the presence and agency of spirits in the material world is self-evident.[21] They also have an understanding of the active agency of God in their midst through the Spirit of God. This worldview stands as a challenge to many American churches. It is striking to note that the rise of Pentecostalism in the United States represents a vivid counterexample to this trend.

The Marginalization of the Euro-Tribal Christian Faith Traditions

Central Valley Presbytery was considering trying to start a new congregation. Its recent experience with church planting, however, made this controversial. In the late 1990s, it had attempted to plant its last church, Community Presbyterian Church, using the traditional suburban strategy of purchasing land, hiring a staff, and launching a worship service. Initially, there was some growth as members from area congregations joined Community Presbyterian to help out. But after five years, many of these people burned out and returned to their home congregations; within two more years, the presbytery acted to close the church plant. The total investment made by the presbytery by that time added up to over $1 million.

The new debate was about what type of congregation to start and what strategy to use. It was obvious that a traditional church plant was out of the question—since the name "Presbyterian" just didn't carry much weight anymore. Some wanted to try to start an emerging church targeted to Generation X; others argued that such a plan was already passé. A few argued for a church/café strategy that focused on reaching Millennials; others wondered whether it would then really be a church. The Presbytery Council began to realize that many of the assumptions guiding their work just didn't fit reality anymore: the world had changed too much. The basic questions they began to focus on were: What is a Presbyterian identity? What does it mean to be Presbyterian in today's world?

The Rise of the Euro-Tribal Christian Faith Traditions

Most persons trained in American seminaries and schools of theology have learned to frame the story of world Christianity around a number of key turning points. They typically include: the persecution of the church in the

21. Noll, *The New Shape of World Christianity*, 35–37.

early centuries; Constantine's conversion in the fourth century CE; the divide of Eastern Orthodox and Western Roman Catholic churches in the eleventh century; and especially the Protestant Reformation and the Catholic Counter Reformation in the sixteenth century. These latter reformations represent a critical line of demarcation for most Protestants, as well as for many Catholics in both Europe and North America. The various Protestant Reformation faith traditions have their identity narratives deeply embedded in the events of the sixteenth century.

At the time of the sixteenth-century reformations, Christianity in the West operated from the premise of the Nicene Creed: that there was only one holy, catholic, and apostolic church. Both the protestors and the Roman Catholic Church worked from this same narrative, which raised the fundamental question: Which churches are true and which are not? The two *notae*—the pure preaching of the word and the proper administration of the sacraments—eventually became the Reformers' test for answering this question, at least within those Euro-tribal faith traditions that came to represent the Protestant magisterial reformation.[22] The protestors soon consolidated their theological convictions within a variety of confessional documents and accommodated their fragile movements to the cultural-political realities of their day to eventually form state churches.[23]

The Reformation confessions, which theologically consolidated the church, were paralleled by the consolidation taking place culturally and politically in the rise of modern nation-states, which, in turn, led to the formation of state churches. It is crucial to note that these Protestant state churches worked from the assumption of having social, cultural, political, and religious domain in exercising hegemony within their defined territories. Evidence of dissent from this understanding was present among the sectarian groups that challenged this view of the church from the beginning, including such groups as the Anabaptists, Quakers, Mennonites, and Puritans, all of whom paid the heavy price of severe persecution for their alternative views. But historically, this made the point that these Euro-tribal faith traditions that had emerged exercising hegemony as state churches in

---

22. David J. Bosch, *Transforming Mission: Paradigm Shifts in Theology of Mission* (Maryknoll, NY: Orbis, 1991), 248–49.

23. Examples of these confessional documents include: the Augsburg Confession (1530), Calvin's *Institutes* (1536), the Thirty-Nine Articles (1563), the Belgic Confession (1566), and the Westminster Confession (1646). The purpose of such confessions was to define what they believed to be *true*, and they used the confessions to defend their interpretation of the faith over against one another.

Europe were, in fact, fundamentally particular and thus not normative or universally applicable.

Various moves were made by later generations in efforts to overcome this reality, such as mutually affirming a number of historic creeds, or identifying various Reformation *solas* (e.g., *sola Scriptura,* etc.) that are held in common. But these approaches fall short of addressing the core issue: the inherent ethnically diverse and multicultural character of the Christian faith. This historical diversity has been made clear in such recent works as *Constants in Context* by Stephen Bevans and Roger Schroeder, as well as books by Andrew Walls, who was one of the first to label the sixteenth-century reformations as largely the "clan history" of Europe.[24] It is long past time for those of us in the West to recognize that the Euro-tribal faith traditions are, in fact, particular and perspectival within the larger Christian story. But it will likely take continuing voices from the majority church in the Global South joining this discussion before we can adequately turn the historiographical corner that needs turning.

The Rise of the American Version of the Euro-Tribal Faith Traditions

Evidence of the historical particularity of the Euro-tribal faith traditions became manifest when their diverse immigrants began to settle into the British colonies of what was eventually to become the United States. Coming from traditions of domain, some of these faith expressions, such as the Anglicans and Congregationalists, initially acted to establish a similar domain in colonies where they were the majority. But the seeds of the inherent diverse reality of the Christian faith sown in Europe quickly bore fruit in the colonial context. The solution for addressing this increased diversity of Christian faith traditions involved several important organizational developments. It is crucial to understand and assess these developments when we try to deal with the practices of mission and the development of the discipline of missiology in what was to become the United States. We discuss these developments in more detail in later chapters, but it is helpful to briefly examine three of them with respect to their influence.

---

24. Stephen B. Bevans and Roger P. Schroeder, *Constants in Context: A Theology of Mission for Today* (Maryknoll, NY: Orbis, 2004); Andrew Walls, *The Missionary Movement in Christian History: Studies in the Transmission of the Faith* (Maryknoll, NY: Orbis, 1996).

Separation of Church and State

One organizational development occurred in the aftermath of the Revolutionary War when the Founding Fathers agreed that the state and the church needed to be separated. This was codified in the First Amendment through the ratification of the Bill of Rights in 1791. No church was to be established by the state or infringed on from the state. This right enfranchised the Lockean ideal, which envisioned rational, autonomous individuals entering into a social contract to form self-governing organizations—similar to the assumptions underlying the US Constitution. The logic of this understanding was readily applied to the church in the United States, with congregations being formed on a voluntary basis and being governed by democratic church polities.

It is interesting that the Euro-tribal faith traditions with magisterial ecclesiologies and polities soon adjusted to this new understanding by amending the articles in their documents that dealt with magistrates having responsibility for the welfare of the church and managing its public order. The voluntary concept of the church became the normative operational understanding of the church. Subsequently, with the rise of the modern missions movement in the nineteenth century, this understanding was also spread throughout much of the world by missionaries sent out by the mission societies and denominational mission agencies.[25] With these developments, the notion of domain continued to function, but it was now a domain limited to particular faith traditions basically trying to exercise some kind of order among their own members.

Denominations and Mission Organizations

A second organizational development that emerged to address the complex diversity of faith traditions was the creation of the modern denominational form of church following the Revolutionary War.[26] There were

---

25. John Corrigan and Winthrop S. Hudson, *Religion in America: An Historical Account of the Development of American Religious Life*, 10th ed. (Upper Saddle River, NJ: Pearson Education, 2010), 132–39.

26. Craig Van Gelder, "An Ecclesiastical Geno-Project: Unpacking the DNA of Denominations and Denominationalism," in *The Missional Church and Denominations: Helping Congregations Develop a Missional Identity*, ed. Craig Van Gelder (Grand Rapids: Eerdmans, 2008), 12–45.

more than thirty denominations created in the newly formed United States by 1800, a number that increased to more than 200 by 1900, and hundreds added since then.[27] Most of the early denominations were formed out of Euro-tribal immigrant groups who shared a common faith tradition—for example, Presbyterians, Lutherans, Episcopalians, and so on. But they were quickly joined by denominations that were uniquely made-in-America. Many of these latter groups had strong Restoration tendencies in seeking to reestablish a biblical—primarily a New Testament—Christian faith, for example, Congregationalists, Christian Church (Disciples of Christ), and several strains of Baptists.

New structures emerged to engage in mission work as the modern missions movement came of age in the midst of these developments. In Europe, this included the independent mission societies that worked alongside the state churches. Similar independent structures were organized in the United States that worked outside or alongside the emerging denominations, initially organized as interdenominational mission societies. In seeking to maintain a highly competitive confessional identity, most of the nascent denominations had acted, by the 1830s, to bring this growing foreign mission work inside their structures by forming what became known as "denominational agencies."[28] All of these newly created structures for missions worked to spread Christianity around the world throughout the nineteenth and twentieth centuries. The Euro-tribal framing of the conversation has had domain in shaping the unfolding of this story for the past two centuries and more; but it is a domain that is now increasingly being either deconstructed or simply just ignored.

The Modern Project, the Rise of Corporate Culture, and the Postmodern Turn

The Enlightenment of the eighteenth century gave birth to what can be labeled the "modern project." This included the advances being made in scientific discoveries that were increasingly used to exercise control over the physical world. It also involved the coalescence of these creative forces with the harnessing of water and steam power to fuel the Industrial Revo-

---

27. Robert Wuthnow, *The Restructuring of American Religion* (Princeton: Princeton University Press, 1988), 20.

28. Bosch, *Transforming Mission*, 327–34.

lution during the eighteenth and nineteenth centuries. These developments required the creation of new forms of organizations that could arrange the work of the large corporations that were beginning to emerge—for example, bureaucracy as conceptualized by Max Weber.[29] They also required the creation of new ways of managing these organizations—for example, scientific management as proposed by Frederick Taylor.[30] All of these developments took place at the same time that Western powers were colonizing and dominating the rest of the world—politically, economically, and to some extent, culturally.

This same period of time saw the massive expansion of missionary work from the West, as thousands of missionaries were sent out by hundreds of mission societies in Europe, and faith missions and denominational agencies from the United States. The world mission conference at Edinburgh in 1910 represented the high point of this symbiotic relationship between colonialism and foreign missions. But this colonial system was gradually dismantled in the twentieth century, resulting in the mission enterprise in the field having to work more closely with national churches coming into existence, as new nations were formed from the late 1940s through the 1960s. This was the same time that the United States moved into world leadership politically and militarily, with its stand against communism, and economically, with the rise of multinational corporations. This was the same period when there was a resurgence of the evangelical movement in America.

The United States came to exercise a kind of hegemony with regard to power dynamics throughout the world during the last half of the twentieth century. Mission work, in general and from all traditions—but especially mission work among evangelicals—functioned within this hegemonic narrative of American influence. For the most part, the general values, practices, and assumptions embedded in US culture were largely accepted as being normative, with its fruits being used to promote mission work around the globe. The postmodern turn in the last quarter of the twentieth century began to challenge and deconstruct the validity of many of these assumptions, and with this shift in perspective, it has increasingly subjected the assumed superiority of Western culture to scrutiny.

29. Max Weber, *The Theory of Social and Economic Organization* (New York: Free Press, 1947).

30. Frederick Taylor, *The Principles of Scientific Management* (1911; Mineola, NY: Dover Publications, 1998).

This is at the heart of the gospel-and-Western-culture question that Lesslie Newbigin first raised in England in the 1970s, and which the Gospel and Our Culture Network focused on in the 1980s and 1990s in the United States. The critical question for much of the mission work that continues to come out of the United States at the beginning of the twenty-first century is: To what extent are we stewarding the power of the gospel, and to what extent are we basically relying on the power and privileges that US culture provides us in order to engage in mission? The extent to which it is the latter is the extent to which Americans will continually fail to understand the marginalization of the hegemonic influence of the United States in the world church with the rise of the majority church in the Global South.

Something systemic is shifting concerning the relationship of the historical Christian faith traditions in America with the now majority church in the Global South. World Christianity in the twenty-first century appears to be flourishing amid realities that are in some ways analogous to what the church experienced during its first several centuries. First, the world church is rediscovering how to affirm its inherent many-ness in the midst of its essential one-ness.[31] The rich diversity of the church today is almost mind-boggling; the reality of every tribe and tongue praising God is coming to fruition. Second, the global church is being repositioned geographically once more as a majority church in the Global South. This was actually the location of the churches that were in existence in the early centuries.

Recognition of these realities has reframed key narratives of the historiography being used to tell the Christian story. The Western framing of the story of the spread of Christianity as the "history of Western Christian missions," classically told by Kenneth Scott Latourette and summarized by Stephen Neill, is now being retold as the "history of the world Christian movement" by authors such as Dale Irvin and Scott Sunquist.[32] This shift is a clear marker that the lens for framing the Christian story has fundamentally changed. The lens now requires a more holistic crafting that accounts for the growing influence of the majority church in the South and incorpo-

---

31. The early church was very diverse, including traditions that were quasi Jewish, Hellenistic, Syrian, Alexandrian, Coptic, Ethiopian, Orthodox, Roman, Celtic, and so on.

32. Kenneth Scott Latourette, *A History of the Expansion of Christianity*, 7 vols. (New York: Harper and Row, 1937); Stephen Neill, *A History of Christian Missions* (New York: Penguin, 1964); Dale T. Irvin and Scott W. Sunquist, *History of the World Christian Movement*, vol. 1: *Earliest Christianity to 1453* (Maryknoll, NY: Orbis, 2009) and *History of the World Christian Movement*, vol. 2: *Modern Christianity from 1454 to 1800* (Maryknoll, NY: Orbis, 2012).

rates much more about the daily lives of the laity, the role of women, and the voices of suppressed minorities. This lens also acknowledges what is becoming increasingly apparent: we are experiencing the reshaping and marginalization of the too-often-presumed normativity of the Reformation-born, Euro-tribal Christian faith traditions.

Summary

The twenty-first century has brought disruptions to long-established patterns and structures of church life in America. These disruptions are rooted in larger cultural transformations that are sweeping through American society and the wider world, affecting institutions of all kinds. For churches that were birthed and developed in previous eras of a churched culture, or those with deep roots in European Christendom, this is an unsettling moment. At the same time, the Spirit of God is bringing forth a vital and dynamic new moment in the world Christian movement, centered in the Global South. With global population shifts bringing increased diversity into the US context, the vitality and dynamism are becoming more present in American neighborhoods all the time, even as many established forms of church seem disconnected from American life. Deep assumptions and norms in the lives of many churches are being called into question. In order to understand these shifts, we must reflect more deeply on God's missionary engagement with the diverse contexts of human life and culture. We take up that discussion in chapter 2.

Developing a Missiological Approach to the Church in the United States

God's Mission and the Church

The triune God is a missionary God. The biblical narrative tells the story of a Creator who forms the world in love, ordering life for relationships of flourishing. When humanity turns away from God, each other, and the earth, God compassionately and painstakingly seeks to heal and restore humans, calling and sending particular people to embody God's promises to the world. Through Israel, Jesus, and the church, God acts to reconcile and renew an estranged creation so that it might flourish once more. In Jesus, God sends God's own self to join humanity in its suffering and pain, taking that estrangement into God's life and transforming it into a new creation. All of humanity is invited to participate in this new creation as a sign of hope for a future of eternal community with God.

God's mission is the generative, creative, and redemptive sending by which the cosmos first came into being and continues to be healed and restored in the midst of its brokenness. As we shall explore in more detail in later chapters, this mission is above all God's. The God about whom the Bible testifies and whom the church confesses is a sending God—a missionary God. God's communal life as Trinity is open and generative, sustaining created others in all their diversity. God's Spirit forms a people and leads them from bondage to freedom. The people of Israel are called in their common life to witness to God's ordering of human community to the nations. In Jesus, God comes in the flesh to share the place of humanity and embody God's reign, reconciling us to God.

God's mission has a church. This consists of a people of promise called from every tribe and nation to live under God's gracious rule in the power

of the Spirit. The church is sent to witness in word and deed to God's renewal of creation in Jesus. Just as mission is integral to the identity and
life of God, so is it also integral to the identity and life of the church. The
church is a community created by the Spirit, who is intended by God to
fully participate in God's mission. It exists, not for itself, but for God and
for its neighbors both at home and around the world, pointing toward the
horizon of an alternative future of a healed creation.

The Church Is Missionary by Nature

The identity of the church lies within the triune God's mission. Its very nature is inherently missionary. In the way the church has been understood
historically, this is a reality that has often been missed, because for much of
the history of Western Christianity, mission was viewed as an activity that
the church did—for example, the church's sending of specialized missionaries by the church cross-culturally, typically overseas. This understanding of
mission betrays the deeper Trinitarian roots of mission. Being missionary
is, in fact, something the church is. The doing flows out of the being. Jürgen
Moltmann notes that "it is not the church that has a mission of salvation to
fulfill in the world; it is the mission of the Son and the Spirit through the Father that includes the church, creating a church along the way."[1] We should
note that the term "mission" was used in theology up to the sixteenth century to refer exclusively to the sending of the Son and Spirit within the Trinity. The Jesuits were the first to use it to refer to the sending of the church to
spread the Christian faith among those who were not Christian (or at least
not Roman Catholic).[2]

The church is missionary by nature because God's very life as Trinity
is missionary. In *Ad Gentes*, Vatican II articulated it this way: "The Church
on earth is by its very nature missionary, since, according to the plan of the
Father, it has its origin in the mission of the Son and the Holy Spirit."[3] When
you start biblically and theologically with God's mission, you cannot separate the church from mission. Doing so introduces a false dichotomy and

1. Jürgen Moltmann, *The Church in the Power of the Spirit: A Contribution to Messianic Ecclesiology* (Minneapolis: Fortress, 1993), 64.

2. David J. Bosch, *Transforming Mission: Paradigm Shifts in Theology of Mission* (Mary-knoll, NY: Orbis, 1991), 1.

3. Austin P. Flannery, ed., *Documents of Vatican II* (Grand Rapids: Eerdmans, 1975), 814.

separates ecclesiology (the study of the church) and missiology (the study of mission) as if they were two distinct entities. This is the same as separating God's being from God's actions, which introduces a false dichotomy into theology.[4] Mission is at the heart of God's own life and is constitutive of the church's identity.

This understanding of God, God's mission, and the church as being missionary by nature has huge implications for our understanding of the historical development of the church in America, and we will develop these implications in the chapters that follow. Mission is not just one more activity or dimension of the church's life; rather, it flows out of the very identity and nature of the church. This was manifested creatively in different ways as the Spirit formed new communities of faith and renewed others in the story of the church in the United States. But the church can misdirect the missionary impulses that flow from this identity and nature. There are numerous examples of both overcontextualizing and undercontextualizing in the missiological engagements of the American church, which we discuss with respect to each period of time in what follows. It is the church's responsibility to discern carefully the leading of the Spirit both as it bears witness to the good news of the gospel of Jesus Christ and as it seeks to contextualize an understanding of this good news into a particular cultural setting.

The Embodied Word: Incarnation

At the center of the Christian understanding of God's mission is Jesus, the Word made flesh in the power of the Spirit. Jesus is the human face of God, the hermeneutical key to understanding God's life and love for the world and God's vision for human flourishing. The answer to the central question of the relationship between gospel and culture as the church engages in mission lies in how God comes to us in Jesus—that is, the incarnation. The incarnation offers a paradox: the eternal Word, or rational order, of the universe comes into the particular, the local, and the concrete (John 1). God's way of communicating with us in Christ is to join us, where we are in the ordinary embodied human life. God embraces the particular in the incarnation, and by doing so, God enters and critically engages local culture.

The missiologist Andrew Walls uses the metaphor of translation to

4. John Flett, *The Witness of God: The Trinity, Missio Dei, Karl Barth, and the Nature of Christian Community* (Grand Rapids: Eerdmans, 2010).

describe how the incarnation functions. In Jesus, the Word is translated into human flesh. But language is always particular, specific to a cultural context, never abstract or universal, even as it seeks to communicate universal truths. The gospel is universal precisely by being particular and local. God's translation of the Word into an embodied life in Jesus Christ within the cultural situation of first-century Palestine is the prelude to an ongoing pattern of translation into every time and place in every culture in the world.[5]

Therefore, no culture can claim to be more divine than any other: all cultures and all historical moments may bear, as well as distort, God's presence and promises. Lamin Sanneh says that there is "a radical pluralism implied in vernacular translation wherein all languages and cultures are, in principle, equal in expressing the word of God."[6] Christianity thus involves a relativizing of culture at the same time that it embraces particularity of culture as the very means by which God reveals Godself to us in Christ.

The incarnation also disallows the premise that it is possible to have a pure, unadulterated, culture-free gospel. Because the gospel is an enfleshed Word, the gospel is by nature always embodied in cultural particularity, as Lesslie Newbigin observes: "There can never be a culture-free gospel. Yet the gospel, which is from the beginning to the end embodied in culturally conditioned forms, calls into question all cultures, including the one in which it was originally embodied."[7] In the incarnation God both embraces and critically engages culture. This important dimension is vital for the church to cultivate in order to be faithful to its vocation within the local and particular. When the church only embraces culture, without critical engagement, it loses its distinctive witness. At the same time, if the church in mission fails to translate the gospel deeply enough into the particular and local, it will not speak meaningfully to its neighbors.

Lamin Sanneh notes that the process of translation involves reciprocity. When the gospel, Scripture, and the church's life are translated into local vernaculars, the local culture changes even as the missionaries are challenged by new insights into the meaning of the gospel. Both are transformed.[8] San-

---

5. Andrew F. Walls, *The Missionary Movement in Christian History: Studies in the Transmission of Faith* (Maryknoll, NY: Orbis Books, 1996), 27.

6. Lamin O. Sanneh, *Translating the Message: The Missionary Impact on Culture* (Maryknoll, NY: Orbis, 1989), 208.

7. Lesslie Newbigin, *Foolishness to the Greeks: The Gospel and Western Culture* (Grand Rapids: Eerdmans, 1986), 4.

8. Sanneh, *Translating the Message*, 70.

neh traces how, in the history of African Christianity, the places where the indigenous culture and language (including the indigenous name for God) were most alive and intact were the places where Christianity flourished. Christianity, as it is expressed in the vernacular of local language and culture, has the effect of vivifying local culture.[9]

Therefore, Christianity is by its very nature a culturally embodied and culturally dynamic faith. If Christians propagate one culture above others in the name of mission, rather than engaging with their neighbors in the work of cultural translation, they betray their own story. Mission history is full of experiments in translation as well as controversies over the ways in which Christians have attempted to embody, express, and communicate the gospel. America offers a striking case in point of these dilemmas.

The Gospel Is Multidimensional

The gospel is multifaceted. As the good news of holistic salvation, the gospel relates to every dimension of life. But as the incarnation clearly demonstrates, the gospel is also historically embodied as it encounters us in our various and particular cultures and contexts. Thus, the church that is missionary by nature always develops a contextualized understanding of the gospel with respect to its participation in God's mission. This began at Pentecost, with the polyvocal witness unleashed by the Holy Spirit in multiple tongues through many voices. From that moment, Christians have borne witness to a holistic gospel by accenting particular dimensions that speak to their situation. The New Testament itself presents many themes or strains of good news: the coming of God's reign (Mark 1:14-15), with a call to repentance and new life (Acts 1:38); mercy and forgiveness for sinners (Rom. 6:22-23); healing and restoration to community for the sick and demon-possessed (Luke 11:14); the inclusion of outcasts and foreigners in a new household of faith (Eph. 2:12-14); empowerment, liberation, and deliverance for the disenfranchised (Matt. 11:4-6); challenges to social, economic, and political forces of oppression and injustice (Col. 2:13-15); God's joining us in our suffering in Christ (Phil. 2:5-11); and the promise of eternal life (John 10:7-10).

Through history, Christians in a diversity of cultural and social locations have practiced and articulated such multiple dimensions of presenting

---

9. Lamin O. Sanneh, *Whose Religion Is Christianity? The Gospel beyond the West* (Grand Rapids: Eerdmans, 2003), 18.

the good news in Christ and developing missiological engagements. When encountering oppression, the church has presented a gospel that offers good news about liberation. When encountering people who are dispirited, the church has presented a gospel that offers good news of renewal and revival. When encountering issues of the abuse of people, the church has presented a gospel that offers good news of mercy to the afflicted as well as justice regarding systems that distort human life. When encountering people who have no hope, the church has presented a gospel that offers good news about living life now in all of its intended fullness, as well as experiencing life with Christ throughout all eternity.

These various strains illustrate how a holistic gospel relates to all of life. The story of the church in America illustrates that a variety of such strains became manifest as the gospel interacted with particular contexts. It is important to note the ways in which these strains morphed over time, as circumstances changed and new initiatives were begun to respond to or address the issues of the day. But it is crucial to keep in mind that the church, in carrying out its missiological engagements, did not always maintain a sufficiently prophetic stance of critiquing the culture in which it was embedded. All too often, the principalities and powers that the gospel seeks to unmask have resided *in* the church—that is, within the church's relationship with the culture in which it was located. One example: the American church has at times tied Christianity too closely to US national interests, and "God and country" have coalesced too easily into notions of a Christian America. Another example: during slavery, many white churches—on biblical grounds—legitimated rather than rejected slavery. There are countless such instances. The argument we are making in this book is that the church needs to live out of a theological missiology that allows for all the strains of the gospel to be expressed within any and every particular context while also critiquing, where necessary, the ways in which expressions of these strains have become overly captive to the culture.

Contextualization

A common term for this dynamic, incarnational interplay of gospel and culture is contextualization, or bringing to expression the presence and truth of God within particular cultural contexts.[10] The eternal Word became en-

---

10. See A. Scott Moreau, *Contextualization in World Missions: Mapping and Assessing*

fleshed within a particular cultural setting so that the presence and truth of God through Jesus could be experienced as it was seen, heard, and touched. This has made the enduring mission of God both concrete and accessible to the people of that time. This same incarnation confirms the promise of the gospel: that it is inherently translatable to every cultural context as it conveys the eternal and universal truths embedded within it. The gospel has within it the potential of being good news in every context; but to be so, it must be expressed in terms that make sense to those who are hearing it.

Inherent Translatability of the Word

Jesus took on the particularity of his context as the incarnate good news. But even in his particularity, he retained his universal relevance.[11] This is part of the mystery of the good news of Jesus Christ. We find in its particularity the promise and the reality of its universality, what Newbigin refers to as the "scandal of particularity."[12] God's universal mission proceeds through the local and particular, from Abraham and Sarah through Israel, Jesus, and the church. Just as Jesus, the living Word, took on the particularity of a specific context, the good news about him is inherently translatable into every particular cultural context in order to be universally applicable.[13] This means that it can become good news to everyone, everywhere, in language and within cultural expressions that are understandable, knowable, and accessible. Through this inherent translatability, this same gospel of good news invites people to come to know the living and true God and to join the worldwide church.

Inherent Translatability of the Church

Just as the gospel is inherently translatable into every cultural context, the church, which is missionary by nature, is also inherently translatable in the same way. The church that we profess to be catholic (universal) in the Apos-

---

Evangelical Models (Grand Rapids: Kregel Publications, 2012); Stephen B. Bevans, *Models of Contextual Theology*, rev. ed. (Maryknoll, NY: Orbis, 2002).

11. See Lesslie Newbigin, *The Gospel in a Pluralist Society* (Grand Rapids: Eerdmans, 1989), 80–115.

12. Newbigin, *Gospel in a Pluralist Society*, 72.

13. Sanneh, *Translating the Message*.

tles' and Nicene Creeds has the inherent ability to live every place and to become contextual within any and every cultural setting. As the Nicene Creed attests, the church is also apostolic, which means it is missionary, or sent, by its very nature. A church that is missionary by nature seeks its contextuality in order to make God's promises in Christ understandable and accessible. While stewarding the truths of the faith, the church seeks to become relevant and responsive within every context in which it finds itself; to do so, it must engage the cultural narratives that shape a particular context.[14]

Embodied Cultural Narratives in the United States

The Christian confession of an incarnate Jesus within a culturally embodied faith points toward a deep truth: all human life is shaped by cultural narratives. The stories in which we live shape our perspective and experience, even as experience shapes those stories. We make sense of the world by virtue of frameworks, assumptions, and a given repertoire of meanings, much of which we rarely notice or reflect on. They are like the air we breathe.

Charles Taylor uses the term "social imaginary" to describe these deep structures of meaning within communities. They are the ways in which people imagine their life together, how they develop relationships with others, the expectations that are normally met, and the deeper ideas and images that underlie those expectations.[15] Taylor writes: "It is in fact that largely unstructured and inarticulate understanding of our whole situation, within which particular features of our world show up for us in the sense they have."[16] In other words, shared cultural and social assumptions function as a framework in shaping the meaning we give to experiences.

We all interpret situations by way of weaving stories from a cultural repertoire of meanings.[17] The actions we take follow paths that are pre-legitimated by the stories in which we dwell. The cultural resources at hand influence how we frame and make sense out of our experiences. This means that people in different cultural and social locations often draw contrasting

---

14. This is the argument developed in Craig Van Gelder, *The Essence of the Church: A Community Created by the Spirit* (Grand Rapids: Baker, 2000).

15. Charles Taylor, *A Secular Age* (Cambridge, MA: Belknap Press of Harvard University Press, 2007), 171.

16. Taylor, *A Secular Age*, 173.

17. Scott Cormode, *Making Spiritual Sense: Christian Leaders as Spiritual Interpreters* (Nashville: Abingdon, 2006), 14–47.

interpretations out of their experiences, and these interpretations lead to alternative actions.

Christianity is a repertoire of meanings: of narratives, images, practices, and shared assumptions. But it is also always embedded within specific cultural repertoires, leading to divergent interpretations and practices, as well as to many conflicts within the church. This inherent pluralism accounts for much of the richness and diversity of Christian life and witness. It also involves ambiguity surrounding what is, in fact, a faithful expression of the Christian story (a contextualized gospel) in particular cultural form, and what is a betrayal of that story (over- or undercontextualization).

Christian communities, at various points in history, have thus operated with cultural assumptions in mission that other Christian communities would deeply challenge. It is worth highlighting a few of the distinctive cultural threads or deep narratives that continue to function in contemporary American culture. These threads account for some of the uniqueness of the church in an American setting as well as some of the challenges the church faces. They manifest themselves in various ways in American Christianity and are bound up with provocative contradictions. Each has important missiological implications.

New Humanity in a New Land

American self-identity is grounded in a sense of expansive possibility. There is an abiding belief that human life can begin anew in this land, that America is an exceptional place and Americans are exceptional people. The Puritans expressed this with their vision of a "holy commonwealth" where humans could attain a kind of communal Christian perfection that was impossible in Europe. Governor John Winthrop asserted that the American colony would be a "city on a hill" for the world to see.[18] Somehow, America could be freed from the long and tortured history of the world. There is in American history a deep primordialism, a sense that in America it is possible to escape original sin, to start humanity over from scratch.[19] The national seal articulates it this way: Novus ordo seclorum ("a new order of the ages").

18. As quoted in Sydney E. Ahlstrom, *A Religious History of the American People* (New Haven: Yale University Press, 1972), 147.

19. Ephraim Radner and Philip Turner, *The Fate of Communion: The Agony of Anglicanism and the Future of a Global Church* (Grand Rapids: Eerdmans, 2006), 29-33.

Known as "American exceptionalism," this impulse is a strain of American identity that fuels a deep, intrinsic sense of optimism and has fostered great innovation and creativity. This played itself out in modernity as a "can do" attitude that has emphasized human agency and initiative, particularly when coupled with technological innovation. There was—and still is—a sense that nothing can get in the way of what America can accomplish. This exceptionalism, when tied to pragmatism, has become a signature feature of American life and a defining influence shaping American missiology.

There is also a strong sense of power and domain operative in this ideal of new humanity in a new land. Various forms of American colonialism tried to work out of the assumption that America was inherently good and deserved to expand and share its blessings with other peoples—even while subjugating them. This points to the deep irony in this ideal: to native peoples, of course, there was nothing *new* about America when the first European settlers arrived. They had lived here for many generations, and the newness of the colonial experiment was predicated on displacing them and eviscerating their way of life. Native Americans were idealized as "noble savages" who were at the same time assumed to be inferior to Europeans and were treated as such.

The ideal of American exceptionalism has a dangerous blind side. It exalts humanity as being capable of achieving perfection, even while sanctioning violence and destruction, sometimes in the name of God, the church, and mission. Americans seem to assume the best about themselves in their missionary or imperial endeavors, and thus they often seem surprised when things don't turn out as planned.[20] It seems difficult for Americans to reflect on their own sinfulness as a nation; they want to believe that the forces of corruption don't apply to them.

Dreaming of Freedom

Freedom is a powerfully recurring theme in American life. The first English settlers came to America to exercise religious freedom, followed by waves of peoples from around the world who saw America as a place where they could express their faith without government interference. This has fostered

---

20. The American invasion of Iraq in 2003 and its aftermath is an instance in recent memory of how persistent this ideal is.

a sense of openness in American religious life that continues today. Freedom to define, speak, worship, assemble, publish, and otherwise express one's religion and spirituality is a bedrock of American national identity.

As articulated in the Declaration of Independence, the Constitution, and other founding documents of the United States, the American understanding of freedom is deeply indebted to the Enlightenment idea of individual expression—freedom *from* restraint. With the individual as the basic unit of society, America has tended to define freedom in individualistic rather than communal terms. Religious communities are seen as voluntary societies along the lines of John Locke's definition, where individuals contract to meet their spiritual needs and are free to dissolve such contracts when those needs are not being met.[21] This has encouraged a variety of consumerist approaches to church, especially in recent decades.

Like the ideal of American exceptionalism, the ideal of freedom also has a deeply problematic underside. American history is full of oppression and the denial of freedom to some members of society—based on race, ethnicity, gender, sexual orientation, and other factors. The cardinal example, of course, is slavery. For those enslaved or oppressed, freedom is something to dream about and long for. The church within oppressed communities in American history has powerfully articulated a missiology of freedom that stands against the dominant culture's sense of freedom as privilege. While the dominant culture has emphasized the freedom of human self-actualization and individual expression, the African American church and other minority communities have prayed, preached, and sung stirring dreams of deliverance by a liberating God, holding the rest of the country accountable for making it so difficult to live out its own ideals.[22]

Self-Invention and Choice

Amidst this sense of exceptional possibility and expansive freedom, American culture has embraced the view that one can be whatever one wants to be. One's family roots need not determine one's own future. The self can be invented or reinvented through ingenuity, luck, and hard work. Pervading

---

21. John Locke, "A Letter Concerning Toleration," in *Locke on Politics, Religion, and Education*, ed. Maurice Cranston (New York: Collier, 1965).

22. Martin Luther King Jr. is a hallmark example of a Christian voice in American history calling the country to live up to its own ideals.

this ideal is the assumption of choice: America is a land of endless choices that offer the promise of shaping a new identity. Religious faith and practice constitute matters of choice for an increasing number of people, as the bonds of family loyalty and religious tradition weaken in an increasingly discretionary culture. Baby boomers were the first generation to drop out, on a large scale, of the religion or denomination of their own family of origin and switch between churches or faiths in trying to have their own perceived needs met.[23] This trend has continued in subsequent generations, where the bonds of duty and loyalty to a denomination or faith community have further weakened. American culture is now a culture of what is discretionary—in religion as well as in most other things.

Late modernity has brought an existential deepening of this sense of self-invention, in which personal identity is no longer given by birth into stable communities (family, neighborhood, religious community, workplace). Rather, it must be created and maintained through endless choices in the midst of rapid flux and change. Anthony Giddens observes that "we are, not what we are, but what we make of ourselves."[24] Marriages break down when people no longer feel personally fulfilled by them. Nomadic citizens are relocated by corporate systems, economic opportunities or lack thereof, or their own wanderlust. Over the course of a lifetime, people switch, not just their jobs, but whole careers—multiple times. Personal identity is the subject of a lifelong struggle of self-invention.[25] Traditional forms of authority break down amidst a new pluralism in which the individual must decide what and whom to obey. Underneath it all is the lurking threat of meaninglessness.

These examples illustrate the power of the deep cultural narratives that are part of America's "social imaginary." They also illustrate that it is always a challenge to render a clear distinction between gospel and culture. This is because the church is embedded within political, social, and economic power structures where its capacity for critical self-reflection can be compromised all too easily. The exploration of mission in the United States that follows in the second section seeks to draw out and reflect critically on

23. Robert Wuthnow, *After Heaven: Spirituality in America since the 1950s* (Berkeley: University of California Press, 1998). See also Dean R. Hoge, Benton Johnson, and Donald A. Luidens, *Vanishing Boundaries: The Religion of Mainline Protestant Baby Boomers* (Louisville: Westminster John Knox, 1994).

24. Anthony Giddens, *Modernity and Self-Identity* (Stanford: Stanford University Press, 1991), 75.

25. Giddens, *Modernity and Self-Identity*, 195–201.

these questions and dilemmas of contextualization. They remain central to the challenges of mission in twenty-first-century America.

Spirit-Led Mission in Context[26]

The Holy Spirit is the Christian way of talking about God's power and presence in the here and now. In this sense, the Spirit is the primary actor in God's mission today. From the beginning of creation, the Spirit of God acts to bring forth the world, to form people into community, and to call them into the adventure of God's mission. This plays out in the Old Testament through Abraham and Sarah, Moses and Miriam, Israel, and the judges and prophets through whom the Spirit empowers, unifies, and leads God's people. Jesus's own ministry is Spirit-shaped, and at Pentecost the Spirit brings forth a new community of multilingual and multicultural witness to God's power.

The Spirit leads that community, the church, into cross-cultural witness in the book of Acts. This witness is dynamic, improvisational, and fluid as the apostles encounter resistance and persecution. The Spirit calls them via dreams, visions, and discernment as they translate the message about Jesus into new cultural vernaculars. What had originated as a Jewish movement quickly takes on Greek and Roman cultural expression. Along the way, the Spirit connects people across cultural differences into a new community.

The Spirit leads the church to embody Jesus's witness as the body of Christ within diverse contexts, contexts that are always undergoing some level of change—since change is of the very nature of life. Contextualization is thus an ongoing process that needs to be shaped through the Christian community's discernment of the Spirit's leading. It is important for a church to anticipate that its context will change, so that it can intentionally continue to recontextualize its ministries to address new conditions as these emerge. The challenge is that the church can easily fall into two ditches on either side of faithful contextualization: *overcontextualization* and *under-contextualization*. What is it about the church that, on the one hand, it can

---

26. Most of the material in this section, now substantively revised, first appeared in "How Missiology Can Help Inform the Conversation about the Missional Church in Context," in *The Missional Church in Context: Helping Congregations Develop Contextual Ministry*, ed. Craig Van Gelder (Grand Rapids: Eerdmans, 2007), 12–43.

be so creative and innovative in seeking out new opportunities for ministry, and, on the other hand, that it can so often be reactive and resistant to change? How are we to understand these dimensions as being part of the same church of Jesus Christ?

Complicity or Relevance—Overcontextualization

Historically, the church has often incorporated the deep narratives and practices of the broader culture and assumed that these were Christian. This has led to overcontextualization, where the church becomes too culturally adaptive, too complicit in compromising aspects of the gospel, as illustrated in the previous section. Also typical of many churches in the United States over the past half century is a response strategy that attempts to incorporate elements of new cultural patterns into the life of the church. This can be a helpful instinct to pursue in working at contextualizing or recontextualizing a church's ministry as changes take place. However, this strategy can become problematic if a church relies on it too heavily to provide a solution for pursuing effective ministry. This is evident in the pattern among many churches today of always seeking for what might be called the "new and the next."[27] Multiple books have been written in the first two decades of the twenty-first century that focus on the church's need to change in order to respond to and engage a changing context.[28]

The tendency is to look for methods that work or to find models of ministry that can be applied in different locations. They utilize primarily the framework of the relationship of church and culture to develop their understanding of the church's responsibility in the world, with the church needing to engage a changing culture as their primary focus. A deeper

27. A helpful introduction to this concept can be found in Charles Trueheart, "Welcome to the Next Church," *Atlantic* 27, no. 2 (Aug. 1996): 37–52.

28. Examples include: Rick Rusaw and Eric Swanson, *The Externally Focused Church* (Grand Rapids: Group Publishing, 2004); Dave Browning, *Hybrid Church: The Fusion of Intimacy and Impact* (San Francisco: Jossey-Bass, 2011); Neil Cole, *Organic Church: Growing Faith Where Life Happens* (San Francisco: Jossey-Bass, 2005); Neil Cole, *Church 3.0: Upgrades for the Future of the Church* (San Francisco: Jossey-Bass, 2010); Jim Belcher, *Deep Church: A Third Way beyond Emerging and Traditional* (Downers Grove: IL: InterVarsity, 2009); Mark Dever, *The Deliberate Church: Building Your Ministry on the Gospel* (Wheaton, IL: Crossway, 2005); Tim Chester and Steve Timmis, *Total Church: A Radical Reshaping around Gospel and Community* (Wheaton, IL: Crossway, 2008); Reggie McNeal, *The Present Future: Six Tough Questions for the Church* (San Francisco: Jossey-Bass, 2009).

framework is required in order to get to the heart of the problem. This involves focusing on the relationship between gospel and culture, not just church and culture.

Resistance—Undercontextualizing

Many churches, in the face of significant change in their contexts, unnecessarily resist changes to which they should adapt, seeking to stave off change of any kind. Depending on the changes that are taking place, this response often takes on a reactive character. Typically, churches pursuing this approach make efforts to maintain the status quo or even, at times, to recover a former approach to ministry from another historical time. For example, some churches continue to emphasize particular practices that emerged within a different period of time but which no longer fit the cultural ethos of the day, for instance, the continued scheduling of a yearly revival to reach their community, or the standard practice of using only hymns that were mostly produced in previous centuries.

The manifest logic they use to justify an approach of resistance is that maintaining things the way they have been is a function of being faithful and obedient to the call and purpose of God. The embedded logic of this approach is that familiarity with *our way of doing things* represents a type of biblical fidelity that must be preserved. Churches that take this approach to change usually fight an endless battle of retrenchment and are often able to attract only disaffected persons from other churches who hold similar values. They fail to grasp the dynamic process of ongoing, Spirit-led contextualization that is integral to Christian mission.

The Church Living within a Changing Context

In view of these strategies, which tend to position the church within its context as being either overcontextualized or undercontextualized, it is helpful to further consider the missiological engagement of the gospel with culture. The church always faces the task of living and becoming embodied within a particular context; and, as such, it faces the challenge of stewarding its identity so that it can maintain the strengths of a tradition, while also trying to respond to new cultural realities that are emerging. One way the church historically attempted to address this challenge surfaced in the aftermath of the Protestant

Reformation and became known by the shorthand Latin phrase *ecclesia reformata, semper reformanda* ("the church reformed and always reforming").[29]

The concept that the church is "always reforming" provides an important insight into how the church needs to respond as it continues to become embodied within any changing context. Doing so requires a return to the biblical and theological roots that initially shaped the church. But this response tends to address only one side of the issue of change—by bringing insights from Scripture and the historic Christian faith to bear on renewing the church when it has become overcontextualized. What we must also address is how the church needs to learn from what is occurring in its changing context and then to recontextualize itself to respond to new realities. This introduces the important reciprocal relationship between gospel and culture, in which the church must be understood as always both *forming* and *reforming*.

The Church as Always Forming and Reforming

This understanding reflects the truth about the inherent translatability of the church into any and every cultural context. It helps to address the problems inherent in those approaches to cultural change in which the church either tends to overcontextualize or undercontextualize. Understanding that the church is always forming and reforming reinforces the logic that the church always needs to be both missional and biblical/confessional. A church that is forming is missionally engaging its context; a church that is reforming is reflecting carefully on its biblical and/or confessional heritage. The historical Reformation watchword for the church needs to be complemented by another perspective:

> The church is always forming—*ecclesia semper formanda*
> The church is always reforming—*ecclesia semper reformanda*.

This framework offers a deeper truth about the church and the ministry of the Spirit, a truth that draws together the better impulses of each approach and understands them as a polarity where both are accepted as

29. The phrase is credited to Jodocus van Lodenstein in 1674, who was seeking to bring further reform to the church—during what is known as the Dutch Second Reformation. See Michael Bush, "Calvin and the Reformanda Sayings," in *Calvinus sacrarum literarum interpres: Papers of the International Congress on Calvin Research*, ed. Herman J. Selderhuis (Göttingen: Vandenhoeck and Ruprecht, 2008), 286.

true.[30] This polarity creates a dynamic and healthy tension between change and continuity, as well as between mission and confession. The leading of the Spirit maintains the tension line in this polarity between the challenge of recontextualizing the church's ministry in the midst of a changing context and the challenge of continuing to maintain the truths of the historic Christian faith as understood by the church. The issue is really one of living in the tension between the two logics of *outside-in* (forming) and *inside-out* (reforming). On the one hand, this means that the church seeks to become contextualized even while it seeks to maintain the historic Christian faith, an outside-in logic. In doing so, the church invites change even while it seeks to maintain continuity. On the other hand, the direction of the church's effort to always reform even as it is continuously forming is to help the church become more responsive to its heritage by focusing on the inside-out. It is understood that, by recovering something from its past through reform, the church will become more responsive to its present situation. It is crucial to maintain a dynamic balance between the two. Of course, this has not always been the case. That will become clear in later chapters, where we summarize and review the historical development of the church in America.

Missiological Capacities for Contextualization

There are certain inherent missiological capacities embedded within the church's missionary nature that need to be cultivated as it pursues the tasks of both forming and reforming. This is based on the work of the Spirit of God, who not only creates the church by calling it into existence, but who also leads and teaches the church by sending it into the world to participate fully in God's mission in all of creation. As local churches seek to engage in ministry within the contexts in which they are located, they would be well served by seeking to develop the following capacities to guide them on this journey.

1. The Missiological Capacity of Learning to Interpret a Context

It is crucial for the church to develop the ability to understand its context. The church, which is missionary by nature, has within it the impulse to seek

---

30. Barry Johnson, *Polarity Management: Identifying and Managing Unsolvable Problems* (Amherst, MA: HRD Press, 1992).

to be contextual in engaging its location. The importance of this aptitude for reading a context has become increasingly recognized in recent decades, and many tools have been developed to assist congregations in this work.[31] The key to interpreting a context should not be limited, however, to the sociology and demographics of a context; it should also include a theological reading of the sociological and demographic findings. This is where the faith/discernment responsibility of the church comes into play—as it is led and taught by the Spirit. The church must continue to ask: What might God be up to within these contexts? How are we gifted and called to join what God is doing? Answering these questions involves a lot of listening— to Scripture, to the Spirit in discernment, to neighbors, and to one another.

2. The Missiological Capacity of Anticipating New Insights into the Gospel

As the gospel engages diverse cultures within various contexts, and as the translation of the gospel takes place with respect to these new cultures, the church must cultivate the missiological capacity of anticipating new insights into the fuller meaning of the gospel. The very act of translating the gospel into different worldviews often opens up fresh understanding and insights regarding the meaning of Scripture. This was certainly true of the New Testament church when the gospel was translated into a Hellenistic worldview in the church at Antioch. The Hellenized version of the gospel helped break Jewish Christianity out of its provincialism and later became the normative expression of the faith for centuries to come.[32]

Lamin Sanneh makes this same point regarding the translation of the gospel within the African context. Here, despite all the transposed Western forms of Christianity laid on the young churches by the missionaries, the gospel found its indigenous voice within the cultures of the African peoples and gave new expressions to the faith and forms to the churches.[33] For the church to anticipate and appreciate new insights into the gospel as they emerge within a different context, it must listen deeply, patiently, and with careful discernment. This is part of the *forming* work

---

31. See, for example, Nancy Ammerman et al., *Studying Congregations: A New Handbook* (Nashville: Abingdon, 1998).

32. Andrew F. Walls, *Missionary Movement in Christian History*.

33. Sanneh, *Translating the Message*.

of the church that often releases fresh resources for understanding and living the faith.

3. The Missiological Capacity of Anticipating Reciprocity

One of the interesting things about the leading and teaching of the Spirit in the church over time is that the gospel often brings about reciprocity: a mutual reconciling of relationships amid differences. Reciprocity occurs when the cultural group that has brought the gospel into another context is itself changed by the receiving culture.[34] An example of this is the story of Peter's encounter with Cornelius (Acts 10); it is as much about the continuing conversion of Peter as it is about the conversion of Cornelius. Another example is the spillover effect of the persecution of the church in Acts 8 that resulted—circumstantially, it would seem—in the development of the Gentile church in Antioch (Acts 11). Given time, the gospel that was proclaimed in Antioch as salvation by grace through faith, without cultural conversion to Judaism, came to be the accepted understanding of the gospel by the entire church (Acts 15).

In the latter example, what began on the margins came to the center. This is often the case with reciprocity. A present example of this in the American context can be seen in many of the newer immigrant communities. Coming from indigenous churches in what were formerly foreign mission fields of Western churches, many new immigrant congregations are now locating in established communities across America. These congregations are often inviting people into a deeper level of understanding of the gospel's call for reconciled unity among Christians. Often, they are also bringing their own missionary activity to the US context, where they view many of the persons in their new location as needing to hear the gospel, once again, for the first time.

4. The Missiological Capacity of Understanding That the Church Is Local and Therefore Also Particular

Our language illustrates this point whenever we refer to a congregation as a "local church." Local means that, by necessity, a congregation is particu-

---

34. Sanneh, *Translating the Message.*

lar to its time and place. While it is also catholic (universal), representing the historic Christian faith, it is profoundly local in contextualizing these realities within the setting it seeks to serve. This means that there is always a certain provisional character to a local church as it lives within a specific location.

As contexts change, the church should expect to change as well, even as it attempts to live out the tension inherent in being faithful to the gospel and also being responsive to its context—always forming while also reforming. This missiological capacity challenges the way that *models* of church are often promoted. In reality, there can be no model church. While there can be illustrative examples of a contextualized church in ministry that might help to inform others, no church can be duplicated within a different context. It is important to remember that it is the work of the Spirit to lead and teach a church to contextualize itself within a particular location.

5. *The Missiological Capacity of Understanding That Ministry Is Always Contextual and Therefore Also Practical*

This missiological capacity understands that the practice of ministry is always normed by Scripture, but it also understands that this takes place in the particular contexts where churches serve. Just as churches are always contextual, their ministries are also always contextual: the Spirit leads and teaches a church within a particular context. Ministry can take place only in relationship with that context, and as ministry takes place, a church develops specific practices to carry out that ministry.

This means that all forms of ministry are going to bear the patterns and shape of the cultural context in which a church is ministering. The necessary practices that it develops are a practical outworking of this ministry. This point introduces the important issue of how *programs* have come to function in many churches. Modern American culture shapes people to look for a standardized recipe or program for success—regardless of context. In reality, there can be no common program that works the same way in each church and context. While a basic programmatic framework may inform the development of ministry, each church is best served when it thinks carefully about how to practice the Way of Jesus within the realities of the particular context it serves.

6. The Missiological Capacity of Understanding That Doing Theology Is Always Contextual and Therefore Also Perspectival

A church articulates its confessed faith in what is generally referred to as "theology." This represents its understanding of the eternal truths of Scripture within a form that conveys a historical confessional perspective. This aptitude helps a church understand that these confessional perspectives have embedded within them elements of the culture and context in which they were initially formulated. While these theological expressions bear witness to the realities of truth found in Scripture, they must always be understood as also being tied to a particular time and place. While the theological expressions of a particular time and place can have great relevance for many other contexts, there is always a need to interpret and translate them with respect to new contexts.

This point introduces the important issue of how *confessions* function within a church's life and ministry. In reality, there are no universal confessions that can speak to every church for all time. Even the most basic confession, "Jesus is Lord," draws on (and subverts) cultural categories of lordship that have varied in time and place—from the ancient Roman empire to medieval Europe to contemporary Africa and beyond. Every church is responsible for making use of its historical confessional heritage while also continuing to engage in the task of confessing the faith with respect to the issues and challenges of its particular context. It needs to actively engage in translating the themes and insights of historical confessions in order to address its own time and place.

7. The Missiological Capacity of Understanding That Organization Is Always Contextual and Therefore Also Always Provisional

As a church develops organizational forms to carry out its ministry and to structure its life, this missiological capacity helps a church understand that these forms also bear the imprint of particular contexts. Therefore, organization in the church always has, to some extent, a provisional character about it. While biblical principles of church organization function across a wide range of contexts, the particular forms that emerge must be seen as being particular to specific contexts. This is part of the good news of the gospel: that a church is able to relate to any culture and develop its organizational life and ministry in any context.

The challenge for the church is to bring the gospel into diverse contexts and allow for the leading and teaching of the Spirit to give birth to organizational forms that are informed by both the historical Christian faith and the realities of the context in which the church is taking root. Church polities need to be adaptive and flexible as they consciously take context and culture into consideration in the midst of the continuous processes of forming and reforming.

Taking a Missiological Approach

What does it mean, then, to take a missiological approach to the church in the American context? The history of missiology as it emerged in Western Christianity within the past few centuries reflects its historical context: the rise and decline of foreign missions by Western Christians during a period in which the church was for the most part aligned with Western colonialism. As we introduced it in the Introduction—and will continue to illustrate in the historical chapters that follow—missiology developed as a "practical" discipline that was meant to assist the church's missionary endeavors, which were themselves on the margins of the church's established life in the European and North American contexts. From the perspective of the great majority of Western Christians, mission was largely something done by someone else, somewhere else, and missiology's place in the theological academy was accordingly marginal.

However, as Martin Kähler famously observed over a hundred years ago, "Mission is the mother of theology."[35] The Christian movement began with the early church being in mission. Theology has been—and is—the church's reflection on its unfolding participation in God's mission in various times and places. The political and economic circumstances that led to the rise of the era of colonial missions from the West are now long past. Christianity is thriving as a religion of the majority world, while it continues to weaken in Europe, North America, and other Western societies. The white Protestant churches (both mainline and evangelical) that saw themselves at the center of American society and religious life for so long are rapidly being displaced in a new moment of increasing cultural, religious, and ethnic diversity—and a significant generational abandonment

---

35. Quotation translated from the original German and quoted by David J. Bosch, *Transforming Mission: Paradigm Shifts in Theology of Mission*, 16.

of religion in the United States. The twenty-first century calls for a different kind of conversation about the gospel, the church, mission, culture, and the American context.

This book is an attempt to frame and contribute to such a conversation. It is instructive, as we engage in this conversation, to revisit the long and complicated history of Christian missionary engagement on these shores, which we do in Part 2 (chapters 3–7). It is a story of the contextualization of the gospel through numerous missiological engagements with local cultures over the centuries, as well as painful moments and patterns of over- and undercontextualization. This mission history is the legacy on which much of the churches' missionary engagement with their American neighbors still rests. It warrants critical reflection so that we can claim and carry forward elements of a usable past, and so that we can repent of and address past injustices and errors.

Yet, the triune God's mission in the US context continues to unfold, and the church is called now as much as ever to give witness to God's creative and renewing work of forming communities of love, reconciliation, and hope in Christ through the power of the Spirit. Part 3 of this book takes seriously the presupposition with which this chapter began: God's mission has a church. What does it mean to interpret this cultural moment in American life? How might the gospel speak to it? How might forms of church life and organization be faithfully recontextualized for the world in which we find ourselves?

For too long in Christian theology, mission has been an ancillary topic of conversation: missiology has often been located on the margins and addressed with little theological reflection. But if God's mission has a church, then God is the primary missionary, and God's mission relates to the whole of creation. This makes the study of Christian mission a deeply theological task. It means the church's identity is fundamentally missionary because it is rooted in the triune God's own missionary sending in all of creation. This means, first, that missiology and ecclesiology can no longer be separated, and, second, that theology and missiology cannot be separated either. These are inherently interrelated in what technically can be referred to as a "missiological ecclesiology" and a "theological missiology."

It is essential to shift the focus of the primary questions many have been accustomed to asking. Instead of wondering how the church can either remake itself to be relevant again to a changing culture or try to recover a lost past, we must begin with wondering what God might be up to in the world, particularly whatever local context we find ourselves inhabiting, and how we are gifted and called to participate in God's mission. Instead of focusing on strategies and techniques that would attract people who are leaving the church back to it—or working to reclaim a once powerful privilege in society—the church must deepen its discernment about what it means to practice Jesus's Way as it faithfully translates the gospel into relationships of reciprocity with its neighbors. This is a different agenda from that of those who have driven many American churches over the past few generations. It pushes us beyond the questions that consume so many church leaders today, about how to do church differently, and invites us to explore more deeply the cultural context in which we find ourselves.

Summary

The themes developed in this chapter deeply inform the possibilities and the challenges associated with American church life and missiology. They offer rich openings for Christian engagement, and they provide a stance for making a critique. The chapters of Part 2 take up the story of mission in American history with an eye toward addressing the present moment in its complexity. In doing so, we use the polarity of forming and reforming as those two realities have played out in the story of the American church. There is much genuinely new in American Christianity over the centuries—moments of forming—encouraged in part by the themes named above. There are also moments in which the distinctiveness of the gospel gets lost amid other ideals, values, and commitments—moments that call for reforming.

PART 2

Understanding the Challenge

In the following five chapters we use the missiology developed in chapter 2 as a lens for reviewing and retelling the story of the church in the United States from the colonial period to the present. This is especially helpful in identifying how the church developed as it did and why it pursued its various public missiology engagements. The five periods represent the typical divisions many historians use to define the development of the church in the United States: colonial, frontier, urban growth, suburbanization, and late-modern success. Each of these periods was followed by a major transition, which contributed to the existing church's continuing to evolve into new expressions. These transitional periods include: the Revolutionary War, the Civil War, the Great Depression and World War II, the cultural revolution of the 1960s and '70s, and the "great unraveling" of the contemporary era.

Each of these periods, and the transitions that followed, presents some unique themes regarding the development of the church; those, in turn, were shaped by significant changes occurring in the broader context. A general summary of the themes in these periods is:

- *Colonial Experience*: The church in the colonial period, followed by the Revolutionary War, experienced the emergence of denominations—which were the result of the earlier Euro-tribal immigration— as a new organizational form of the church, since other early efforts to establish the church failed.
- *Expanding Frontier*: The church during the frontier period, followed by the Civil War, experienced a rapid increase of congregations pop-

ping up as the upstart, made-in-America denominations quickly out-paced the existing church forms.

- *The Church in the City*: During the period of urban growth, followed by the Great Depression and World War II, the church experienced massive growth from the shifting patterns of European immigration and rural-to-urban migration, along with an increased professional-ization that contributed to its significant fragmentation.

- *Suburban Success*: The church in the period of suburban success, fol-lowed by the cultural revolution of the 1960s and '70s, experienced a major relocation to the suburbs of primarily white people moving out of the cities and meeting up with those from rural areas and forming suburban congregations as the corporate denomination form reached its peak.

- *Late-Modern Success Strategies*: The church during the period of late-modern success, followed by the current "great unraveling," expe-rienced the important shift from the earlier norm of the geographic-neighborhood church to the attractional-lifestyle church, with its emphasis on using ever-evolving strategies in an endless search for success.

We have further used the missiological lens from chapter 2 to assess key interpretive frameworks that we use to fill out the story of the church within these periods. We begin each chapter by summarizing the *development of the church in each period* with respect to its particular context, and then sketching its interaction with important historical developments and cultural narratives during that period. This provides an understanding of the shifting focus of the church with regard to the broader society as it con-tinued to evolve organizationally over time. Second, we examine the influ-ence of these historical developments and cultural narratives by highlight-ing some of the key themes, events, and population shifts taking place at the time. This helps to explain the increasing diversity, as well as the growing complexity, that the church continued to experience.

We follow this framework for understanding the social location of the church during each era by paying attention to the organizational changes that were taking place.[1] First, we pay specific attention to the changes oc-

---

1. The sections within each of these five historical chapters that deal with the changing system of congregations, the development of the denominational church, and developments in theological education previously appeared in chapters written by Craig Van Gelder in the

curring in the *system of congregations*. We note how the number of congregations in the overall system continued to increase and how existing congregations continued to morph to respond to their new realities. Second, we pay attention to the ongoing evolution of the *denominational, organizational church* as it adjusted its purpose and structure to respond to the changes taking place in the larger context and with congregations.

We follow the discussion of the organizational changes taking place in each period with three additional perspectives that help to clarify why and how the church in the United States developed as it did. The first perspective deals with the growth and maturing of *missiology as a discipline* in response to the changes occurring in the relationship of the church to the broader society. This part of the story helps explain why the church was slow to develop and use a theological missiology to shape its life and ministry. The key connection is that the missiological engagements pursued by the church are basically formed by the theological imagination the church possessed at the time, especially with respect to the important issues of ecclesiology and the relationship of the church to the world.

The second perspective deals with the diverse *public missiologies of the church* that were developed and used as the church sought to engage its changing context. These missiological engagements have distinctive characteristics that are associated with each period; but there is also continuity of broader themes as the multifaceted gospel came to expression. The third perspective deals with the primary practices associated with *theological education and leadership formation* during each period in response to changes taking place in the church and the broader context. This history helps to explain why and how the pastors that were formed helped to lead the church to pursue the public missiologies that it did.

At this point we remind the reader of the two different ways to read this book that we suggested in the introduction. We encourage you to proceed through each chapter in the normal sequence, in which the narrative of the church in America unfolds historically. This will help you understand the evolution of the complex dynamics that have shaped the church as it

---

following books: "An Ecclesiastical Geno-Project: Unpacking the DNA of Denominations and Denominationalism," in *The Missional Church and Denominations: Helping Congregations Develop a Missional Identity*, ed. Craig Van Gelder (Grand Rapids: Eerdmans, 2008), 12–45; and "Theological Education and Missional Leadership Formation: Can Seminaries Prepare Missional Leaders for Congregations?," in *The Missional Church and Leadership Formation: Helping Congregations Develop Leadership Capacity*, ed. Craig Van Gelder (Grand Rapids: Eerdmans, 2009), 11–44.

exists in America today. On the other hand, you may want to proceed from here to chapter 7, in order to examine the church in relation to our own time—if that is your primary interest. After you have finished Part 3 in that strategy, we invite you to come back here to examine chapters 3 through 6/7 and explore in more detail the influences that brought about the church as it exists in America today—and the changing context as we now know it.

CHAPTER 3

The Colonial Experience, 1600s to 1780s

The Church during the Colonial Period

The church in the colonial period developed primarily because of European invasion, conquest, immigration, and settlement within territories that were already inhabited. As a result, the public missiologies that the church engaged in reflected these realities. On the whole, they represent one of the darker eras of the history of Christian mission. Telling this story requires a basic understanding of what was taking place in the church in Europe during the fifteenth and sixteenth centuries. While the details of this story are important, it is necessary to sketch only several key developments in order to frame the argument we are making in this chapter. There were two that especially shaped the conditions giving rise to the church in the colonial period.

The first key development was the continued strengthening of the emerging nation-states of Western Europe, which had become major maritime powers by the late 1400s, especially Spain and Portugal. Their ships were soon exploring the coastlines to the south and around Africa, and then to the east. Some traversed the vast ocean to the west, where they encountered lands that were already inhabited by native peoples. Wherever these explorers traveled, they planted their national flag to claim these new territories for their respective countries. Since these were Catholic countries, their monarchs worked in concert with the papacy to extend the Catholic faith to the people they encountered.

Their approach typically involved military conquest, which was especially true of Spain in South and Central America, islands in the Caribbean, and the territories along the southern and southwest border of what was to become the United States. France emerged as a major maritime power by the late 1500s, and also joined in the activity of invading and claiming new territories for the crown. Included in French explorations and land claims was the building of settlements in the area that would become Canada. The priests of the French missionary orders were soon traveling down the inland rivers into the territory that would become the United States.

The second key development was the Protestant Reformation, which began in the early 1500s in Germany and then rapidly spread to other northern European countries. Eventually, the control the Roman Catholic Church had over these countries was broken; these nation-states each created a state church that reflected the unique development of the Protestant faith within their country: Germany and Scandinavian countries became Lutheran, the Netherlands became Reformed, and England became Anglican. But alongside these state churches, a variety of sectarian groups emerged that sought to form a church that would be free from state control—for example, Anabaptists and Mennonites on the continent, Quakers and Puritans in England.

These developments led to the outbreak of religious wars across Europe during the second half of the sixteenth century. The religious wars culminated in the (later named) Thirty Years' War, which was waged between Catholic and Protestant territories between 1618 and 1648. Also featured in this warfare was the persecution of the sectarian groups—by both Catholics and mainstream Protestants. During the same period, England and the Netherlands emerged as major maritime powers, and they began to colonize distant lands by way of the same processes of invasion, conquest, immigration, and settlement. It was in this context that a series of colonial settlements were started, primarily by the British in the territories that eventually became the United States.

The church that developed in the 1600s in colonial America reflected all the diversity of the church in Europe, but there was one major difference. The territorial religious warfare that was being waged across Europe did not find its way into the colonies. The diversity of faith traditions emerging within the colonies eventually required a new way of understanding the church and its relationship to the state by the end of the seventeenth century.[1] The results were: (1) freedom of religion was legitimated by the

---

1. Mark A. Noll, *The Old World Religion in the New World: The History of North American Christianity* (Grand Rapids: Eerdmans, 2002), 31-32. Noll observes that, "even as the

end of the colonial period in the legal separation of church and state, and (2) the formation and legitimation of the denominational form of the church became the norm. The rest of this chapter provides some perspective on why and how these developments took place, and their implications for the church that emerged in America.

Key Themes, Events, and Population Shifts

Native Americans as First Inhabitants

The European invaders who came into what became known as North America encountered a population that had occupied the land for centuries—the Native Americans. Population migration over that land mass actually dates back thousands of years. Tribes from Eurasia who came to be called American Indians were the first to populate this vast territory. It is theorized that the original migrants passed over a land bridge between Asia and modern-day Alaska that once connected the two continents roughly 12,000 years ago.[2] A great diversity of tribal cultures developed and settled within Central America and North America over the centuries.[3] By the time the European invasions began, the numerous tribal nations to the north "had occupied and shaped every part of the Americas, establishing extensive trade networks and roads."[4] The Europeans were largely unaware of it, but they had entered an extensively inhabited landscape.

The narrative of European powers "discovering" the territories of the New World was the predominant way of telling the American story up until the past few decades. This approach draws deeply on the Western tradition

Puritans and Anglicans strengthened their positions, a rising number of alternatives—either to the Protestantism of the English colonies or the assumptions of establishment—were emerging as well."

2. Spencer Wells, *The Journey of Man: A Genetic Odyssey* (New York: Random House, 2004), 138–40.

3. Roxanne Dunbar-Ortiz, *An Indigenous Peoples' History of the United States* (Boston: Beacon, 2014), 15. The author notes that, in about 8500 BCE, "domestication of plants took place around the globe . . . based on corn," with three of these settlements located in the Americas.

4. Dunbar-Ortiz, *An Indigenous Peoples' History*, 27–29. The roads were typically "developed along rivers, and many Indigenous roads in North America tracked the Mississippi, Ohio, Missouri, Columbia, and Colorado Rivers, the Rio Grande, and other major streams." These roadways also ran parallel along the seacoasts.

of the formation of modern nation-states. The maritime European nations in the fifteenth through seventeenth centuries quite arrogantly planted their flags on newly encountered territories as being the first to "discover" them and then proceeded to make colonial claims of ownership of these territories for their king and country. In doing so, they brought assumptions about private ownership of land that stood at odds with those of the native peoples. This European invasion, beginning in the late fifteenth century, actually represented a "settler colonialism," in which the land was possessed and the rights of private ownership were enforced. But this "discovery" narrative has been substantially deconstructed in recent decades.[5] Rather than being "discovered," the portion of geography that eventually came to be known as the United States is better understood as a narrative of being a *contested territory* over the centuries, and especially so in the past five hundred years. The European powers were but one set of players who competed to occupy it.

The size of the Native American population of what became the United States in the sixteenth century is a subject of debate among historians: estimates vary greatly, ranging from 2.1 million to 18 million.[6] Trading relationships between the Native Americans and Europeans were developed to some extent in the 1600s, but warfare between the colonial invaders and the tribes all too often became the norm, as the European invaders enforced the displacement of the Native Americans from their lands. Several European nations were implicated in this pattern of invasion, conquest, immigration, and settlement that took place. The initial settlements by the Spanish were located in the Southeast along the seacoast of what is today Florida and the Gulf Coast. These settlements were soon followed by others, with the Spanish pushing north from Mexico into the Southwest. The French arrived on the continent from a different location, settling along the northern Atlantic seacoast of what is today Canada and then traveling and trading with native populations along the rivers into the heartland of the continent.

The British represent the third major European incursion into native lands: they created permanent settlements along the Eastern Seaboard all

---

5. Dunbar-Ortiz, *An Indigenous Peoples' History*, 1–14. This continues to take place as the legal rights of the indigenous tribes who actually occupied these territories are legitimated. Furthermore, no one term of definition has been agreed on to define these tribal populations. Some prefer being referred to as American Indians, while others identify as Indigenous or Aboriginals, while still others use Native American.

6. Russel Thornton, *American Indian Holocaust and Survival: A Population History since 1492* (Norman: University of Oklahoma Press, 1990), 26–32.

the way from what now is Georgia in the South to Nova Scotia and New-foundland to the north. Engagement with the Native Americans by these various European newcomers varied in these regions—all the way from cooperative trade to open conflict. However, the primary pattern over the next several hundred years was a systematic displacement of native populations by means of wars and treaties, a process greatly facilitated by the decimation of the Native American population base via diseases that the Europeans introduced, especially smallpox.[7]

The church was actively involved in all of the early settlement patterns of the Europeans as they encountered the Native American populations. The primary pattern introduced by the Spanish was one of conquering and colonizing: the Jesuit and Franciscan priests usually worked hand in hand with the conquistadors to conquer, settle, convert, and govern the native population. The primary pattern that the French used was seeking to co-exist with the native tribes and trade with them. The priests from various Catholic orders usually worked alongside the French explorers, traders, and merchants as they established alliances with the indigenous population. The pattern within the British settlements was a bit more diverse: some, such as John Eliot, tried to domesticate the Native Americans by having them live in "praying towns" under the pretext of protecting them from being massacred.[8] But the dominant pattern was one of conflict and warfare: the white settlements continued to encroach on Indian lands and to displace the inhabitants.

Some efforts were made to introduce the Christian faith to the native population without the use of force. But until the 1760s (at least), Europeans generally assumed that introducing Christianity to Native Americans was synonymous with introducing them to European culture. Therefore, the natives were viewed as needing to be "civilized" before they could be converted, a view that has now been severely criticized by Native Americans

---

7. George C. Kohn, *Encyclopedia of Plague and Pestilence: From Ancient Times to the Present* (New York: InfoBase Publishing, 2008), 33.

8. Changing historiographical approaches to mission history in the 1970s and 1980s brought many of the practices of Eliot under critical review and substantial criticism, and, to some extent, helpfully so. See, e.g., the substantive critique of Eliot's mission work by George E. Tinker, *Missionary Conquest: The Gospel and Native American Cultural Genocide* (Minneapolis: Augsburg Fortress, 1993). Some recent scholarship, however, has sought to restore more balance in the overall assessment of Eliot's work in general and his "praying towns" in particular. See also Richard W. Cogley, *John Eliot's Mission to the Indians before King Philip's War* (Cambridge, MA: Harvard University Press, 1999).

such as George Tinker.[9] Ironically, the Native Americans became effective missionaries in attracting the French and English to adopt some aspects of their culture and practices.[10] Treaties that were eventually reached typically led to the displacement of native peoples to other territories, usually further inland, where whites had yet to settle. This invasion by new settlers into Native American lands, of what was to become the United States, was well under way by the early 1600s and continued all the way into the late 1800s.

European Settler Colonialism

A number of important developments took place within these territories during the colonial period. These include the competing interests of Spain, France, and England, all of which made claims regarding various areas within these territories. As we have noted earlier, the Wars of Religion taking place in Europe, which broke out during the Protestant Reformation in the 1500s, continued well into the late 1600s and led many to immigrate, as new colonies were being established. Numerous people from Christian sectarian groups who had been persecuted by the emerging Protestant state churches also immigrated to the newly established colonies, where they became disproportionally greater in number than they had been back in Europe.

The church that emerged in these colonial settlements reflected all the diversity of the now divided church in Europe. There were five colonies in the north that became the refuge and domain of the Puritans from England; they proceeded to establish the Congregational Church in what became New England.[11] The mid-Atlantic and southern colonies were developed as chartered colonies of the crown and saw the establishment of the Anglican Church.[12] The middle colonies became home to many of the sec-

---

9. James Axtell, *The Invasion Within: The Contest of Cultures in Colonial North America* (New York: Oxford University Press, 1985); Tinker, *Missionary Conquest*, 4. Tinker notes that European missionaries failed to distinguish the gospel from their own culture and that "the Christian missionaries—of all denominations working among American Indian nations— were partners in genocide. Unwittingly no doubt, and always with the best of intentions . . . [they] blurred any distinction between the gospel of salvation and their own culture."

10. Axtell, *The Invasion Within*, 302.

11. Noll, *The Old World Religion*, 29-30. These were Plymouth (1620), Massachusetts Bay (1630), Connecticut (1636), New Haven (1638), and New Hampshire (1629).

12. Noll, *The Old World Religion*, 31. The establishment of the Anglican Church in the

tarian groups from England, as well as immigrants from across Europe who sought a place to practice their faith without persecution. But some of them settled within the other colonies as well. New Amsterdam was founded by the Netherlands, and the Reformed Church became the church of that colony. And Lord Baltimore received a charter from the English crown to establish the colony of Maryland as a safe haven for Roman Catholics during the seventeenth-century wars of religion.

The later European wars, those of the late seventeenth and eighteenth centuries, were transposed onto the North American continent, and various Native American tribes were caught up in the conflicts due to alliances they made with one or more of the European powers.[13] The French and Indian War (1754–1763) was consequential for a number of reasons relative to the emerging thirteen colonies. It expanded English control of territories that would eventually become Canada, while it reduced French control in lower Canada. It also displaced the French from the interior of what would soon become the extended territories of the new states. In addition, it served as a training ground for a new generation of colonists, those who would soon revolt against England and engage in their own Revolutionary War (1775–1783).

African American Population as a Subculture

Another kind of contesting for the land came as a result of the introduction of slavery, which resulted in the creation of an intentional subculture consisting of an enslaved population. The first African slaves were introduced into the Jamestown settlement in 1619, arriving on a Dutch ship that had taken them from a Spanish slave ship.[14] Initially, they were treated as indentured servants, similar to those who came to the colonies from Europe to work for a period of time in paying off their indenture commitment before being freed. Within a few decades, however, it became increasingly clear

---

colonies included first Virginia (1619), which was joined by the Carolinas (founded 1636 and established 1706), Maryland (1691), and parts of New York City (1693).

13. These wars took place from time to time between 1688 and 1763. The final war of these extended campaigns, known as the French and Indian War, took place between 1754 and 1763 and was actually a subset of the larger conflict between France and England in their Seven Years War on the continent.

14. Darlene Clark Hine et al., *African Americans: A Concise History* (Boston: Pearson Education, 2012), 53.

that a larger labor force was required for agricultural work than could be provided by this means. The imporation of slaves, which had been practiced by the Spanish for some time, soon spread into the British colonies all the way from the Carolinas and Georgia in the South to Massachusetts in the North.

The system of enslaving African peoples and relocating them to the New World was extensive and involved a number of European countries. But the total percentage of enslaved Africans caught in this system who actually ended up in the British colonies that became the United States was quite low: estimates place it at about 4 percent of the total number of Africans sold into slavery in the Americas. This relatively low percentage of the total, however, actually represented several hundreds of thousands of slaves, which indicates how extensive the whole system was, especially throughout the Caribbean. It was particularly in the southern colonies of what became the United States that the practice of slavery became deeply embedded over time within the agricultural system of raising the cash crops of rice, tobacco, and cotton. The colonial version of slavery developed modestly during the 1600s, but it became much more extensive in the first decades of the 1700s, as Southern agricultural practices that were based on slavery were maturing.[15]

Various churches became implicated early on in this system of slavery. Many of the owners who purchased slaves in the Eastern markets chose to have their slaves baptized, a practice that churches accepted as a way of trying to help Christianize (and control) those slaves. Christianity thus became an important part of the slave experience in the colonies; some aspects of it were under the control and watchful eye of the owners, and other aspects became part of a hidden slave version of church. "In the slave quarters, African Americans organized their own 'invisible institution' . . . they called believers to 'hush harbors' where they freely mixed African rhythms, singing, and beliefs with evangelical Christianity."[16] This deep connection between African Americans and Christianity became a critical part of the story line of the United States regarding the continued *contesting* taking place in this land. The challenge it presented to the church was unique because "American forms of racial division *within the same forms* of Chris-

---

15. This was especially true in the early 1800s, when Eli Whitney's cotton gin was perfected and became operational, thus ensuring the economic viability of a slave plantation economy in the states of the South.

16. Laurie F. Maffly-Kipp, "An Introduction to the Church in the Southern Black Community," http://www.docsouth.unc.edu/church/intro.html (accessed June 10, 2016).

tianity had no direct counterpart in Europe."[17] It was painfully and divisively worked out over time in constitutional compromises, the Civil War, reconstruction, Jim Crow legislation, and the civil rights movement—and continues to this day with movements such as Black Lives Matter.[18]

The African American population increased dramatically by the time of the American Revolution—both from further slaves being imported and purchased as well as from natural growth through the birth of children. By 1790 there were 750,000 people of African descent, mostly slaves, within the newly formed states, representing 19 percent of the total US population of 3.9 million at the beginning of the new republic.[19]

European Immigration

It was the immigrants from European countries, primarily England, who brought to the fore the further contesting for the territories that became the United States. These invading settlements by the end of the seventeenth century had become organized as thirteen colonies ranging from the "colony" of Georgia in the South to the "province" of Massachusetts Bay in the North. The population in the thirteen original colonies stood at 3.9 million by 1790: 3.1 million of that total was white European.[20]

It is important to note that diversity was a part of the story of the church in these colonies from the very beginning. At least five different cultural regions with distinctly different social imaginaries or cultural frameworks emerged within the thirteen original colonies that influenced the development of the church. These diverse cultural regions held competing views during the colonial period, though they eventually united to support the Revolution and, by making the necessary compromises, to create the United States. In many ways, these differences continue to this day and help us understand some of the social, political, and religious distinctives that exist between geographic regions in the United States today.[21]

17. Noll, *The Old World Religion*, 17 (italics in original).

18. Keeanga-Yamahtta Taylor, *From #BlackLivesMatter to Black Liberation* (Chicago: Haymarket Books, 2016).

19. The African American percentage of the overall population today stands at approximately 11 percent.

20. Note that all population figures used in chapters 2 and 3 are taken from official US Census documents.

21. Colin Woodard, *American Nations: A History of the Eleven Rival Regional Cultures*

The northern colonies consisted of what Woodard refers to as "Yankeedom," which was settled largely by English Puritans who sought to form the equivalent of a Protestant theocracy, and they established the Congregational Church in their colonies (57, 60). Perry Miller referred to this as their "errand into the wilderness," where they attempted to use the powers of government to build a better society, one that focused on civic responsibilities and maintained public morality.[22] Located in close proximity to these colonies, but representing a contrasting culture, was the territory of New Netherlands, originally settled by the Dutch (now New York). It maintained a Reformed church that was connected to Classis Amsterdam in the old country. This settlement was taken over in 1664 by the English, who introduced the Anglican Church—while also allowing for religious diversity. The social imaginary, as well as the economy of this area, was based on global trade, resulting in the creation of a society where "diversity, tolerance, upward mobility, and an overwhelming emphasis on private enterprise" was the order of the day (Woodard, 66).[23]

The middle colonies, referred to by Woodard as "The Midlands," had been originally settled by the Quakers, who openly welcomed other sectarian groups that were persecuted by the state churches of Europe. The social imaginary of this area was shaped by a "tolerant, multicultural, multilingual" religious population of modest means "who desired mostly that their government and leaders leave them in peace" (92). Just to the south lay the colony of Virginia, which is referred to by Woodard as the "Tidewater" area. These settlers had come to "conquer and rule," by contrast to the small-scale farmers of The Midlands to the north and those who sought to build a new society further north in New England—Yankeedom (44–45).

In the middle of the colonies, the Tidewater area was developed as a plantation society by Anglican gentry who embraced a "*classical* republicanism" and sought to emulate ancient Athens as a slave-holding elite (54). Further to the south lay the area known even today as the "Deep South," where a society developed that was tied deeply to the West Indian slave

---

of North America (New York: Penguin, 2011), is helpful in mapping these differences. Hereafter, page references to this work appear in parentheses within the text.

22. Perry Miller, *Errand into the Wilderness* (Cambridge, MA: Belknap Press, 1956).

23. See also Roger Panetta, *Dutch New York: The Roots of Hudson Valley Culture* (New York: Fordham University Press, 2009), for a helpful discussion of Dutch contributions in shaping what later became the basic principles of the Revolution and the founding of the nation.

culture and slave trade. Here there were "radical disparities in wealth and power, with a tiny elite" controlling the rest of the population and using it to promote their own extravagant welfare (82). From its center in Charleston, in the colony of South Carolina, this slave-holding elite, initially mostly Anglican in religion, would be joined in the next century by Baptists and Methodists in spreading this slave-based society across what would become all of the states of the South.

The English represented the majority of immigrants along the Eastern Seaboard during the colonial period, coming as part of the established Anglican church, the dissenting Puritans, or various other sectarian groups from the English state church, such as the Baptists, Quakers, and Shakers. These were joined by immigrants from other European state churches, as well as persecuted sects from across Europe, especially from German territories, such as the Moravians, Mennonites, Amish, Schwenkfelders, and Dunkers. It took some time, but the gradually increasing numbers of these new settlers came to realize that their shared plurality of Christian faith expressions required a different organizational identity from that of the *establishment* in order for each expression to be able to claim legitimacy as a valid church.

This alternative conception of the church came into existence as the denominational, organizational church. It emerged as a *voluntaristic ecclesial body* that presupposed "a condition of legal or de facto toleration and religious freedom."[24] It can best be understood as having an *organizational self-understanding around a purposive intent.*[25] By the mid- to late 1700s, the denominational view of the church in the colonies—soon to become states—became the normative understanding of the diverse associations of churches that were being formed within the growing system of congregations. At that time the Roman Catholic Church that settled in Maryland resisted this understanding in its efforts to maintain a sense of establishment, which continued for many decades. Their establishment was limited to maintaining tight control over their own membership and by building extensive institutions to serve them. Over time, however, the Catholic Church had to accept the reality that it was, in fact, functioning much like any other denomination within the setting of the United States.

---

24. Russell E. Richey, *Denominationalism Illustrated and Explained* (Eugene, OR: Cascade Books, 2013), 2.

25. Craig Van Gelder, "An Ecclesiastical Geno-Project," 12–45.

System of Congregations

Immigrants came to the colonies for many reasons. But large numbers of them came for religious reasons, especially those sectarian groups that had been persecuted in Europe. The Puritans who settled in the New England colonies—Yankeedom—became the first and largest concentration of this type of immigration. The churches they initially established in these colonies tried to exercise tight control over every facet of life. The Anglicans, who settled primarily in the Tidewater area and the Deep South, were able, for a time, to establish the Anglican Church, with its parish system exercising a kind of religious domain.

These efforts at establishment, however, were only partially successful in controlling the development of the church within the respective territories, partly because of the presence of dissenting groups. The establishment approach became increasingly obsolete by the early decades of the eighteenth century, especially as the Great Awakening, through the revival efforts of George Whitefield and others, helped foster the growth of diverse expressions of the faith, which became more evangelical in character.[26] This shift "marked the passing of Puritanism and the rise of evangelicalism as the dominant Protestant expression in America." It was a form of the faith that would become readily transportable to the frontier by the end of the eighteenth century.[27]

The middle colonies—The Midlands—were settled initially by sectarian groups such as the Quakers, Mennonites, and English Baptists, along with other settlers coming from the established churches of Europe, for example, Reformed immigrants from the Netherlands, Lutheran immigrants from Germany and Scandinavia, and Scots-Irish Presbyterians from Scotland and Northern Ireland. The congregations related to the state churches of Europe, such as the Reformed and Lutheran, continued to look to the churches of their respective home countries to provide congregational leadership. By contrast, the sectarian immigrant groups had to rely on leadership to emerge in whatever form it could from within their own ranks.

An important shift had begun to take place in the emerging system of congregations in the late 1600s, which was furthered by the Great Awakening in the early 1700s: the growing obsolescence of enforcing an estab-

---

26. Noll, *The Old World Religion*, 51; see also Thomas S. Kidd, *The Great Awakening: The Roots of Evangelical Christianity in Colonial America* (New Haven: Yale University Press, 2009); and Robert Philip, *Life and Times of the Reverend George Whitefield, M.A.* (San Bernardino, CA: Ulan Press, 2012).

27. Noll, *The Old World Religion*, 52.

lishment approach as practiced by the Congregationalists and Anglicans. This was also the case in England, where the Act of Toleration was passed by the English Parliament in 1689. It provided for freedom of worship for the Nonconformists in Great Britain, where these groups continued to represent only a minority within England. This same principle of toleration increasingly took root in the American colonies, especially in light of the Great Awakening; the congregations that expected to be able to practice freedom of worship in the colonies soon became the majority. Their viewpoint became legally represented in Article 3 of the Bill of Rights, passed in 1791, which created a wall of separation between the church and the state.

The majority of the immigrants brought with them two distinctive realities: (1) their ethnicity and (2) their distinct version of the Christian faith. During the colonial period, the congregations of all the diverse forms that emerged represented what might be called the *ethnic-immigrant congregation*. The core identity of this type of congregation was largely its ethnic makeup and the faith tradition it practiced; often whole congregations migrated from the old country. Most of these congregations functioned as intergenerational extended family systems within which the young people usually intermarried. This expanding system of congregations was quite substantial by the time of the Revolutionary War: roughly 3,200 congregations had come into existence over the preceding 150 years.[28]

Development of the Denominational, Organizational Church

What is important to note about the church in the United States is that it was within the crucible of the colonial experience that a new organizational expression of the church was born: the denominational-organizational church. This development marked a distinctive shift in understanding from the entire previous history of the church.[29] Mark Noll observes that "the 'denomination' in America is neither a 'church' nor a 'sect.' Rather, it is a singular product of an environment defined by great space, the absence of formal church-state ties, and competition among many ecclesiastical bodies."[30] A number of important influences were associated with its coming into being.

28. Roger Finke and Rodney Stark, *The Churching of America, 1776–2005: Winners and Losers in Our Religious Economy* (New Brunswick, NJ: Rutgers University Press, 2005), 28.
29. Martin E. Marty, *Righteous Empire: The Protestant Experience in America* (New York: Dial Press, 1970), 67–68.
30. Noll, *The Old World Religion*, 23.

The Two Strains of Reformation and Restoration

There were two diverse groups that made up the faith communities that became fully developed denominations.[31] One group represented denominations deriving from the established state churches of the magisterial Protestant Reformation of Europe. These churches worked from the premise of having territorial domain, and they embraced a theology of *ecclesia semper reformanda* (the "church is always reforming") from the Reformation. In the context of the colonies and emerging states, they had to recontextualize their European understandings of ecclesiology, polity, and liturgy to fit the new setting. For example, the Anglicans, who were renamed Episcopalians in 1785, soon found that they had to forgo the practice of parish boundaries that was so basic to church life in England.[32]

Other groups offered an alternative to that pattern. They sought to create something new within the emerging nation, and they took their starting point from the Noncomformists (Independents) in England: the practice of going back to biblical foundations to restore the Christian church to its original intent, or "Restoration." The denominations that came to represent the Restoration impulse stand in contrast to those representing the reforming impulse; they constitute what might be called the first phase of made-in-America denominations.[33]

Free Church Ecclesiology

The formation of this new identity for the church—what we identify as the denominational church with an organizational self-understanding around a purposive identity—drew on a number of historical developments taking place in the Church of England as it clarified its ecclesiology and polity. Russell Richey notes that English contributions toward normalizing toler-

---

31. Sidney E. Mead, "Denominationalism: The Shape of Protestantism in America," in *Denominationalism*, ed. Russell E. Richey (Nashville: Abingdon, 1977), 73–75.

32. Mead, "Denominationalism," 76.

33. Noll, *The Old World Religion*, 53–54. An example is the Baptists in Rhode Island under the leadership of Roger Williams. See also John M. Barry, *Roger Williams and the Creation of the American Soul: Church, State, and the Birth of Liberty* (New York: Penguin, 2012). Numerous other groups would follow this pattern over the next two centuries, as the United States expanded into the frontier territories.

ance included "the Restoration, particularly after the Glorious Revolution, the Acts of Toleration, the writings of John Locke and others, and the path-making efforts of newly tolerated English Presbyterians, Congregationalists, Baptists, and Quakers (recognized as Dissenters or Nonconformists)."[34] It was here that the incorporation of free-church ecclesiology became central to understanding the denominational expression of the church. All of these influences proved to be formative for the emergence of the denominational form of the church in the colonies.

Free-church ecclesiology had emerged during the Protestant Reformation among the Anabaptists, who conceived of the church primarily as a gathered social community of professing believers that had the freedom to associate and the right to govern its own affairs.[35] Also influential was the work of English Baptists, who formulated their foundational principles in the Savoy Declaration of 1658.[36] In time, the churches in the colonies with ecclesiologies and polities deriving from European state churches were required to make adjustments.[37] The primary adjustment made by all colonial churches toward the end of the 1700s, with the formal separation of church and state, was the adoption of free-church ecclesiology, at least as an overlay of it on their previous ecclesiologies.

Church as Voluntary Organization

A parallel development that fed into the conception of the denominational church during the colonial experience was the understanding that religious freedom required the church to be developed on a voluntary basis. By the

---

34. Richey, *Denominationalism Illustrated and Explained*, 154.

35. See, e.g., the Dordrecht Confession (1632), which was adopted by the Mennonites, especially article 7 concerning the Church of Christ.

36. Sydney E. Ahlstrom, *A Religious History of the American People* (New Haven: Yale University Press, 1972), 94. An earlier representative figure of this tradition, John Smyth (1554–1612), had developed a free-church view of the church first in England, and later in exile in the Netherlands. He emphasized the importance of obedience and a biblical form of church organization as being essential for the church in addition to the word, sacraments, and the gathered assembly of God's people. See Miroslav Volf, *After Our Likeness: The Church as the Image of the Trinity* (Grand Rapids: Eerdmans, 1998), 23–24, 131–34.

37. A helpful discussion of the shift to the gathered church as a voluntary organization in the midst of the breakdown of the parish system is provided in John Corrigan and Winthrop S. Hudson, *Religion in America,* 10th ed. (Upper Saddle River, NJ: Pearson/Prentice Hall, 2010), 40–42.

late 1600s and early 1700s, the concept of voluntary associations was increasingly appropriated for this purpose.[38] The notion of the voluntary character of the church was conceptualized by John Locke in 1689 in A Letter Concerning Toleration.[39]

> A Church I take to be a voluntary society of men, joining themselves together of their own accord in order to the public worshipping of God in such manner as they judge acceptable to Him. . . . I say it is a free and voluntary society. Nobody is born a member of any church; . . . since the joining together of several members into this church-society . . . is absolutely free and spontaneous, it necessarily follows that the right of making its laws can belong to none but the society itself; or at least to those whom the society by common consent has authorized thereunto.

Locke used the notion of social contract to conceive of the church similar to what he had done with regard to developing the social order of civil society. This view was ratified within the English experience that same year with the formal adoption of the Act of Toleration in 1689. The freedom to develop the church on a voluntary basis became first legitimated in England. But it came to its more prominent expression in the emerging colonies that would become the United States, where it was married to a free-church ecclesiology and became "the great point of distinction for the American church."[40] As a result, the emerging voluntary associations of congregations in the colonies became formal denominations by the late 1700s—when the United States was formed. The pattern of understanding church life in America as voluntary in nature quickly became married to the emerging denominational form of the church.

---

38. Richey, *Denominationalism Illustrated and Explained*, 126–33; see also Ahlstrom, *A Religious History*, 217–29.

39. http://www.constitution.org/jl/tolerati.htm (accessed November 28, 2016). Locke wrote this letter to his Dutch friend Philip von Limborch while in exile there in 1685, and in it he called for an end to the oppression of people who held unorthodox religious beliefs. The letter was published without Locke's permission after he returned to England following the "Glorious Revolution" of 1688.

40. Richey, *Denominationalism Illustrated and Explained*, 126.

Divine Destiny or Noble Experiment

Many of the immigrants into the colonies in the 1600s brought with them the expectation of being able to exercise religious freedom. But a number of them, especially those trying to restore the church to its biblical roots, brought a keen sense that it was God's divine providence that was providing them with an opportunity to do so in this new land. This was especially true of the Puritans in Yankeedom, though the Quakers in the colony of Pennsylvania held similar views. The Puritans under John Winthrop's leadership arrived at the conclusion that they "could 'tarry for the magistrate' no longer, lest they be extinguished altogether. As a saving remnant, they left England behind, to become a kind of Church of Christ in Exile, a 'city on a hill' for all the world to see."[41]

The biblical narrative of the Exodus played large in this vision as the Puritans immigrated to the Promised Land. Finally, they were free to form a society where church and state worked together to re-create humanity—what they conceived of as *divine destiny*. This perspective represents a rather high view of God's unique blessing, leading the Puritans to legislate strong communal norms of moral sanctification in order to usher in the millennial kingdom. It is also a strain of Christianity that introduced into denominational church life in America the concept of "Christian" as an adjective to define America, a strain that is still very much alive and contested to this day.

Their vision of community was eschatological in character: they believed that establishing a society without sin would bring a new era for all of humankind.[42] Central to this approach was discipline: bringing all of life under what they understood to be biblical norms of behavior and control. It was a social imaginary that gave birth to one version of what became known as American exceptionalism: (1) that America's history and setting was unique in its being formed as a new nation; (2) that the political ideology of personal liberty and responsibility are central to its core identity; and (3) that America possesses unique traits and has a mission to serve as an example for the broader world to follow.[43]

Another version of American exceptionalism drew more from En-

---

41. Ahlstrom, *A Religious History*, 145.

42. See Ernest Lee Tuveson, *Redeemer Nation: The Idea of America's Millennial Role* (Chicago: University of Chicago Press, 1968).

43. Charles Murray, *American Exceptionalism: An Experiment in History* (Washington, DC: AEI Press, 2013), 7–37.

lightenment ideals that held to a deistic view of God. Founding fathers such as Thomas Jefferson championed the exercise of human reason in constructing a social contract to form a better society relative to the unique situation of the colonies. They held to a sense of civic responsibility that increased in importance during the mid-1700s, as tensions with England began to grow and calls for independence began to increase. The call for patriotic loyalty in the support of the revolutionary cause came to be nurtured by many within these churches, as it was among churches that developed from sectarian roots.[44]

In what was assumed to be a Christian society (even though diversely expressed in the American context), the church's mission was focused on upholding morality, assisting the vulnerable, and sanctifying society from the center. This was the more secular version of American exceptionalism and became known as the "noble experiment." The result of this was a conflict over how best to frame the national narrative. Was it to be told primarily in terms of divine destiny or noble experiment?[45] The majority of the churches on both sides, regardless of how they framed the narrative, viewed America as unique in the world, and they accepted supporting the nation as their patriotic duty.

Developments Regarding the Discipline of Missiology

It is important to understand that the formal discipline of missiology developed only slowly in the Protestant church in the aftermath of the Protestant Reformation of the sixteenth century. When it did begin to develop, it emerged within a Protestant Christendom worldview. This had significant implications for the church, as well as the fledgling discipline of missiology, since various public missiologies were developed in relation to the worldview of Christendom. It would take several centuries for the discipline to move beyond this framework, and even then some of its vestiges lingered on.

The emergence of the discipline finally began to take place for Protestants in the eighteenth century, two hundred years after the Protestant Ref-

44. This was more complicated for the Anglican clergy, since they were initially loyalists who had sworn an oath of allegiance to the king at their ordination. Large numbers of them left for England during the Revolutionary War.

45. These competing narratives have continued to be part of the US story since that time and in many ways have coalesced around particular political parties since the twentieth century.

ormation had used a Christendom worldview for shaping the relationship of the church to the world. This worldview made the primary focus of theology one of helping the state church relate to what was assumed to already be a Christian society, with the church working in tandem with a presumably Christian magistrate to carry out its ministry. When Protestant state churches began to become involved in cross-cultural missions, they carried them out via the initiative and under the oversight of the magistrate/king, an understanding that changed only slowly over the decades that followed.

However, there were some important developments in the Roman Catholic Church that took place during the two centuries following the Protestant Reformation that helped to shape the discipline of missiology as it later emerged among Protestants. The Catholic Church also operated in relation to a Christendom worldview, so the extensive engagement in missions by Catholic nations throughout the larger world took place as inhabited lands were invaded and settlements were established.

Roman Catholic Developments: Post-Reformation

The Catholic Church began to bring focused attention to the field of missiology during the sixteenth through eighteenth centuries in the aftermath of the Protestant Reformation, by way of the Catholic countries of Spain and Portugal, and later France.[46] The mendicant orders, as well as the newly formed Jesuit Order in the seventeenth century, provided the personnel for this global mission enterprise. An interesting development in the seventeenth century was that Marie of the Incarnation led a group of nuns to New France to establish the Ursuline Order and founded the first girls' school in the New World. Several organizational changes and other developments within the Roman Church in Europe worked to support and give direction to Catholic missions during this period.

- *Sacred Congregation of the Propagation of the Faith (Propaganda)*: Formed by Pope Gregory XV in 1622, this entity was responsible for propagating the Catholic faith around the world by collecting information, developing mission policy, and promoting the development of an indigenous clergy within the mission fields.

---

46. These countries provided the political and military support for the spread of the Catholic faith around the world as their seafaring enterprises encountered already populated lands.

- *Vicars Apostolic*: These bishops were appointed by the pope to serve at large and were directly responsible to the papacy. They helped overcome the inertia in mission fields where insufficient numbers of bishops and priests were provided by Spain and Portugal, and they worked to take power from local governments and give it to the church.
- *Seminary in Paris (Société des Missions Étrangères)*: Formed in 1663, this seminary trained missionary personnel, focusing especially on training persons in ecclesiastical orders to participate in mission throughout the Catholic world.
- *Mission as Contextualization*: Significant cross-cultural missionary work was accomplished in the sixteenth and seventeenth centuries by missionaries such as Francis Xavier, Matteo Ricci, Roberto de Nobili, and Alexandre de Rhodes, who worked to accommodate the faith within diverse cultural contexts.

Several centuries of practicing a missiology of contextualization gradually led to significant controversy within the Roman Catholic Church. This became especially manifest in the Chinese Rites Controversy, which was concerned with such matters as the naming of God, the veneration of ancestors, and the use of vernacular languages. Finally, Pope Benedict XIV issued a papal bull in 1742 that standardized Roman traditional practices and the use of Latin, thus ending two centuries of experimentation. This decision was reinforced in 1773, when Pope Clement XIV disbanded the Jesuits, resulting in at least three thousand missionaries being withdrawn from fields throughout the world.[47]

Protestant Developments: Post-Reformation

Even with the substantial precedents available from the Roman Catholics to inform their work, Protestants were slow to take up the task of engaging in missions following the Reformation. The greater part of their initial energies, shaped by a Christendom worldview, were focused instead on

47. David Bosch, *Transforming Mission* (Maryknoll, NY: Orbis, 1991), 449–50. See also Stephen B. Bevans and Roger P. Schroeder, *Constants in Context: A Theology of Mission for Today* (Maryknoll, NY: Orbis, 2004), 192–95. This controversy came to a head concerning the work of T. M. de Tournon in the Far East in the early 1700s, when he opposed efforts to make the faith more indigenous. A papal bull is a particular type of letter or charter issued by a pope and carrying the authority of the Catholic Church.

pursuing a public missiology of strengthening the gains made in bringing former Catholic territories under Protestant domain. The Peace of Westphalia in 1648 ended the Thirty Years' War and resulted in these energies being redirected toward a public missiology of strengthening particular confessional traditions, often over against one another. It was not until the eighteenth century that significant developments began to take place that brought Protestants into engagement with the growing missions enterprise in the broader world that had been pioneered and developed by the Catholic Church. With this engagement came the development of the theological discipline of missiology.

The Protestant Reformation in the sixteenth century represented a significant shift in the development of Christianity by giving birth to Protestant state churches, which proceeded to persecute the other organizational expressions of the church that had emerged, which they viewed as sects.[48] A primary focus for all was clarifying what they believed, as well as justifying the legitimacy of their historical existence. This produced a variety of confessions, all of which included major articles explicating their understanding of the church—their explicit ecclesiologies.[49] Developing an explicit missiology was not yet a part of their horizon for the state churches.

The Christian groups referred to as "sects" had to work, by default, within the same worldview of Christendom, and they developed a believers' church understanding of the faith, which they used to begin to experiment with cross-cultural missions. Illustrative developments during the seventeenth and eighteenth centuries informing the development of the discipline of missiology for Protestants include the following:

- *Justinian von Welz*: In the mid-seventeenth century, von Welz worked contrary to consensus opinion by offering an argument to the ecclesiastical authorities, largely unsuccessfully, that the Great Commission was still valid.
- *Seminary of Dutch East India Company*: In the early 1600s, this commercial enterprise trained pastors to serve company personnel in

48. The magisterial-led reform movements included the Lutheran churches in Germany and Scandinavia, the Reformed churches in the Netherlands and Scotland, and the Anglican Church in England. The sectarian groups these state churches persecuted included such groups as the Anabaptists, Mennonites, Amish, Puritans, Quakers, and Independent Baptists.

49. Examples include the Augsburg Confession in 1530 (Lutheran); Belgic Confession in 1561; the Heidelberg Catechism in 1563 (Continental Reformed); the Dordrecht Confession in 1632 (Anabaptist); and the Westminster Confession in 1646 (English Reformed).

their expanding colonies, but these pastors were also offered a cash bonus for converts won from among the native populations.

- *John Eliot*: During the seventeenth century, Eliot championed the cause of the Iroquois Indians in the Massachusetts colony, translating the Bible into their native language and forming "praying towns" to help them adjust to the forces of change. His legacy, however, is controversial.
- *Anne Hutchison*: The controversial female preacher in colonial New England in the 1630s was openly critical of certain Puritan ministers. She was a serious student of Scripture and worked primarily with other women, but she was charged with being a heretic and banished from the Bay Colony by Governor John Winthrop.
- *Pietism in Germany at Halle*: Philipp Jakob Spener and August Herman Franke provided the missionaries Zieganbalg and Plütschau, who were sent by King Frederick IV of Denmark to the Danish settlement of Tranquebar off the coast of southeast India in 1705. (Note that the role of the magistrate was required to legitimate this project within Danish territory.)
- *Count Zinzendorf and the Moravians*: In the early eighteenth century, Zinzendorf helped organize the Moravians, who settled on his property in Herrnhut, Germany, as a missionary community; they were then sent to various mission fields around the world.

The seeds for the development of a discipline of missiology planted by these Protestant precursors were substantial, but the flowering of a formal discipline was still missing. Protestants had chosen to cancel out the monastic orders that were common within Catholic ecclesiology; these had historically engaged in missions on behalf of the church. Extensive missionary work by Protestants would have to await the fuller development of the foreign missionary enterprise in the nineteenth century, which was eventually built around the mission society when it emerged.[50] This meant that what became known as the "modern missions movement" came into existence largely from *outside*, and to some extent *alongside*, the established churches of Europe that operated within a Christendom worldview. An organizational structure that was able to function beyond the Christian duties assigned to the magistrate was required for missions to come into their

---

50. See, e.g., Bosch, *Transforming Mission*, 262–345; see also Bevans and Schroeder, *Constants in Context*, 210–12.

own. But the creation of this alternative structure for Protestant missions continues to have huge implications for the church because of the separating of mission and church into two distinct entities.

Protestant Mission Structure: The Mission Society

The formation of the mission society as a specialized voluntary organization to engage in missions began in the seventeenth century and was further developed in the eighteenth century. An early example of a separate mission society in the colonies was the one formed in 1649 by John Eliot to structure his work among the Indians in the Massachusetts colony: the Society for the Propagation of the Gospel in New England.[51] Mark Noll observes that "Protestant voluntary societies had existed in Britain for some time, but they came into their own in America during the early decades of the nineteenth century.[52] Examples of early English mission societies created to work alongside the church were those formed by the Anglicans: the Society for Promoting Christian Knowledge (SPCK, 1698) and the Society for the Propagation of the Gospel in Foreign Parts (SPG, 1701). These proved to be quite strategic for the spread of Anglicanism within areas under British rule around the world, but especially in the American colonies. However, the fuller development of the independent mission society would only take place at the end of the eighteenth century and into the next.

Public Missiologies in the Colonial Period

The church's understanding of the gospel is always contextual, as we discussed in chapter 2. This means that it is tied to particular perspectives and narratives that shape how people relate to the world in which they live. The

51. The English Parliament, on July 27, 1649, enacted an "Ordinance for the Advancement of Civilization and Christianity among the Indians," which created The Society for the Propagation of the Gospel in New England, the first Protestant missionary society: http://www.solagroup.org/articles/historyofthebible/hotb_0005.html (accessed June 10, 2016).

52. Noll, *The Old World Religion*, 67, where he discusses the rise of this important vehicle that Protestants used to engage in missions. See also Bosch, *Transforming Mission*, 280, where he notes that William Carey was an important early proponent, though not the only one, of forming an independent mission society to engage in mission work. He proposed such in his *Inquiry* in 1792.

basic pattern in the United States is for there to emerge a majority cultural narrative, one that is legitimated socially and often institutionalized politically.[53] Churches use various biblical and theological perspectives to frame their particular understanding of the gospel while interacting with the dominant narrative, often in support of some aspects of it while challenging others. Varieties of subculture narratives typically emerge in the midst of these majority narratives that challenge the dominant narrative in some way.

This diversity gives rise to a variety of public missiologies of the church's engagement with its context. Several cultural narratives with differing gospel strains emerged within the colonial period, all operating within or in reaction to a Christendom worldview. Each of these strains influenced how the gospel was understood and expressed in relationship to the context and the key narratives embedded in the culture. The public missiologies that emerged during the colonial period are displayed in the following table:

Table 3.1 Public Missiologies of the Church in the Colonial Period

Missiology Strain	Colonial Period	Frontier Period	Urban Growth Period	Suburban Success Period	Strategies for Success Period
Focus on Nation	Conquest to Civilize and Christianize -Established -Religious Freedom				
Focus on Tradition	Maintain Traditional Faith -Immigrants				
Focus on Engaging in Missions or Mission	Native American Missions				
Focus on Social Reform	"True" Christian Society				
Focus on Justice and Liberation	Pursuing Freedom from Margins -Slavery				
Focus on Revival and Renewal	Revival and Renewal -Great Awakening				
Unique Focus					

53. Charles Taylor, *Modern Social Imaginaries* (Durham, NC: Duke University Press, 2003). Such a cultural narrative, as we discussed earlier, reflects one form of what is known as the "social imaginary."

Many of the original charters approved by the British government for the establishment of colonies in the so-called New World included some aspect of converting the native populations.[54] The assumption was that the nation (England) granting the charters had the authority to direct such activity. This particular effort functioned in practice as *a missiology of conquest to civilize and Christianize* the Native Americans. The operating assumption was that the Indians would best be served by being "Europeanized," even as efforts were being made to Christianize them. Differing views about ownership of property made mutual coexistence impossible: the settlers personally owned property by way of legalized deeds; the Native Americans communally used the land without owning it.[55] The churches transplanted from Europe to the colonies made significant efforts to "civilize and Christianize" the native population, but the typical result of those efforts was hostility, conflict, war, conquest, and displacement.

A variation of this missiology became operative during the period among two other groups: the Anglicans and, to some extent, the Congregationalists. Many of the immigrant colonial congregations came from the European reforming tradition of state churches and were organized according to the ecclesiologies and polities of those state churches, typically along national, ethnic lines. This was especially true of the southern colonies, where the Anglican Church was established. But it was also true of Congregationalists in the New England colonies, who sought to enfranchise the church in society to conform to their religious ideals. The missiology at work can be labeled a *missiology of establishment*. The members of the immigrant churches were given a privileged place in society in return for being good citizens.[56] This approach worked to some extent during the colonial period, but it soon encountered significant challenges as other immigrant groups from different European state churches, such as the German and Scandinavian Lutherans, the Dutch Reformed, and the Scottish Presbyterians, began to settle within their parishes.

Another variation of this missiology became operative for those groups who were opposed to establishment. The seeds of religious diversity in all the colonies were planted by the mid-1600s and began to take deep root

---

54. See, e.g., Anonymous, *The Charters of Massachusetts Bay* (Colorado Springs, CO: CreateSpace Independent Publishing Platform, 2015).

55. Dunbar-Ortiz, *An Indigenous Peoples' History*, 32–44.

56. The cultural understanding supporting a missiology of establishment was adapted from the English pursuit of empire and its expectation of exercising hegemony. Attempting to manage the various colonies politically, economically, and even religiously was the order of the day.

by the early 1700s.[57] The immigrants representing the established churches of Europe, such as Lutheran, Reformed, Presbyterian, and Anglican, soon found themselves living alongside other Christian faith traditions. These included members of the sects who had also emigrated from Europe, such as the Quakers and Mennonites, as well as new groups that emerged from within the colonies, such as the Baptists. Many people from these groups ended up residing within the territories of the established churches; but in the Midlands (Rhode Island, New Jersey, Pennsylvania, and Delaware) it was impossible for any one group to become dominant.[58] The religious freedom-seeking tradition quickly gained currency in these colonies and, over time, came to functionally represent what might be described as a *missiology of religious freedom*. Even in those colonies that made either the Anglican Church or the Congregational Church the established religion, the continued influx of immigrants increased religious diversity and soon led to a call for religious freedom in those areas.[59]

The Roman Catholic Church functioned as the established church in Maryland at that time, and it expected to have domain. But political realities in the colonies soon made it necessary for the Roman Catholic Church to function alongside other churches—that is, largely as another organizational expression of the church. They did so largely by engaging in a *missiology of maintaining the traditional faith*, where they turned inward to practice their own way of life, which acknowledged the de facto acceptance of religious diversity. This required a new imagination of how to conceive of the church as well as how to organize congregations. The old formula of a state church with a privileged establishment identity was becoming increasingly obsolete by the time of the Revolutionary War, though some vestiges of it lingered into the early 1800s.[60]

A number of the colonial charters included the expectation that the colonists would convert the Native American population, and this expectation, as we have noted above, typically resulted in a strategy to Europeanize and civilize them as they Christianized them. However, there was a variation of this strategy by some individuals, who sought to bring the gospel

57. Corrigan and Hudson, *Religion in America*, 45–51.

58. Ahlstrom, *A Religious History*, 200–213; see also Corrigan and Hudson, *Religion in America*, 50–51.

59. Ahlstrom, *A Religious History*, 184–99; see also Corrigan and Hudson, *Religion in America*, 46–50.

60. Ahlstrom, *A Religious History*, 114; e.g., Massachusetts retained vestiges of establishment until 1833.

to the various tribes by engaging in evangelism. This included the work of such pioneers as John Eliot and David Brainerd, who implemented a *missiology to evangelize Native Americans* as a kind of cross-cultural mission, which would later emerge as "foreign missions." These efforts were often misunderstood by other colonists, who took a more militant stand against the Native American tribes.

The formation of the American colonies was the result of diverse interests. Many of the more radical sectarian groups in Europe immigrated to the colonies to secure their religious freedom, especially the Puritans, Baptists, Quakers, and Mennonites. One group in particular—the Puritans in the New England colonies (Yankeedom)—attempted to set up their own version of what can best be described as an effort to form the true believers' church within the social order. Noll notes that the Puritan "leaders translated their aspirations into reality by constructing a society governed by a comprehensive theology of *covenant.*"[61] This extended beyond the principle of establishment in pursuit of what can be described as a *missiology of creating a "true" Christian society.* The focus was on church members living as Christian citizens in public life as they came under the discipline of the law in order to ensure moral behavior. Every effort was made to develop their emerging social order on Christian teachings, and opportunities were regularly found in claiming God's providence for their doing so.

There was another missiological approach that emerged among the African slave community during the colonial period, mostly a result of trying to survive. As we have noted above, the enslavement of this population was often accompanied by the owners having their slaves baptized, usually as a way of better controlling them. But the gospel often offers its own surprises as people come to understand and interact with it. While the slaveowners sought to promote subservience, the emerging black church (largely invisible to whites) developed its own understanding and practices of subversion. The practice of what might be called a *missiology of pursuing freedom from the margins* was the result. Its capacity to foster change in the broader culture was quite limited during the period of slavery, but the seeds planted at that time eventually bore substantial fruit in the cultivation of a black church missiology. This missiology intertwined pietistic and liberationist strains that engendered a movement toward social equality and political change.[62]

---

61. Noll, *The Old World Religion*, 38; see also Ahlstrom, *A Religious History*, 146–50.

62. Raphael G. Warnock, *The Divided Mind of the Black Church: Theology, Piety, and Public Witness* (New York: NYU Press, 2014), 3.

The Great Awakening (early 1730s up to 1740) caught many people in the colonies by surprise. Revival and renewal movements had been known to occur alongside—and even from the underside of—European state churches, often led by laypeople. Now such a movement was afoot in the colonies and was being led by various church leaders, such as Jonathan Edwards, a Congregational pastor, and George Whitefield, an Anglican cleric, both of whom preached a Calvinistic theology. This awakening introduced into the life of the American church what might best be labeled a *missiology of revival and renewal*—similar to what was happening across Europe—an approach to church life that believes that the church is constantly in need of being revived and renewed. This missiological strain has had an enduring presence in the life of the church in the United States ever since.

Theological Education and Leadership Formation

Leadership in the church is always a matter of crucial importance for shaping its ministry. The public missiologies the church engaged in during this period were embedded within a Christendom worldview or emerged in reaction to it. This directly influenced the practices used by the church in forming persons to provide leadership, practices that became quite influential in establishing a framework for theological education for the next several centuries.

It was clear early on that the diverse, ethnic-immigrant congregations in the colonies required qualified leaders, and they pursued different approaches for supplying those leaders. Initially, most of the churches that were derived from state churches continued to look to Europe to supply the necessary ministerial leadership for their congregations. But they often encountered problems in securing an adequate supply of qualified personnel and soon recognized that schools needed to be built along the lines of European approaches to theological education. Glenn T. Miller argues that the Reformers had concluded that "schools were the means of cultural change, and Protestants staked the future of their movement on the ability of teachers to transform habitual patterns of thought."[63]

The charter of the Virginia Company initially envisioned the establishment of an Anglican college to serve the colony. Circumstances, how-

---

63. Glenn T. Miller, *Piety and Intellect: The Aims and Purposes of Ante-Bellum Theological Education* (Atlanta: Scholars Press, 1990), 17.

ever, delayed the founding of the College of William and Mary in Williamsburg until 1693, when it finally came into operational existence for the purpose of educating men in grammar, philosophy, and divinity. A number of those being educated were intended to serve as ministers in Anglican congregations.

The churches representing sectarian theological views, especially the Puritans, also recognized early the need for training ministerial personnel. Harvard College was, in 1636, the first college established in the colonies, and it was founded for the purpose of providing leadership for the expanding system of Congregational congregations. Yale was founded for this same purpose in 1701, when the more conservative elements in the Congregational church lost confidence in Harvard as it increasingly came under the influence of Unitarian theological positions.

These early schools were formed largely for the purpose of training ministerial personnel, though they always pursued a broader mandate of educating leadership with a classical liberal education in the arts and sciences. Ministerial training involved primarily memorization as one read theology with a mentor/teacher, along with learning the classical languages for the study of the Bible.[64] Pastors were formed primarily to serve as *resident theologians* in a congregation and its broader community. Typically, a theologian was one of only a few individuals in a colonial community to have an advanced education, and he often spoke not only to issues related to church life but also to issues related to the civic life of the larger community.

These early educational approaches to training ministers were complemented by less formal efforts. The tradition of the log college in New Jersey that was established by William Tennent in the 1720s (which eventually became Princeton University) is an example. The Great Awakening further influenced the development of theological education. The emphasis on revival and personal conversion became a deep and enduring value within American Christianity. Theological education was charged with shaping both the minds and the hearts of those being prepared for ministry.

By the time of the Revolutionary War, three patterns of theological education were in place within the colonies. First, the Anglicans, Dutch Reformed, Scottish Presbyterians, and Lutherans continued to rely on Eu-

---

64. Latin continued to be the common language of the scholar. Little attention was given to the formal teaching of the practice of ministry, since this was to be learned through on-the-job training. It was largely assumed that, through the formation of the mind and character of an emerging minister, that person would be able to provide the necessary leadership for a congregation.

ropean churches to supply ministers for their growing number of congregations. (The Roman Catholic Church also relied on the European church: it sent its young men back to Europe to be trained as priests.) A second pattern was the establishment of colleges in the colonies themselves—Harvard and Yale for the Congregationalists and William and Mary for the Anglicans. And a third pattern was the development of what today would be called "nonformal" approaches to training ministers. These approaches were especially prevalent among the emerging groups that were shaped by the revivalist side of Christianity, which by the end of the 1700s included a growing number of Baptists and Methodists, along with splinter groups from the Presbyterians.[65]

Time of Transition

The outlines of the denominational church were beginning to come into focus by the mid-1700s. The War of Independence, along with the adoption of a national constitution following the war, furthered its emergence. The formal separation of church and state in the Bill of Rights in 1791 institutionalized this pattern of what we now know as denominationalism: no church would be established by the state, and every church would be protected to practice religious freedom.

The organizing principle of denominationalism was affirmed with this decision, which gave impetus to the further development of the denominational, organizational church. The predominant type of denomination that emerged came to expression as the *ethnic voluntary denomination*.[66] The formation of this new institutional expression of the church took place during the last two decades of the 1700s, during which representatives of numerous church bodies in the brand-new country, the United States of America, met to form national organizations.[67] The number of newly

65. Miller, *Piety and Intellect,* 23. This involved the Old Light–New Light Presbyterians, who existed as separate churches in the aftermath of the Great Awakening (1741–1758).

66. Richey, *Denominationalism Illustrated and Explained,* 4–7. An earlier version of this typology of denominational forms was originally published in Russell E. Richey, "Denominations and Denominationalism: An American Morphology," in *Reimagining Denominationalism: Interpretive Essays,* ed. Robert Bruce Mullin and Russell E. Richey (New York: Oxford University Press, 1994), 74–98.

67. Corrigan and Hudson, *Religion in America,* 112–17. This included the Methodists in 1784, Episcopalians in 1785, and Presbyterians in 1789.

formed denominations stood at thirty-six by 1800.[68] All of these emerging denominations, whether stemming from European state churches or formed in protest against state churches, had to contextualize or recontextualize themselves within the dynamic setting of the very young country.

The church in the colonies had undergone substantial changes during the eighteenth century—in ethos, in composition, and in regard to opportunities before it. Its ethos had become increasingly more evangelical, and its composition increasingly made up of congregations that pursued a free-church ecclesiology.[69] The opportunity the church faced in the newly created United States was that of extending the Christian faith to the frontier, which was opening up to the west and being quickly settled by increased immigration.

68. Robert Wuthnow, *The Restructuring of American Religion* (Princeton: Princeton University Press, 1988), 20.

69. Noll, *The Old World Religion*, 50. Noll observes that, "in 1700, Congregationalists and Anglicans constituted almost two-thirds of all churches in the thirteen colonies"; by 1780, their numbers were reduced to roughly one-third of the churches.

CHAPTER 4

The Expanding Frontier, 1790s to 1870s

The Church in the Frontier Period

The church developed during this period primarily in relation to the expanding frontier and increased immigration from Europe. It also became more evangelical in ethos amidst the rapid growth taking place in many of the newly forming denominations. This growth represented a very real success for the church in terms of starting new congregations; but on the more problematic side, the church also struggled greatly with the slavery issue. This led eventually to a divided country, to the Civil War, and then to Reconstruction, during which freed slaves formed a number of their own denominations. The public missiologies the church pursued reflected all of these realities—those that were more positive as well as those that were more negative.

The process of forming the United States of America took place between the issuing of the Declaration of Independence in 1776 and the adopting and ratifying of the Constitution in 1789. Politically, this marked a major transition in the colonies: the orientation of the country now turned to governing and managing its own interests and welfare as it redefined its relationship to the broader world; meanwhile, the church responded to this shift by creating, in a parallel development, national denominational structures to govern and manage the affairs of church life.

The orientation of the United States was now focused not only in a more inward direction but also in a westward direction. The territories beyond the Allegheny Mountains were soon opened for settlement, and with the Louisiana Purchase in 1803, the new nation engaged in a movement west for the rest of the century—all the way to the Pacific Ocean. Three issues deeply shaped this westward expansion. First, both the country and the church had to deal with the increased influx of immigrants from across Europe, who brought with them increased diversity. Second, both the country and the church had to address the issue of Native Americans, who already inhabited these territories, which became a continued story of invasion, conquest, displacement and resettlement of these peoples onto reservations. Third, both the country and the church had to come to grips with the injustices associated with slavery, the divisions it created, the war it eventually led to, and the aftermath of working to become reunited.

A Changing Church

The situation for the church in the former colonies (which had now become states) changed substantially during the latter half of the eighteenth century. The Great Awakening had planted the seeds of a more evangelical faith in the soil, and they had taken root especially among the more sectarian groups. The struggle for independence during the Revolutionary War helped to foster a growing democratic ethos in the population that was more egalitarian in spirit. This contributed to what became a growing crisis of authority, as further ties to the legacy of European authority structures and practices were broken, especially on the expanding frontier.[1] The rise of a democratic popular culture that promoted self-government for the nation also shaped the governing church structures that were becoming organized as official denominations beginning in the 1780s. Most of these new organizational expressions of the church readily engaged in the responsibility of spreading the faith to the frontier that was opening up.

The Christianity that was developed after the Revolutionary War and carried to the frontier was a more evangelical faith. It was spearheaded especially by the Methodists, who had only about 5,000 members in 1776, but had grown to more than 130,000 by 1806. The Baptists experienced a similar growth, increasing from roughly 35,000 in 1784 to over 172,000 in 1810.[2]

---

1. Nathan O. Hatch, *The Democratization of American Christianity* (New Haven: Yale University Press, 1989), 17–46.

2. Roger Finke and Rodney Stark, *The Churching of America, 1776–2005: Winners and Losers in Our Religious Economy* (New Brunswick, NJ: Rutgers University Press, 2005), 59.

They were soon joined in such frontier growth by the Christian Church (Disciples of Christ), which emerged out of the Restoration tradition.[3] The Congregationalists, Presbyterians, and Episcopalians also increased in membership during that period, but their growth rate was more modest than that of what Finke and Stark call the "upstart denominations." By 1850, the Methodists had become the largest denomination in the United States, followed by the Baptists.[4] What accounts for such rapid growth and the important shift within the emerging denominational system?

Scholars identify at least seven reasons that led to this rapid growth in the first decades of the nineteenth century and the accompanying changes it introduced into the life and ministry of the church. First, the formation of the new nation, with its decision to separate church and state gave rise to what has been labeled a "free-market religious economy."[5] Competition between the newly formed denominations became the order of the day.

Second, the growing democratic spirit increasingly brought the common person into active participation in spreading the faith. This "passion for equality" included for the upstart denominations the blurring of the distinction between clergy and laity, as the religious experience of ordinary people was legitimated.[6]

Third, leadership roles for the new congregations were filled by those felt called into ministry, whether they had formal education and training or not. Many did not. It was estimated "that in 1823 only about a hundred out of the two thousand Baptist clergy had been 'liberally educated,'" and that for Methodists in "1844 fewer than fifty (of . . . 4,286 traveling ministers) 'had anything more than a common English education [grade school], and scores of them not that.'"[7]

Fourth, there was a great increase in the publication and availability of religious literature. Hatch notes that this contributed significantly to the popularization of the faith among the common people—something that has often been overlooked by historians.[8]

---

3. The original Stone Movement (1803) emerged out of the Presbyterian church during the Cane Ridge revival, and the Campbell Movement (1811) emerged out of the Presbyterian church in Pennsylvania and merged into the Christian Church denomination in 1831.

4. Finke and Stark, *Churching of America*, 55–116.

5. Finke and Stark, *Churching of America*, 60–64.

6. Hatch, *The Democratization of American Christianity*, 9–11.

7. Finke and Stark, *Churching of America*, 76–77.

8. Hatch, *The Democratization of American Christianity*, 11. Hatch notes that the evangelical "leaders were intoxicated with the potential of print. The rise in a democratic religious

Fifth, this democratic religious culture in print was simply a manifestation of a growing populism that had emerged during the long struggle for independence and spread across the frontier. The informally trained preachers of the evangelical denominations connected with this populism by appealing to common people in their preaching, often with messages that criticized and even ridiculed the ordained clergy of the colonial denominations. They understood the power of the spoken word, a word that "was personal rather than abstract . . . [that] expressed a preacher's deepest personal feelings."[9] This kind of religious populism, "reflecting the passions of the ordinary people and the charisma of the democratic movement-builders, remains among the oldest and deepest impulses in American life."[10]

Sixth, the methodology developed for spreading the faith on the frontier differed greatly from the practices of the churches in the east. The frontier churches developed the camp-meeting revival and used it with organizational proficiency. This new method began with several earlier meetings in 1800 in Kentucky, which influenced Barton Stone to organize well-planned camp meetings, the first one at Cane Ridge, Kentucky, in 1801.[11] The Methodist circuit riders used this methodology extensively, and the Baptists and Restoration leaders quickly followed suit in efforts to spread the faith on the frontier.

Seventh, there was the gradual development of what became known as the "new measures," pioneered by Charles G. Finney, an ordained Presbyterian layman who "used techniques of hard-sell persuasion such as the 'anxious seat,' a special bench in the front of the meeting hall" for those under spiritual conviction.[12] The development of the revival and these new

---

culture in print after 1800 put obscure prophets . . . on an equal footing with Jonathan Edwards or Timothy Dwight."

9. Hatch, *The Democratization of American Christianity*, 137; Finke and Stark, *Churching of America*, 86. The authors observe that these preachers "looked like ordinary people because they were, and their sermons could convert and convince ordinary people because the message was direct and clear . . . [and] seemed to issue directly from divine inspiration."

10. Hatch, *The Democratization of American Christianity*, 5.

11. Hatch, *The Democratization of American Christianity*, 97, 49–56. This meeting lasted for a week and involved "at least 10,000 and perhaps as many as 20,000 . . . [where] an estimated 3,000 were converted." The Methodists soon adopted this approach, and "Methodist circuit riders soon promoted camp meetings everywhere."

12. Hatch, *The Democratization of American Christianity*, 196, 199. Finney became "a crucial figure in American religious history . . . [who] conveyed the indigenous methods of popular culture to the middle class" and made them respectable.

measures to reach people with the gospel also included the extensive use of the Sunday school.[13]

The successes of the upstart denominations did not go unnoticed by the earlier colonial denominations, which included the Congregationalists, Presbyterians, and Episcopalians, as well as a growing number of ethnic Lutheran denominations. This was a contentious period for them: they struggled to respond to the revivalists, and they grappled with developing their own efforts to start new congregations and come to grips with frontier realities. It is important to note that the regions of the country identified in chapter 3 continued to reflect the dividing lines between these two types of denominations as the population moved west. The reality of this divide later became pronounced over the issue of slavery, especially when the Methodists and Baptists (in the 1840s) and the Presbyterians (in the 1860s) formed separate Northern and Southern denominations.

Key Themes, Events, and Population Shifts

The population of the United States grew significantly during this period, and the population concentrations changed dramatically within the expanding geography of the new nation. Over 90 percent of the 3.5 million Americans in 1790 lived east of the Allegheny Mountains, whereas, by 1880, well over 50 percent of the 50.2 million American citizens lived west of that mountain range. The diverse regional cultures that had emerged in the colonial period on the Eastern Seaboard were carried west, as migrants from the newly formed states, along with new immigrants from Europe, settled the frontier.

Cultural patterns of Yankeedom continued to spread to the west through the northern territories as they became states: Vermont (1791), Maine (1820), Michigan (1837), Wisconsin (1848), and Minnesota (1858). People settling in those states continued to place an emphasis on the "greater good of the community" with their "desire to build a more perfect society."[14] It was in these territories that many immigrants from European state churches, along with their pietistic dissenters, settled and soon formed

13. See Martin E. Marty, *Righteous Empire* (New York: Doubleday, 1971), 68; see also Sydney Ahlstrom, *A Religious History of the American People* (New Haven: Yale University Press, 1972), 425.

14. Colin Woodard, *American Nations: A History of the Eleven Rival Regional Cultures of North America* (New York: Penguin, 2011), 5.

their own denominations, especially the Lutherans from Germany and the Scandinavian countries. The Congregationalists and Presbyterians entered into a Plan of Union in 1801 to jointly develop churches on the expanding frontier, working especially across these territories to organize new congregations as these territories became new states. Joining them in this work were the Methodists and Baptists, the upstart denominations who prospered most as a result of the Second Awakening.

Across the center of the country, the region known as the Midlands continued to be settled and to become states: Ohio (1803), Indiana (1816), Illinois (1818), and Iowa (1846). The people who settled here were more pluralistic in outlook and skeptical of top-down government.[15] The same pattern of organizing new congregations developed in this region, similar to those in the North with respect to Lutherans and Presbyterians, as well as the Baptists and Methodists. They were soon joined in these territories by the restorationist Christian Church (Disciples of Christ).

Further to the south, but north of the Deep South, a flood of settlers crossed the Cumberland Gap into what became known as Greater Appalachia. It was a territory that spread west along both sides of the Ohio River and gradually became the states of Kentucky (1792), Tennessee (1796), Missouri (1821), Arkansas (1836), Kansas (1861), and West Virginia (1863). The early settlers were predominantly Scots-Irish and Scottish immigrants, mainly Presbyterians, who held a suspicion of "aristocrats and social reformers."[16] They placed an emphasis on freedom, choice, hard work, and personal initiative that coalesced with the principle of the voluntary association as a preferred way to shape a new social, political, and religious order.[17]

The immigrants into these territories, which constituted the initial center of the Second Awakening beginning at Cane Ridge, Kentucky, greatly influenced the changing character of the Christian faith that came to be shared across much of the frontier.[18] Greater Appalachia became the seedbed for evangelical Christianity, with its emphasis on revivals and personal

---

15. Woodard, *American Nations*, 6–7.

16. Woodard, *American Nations*, 8.

17. Ahlstrom, *A Religious History*, 386. This pattern was documented by the Frenchman Alexis de Tocqueville in *Democracy in America* (1835; New York: CreateSpace Independent Publishing Platform, 2014), when he identified the extensive formation of voluntary organizations as one of the more unusual and distinguishing features of the emerging American society.

18. Noll, *The Old World Religion*, 62–63.

conversion, complemented by people who held to a political philosophy of commonsense reason and individual responsibility. It was here that the "upstart denominations" that were "made in America" flourished—Methodists, Baptists, and the Disciples of Christ.[19]

The Deep South spread from its base in South Carolina and Georgia across the Southern territories as they became states: Louisiana (1812), Mississippi (1817), Alabama (1819), Florida (1845), and Texas (1845). Here, the emphasis continued to be on "white supremacy, aristocratic privileges, and a version of classical Republicanism modeled on slave states of the ancient world."[20] These states created a political and religious culture that was more conservative in character, that developed primarily around an agricultural economy, that required slavery to function. It was in these states that the Baptists and Methodists—and to some extent the Presbyterians—were especially successful in starting new congregations. This was also where these denominations, beginning in the 1840s, all split from their national bodies and formed separate and distinctly Southern denominations. The growing divide between North and South became openly expressed in the decisions by the Baptist and Methodist national churches to split into two denominations in 1845; the Presbyterians followed suit in 1861. The church in this area has maintained aspects of the distinctive Southern culture and has become known over time as the Bible Belt.

The population growth and its geographical shift to the west that took place in the first half of the nineteenth century was related to a number of important developments from the end of the Revolutionary War (1783) to the end of Reconstruction (1877). The Louisiana Purchase territory that President Thomas Jefferson acquired from France in 1803 not only greatly expanded the amount of land available for settlement in the West; it also, on a symbolic level, played into the American people's imagination of becoming an expansive and great nation. The War of 1812, in which the newly formed United States defeated England, redressed the continued restrictions England was placing on US commerce. It also symbolically demonstrated the strength of the United States as a legitimate power on the world stage. This position was further reinforced in 1823, when the US government adopted the Monroe Doctrine, which called for an end to any further European interventions in the Americas.

Jacksonian democracy emerged on the frontier in the early 1800s

---

19. Finke and Stark, *Churching of America*, 55–116.
20. Finke and Stark, *Churching of America*, 9.

and came to influence the whole nation when Andrew Jackson was elected president in 1828. During this period, Congress passed his proposed Indian Removal Act of 1830, which solidified control of the Southeastern states via a policy of relocating Indians to Western lands.[21] The Texas revolution of 1836 further expanded the territory of the new country into the Southwest and also began to define the border that extended across what Woodard calls the "El Norte" territory (northern Mexico).[22] The Compromise of 1850, which brought California into the union, solidified the growing expectation—and reality—that all the Western territories would eventually be brought into statehood.

But it was slavery that increasingly took center stage in national affairs during this period: the expansion of the agricultural slave system across the Southern states and the rise of an antislavery movement in the Northern states. The decision about whether new states forming in the West would enter the union as slave or free states served as the arena for this contest between Northern and Southern states for several decades. With the election of Lincoln in 1860, the battleground shifted back to the east, and the Southern states seceded from the union to form the Confederacy, resulting in five years of civil war. For the ten years after hostilities ended in 1865, the North pursued a punitive policy of Reconstruction, in which they attempted to bring some equality to members of the black population who had become free citizens. It was a policy fraught with complexities.

African American Population

A further version of contesting for the land took place during this time between the Northern and Southern states with the spread of the slave plantation system across the South and efforts to extend it to other new states. The number of African American slaves in the Deep South increased from 750,000 in 1790 to 4.4 million in 1860. This contesting came to involve the entire nation, as these divisions eventually extended to several of the larger denominations. The contesting between the churches was polarized even more as the abolitionist movement gained momentum in the North in the early decades of the nineteenth century.

It is important to note, however, that not all African Americans were

21. Noll, *The Old World Religion*, 105.
22. Woodard, *American Nations*, 208–15.

slaves. Though they represented only a modest portion of the total population in the North, more than 83 percent of African Americans living there were free in 1820; and it is worth noting that more than 10 percent of those living in the upper South, the Tidewater states, were free.[23] The first independent African American denomination came into existence in 1816: it was the formation of the African Methodist Episcopal Church in Philadelphia under Bishop Richard Allen's leadership. Numerous Methodist churches were formed also, and this effort was joined by the formation of black Baptist churches in various Northern cities throughout the first half of the nineteenth century.[24]

This period experienced two phases of *contesting* by the African American slave population (eventually emancipated): the first phase took place *during* slavery, as African Americans struggled against the legalized oppression they experienced. Limited options were available to slaves, and the penalties for violating enforced laws were harshly administered. But some slaves were able to escape north to Canada by means of the "underground railroad"; over 100,000 used that means toward freedom between 1810 and 1850.[25]

A second phase of *contesting* by African Americans took place with the freeing of the massive slave population in the aftermath of the Civil War. The vast majority of those living in the Southern states moved from slavery to sharecropping. Even though this changed their political status, it did little to improve their economic well-being or their social status. Some initial gains were made in various states during Reconstruction; but when that policy was ended during the Hayes administration in 1877, segregation quickly became the order of the day, and Jim Crow laws were passed and enforced throughout the South.[26] In the midst of this flux, the African American church emerged as a place of refuge and political activism, and new black denominations came into existence during this period.[27]

---

23. Darlene Clark Hine et al., *African Americans: A Concise History* (Boston: Pearson, 2012), 103.

24. Hatch, *Democratization of American Christianity*, 102–13.

25. Hatch, *Democratization of American Christianity*, 199–201.

26. We develop this part of the story in more detail in the following chapter.

27. Noll, *The Old World Religion*, 113–18; see also Henry H. Mitchell, *Black Church Beginnings: The Long-Hidden Realities of the First Years* (Grand Rapids: Eerdmans, 2004). This is what whites had largely missed as the "invisible church" during slavery became organized institutionally under African American leadership. And with this development, the long quest for equal rights for African Americans as full citizens began in earnest.

Native American Population

The Native American population also experienced massive changes during the frontier period. These changes led to the tribes further experiencing a contesting for territory, which led to the creation of a system of reservations. Several key political decisions brought this about. Working with Henry Knox during the late 1700s, George Washington had supported the policy of a six-point "civilizing" process that tried to deal fairly with American Indians. But it was clearly designed to support white majority interests; indeed, its concluding principle gave permission to the white authorities to punish those Native Americans who did not cooperate.[28] Federal policy changed direction with the passing of the Indian Removal Act of 1830, which legalized the practice of relocating Indians to reservations, often to distant, underpopulated areas that were also underresourced.[29]

Many of the newly formed denominations became involved in Indian missions, and this work increasingly focused on missionaries working on the reservations in the early 1800s. Those efforts focused on imposing Christianity and white cultural values on the American Indian tribes, a move, George Tinker argues, that resulted in cultural genocide.[30] The federal policy toward Native Americans changed by the late 1860s: by then it became one of forced assimilation, as all tribes were relocated to predetermined reservations. There was initially government oversight by way of religious leaders providing for the management of these reservations; the Quakers were especially active in this role. But by the late 1870s, this approach proved to be problematic, and by 1882, leadership transitioned from religious leaders to personnel serving within the Indian Service of the government. The Indian wars in the West were coming to an end by the late 1870s and early 1880s, as the Sioux War—which included the Battle of Little Bighorn—played itself out, though continued struggles for independence by various tribes would occur over the next several decades.

28. Eric Miller, "George Washington and Indians: Washington and the Northwest War, Part One," 1994, http://www.dreric.org/library/northwest.shtml (accessed December 30, 2015).

29. Patrick Minges, "Beneath the Underdog: Race, Religion, and the Trail of Tears," 1998, http://www.us-data.org/us/minges/underdog.html (accessed June 10, 2015). Associated with this Act was the Trail of Tears, which included the forced relocation of several tribal nations from the Southeastern states to Indian territory west of the Mississippi—Cherokee, Muskogee, Seminole, Chickasaw, and Choctaw.

30. George E. Tinker, *Missionary Conquest: The Gospel and Native American Cultural Genocide* (Minneapolis: Fortress, 1993).

A dominant culture narrative began to emerge at this time concerning the concept of "Manifest Destiny": that it was the right of the expanding United States to occupy the continent from coast to coast.[31] Building on the earlier concept of American exceptionalism, leaders legitimated this notion by tying it to divine providence, a connection that continued to be developed throughout the nineteenth century as a part of the American story.[32] But not all Americans held this view; some, like Lincoln and Grant, along with other Whigs, saw "America's moral mission as one of democratic example rather than one of conquest."[33] The dominant voices of the postwar period, however, argued that it was America's destiny to occupy the continent. The consequences for the Native American populations were devastating, as tribe after tribe were forced to sign treaties—either peaceably or as a result of hostilities—that turned over most of their ancestral lands to white settlers.

Increasingly Diverse Immigration and Religious Pluralism

Significant changes also occurred within the white population during this period. In 1790, more than 80 percent of the white population still had English ancestry. But immigration patterns shifted in the first half of the nineteenth century, which saw dramatic increases of Irish and German immigrants, which greatly added to the membership of Catholic and Lutheran churches. Also noteworthy were the 105,000 US residents in 1880 who were from the Pacific Rim, many of them immigrants from China who were working on the expanding American railroad network. Overall, this influx of immigrants during those years introduced a further phase of contesting for the land, as the immigrant population became more diverse. This growing diversity included Irish Catholics from Europe and Mexican American Catholics who settled in the Southwest, along with persons from different racial and religious backgrounds, such as East Asians who adhered to Buddhism, Confucianism, Taoism, or Shintoism.

This increased diversity increasingly challenged the assumption that

31. Ernest Lee Tuveson, *Redeemer Nation: The Idea of America's Millennial Role* (Chicago: University of Chicago Press, 1980), 91.

32. Ahlstrom, *A Religious History*, 849–50. A later example of this is the song "America the Beautiful," which was written in 1895 and soon became a national patriotic favorite.

33. Daniel Walker Howe, *What Hath God Wrought: The Transformation of America, 1815–1848* (New York: Oxford University Press, 2007), 705–6.

America was to be primarily a Protestant nation. But since the overwhelming majority of Christians during this period *were* Protestants, they were able for the most part to assume dominion and engage in building a Protestant nation. This domain was clearly evident within the public education system, where the Bible was regularly used in the curriculum and prayer was commonly practiced. One of the first challenges to this national narrative came as a result of increased Roman Catholic immigration. Coming primarily from Ireland (as well as Germany), the Catholic population grew significantly: from about 30,000 in 1790 to over 600,000 by 1830.

The emergence of the Know-Nothing political party was directly related to this because they viewed these diverse groups of European immigrants as invaders.[34] The Know-Nothings were notably anti-Catholic, and their early activities were instrumental in keeping Catholics largely marginalized within the broader society until the beginning of the twentieth century. At that time a massive Catholic immigration from southern Europe began to overwhelm the Protestant establishment.

In 1800, there were only a handful of Jewish congregations and only about 2,000 Jews in the American population. But that number increased throughout the nineteenth century and stood at roughly 200,000 by 1880. The Jewish population, however, even with that growth spurt, continued to represent only a small proportional presence in the overall population during this period.[35]

Other important features of religious diversity that emerged during that period included a variety of experiments regarding the Christian faith, such as the holiness emphasis of Phoebe Palmer, which focused on creating an inner spirituality; the millennial emphasis on an imminent Second Coming by William Miller; and the Mormon revision of the faith introduced by Joseph Smith.[36] These movements would continue to grow in influence throughout the 1800s. Joining in this experimental work, often related to the religious impulse but also stemming from the influence of Transcendentalism, were numerous communitarian initiatives.[37]

---

34. Bruce Levine, "Conservatism, Nativism, and Slavery: Thomas R. Whitney and the Origins of the Know-Nothing Party," *Journal of American History* 88, no. 2 (2001): 455–88.

35. Ahlstrom, *A Religious History*, 569; see also http://www.jewishvirtuallibrary.org/j source/US-Israel/usjewpop1.html (accessed June 10, 2016).

36. Noll, *The Old World Religion*, 98–103.

37. Ahlstrom, *A Religious History*, 496–501. These include the Amana Society, New Harmony, the Oneida Community, Hopedale, and Brook Farm. Many of these played themselves out within a few decades, but vestiges linger on into the next century for others.

System of Congregations

The system of congregations increased dramatically during this period, as the growing immigrant population spilled across the Allegheny Mountains and as evangelical revivalism took hold on the frontier. The 3,228 congregations that existed in the late 1770s grew into a system of over 70,000 congregations by the 1870s.[38] The original colonial denominations of Congregationalists, Presbyterians, and Anglicans, combined, still held a majority of congregational membership in 1776 at 55 percent.[39] But they were quickly outpaced by the newly formed Methodists and Baptists, along with the newly created Christian Church (Disciples of Christ); these three upstart denominations often worked on the margins of society with those who were disadvantaged socially, economically, and politically, and they led the effort of starting new congregations on the frontier.[40]

An evolved form of congregation emerged during this period, and it helped contribute to the remarkable expansion of the system of congregations. It can best be described as the *village congregation*. The typical village congregation was made up of a cross section of migrants moving into a new settlement, where extended families intermarried and created an intergenerational community over time. The predominant architecture of the village congregation focused on the worship space, usually with seating capacity for up to a hundred or more worshipers. Room was available for fellowship, education, and social life in the basement, typically with poles down the middle supporting the upper floor. Many of these churches also had cemeteries, which helped to ensure loyalty from their members and the longevity of their properties through succeeding generations.

Two versions of the village congregation emerged as the faith spread rapidly across the frontier. The first version was composed of those congregations that were founded by the upstart denominations, with their practice of evangelical revivals. The Methodists led the way with their practice: conducting camp meetings and using circuit riders to organize classes that were led by lay leaders.[41] The Baptists joined them in conducting camp meetings but used the farmer-preacher to provide leadership for the expanding sys-

---

38. For the 1770s figures, see Finke and Stark, *Churching of America*, 28; for the 1870 figure, see Robert Wuthnow, *The Restructuring of American Religion* (Princeton: Princeton University Press, 1988), 22.

39. Finke and Stark, *Churching of America*, 55.

40. Finke and Stark, *Churching of America*, 55–116.

41. Finke and Stark, *Churching of America*, 73–74.

tem of congregations.[42] The practice of revivalism by both focused on a gospel of personal morality, which coalesced well with the social imaginary of individualism and personal responsibility.

The second version was of those congregations that sprang up across the frontier to serve the faithful from the ethnic-specific immigration that was taking place. All the members of these congregations shared the same ethnic background; many of them had actually emigrated together from the old country. This pattern was especially prominent in the Midlands and Yankeedom among the Lutherans. Here, ethnic-specific congregations were formed by the Germans, Swedes, Norwegians, Icelanders, and Finns.[43]

Thousands of both types of congregations were started on the expanding frontier during this period, and the process lasted well into the latter half of the nineteenth century, as additional territories west of the Mississippi River became states. An important development within this changing system of congregations came in the aftermath of the Civil War, when thousands of freed blacks, many of whom had adopted the Christian faith, formed black congregations and soon created their own denominational structures.[44] The black church that emerged contributed to forming an identity and providing a social and political voice for the African American population as it engaged the challenges associated with segregation.[45]

Development of the Denominational, Organizational Church

In chapter 3 we discussed the creation of the denominational, organizational church as a unique new form of organization within the American setting. We noted that this form emerged largely as a pragmatic response to a variety of circumstances. It was usually rationalized biblically and theologically after the fact, if at all.[46] Church historian Martin Marty views this development as a turning point in the history of the church, one that departed from the previous 1,400 years of the church's

42. Finke and Stark, *Churching of America*, 96.

43. Woodard, *American Nations*, 183–88.

44. Noll, *The Old World Religion*, 113–21; Finke and Stark, *Churching of America*, 190–96; see also earlier scholarship by E. Franklin Frazier, *The Negro Church in America* (New York: Schocken [Random House], 1974), 14, 35–51.

45. C. Eric Lincoln and Lawrence H. Mamiya, *The Black Church in the African American Experience* (Durham, NC: Duke University Press, 1990).

46. Russell E. Richey, *Denominationalism* (Nashville: Abingdon, 1977), 19–21.

self-understanding.[47] This organizational innovation prospered in the nineteenth century as the number of such denominations increased from thirty-six in 1800 to over two hundred by the end of the century.[48]

As the newly emerging denominations began to form, they adopted organizational polities to guide their institutional development. Immigrants from the European state churches had brought with them confessional understandings of the church, as well as organizational polities shaped by the assumptions of Christendom and the established church. For the most part, these denominations simply adapted with minor adjustments their European national church polities as they formed their local, regional, and national assemblies in the United States.[49] Those churches observing a free-church ecclesiology tended to follow the same pattern of developing a series of ascending assemblies, but gave much less authority to regional judicatories and national assemblies. The early African American denominations organized with these same structures, and those formed following the Civil War were added to the expanding denominational system.[50]

The diverse religious context of the United States deeply challenged some of the underlying assumptions of European state church assembly-structured polities, especially the notion that if you were born into the parish you were baptized into the church. There were no structures in place for reaching persons outside of the church. The new situation of religious diversity and the challenge of reaching vast numbers of unchurched persons on the frontier led some newly formed denominations to form special interdenominational organizations to engage in this work on their behalf. These became known as *mission societies.*[51] This work of evangelism and church planting on the frontier—*home missions*—was paralleled by the other mission societies forming to engage in what became known as *foreign missions.* The formation of such mission societies in the early 1800s in the United States represented a remarkable organizational development in the life of the church that in many ways paralleled the development of denominations.

47. Marty, *Righteous Empire*, 67–68.

48. Wuthnow, *Restructuring of American Religion*, 20.

49. We find, for example, the Presbyterians adapting and adopting the Book of Order developed by the Westminster divines in the 1640s, and the Reformed Church in America adopting the polity of Dordt developed in 1619. The descendants of these European state church polities are today part of the great unraveling that is taking place.

50. Noll, *The Old World Religion*, 113–21.

51. Noll, *The Old World Religion*, 67–70; Finke and Stark, *Churching of America*, 65–67; Ahlstrom, *A Religious History*, 382–83.

An important development in the American church took place as mission work increased through both the societies and denomination agencies. These structures "opened up unusual opportunities for religious women" to become involved in providing leadership with respect to missions.[52] Initially this included primarily the wives of missionaries, who contributed substantially to the mission work being conducted in foreign fields.[53] They were soon joined by many other women, most of whom served as teachers in the schools that were started in mission communities.[54] As the sending of missionaries gained momentum after midcentury, particularly with the formation of independent evangelical societies, single women joined the expanding foreign mission enterprise and were increasingly sent to engage in the work directly.[55]

While hundreds of such voluntary religious societies were formed locally or regionally, seven of them managed to gain national prominence by the early 1820s: American Board of Commissioners for Foreign Missions (1810), American Bible Society (1816), American Education Society (1816), American Colonization Society (1816), American Sunday School Union (1824), American Home Missionary Society (1826), and American Temperance Society (1826).[56] These structures, while reflecting the democratic principles being nurtured in the still-developing United States, were also the natural extension of the logic of the voluntary basis of the church with regard to a free-church ecclesiology.

Developing alongside the mission societies in the early 1800s were internal denominational organizational structures for engaging in missions and ministry, structures that were initially formed as committees and boards.[57] Representative of this trend were the Presbyterians, who formed a standing committee on missions in 1802 and then, more formally, a Board of Missions in 1816. These structures initially sought to coordinate and integrate their efforts with the interdenominational mission societies.[58] These

52. Noll, *The Old World Religion*, 69.

53. Dana L. Robert, *American Women in Mission: A Social History of Their Thought and Practice* (Macon, GA: Mercer University Press, 1997), 39–48. Some of the pioneer missionary wives in the early 1800s were Harriet Newell, Ann Judson, and Roxana Nott.

54. Robert, *American Women in Mission*, 81–124.

55. Robert, *American Women in Mission*, 189–205

56. Fred J. Hood, "Evolution of the Denomination among the Reformed of the Middle and Southern States, 1780–1840," in Richey, *Denominationalism*, 145.

57. These committees and boards functioned under the authority and oversight of the national assemblies and became responsible for helping to manage the growing mission work taking place both at home and abroad.

58. Hood, "Evolution of the Denomination," 147.

initiatives led to the development of the recently formed denominations into what has become known as the *purposive missionary denomination*.[59] Its core identity became deeply embedded in what it tried to accomplish by way of its missionary purposes.

This growing system of agencies and boards also increasingly developed a standardized, programmatic approach to ministry. More and more, the central headquarters took on the task of developing materials for all their member congregations to use in their local ministries. The classic example of this is the Sunday school, which began in England during the late 1700s outside the church to provide at least some rudimentary education for working-class children who were caught up in the hard life of the expanding Industrial Revolution. This approach was brought into the American church in the early 1800s.[60] Over time, the denominations took it over and developed standardized lesson plans and curricular materials by the 1870s. This kind of approach served as a template for an expanding denomination system of programming over the next hundred years.

With these changes, the basic structure of the modern denomination was now in place: a series of representative assemblies that governed the work of denomination-specific boards, which in turn provided oversight of the agencies with professional staff. The biggest question left unresolved in this formulation was the relationship between the formal denominational boards and agencies to the previously formed assembly structures of the new national denominations. Which one would lead, and which would be subordinate? It soon became clear that the assembly structures would maintain primary control. Therefore, engaging in mission came under the governance of ecclesial assemblies in these denominations, which eventually led to problems of too much Western control for too long over the churches started on numerous foreign mission fields.

59. Russell E. Richey, *Denominationalism Illustrated and Explained*, 4–7, 159–61.

60. Typically, the Bible was used as the primary curriculum. This practice soon spread to the frontier, especially in the rural areas, and denominations soon joined this effort by organizing their own internal Sunday school systems for their congregations. See Anne M. Boylan, *Sunday School: The Formation of an American Institution, 1790–1880* (New Haven: Yale University Press, rev. ed. 1990).

Developments Regarding the Discipline of Missiology

The focus of missiology changed in orientation during this period, as the church moved beyond a Christendom worldview in understanding its relationship to the world. The separation of church and state led to replacing the role of the magistrate/king with the formation of separate structures to engage in missions to the world. Most denominations did not initially create their own structures; instead, they participated in working with independent mission societies that were then emerging. But within a short time they acted to form their own internal agencies, which were governed by boards. The combination of these societies and agencies soon produced what became known as the "modern missions movement," which fostered a dichotomy between church and mission—as if they were two distinct entities. This movement also placed a focus on human and/or church agency as the primary motivation for engaging in mission work—which involved obedience to the Great Commission. The emerging discipline of missiology was deeply shaped by both of these realities, and it would struggle greatly over the next century and a half trying to address them.

Protestant missions had gradually begun to take root in the European churches during the eighteenth century, not only via the state churches but also alongside them, especially the dissenting groups.[61] It was in this milieu that William Carey emerged as a Particular Baptist and made a contribution to the growing cause of missions. David Bosch notes that, while "there is some validity to . . . singling him out, it has to be remembered that he was only one of many similar figures from this period and as much a product as a shaper of the spirit of the time."[62] However, he does serve as a helpful "representative of this missionary period."[63]

The contribution of Carey was in serving as a transition figure in helping to frame a larger conception of the missionary task for Protestants and lay a foundation for the emergence of the formal discipline of missiology.[64]

---

61. These included the work of the Pietists on the Continent, especially in Germany, who also influenced Zinzendorf and his work with the Moravians. Other important influences were at work in England because of Wesley and the growth of the Methodists, as well as increased interest in missions among the numerous Nonconformist groups.

62. David J. Bosch, *Transforming Mission* (Maryknoll, NY: Orbis, 1991), 280.

63. Stephen B. Bevans and Roger P. Schroeder, *Constants in Context* (Maryknoll, NY: Orbis, 2004), 211.

64. William Carey, *An Enquiry into the Obligations of Christians* (Leicester: printed by Ann Ireland, 1792); John Clark Marshman, *The Life and Times of Carey, Marshman, and*

Drawing on earlier rationales, he proposed the necessary obedience to help fulfill the Great Commission (Matt. 28:18–20) as the primary biblical foundation for engaging in mission, a view that continued to be influential well into the next century.[65] Soon there were other societies within Europe that worked alongside the state churches, especially in the British Isles.[66]

With the development of the independently governed and voluntarily funded mission society, the organizational deadlock of the state-church magistrate being the authorizer of mission work was finally broken. But what was left unanswered was the question of the relationship of the new church on the mission field to the mission society operating back home. It would take a century and half to resolve this. That same organizational framework and the issues it generated also came to the fore in America, first in the colonies with regard to Indian missions and after independence with respect to the newly formed mission societies and denominations.[67]

The early expansion of the Protestant mission enterprise in the United States and its pursuant public missiological engagements took place primarily via the mission societies. Numerous *interdenominational* mission societies mobilized cooperative denominational mission activities among the thirty-plus national denominations that had come into being by the early 1800s.[68] Internal church politics, however, soon led increasing numbers of denominations to withdraw from these cooperative agreements in order to form their own internal denominational agencies, with governing boards, like, for example, the American Baptist Foreign Mission Society (1814), the Methodist Missionary Society (1819), and the Presbyterian Board of Foreign Mission (1837). Now mission societies existed in two forms, one version being independent of the denominational churches (later taking on names such as "faith missions" and "parachurch organizations") and the

---

Ward: *Embracing the History of the Serampore Mission* (London: Longman, Brown, Green, and Roberts, 1859). These works contributed to the development of a fuller theory and practice of missions.

65. Bosch, *Transforming Mission*, 251. Justinian von Welz, e.g., had proposed the continued validity of the Great Commission in tracts published in 1663–64.

66. These included the London Mission Society (1795), the Scottish Missionary Society (1796), and the Church Mission Society (1799)—and later the Berlin Missionary Society (1824).

67. See William R. Hutchison, *Errand to the World: American Protestant Thought and Foreign Missions* (Chicago: University of Chicago Press, 1987).

68. Wuthnow, *The Restructuring of American Religion*, 20. The societies that were formed included: the American Board of Commissioners for Foreign Missions, American Bible Society, American Education Society, American Colonization Society, and American Sunday School Union.

other form being an organizational structure within these denominations (becoming known as "denominational agencies," with internal governing boards).

The formation of mission societies contributed to the separation of mission and church—that is, of missiology and ecclesiology, an issue that still plagues the church today. These developments took place just as missiology was on the threshold of beginning to be conceived of as an academic discipline to support the expanding work of foreign missions in both Europe and the United States.[69] Some of the important developments impacting the emergence of the discipline of missiology during the nineteenth century include the following:

- *Missiology as a Practical Discipline*: The conception by F. D. Schleiermacher in his 1811 proposal to the University of Berlin for a theological curriculum of placing missions within the study of theology as a subdiscipline within practical theology.
- *Breckenridge*: The appointment in 1836 of Charles Breckenridge at Princeton as the professor of practical theology and missionary instruction (the post was discontinued in 1839).
- *Duff*: The creation in 1867 of the chair of evangelistic theology at Edinburgh for Alexander Duff, which he held until 1878 (the chair came to an end with his death).

It is important to understand that the Protestant version of the modern missions movement emerged largely outside the established, institutional church. As a result, missiology came to the theological academy with the second-class status of an *applied* discipline, which was usually taught by missionary practitioners. In addition, the recruitment of future missionaries, especially in the United States, was largely the work of voluntary associations of students, which networked across the various theological

69. William Richey Hogg, "The Teaching of Missiology: Some Reflections on the Historical and Current Scene," *Missiology* 15, no. 4 (1987); Olav Guttorm Myklebust, *The Study of Missions in Theological Education: An Historical Inquiry into the Place of World Evangelisation in Western Protestant Ministerial Training, with Particular Reference to Alexander Duff's Chair of Evangelistic Theology* (Oslo, Norway: Egede Instituttet; Hovedkommisjon Land og kirke, 1955); James A. Scherer, "The Future of Missiology as an Academic Discipline in Seminary Education: Attempt at Reinterpretation and Clarification," *Missiology* 13, no. 4 (1985); see also Scherer, "Missiology as a Discipline and What It Includes," *Missiology* 15, no. 4 (1987).

schools.[70] The focus was on developing efficient practices to support the training and sending of mission personnel to other parts of the world.

Some denominations in the United Sates also established home mission boards, but these tended to focus on starting new congregations as denominational franchises on the expanding frontier, and they gave little attention to matters of context. This formative period in the development of the discipline of missiology paid little attention to congregations, either theologically or theoretically, whether at home or abroad.

Congregations at home were assumed to be the primary constituents for supporting the work of foreign missions. The denominations created substantial organizations to support this work; these were especially developed by women.[71] Congregations on the mission field were, for the most part, the byproduct of the primary work of evangelism, which focused on winning converts to the faith. This lack of attention to the development of indigenous congregations was complicated by the fact that missionaries often maintained primary leadership roles for decades within the newly planted churches. These same missionaries also tended to bring into the new congregations—somewhat uncritically—many of the practices of traditional church life as they existed back home.

There were a few exceptions, for example, Henry Venn and Rufus Anderson—that is, individuals who began to formulate other ways of developing new congregations in their efforts to avoid the problem of Western domination in the various mission fields.[72] The newly evolving discipline of missiology among Protestants was beginning to focus on the formation of congregations, at least on the mission field. But overall, foreign missions throughout this period pursued a missiological approach that tended to transpose predominantly Western forms of congregational life into the various mission areas.

70. Michael Parker, *The Kingdom of Character: The Student Volunteer Movement for Foreign Missions, 1886-1926* (Lanham, MD: American Society of Missiology and University Press of America, 1998).

71. Robert, *American Women in Mission*, 125–88. Here Robert presents the formation, development, and ministries of various denominational mission-support organizations that were created by women in the 1800s.

72. Wilbert R. Shenk, "Rufus Anderson and Henry Venn: A Special Relationship?," *International Bulletin of Missionary Research* 5, no. 4 (1981). See also Bosch, *Transforming Mission*, 331–34; and Bevans and Schroeder, *Constants in Context*, 213. By the middle of the nineteenth century, Henry Venn in England and Rufus Anderson in the United States independently proposed what became known as the "three-self formula" for establishing new churches (self-governing, self-supporting, and self-propagating).

Public Missiologies in the Frontier Period

There were several nuances added to the larger social imaginary of the dominant culture in the frontier period as the demographic shifts took place and the West was settled. These included: a deep commitment to democracy and democratic ideals; the emergence of a national identity; and the beginning of a notion of manifest destiny as Indian populations were removed in the ceaseless westward expansion. The public missiologies that were used by the church to engage its context on the frontier can be seen in the following table.

Table 4.1 Public Missiologies of the Church in the Frontier Period

Missiology Strain	Colonial Period	Frontier Period	Urban Growth Period	Suburban Success Period	Strategies for Success Period
Focus on Nation	Conquest to Civilize and Christianize -Established -Religious Freedom	Protestant Nation-building			
Focus on Tradition	Maintain Traditional Faith -Immigrants	Maintain Traditional Faith -Immigrants			
Focus on Engaging in Missions or Mission	Native American Missions	Foreign Missions			
Focus on Social Reform	"True" Christian Society	Social Reform -Morality -Slavery			
Focus on Justice and Liberation	Pursuing Freedom from Margins -Slavery	Pursuing Freedom from Margins -Slavery			
Focus on Revival and Renewal	Revival and Renewal -Great Awakening	Expanded Revival and Renewal -Second Great Awakening			
Unique Focus					

The colonial period had required either that adjustments be made to existing European understandings of church or that new approaches be created. Now that the United States was formed as a nation, many of the earlier missiologies evolved with respect to the changing realities. The former missiology of conquest and civilizing continued into this period, as can be seen from the displacement of the Indian tribes. But much of the focus during this period shifted to one of pursuing a *missiology of Protestant nation-building*, one that could build on the notion of American exceptionalism introduced from Yankeedom. The formation of Protestant denominational churches following the Revolutionary War led fairly quickly to efforts to bring the church to the expanding frontier. The church and the public school were often closely linked together in these efforts: Protestants engaged in the support of public education as an extension of their efforts to build a Protestant nation. Their understanding of the gospel became deeply commingled with the new nation's guarantee of individual rights, which was tied to the fervor of revivalist zeal; that, in turn, framed a culture of individual responsibility. This emphasis on individual responsibility, drawing on the premises of the newly adopted US Constitution, worked toward creating a nation that would be largely Protestant in makeup and evangelical in spirit, as personal piety was promoted via the methodology of revivals.

The dominant Protestant society marginalized some newly arriving non-Protestant immigrant groups, such as Catholics and Jews; these groups continued to practice what had developed earlier as a *missiology of maintaining the traditional faith*. The Roman Catholic Church focused attention on building a comprehensive system of institutions that would keep members and their children from direct interaction with the broader society, where Protestants ruled the day.[73] The anti-immigrant segment of Protestants found it necessary to protect their members via the active efforts of some, such as the Know-Nothing Party, to intentionally restrict Catholic participation in society. Other immigrant groups, including the many German Lutherans, also practiced a version of this missiology of maintaining the traditional faith as they sought to preserve the familiar practices of their native country. But they often struggled in relating to the next generation in their own faith community who sought to Americanize this traditional faith. That pattern became a recurring theme—within many denominations throughout the nineteenth and well into the twentieth century—among those already in the country and those who were newly arriving, both of whom shared the same faith tradition.

This mission work of helping to form churches on the frontier of the United States was paralleled by the formation of various independent societies, along with the development of denominational agencies to engage in

---

73. An example of this was the work of the order of Scalabrinians that was created in the late 1800s to help immigrants maintain the Catholic faith in the new world.

what became known as a *missiology of foreign missions.*[74] This missiology was more formal in character, and calls were increasingly being made to participate in fulfilling the Great Commission. This emphasis was, in many ways, a natural extension of the cultural strain that emphasized individual responsibility. At first, the organizational structure of choice to accomplish this work was the independent, interdenominational mission society. They were later joined by their cousin, the denominational agency. The formation of such mission societies in the United States in the early 1800s represented a remarkable organizational development in the life of the church that was paralleled in many ways by the development of denominational agencies. The religious expression of such organizational structures was the natural extension of the logic of the voluntary basis of the church within free-church ecclesiology.

During this time, the earlier missiology that sought to build a true Christian society morphed into an organization focused on addressing specific moral agendas. This was especially true of the antislavery movement and the Temperance issue that focused on individual morality. These moral crusades sought to transform personal views *and* reshape public policy. Related to the earlier missiology of a Christian society, this strain of church life in America developed into what might best be described as a *missiology of social reform.* The involvement of churches in such moral crusades was a common theme throughout the nineteenth and twentieth centuries—and continues to this day. There is an expectation among most denominations in America that they are responsible to help shape public behavior, especially individual moral behavior. There was also an expectation that they would use the democratic political process to achieve this end.

In the unfolding story line of the denominational, organizational church in the United States, it is very important to note that there was a continuation of an earlier missiological expression. This involved the enslaved African American population and the continuation of a *missiology of pursuing freedom from the margins.* Prior to the Civil War, some members of the slave population were included within existing white congregations as marginalized participants. Others developed a religion of protest by functioning with their own forms of the church in the midst of their bondage. These forms were often patterned on white precedents, especially those of the Baptist and Methodists. This quickly changed following the

---

74. Bosch, *Transforming Mission,* 262–345; Bevans and Schroeder, *Constants in Context,* 206–21.

Civil War, as formal black denominations began to emerge and take on an institutional expression.[75]

Much of the spiritual fuel that fed the movements of nation-building, foreign missions, and social reform came from the energy released in the Second Great Awakening. This awakening took place on the frontier, where its energy was picked up and used by numerous denominations and their churches; it was especially true of the Baptists and Methodists, though it also included other newly defined denominations on the frontier, such as the Christian Church (Disciples of Christ). This spiritual awakening was similar in focus to the earlier one, but it became more widespread as it developed a substantial methodology involving such practices as camp meetings, evangelism, church revivals, and the "anxious bench." This *expanded missiology of revival and renewal* was reinforced by the new nation's ethos of democracy, with its emphasis on individual rights and personal responsibility. It also incorporated well the earlier emphasis developed within a missiology of religious freedom.

Theological Education and Leadership Formation

The emerging denominations and their expanding congregational systems continued to adapt their practices of leadership formation as they grew and changed. Pastors usually led their churches in pursuing their public missiological engagements. Providing trained pastors who could lead in this work was partly addressed when the denominations developed self-standing theological seminaries, which soon took on the task of training individuals to be missionaries. But what was largely left unanswered was the question about the relationship between church and mission—that is, between ecclesiology and missiology. Another question that emerged had to do with what constituted the proper motive for mission. This question assumed the primacy of human agency and was an issue that the church and missions struggled with for decades.

The seminary was an institution that became a unique contribution of the US Protestant church regarding the process of leadership formation. This approach to training pastoral leadership was based largely on the European model, which had been copied by the earliest institutions of higher

---

75. Noll, *The Old World Religion*, 113–21; see also Frazier, *The Negro Church in America*, 14, 35–51.

learning in colonial America, such as William and Mary, Harvard, and Yale. But what now emerged was the use of the school model to focus exclusively on preparing individuals for ministry. It is interesting to note that the formation of denominations was being driven substantially by the need of various groups to establish clear confessional or theological identities.[76] This was the context in which theological seminaries came into existence in the United States, within the intense furnace of confessional debates that served to reinforce distinctive sectarian perspectives.

The first seminary was Andover, which was founded in 1807 by a group of Congregationalists who had become concerned, once again, about the steady rise of Unitarian views within their church. The founding of Andover marked a new direction for graduate theological education in the United States: the development of a free-standing seminary. This new kind of Protestant institution was, in fact, patterned after the free-standing Catholic seminaries in Europe. What made Andover identifiable as the first true theological seminary were the following characteristics, as they were identified by Yale's President Timothy Dwight in his 1808 address at the opening of Andover: it had "(1) adequate funding; (2) a program sufficient in length to allow mastery of the subject [. . . three-year course of studies]; (3) a scholarly understanding of Christian theology . . . ; (4) a professional [and specialized] faculty; (5) a large, committed student body; (6) sound principles of trustee management; and (7) an extensive library collection" (68–69).

These characteristics became the normative framework for the numerous theological seminaries that soon joined Andover. The Presbyterians founded Princeton in 1812, a school that had roots going back to the log college days of Tennent (99–113). Other new seminaries included: Bangor (1816), General (1817), Pittsburgh (1818), Virginia Union (1823), Mercersburg (1825), Gettysburg (1826), Newton (1826), Southern (1832), Union New York (1836), Oberlin (1838), and Lane (1839)—to name a few. In all, at least thirty-two seminaries were founded in the United States between 1808 and 1840 (201–2).

There were also developments in the formation of divinity schools, or schools of theology, as departments or unique entities within a secular university. Harvard developed its first graduate program for ministerial candidates in 1811; it then formed a separate Harvard Divinity School in

---

76. Glenn T. Miller, *Piety and Intellect: The Aims and Purposes of Ante-Bellum Theological Education* (Atlanta: Scholars Press, 1990), 21–22. Hereafter, page references to this work appear in parentheses within the text.

1816, the first nonsectarian theological school in the country. Its purpose was to ensure that "every encouragement be given to the serious, impartial, and unbiased investigation of Christian truth."[77] As early as 1746, Yale had recognized the need to establish a specific professorship of divinity; this shift in focus eventually led to the founding of a separate department by 1822 in what became the Yale University Divinity School.[78] These early schools of theology proved over time to be quite influential in shaping the establishment of multiple schools of divinity when the modern graduate research institution came into existence in the latter half of the nineteenth century.

Most of the seminaries and schools of theology started prior to the Civil War were quite small. A typical school had between two and five faculty members and fifteen to seventy-five students; only Andover and Princeton had more than 100 students by 1840 (201–2). Notably, many of these early seminaries did not survive the nineteenth century, and none was offering a formal educational degree. Compounding this situation was the gradual standoff between the Northern and Southern states over slavery, which led denominations such as the Presbyterians, Methodists, and Baptists to each split into two separate churches, respectively, between the mid-1840s and early 1860s.[79]

The curricular framework used by these newly formed seminaries followed the European pattern of the theological encyclopedia and its fourfold curriculum: Bible, history, systematic theology, and practical theology (51–53).[80] The basic approach to the educational process focused on the development of the mind and the character of the pastor being prepared for ministerial leadership in a congregation. The goal was the formation of what might be called the *gentleman pastor* who had a prepared mind. This kind of pastor served well in the congregations of denominations that required formal education for the ordination of their leaders. However, as before, little attention was being paid in any of the schools to providing educational training in the actual practices of ministry (26–28).

Denominations also continued to form pastors for congregational leadership in nonformal ways, especially in the upstart denominations. The typical congregational leader who emerged to be called as a pastor

77. http://hds.harvard.edu/about/history-and-mission (accessed March 30, 2017).

78. http://divinity.yale.edu/about-yds/mission-history (accessed June 10, 2016).

79. Noll, *The Old World Religion*, 108.

80. See also Glenn T. Miller, *Piety and Profession: American Protestant Theological Education* (Grand Rapids: Eerdmans, 2007), 48–49.

usually possessed natural leadership gifts, gave evidence of being called by God, and was able to reach people with his preaching—the *revivalist pastor*. Some attained more schooling over time as these denominations became involved in education. The typical pattern was that, when colleges were founded, they provided a basic education for potential ministerial personnel. Complementing this basic education was the practice of having candidates who appeared to be called by God associate with a mentor, who provided exposure to ministry and guidance in how to interpret the Bible and how to prepare sermons.

After the Civil War ended, the African American denominations, following the pattern of the predecessor white denominations, also formed schools to prepare their ministers. Work in this area had been done by the African Methodist Episcopal denomination (formed in 1816), which established its first college, Wilberforce, in the 1850s in Ohio.[81] The initial establishment of literacy initiatives, along with the later building of colleges, continued apace for the first several decades following the Civil War. Many colleges were founded by Northern denominations and mission societies working in the Southern states.[82] As soon as the newly formed African American denominations gained some financial stability, they also started up numerous colleges, most begun from 1880 to 1900.[83]

The Catholic experience paralleled to some extent that of the Protestant churches. The Roman Catholic Church, from the time of the Middle Ages, had developed and relied on a system of schools to educate its laymen while also preparing clergy leadership for the church. This included the development of seminaries after the Council of Trent (1545–1563). Formal theological education for Catholics in the United States had its origin in 1791, when French Sulpicians established in Baltimore the first Catholic seminary in the United States.[84] Additional Catholic seminaries were founded—and scores of new dioceses were established—as the Catholic population increased through immigration.

---

81. Miller, *Piety and Profession*, 341, 347.

82. Miller, *Piety and Profession*, 367. Examples include: Talladega, Tougaloo, Bennett, Clark, Clafin, Meharry Medical, Morgan, Philander Smith, Rust, Wiley, Benedict, Bishop, Morehouse, Shaw, Spelman, Virginia Union, Biddle, Knoxville, and Slip-on Seminary.

83. Miller, *Piety and Profession*, 367. Examples include: Morris Brown, Paul Quinn, Allen, Shorter, Kettle, Edward Waters, Payne, Campbell, Turner, and Lampton.

84. Patrick W. Carey and Earl C. Muller, SJ, eds., *Theological Education in the Catholic Tradition: Contemporary Challenges* (New York: Crossroad, 1997), 1.

Time of Transition

The various denominations that had proliferated by the time of the Civil War developed clear identities and practices for their ministries, which also included their approaches to theological education. The Civil War and Reconstruction, however, contributed to a transition in a number of ways for denominations and their congregations—as well as for theological education. Denominations that had divided along Northern and Southern lines over the issue of slavery now had to consider how they would once more relate to one another; meanwhile, people training for ministry had to decide where to go to secure that training.

The frontier continued to expand westward, and new congregations continued to be formed within the new denominations coming into existence. A number of new seminaries were started by these denominations, as well as by the older denominations, to prepare candidates for pastoral leadership, with Chicago becoming the center of much of this activity.[85] Accompanying these changes were the increasing efforts by many of the upstart denominations, especially the Methodists, to make their faith practices and congregational leadership more respectable and professional. This move toward respectability dramatically changed the evangelical and revivalistic character of the faith developed earlier on the frontier; furthermore, this change was accompanied by a remarkable slowing of their exponential growth.

A major transition in the ethos of national identity also occurred, as efforts to deal with the divisions engendered by the Civil War began to be addressed. The efforts initiated by Reconstruction were toward bringing the newly freed slaves more fully into American life; but that only exacerbated tensions with white Southerners. Freed blacks did begin to participate more fully when Reconstruction was ended, but with this shift the struggle for integration and equality for the African American population took several steps back. Although the war was over, the distinct regional differences within the country continued to exist. Amid these shifting developments, the African American church emerged as a central institution in the life of the black community.

The Civil War and Reconstruction also marked a transition in immigration and migration patterns. The population continued to diversify,

---

85. Miller, *Piety and Profession*, 40. These developments included the establishment in Chicago of such schools as McCormick Seminary by the Presbyterian Church and Chicago Theological Seminary by the Congregational Church.

and by the latter part of the nineteenth century, people were increasingly migrating to the growing cities, where these rural migrants encountered increasing numbers of immigrants coming from southern and eastern Europe. Over time, this stimulated a shift in focus to a more urban perspective for denominations and their agencies, as well as for many seminaries and schools of theology. But perhaps most important for denominations and theological education, the Civil War and Reconstruction began to mark a time of transition in the method and spirit that theologians used to read and interpret the Bible.

Significant developments began to take place—and for several reasons. First of all, many seminaries and schools of theology gradually adopted the methodologies of higher criticism that had been pioneered in Germany. This new approach to biblical studies eventually would send "shock waves" through the theological educational system and would "[redraw] the theological landscape."[86] The traditional view of reading Scripture as divine revelation was profoundly challenged. Second, coupled with this challenge was the increasing influence of evolution for reinterpreting human existence after the publication of Darwin's *On the Origin of the Species* in 1859, which represented a competing narrative that deeply challenged the biblical story.

86. Miller, *Piety and Profession*, xxii.

CHAPTER 5

The Church in the City, 1880s to Early 1940s

The Church during the City Period

The church in the city period continued to grow in size, while it also diversified in its membership; much of this increasing diversity was the result of expanded immigration and internal migration. As a result, the church also experienced a significant relocation of its members, as this influx of immigrants and migrants settled within the expanding cities, where a new form of the church came into existence: the city-neighborhood congregation. The church continued to become more pluralistic in its faith expressions; the earlier upstart denominations worked to professionalize their ministry; various denominational splits took place; and new movements emerged, such as Pentecostalism. All of these changes greatly influenced the public missiologies that the church pursued, and some important trends associated with these developments emerged.

The settling of the frontier west of the Mississippi River—all the way to the edges of the Rocky Mountains—continued into the territories that would become states in the second half of the nineteenth century and the first decades of the twentieth. This area was settled largely by those seeking to farm or ranch. Continuing the pattern of church establishment in the previous decades, new village congregations were started by the thousands throughout the rural areas of the West, some by denominations that already existed, others by ethnic-specific denominations that were being formed by the immigrants moving west in their quest for land.

The distinctive cultures of the various regions that first emerged during the colonial period and then spread into the opening frontier, continued to be carried further west into the heartland as these territories were settled and became states. But the settling of these areas required the displacement of the Native American tribes, usually by force of military action. Beyond the heartland regions, settlers went into the mountain areas west of the Rockies, settling in the Southwest and the territories along the Pacific Ocean. But the Christian faith that was spread by all the denominations, across the frontier and up to the Rockies, did not make it into these areas in proportionate numbers. The Western region is something of an anomaly in its relative lack of church development—to this very day.

The force of immigration greatly increased in number by the end of the nineteenth century, when it rose to over a million new immigrants a year. And a significant change took place in the ethnic makeup of these immigrants. The majority were now coming from southern and central Europe, which meant that many of them were Roman Catholic; but there were also large numbers of Jews and Orthodox believers. This resulted in a challenge to the notion that the United States was primarily a Protestant nation, a view that increasingly had to give way to a growing Judeo-Christian ethos that included Protestants, Catholics, and Jews.

The growth of American cities during this period was dramatic. Much of this came from increased immigration itself; but a good part of it came from migrants who moved from rural to urban areas. Some were displaced as farm workers due to improvements in agricultural technology; but many came to the cities for the new opportunities that the cities offered. The expanding industrial economy fueled the growth of the cities, especially in the Northern states, from the East Coast through to the Midwest. New city-neighborhood churches were built by the thousands to serve these immigrants and migrants.

A significant change took place in the African American population in the early 1900s, and it interacted with the expanding industrial economy and the growing cities in the North. The pervasive racial segregation in the South continued to be burdensome to blacks, even as job opportunities opened up in the North, leading to what became known as the Great Migration in America: the exodus of thousands of African Americans out of the South to Northern cities, where they experienced new opportunities for employment, though they continued to experience the realities of the segregated society they thought they had left behind. Several thousand new black churches were built to serve this relocated population.

Another change in the ethos of the Christian faith marked this period: it involved the growing divide between those seeking to professionalize the church as they came to grips with modernity over against those who reacted to and resisted these trends. Various denominational splits occurred over this issue, and new denominations came into existence in this milieu. Those included denominations started up by fundamentalists, as well as those resulting from the newly formed Holiness and Pentecostal movements.

Key Themes, Events, and Population Shifts

The population of the United States in 1880 stood at just over fifty million; by 1940, it had more than doubled—to over 132 million. Accompanying this significant growth was a remarkable shift in where this population lived— relocating increasingly from rural areas to cities. The urban population of the US grew from 28 percent in 1880 to 56 percent in 1930. The urbanization of America was by then well under way.

Changes taking place in the broader American society also influenced the growing denominations and their congregations. The population now stretched from coast to coast, as new states were added to the nation in the latter decades of the nineteenth century: Nevada (1864), Colorado (1876), North and South Dakota (1889), Montana (1889), Washington (1889), Idaho (1890), Wyoming (1890), Utah (1896), Oklahoma (1907). The majority of these states are located in the area that Woodard describes as the "Far West." It consisted of territories that were made up largely of mountain ranges or open desert, areas that were not conducive to significant settlement and could not support a large population. This vast area with sparse population was settled mostly by ranchers, who owned large spreads, or by major corporations, with headquarters usually located outside the region, using capital-intensive technologies—the extraction industries.[1] The churches started in these areas were often built to serve company towns. Overall, the Christianity that took root here was not proportional in size to that of the regions that lay to the east, a pattern that would continue throughout the twentieth century.[2]

Along the southern border of the United States were the last states to enter the union in the lower forty-eight contiguous states: New Mexico

1. Colin Woodard, *American Nations: A History of the Eleven Rival Regional Cultures of North America* (New York: Penguin, 2011), 244.
2. Roger Finke and Rodney Stark, *The Churching of America, 1776–2005: Winners and Losers in Our Religious Economy* (New Brunswick, NJ: Rutgers University Press, 2005), 202–3.

(1912) and Arizona (1912). This area represents a commingling of Mexican culture and US Anglo culture.[3] Here the church was largely Roman Catholic, and Protestants were initially very much in the minority. In both areas of the Far West and El Norte, the remaining Indian tribes either voluntarily made peace or were defeated by military action and then relocated to reservations. This brought an end to the Indian wars in the West and clearly was intended to help facilitate the process of bringing the extensive Western territories into statehood. But it took place at the expense of the Native American population.

The fuller development of the Industrial Revolution in America occurred during this period, when a large-scale, labor-intensive industry was developed. This expansion was fueled primarily by the raw materials of iron ore and coal that were required for the production of steel; that, along with the discovery of oil, facilitated an expanding economy of manufacturing. This resulted in what became known as the Gilded Age, an economic reality that saw the rise of barons of industry and their accumulation of massive personal fortunes. The emergence of the labor movement soon paralleled these developments in industry, leading to several decades of labor unrest, strikes, and strikebreaking. The battle was waged primarily over the issues of what constituted the personal property rights of owners and, for the employees, the reality of worker exploitation. That, in turn, contributed to some Northern church leaders articulating a Social Gospel theology by the late 1800s, which sought to redress the abuses of industrialization. For example, Washington Gladden, a Congregationalist, argued for "better wages and working conditions," and Walter Rauschenbusch, an American Baptist, proposed "new models for the organization of society."[4]

Many of the new city-dwellers located within distinct ethnic neighborhoods that were being built along expanding streetcar lines, especially in Northern cities. Most brought with them from Europe their national Christian faith and joined or started congregations that spoke the native tongue. For example, in 1916, "approximately half (49 percent) of all Catholics attended a parish where a language other than English was used in religious services."[5]

---

3. Woodard, *American Nations*, 208–15.

4. Mark A. Noll, *The Old Religion in a New World* (Grand Rapids: Eerdmans, 2002), 132–33. See Washington Gladden, *Working People and Their Employers* (Boston: Lockwood, Brooks, 1876); see also Walter Rauschenbusch, *Christianity and the Social Crisis: The Classic That Woke Up the Church* (1907; San Francisco: HarperOne, 2008).

5. Finke and Stark, *Churching of America*, 134.

What became known as the Progressive Era emerged in the midst of these changes, with attention being given to the trustbusting of many of the industrial monopolies that had been established. Other causes taken up included the Good Government Movement, which attempted to address urban electoral reform; Prohibition, which passed in 1920; and the woman suffrage movement, which also passed in 1920. Standing behind these efforts was a white, largely rural, Protestant political majority that sought to control the national agenda. There was also an increased awareness of the growing role of the United States in world affairs.

All of these developments coincided with the dramatic expansion of foreign mission personnel: by 1900, "Americans outnumbered Continentals by two to one. . . . By 1910 they had also passed the British in financing [and] in number of missionaries."[6] This increase of missionary personnel came as a result of the expansion of mission societies, which grew from sixteen in 1860 to roughly ninety in 1900.[7]

The increased involvement of the United States in the affairs of the world was further enhanced as a result of the Spanish-American War in the late 1890s, in which victory led to the ceding of the Philippines to the United States. During that era, patriotism was blended with missionary zeal and was baptized with the notion of providence. All of this contributed to the eventual involvement of the United States in World War I. But a tempering of an international role occurred in the aftermath of that war, especially in light of the Russian revolution in 1917 and the "red scare" that emerged in America. This signaled a significant shift that was beginning to take place in both world involvement and missionary zeal in the 1920s, as the nation turned inward, as secularization increased, and as questions of the uniqueness of Christianity began to surface. In the midst of these developments, an expanding economy led to an expanding broad-based prosperity that became known as the "roaring twenties." The twenties "roared" until the practices of excessive speculation brought it all to a screeching halt in the stock market crash of 1929. This resulted in the Great Depression of the 1930s, the effects of which continued up to the beginning of World War II.

---

6. William R. Hutchison, *Errand to the World: American Protestant Thought and Foreign Missions* (Chicago: University of Chicago Press, 1987), 93.

7. Hutchison, *Errand to the World*, 91.

The Formation of New National Narratives

The settlement of the country was completed during this time, leading some historians to reflect on this accomplishment. Frederick Jackson Turner proposed his frontier thesis in 1893: he theorized that an egalitarian, common-person democracy had emerged across the expanding frontier of the growing nation, which contributed to the settling of those territories and led to their eventual achieving of statehood.[8] This explanation clearly expressed the spirit of the Protestant denominations and the domain they exercised throughout the 1800s, when they planted thousands of village congregations across the ever-westward-moving frontier. Turner's thesis helped legitimate the notion of American exceptionalism, which "promoted the rugged individualism of which Americans were so proud."[9] The thesis also allowed for the notion that the new states being formed could justify their occupation of these territories as part of and, in fact, representing the democratic tradition.

Others, such as Theodore Roosevelt, argued that the actual story line of the creation of a new nation was primarily one of conquest. This occurred as whites progressively defeated and displaced Native American populations through war, followed by imposing on them a system of disadvantageous treaties in order to occupy their former lands.[10] By the beginning of the twentieth century, the Turner thesis became the popular view, one that the older denominations, along with the upstarts, readily supported. Their democratic ideals supported the view of a manifest destiny in the westward movement to settle this land, a movement in which these denominations had all participated and from which they had all prospered.

This concept of "manifest destiny" developed at the turn of the century built on the earlier notion of American exceptionalism. Ernest Lee Tuveson argues in *Redeemer Nation* that the expanding role of the United States in the world was also supported in the late 1800s by a millenarian ideal that drew on biblical examples to justify the redemptive role played by the United States in international affairs.[11] This narrative

8. Frederick Jackson Turner and Wilbur R. Jacobs, *The Frontier in American History*, 5th ed. (Tucson: University of Arizona Press, 1986).

9. Charles Murray, *American Exceptionalism: An Experiment in History* (Washington, DC: AEI Press, 2013), 11.

10. Richard Slotkin, "Nostalgia and Progress: Theodore Roosevelt's Myth of the Frontier," *American Quarterly* 33, no. 5 (1981): 608–37.

11. Ernest Lee Tuveson, *Redeemer Nation: The Idea of America's Millennial Role* (Chicago: University of Chicago Press, 1968).

was popularized in songs such as "America the Beautiful," written in 1895, which soon became a national patriotic favorite, and "God Bless America," composed by Irving Berlin in 1918, which often serves as a kind of second national anthem at sporting events and the like.[12] This concept of the role of America continues to hold sway in American politics up to the present.

The appeal of this narrative was self-evident to many in the growing population who were settling into the expanding cities of the North. But it was in the cities that the fuller effects of the industrial revolution were also being realized—both positive and negative. The negative effects led to the rise of the Social Gospel. But, in general, this narrative was openly embraced by many of the growing Protestant denominations, especially typified by the thirty-two denominations that initially formed the Federal Council of Churches (FCC) in 1908.[13] Numerous commissions were created by the FCC, all seeking to improve society by addressing the social issues of the day.

Significant changes in population mobility were facilitated by the electrified streetcar systems that began to be built in the cities in the 1880s to replace the earlier horse-drawn cars.[14] These soon became interconnected with the expanding national network of railroads, which increased population mobility and greatly expanded both manufacturing and commerce. Numerous scientific discoveries and technological improvements also took place in such fields as farming, manufacturing, health care, and education, giving rise to an incredible optimism that progress in addressing the human condition was not only desirable but was now, indeed, possible. Things really did seem to be getting a little better every day in every way.[15]

12. Ace Collins, *Songs Sung, Red, White, and Blue: The Stories behind America's Best-Loved Patriotic Songs* (Bel Air, CA: HarperResource, 2003), 82–83.

13. Finke and Stark, Churching of America, 207–8, 216–18; Ahlstrom, *A Religious History of the American People* (New Haven: Yale University Press, 1972), 802–4.

14. Mark S. Foster, *From Streetcar to Superhighway: American City Planners and Urban Transportation, 1900–1940* (Philadelphia: Temple University Press, 1981).

15. This phrase was first used by Frenchman Émile Coué de la Châtaigneraie in 1910 regarding self-improvement. But it was quickly picked up by advocates of the Social Gospel to promote what they saw happening: http://www.quotecounterquote.com/2010/08/every-day-in-every-way-i-am-getting.html (accessed June 10, 2016).

African American Population

The African American population increased during this period from 6.5 million to just under 12 million, with some significant changes taking place within that community. Reconstruction, which began in 1863, had created new political opportunities and opened up space for some participation by African Americans in the broader society of the Southern states. But the Reconstruction experiment was short-lived: the federal government withdrew its forces from the Southern states in 1877, passing to these states the responsibility to work out their own affairs internally. This quickly led to a total white takeover across the South of the machinery of government, from towns and counties all the way up to the state level. It also resulted in the establishment of a segregated society that was enforced by a whole series of what came to be known as "Jim Crow laws"—a system that institutionalized the separation of the white and black societies into two parallel, but totally divided, societies.[16] Most of the black population ended up in an agricultural system of sharecropping rented land; and for most of those who were caught in it, it amounted to little more than an existence in perpetual debt.

As we discussed in the preceding chapter, multiple African American congregations were formed by the freed slaves during Reconstruction; most of them became associated with the new African American denominations that were coming into existence. But the AME, formed earlier in the North, also became very active in working to attract "the churches of the freed slaves, sending seventy-seven missionaries into the South between 1863 and 1870."[17] Joining them were a large number of white denominations that attempted "to start churches for the freed slaves . . . [but] the majority of the membership was found in the black denominations. In 1890, 51 percent of the black population belonged to the nine black denominations and only 8 percent to the predominantly white denominations."[18] The major contribution of the white churches working in the South was to continue to support the earlier investment they had made during Reconstruction, which had to do with the schools and colleges they had started up to provide educational opportunities for African Americans, a pattern that continued through the end of the century.

---

16. David K. Fremon, *The Jim Crow Laws and Racism in the United States* (New York: Enslow, 2014).

17. Finke and Stark, *Churching of America*, 195.

18. Finke and Stark, *Churching of America*, 192.

Black people continued to struggle for their place in society, even though they had become free citizens. As noted earlier, a significant shift in this condition began to occur at the beginning of the twentieth century, when the Great Migration of 1.6 million blacks moved out of the South between 1910 and 1930.[19] They relocated mostly to the Northern cities, where industrial jobs were opening up. The result was the development of large black neighborhoods in most of the large industrial cities, but neighborhoods that developed mostly as segregated communities.

Many of the people involved in the Great Migration brought their denominational faith with them, and hundreds of black churches were built to serve these neighborhoods, which played a major role in socializing this relocated population to urban realities. Frazier helpfully notes that, "like the immigrant faiths, religious freedoms allowed African Americans to use the[ir] churches as institutional safe havens for supporting their members and their culture."[20] It was here that "organized religious life became the chief means by which a structured or organized social life came into existence."[21] This pattern greatly influenced the public missiology that the black church developed.

The growth of African American denominations and their congregations accompanied this migration to the North, even as they continued to expand in the South. By 1906, about 17 percent of the nation's approximately 212,000 local churches were African American, even though they represented only 11 percent of the nation's population of 83 million.[22] An important thing to note is that new centers of power and a different generation of black leaders began to emerge within the black communities of Northern cities. They began to create a new set of black organizations that challenged the practices promoted by Booker T. Washington, the founder of the Tuskegee Institute in Alabama, who was "willing to work within the boundaries set by white society."[23] A good example of the new generation of leaders was W. E. B. Du Bois, the first African American to earn a doctorate from Harvard, who formed the National Association for the Advancement

19. Nicholas Lemann, *The Promised Land: The Great Black Migration and How It Changed America* (New York: Vintage, 1992).

20. E. Franklin Frazier, *The Negro Church in America* (New York: Schocken [Random House], 1974), 36.

21. Frazier, *The Negro Church in America*, 36.

22. Noll, *The Old World Religion*, 121, 155-56.

23. Noll, *The Old World Religion*, 119.

of Colored People in the 1900s.[24] These developments were supported and significantly nurtured by the black churches, especially those in the North.

Native American Population

The remaining Native American tribes living in the West following the Civil War either made peace with the US government or were defeated by the military in the late 1870s, and these tribes were resettled onto reservations. The national reservation system eventually grew to include 554 indigenous groups, located on 310 federally recognized reservations.[25] However, there was a final phase of contesting by Native Americans that involved military action, which consisted of the army using military force to defeat a continued series of uprisings on several reservations among Indians seeking their independence. These actions resulted in several significant massacres of Indian peoples, such as at Wounded Knee in South Dakota in 1890. Uprisings came to an end in that same year, when the US census of that decade put the number of Native Americans in the population at 248,000. This represented a dramatic decline from their numbers at the beginning of the century. Subsequently, the Native American population increased only modestly—to 332,000 in 1930 and 334,000 in 1940.

The federal policy toward the Indian tribes changed significantly during this period. The passage of the Dawes Act in 1887 ended the practice of allocating reservation territory to the tribe as a whole and replaced it with individual allotments, allowing individuals to sell their allotment to outsiders. This practice lasted all the way up to the passage of the Indian Reorganization Act of 1934, when the government terminated it and replaced it with its own imposed design of a heavy investment in infrastructure, health care, and education—policies parallel to those of the New Deal.[26] A shift in the *contesting* for the land by the Native American peoples began to take place at the beginning of the twentieth century: attention was now paid to advocating for treaty justice.

24. W. E. B. Du Bois, *The Souls of Black Folk* (1903; Mineola, NY: Dover Publications, 1994).

25. Roxanne Dunbar-Ortiz, *An Indigenous Peoples' History of the United States* (Boston: Beacon, 2014), 11.

26. For a short time, the leadership of the Bureau of Indian Affairs tried an approach known as "termination," which sought to remove all government involvement with the tribes being compensated to give up their lands in an effort to force their assimilation into mainstream culture. But this practice was soon ended.

A system of government boarding schools had been put in place on the reservations in the late 1800s; the goal was to assimilate the Native American children into the dominant culture by cutting them off from their traditional practices and beliefs. Many denominations started mission work on reservations at that time, planting churches that were typically led by the missionaries; but they were especially involved in working with the schools where missionaries often openly collaborated with government efforts to promote assimilation. The legacy of white control of both education and religious life on the reservations—and the church's involvement in it—has been a legacy that denominations have continued to struggle to own up to and get past well into the twentieth century.[27]

White Population Growth and Continued Immigration

The most substantial population changes taking place at the turn of the twentieth century involved the white population. As immigration from southern and central Europe dramatically increased, it changed the earlier century-long pattern of the vast majority of the immigrants coming from the largely Protestant British Isles and northern European countries. The 1800s saw an increase from an average of roughly 500,000 immigrants per year at midcentury to over 1 million annually in the 1890s and early 1900s.[28]

This expanded immigration from southern and eastern Europe led to significant increases in the numbers of Roman Catholic, Orthodox, and Jewish people joining the US population. The Roman Catholic population represented about 5 percent of the US population in 1850; by 1900 it had grown to 16 percent—to over 14 million people.[29] The Orthodox Church, in both its Greek and Russian expressions, also became a part of the US religious population. The first Russian Orthodox had actually entered the Alaska territory in 1794 and engaged in mission work south along the Pacific seaboard; some of these territories soon became states (Alaska itself was purchased by the United States in 1867). The immigration of the Rus-

27. David Wallace Adams, *Education for Extinction: American Indians and the Boarding School Experience, 1875–1928* (Lawrence: University Press of Kansas, 1995).

28. http://www.americancenturies.mass.edu/turns/theme.jsp?x=3&y=3 (accessed June 11, 2016).

29. http://www.nationalhumanitiescenter.org/tserve/nineteen/nkeyinfo/nromcath .htm (accessed June 11, 2016).

sian Orthodox into Eastern cities began in the late nineteenth century and picked up substantially in the midst of the Russian Revolution. The Greek Orthodox immigration into America also began to take place in the late 1800s; the immigrant church continued to be under the oversight of the Church of Greece. The Jewish population increased from roughly 250,000 in 1880 to more than four million by 1930.[30]

There was also some increase in the Asian and Pacific Rim population during this period: it more than doubled, to just over 260,000, largely as a result of workers being imported to assist in the building of the railroads in the West. But restrictions against Chinese immigration were put into place early when Congress acted in 1882 to pass the Chinese Exclusion Act.[31] Similar restrictions were placed on Japanese immigration by the early 1900s. The exception was Filipinos, who had initially declared independence in the aftermath of the Spanish American War; but the United States waged a brutal war to defeat them and subsequently allowed them to immigrate after the Philippines became a US territory. These populations tended to remain religiously distinct within their own faith traditions; they developed segregated communities and places of worship, which were reinforced by familial and social bonds and by the maintaining of native customs.

The significant yearly increases in immigration continued into the first two decades of the twentieth century, but were temporarily curtailed in 1921. This was partially as a reaction to the red scare following the Russian Revolution. But it was also a reaction to some extent by Protestants to the increasing proportion of Roman Catholics in the overall population, newcomers who engaged in Sunday activities without restriction and who indulged in alcoholic beverages. Immigration was permanently limited in 1924 with the adoption of the National Origins Act, which dramatically limited the number of annual immigrants from any country to only 2 percent of the persons from that country who were living in the United States in 1890. This was clearly a bias in favor of northern European ethnicities, which were disproportionately Protestant.[32]

---

30. Irving Howe and Kenneth Libo, *How We Lived: A Documentary History of Immigrant Jews in America, 1880–1930* (New York: Putman, 1983).

31. John Soennichsen, *The Chinese Exclusion Act of 1882* (Westport, CT: Greenwood, 2011).

32. John Bond Trevor, *An Analysis of the American Immigration Act of 1924: International Conciliation, No. 202, September 1924* (Whitefish, MT: Library Licensing LLC, 2013). The Immigration Act of 1924, also known as the Johnson-Reed Act, limited the number of immigrants who could be admitted into the United States each year. Based on the Census of

All of these shifts meant that the former Protestant domain had to give way eventually to a national narrative involving a shared Judeo-Christian heritage for telling the American story that included Protestants, Catholics, and Jews.[33] This shift represents what has come to be known as the second disestablishment of the Protestant church in the United States.[34] The Progressive Era in the late 1800s and early 1900s represented in many ways the last successful efforts by Protestants to control the national agenda. They focused especially on the moral and legal issues related to Temperance and Prohibition, but also promoted at-large elections in urban areas to neutralize the influence of immigrant-ethnic neighborhoods. Noll notes that the Prohibition movement "could be considered the last gasp of Protestant hegemony," and the repeal of Prohibition in 1933 became the symbolic end of Protestant control over the national agenda.[35]

Much of this expanding immigration, as well as rural migration, settled into the urban centers, especially in the northeast and along the upper Ohio Valley. These growing urban centers expanded geographically through the technology of streetcars into new city neighborhoods being built to house the growing population. This rapid growth of major urban areas was functionally integrated around a well-developed central business district (CBD) with all the amenities of urban life being concentrated there. Thousands of neighborhood congregations were started along the streetcar lines to accommodate this growth, including hundreds of parish churches built to serve the rapidly growing Roman Catholic population. They were joined in this building activity by the old "first" churches from a previous era. The latter replaced their more modest—often wooden—structures with elaborate stone and stained-glass creations. Stephen Cox calls this "the big-church movement."[36]

1890, immigrants were limited to 2 percent of the number of people from that country who were already living in the United States in 1890. This lowered the 3 percent cap that had been set by the Immigration Restriction Act of 1921. Asians were totally excluded.

33. This shift and its importance in American life was well documented by Will Herberg in *Protestant, Catholic, Jew: An Essay in American Religious Sociology* (New York: Doubleday, 1955).

34. Robert Handy, *A Christian America: Protestant Hopes and Historical Realities* (New York: Oxford University Press, 1971). The first disestablishment took place in the decision to separate church and state.

35. Noll, *The Old World Religion*, 135. See also Daniel Okrent, *Last Call: The Rise and Fall of Prohibition* (New York: Scribner, 2011).

36. Stephen Cox, *American Christianity: The Continuing Revolution* (Austin: University of Texas Press, 2014), 50.

System of Congregations

There were approximately 70,000 churches in the United States at the beginning of the 1880s; by the 1920s, more than 225,000 organized churches were in existence.[37] This tripling of the number of congregations was accompanied by a growing diversity among them, illustrated by the following examples: after the Civil War, many African American congregations became organized and joined existing or emerging black denominations; the rise of the Holiness movement in the late 1800s, along with the emergence of the Pentecostal movement in the early 1900s, contributed to the starting up of multiple congregations within both the black and white populations; and the fundamentalist movement away from "modernism" during the first decades of the twentieth century led to hundreds of congregations being founded as members pulled out of their parent Protestant denominations to organize them.

But the major influence that expanded and further diversified the system of congregations came from significant increases of immigrants, many of whom settled in the prairie lands that continued to open up west of the Mississippi as the railroad network expanded. The pattern here was the continued formation of ethnic-specific *village congregations* in the numerous towns that sprang up across the central plains and the ranch lands further to the west.[38] Still, the majority of immigrants coming to America, now from southern and eastern European countries, settled into the rapidly growing industrial cities of the North.

This urban growth led to the development of a new type of church: the *city-neighborhood congregation*. A different kind of facility was built to serve the members of these congregations, one that usually included the following: a large sanctuary/auditorium that could seat several hundred worshipers; a separate multistory Sunday-school building; an expanded ground-level fellowship space; a library; and sometimes even a gymnasium. Thousands of city-neighborhood congregations were started

37. Robert Wuthnow, *The Restructuring of American Religion* (Princeton: Princeton University Press, 1988), 22.

38. An example of this pattern of settlement took place in Osceola County in northwest Iowa, where one of the authors was born and raised. This was the last county in Iowa to be settled, which began with the arrival of the railroad in 1872. The population of the county grew from 2,219 in 1880 to 8,956 in 1910. During this period, sixteen churches were founded in the five towns that were incorporated in the county: five Methodist, four Lutheran, two Christian Reformed, two Presbyterian, one Baptist, one Congregational, and one Catholic.

in the midst of this shift in population patterns and its accompanying growth. The rapid expansion of the system also required more administrative and programming support from regional and national denominational offices, which, in turn, increased financial assistance from the member congregations to the national and regional levels to support that bureaucracy.

This new type of congregation also required pastors to be trained with higher educational and professional standards in order to meet the rising expectations of the urban congregations. The city-neighborhood congregations represented a significant morphing in congregational life with their expanded programming, more elaborate physical plants, and increased staff. The seeds of the *modern corporate denomination* and the formation of the *institutional church* were planted in the midst of these developments. The programmatic approach to church life was developed in response to the rise of a middle-class population that had more leisure time in urban America; church activities were designed to occupy that time. But the institutional church was in many ways simply a more elaborate version of the logic of the village church and its extended families, who intermarried and all lived in close geographical proximity.

Development of the Denominational, Organizational Church

Most denominational congregations during this time developed a more comprehensive programmatic approach to their ministries, which paralleled the expansion of programs being provided by their respective national churches. This led to the further morphing of the earlier purposive denomination into another type, which we can label the churchly denomination. Here the focus was on providing ministry to faithful members from cradle to grave, which included such ministries as educational programs for all ages, youth ministry, camps and conferences, published materials, and Christian colleges.[39]

The pattern that was followed often found denominations either copying or co-opting one of the ministries of an interdenominational mission society and then bringing that activity under the management of their own

---

39. Richey, "Denominations and Denominationalism: An American Morphology," in *Reimagining Denominationalism: Interpretive Essays*, ed. Robert Bruce Mullin and Russell E. Richey (New York: Oxford University Press, 1994).

agencies. This pattern was evident in the earlier mainstreaming of the Sunday school movement within denominational programming by the middle of the nineteenth century, when standardized curricula for the expanding Sunday school systems began to be developed by the denominational publishing houses.[40] Similarly, denominational youth ministries began to appear by the late 1800s, often patterned after the parachurch ministry of Christian Endeavor.[41] Over time, a comprehensive approach to ministry developed that addressed members' needs throughout their lives. The full-service churchly denomination with a growing denominational infrastructure was now coming of age.[42]

This development signaled the initial emergence of what would become the *modern corporate denomination*, with its growing complexity also requiring new ways for structuring and managing the growing church bureaucracy. It is worth noting that the newly emerging field of "organizational sciences" provided answers. Several streams of thought helped birth this new discipline, but the most important for denominations became scientific management.[43] This stream emerged primarily from the work of Frederick Taylor, who published his seminal book, *The Principles of Scientific Management*, in 1911.[44]

An early voice promoting this approach for growing denominations was Shailer Mathews, dean of the Divinity School of The University of Chicago, who in 1912 published *Scientific Management in the Churches*. In utilizing Taylor's work, Mathews notes that "in my judgment the philosophy of efficiency can at least be tentatively applied to the working of churches."[45] The increasingly rationalized world of the modern bureaucracy was starting to become the norm for denominational church life in managing their

40. Sydney E. Ahlstrom, *A Religious History of the American People* (New Haven: Yale University Press, 1972), 741–42.

41. Ahlstrom, *A Religious History of the American People*, 858.

42. Mullin and Richey, eds., *Reimagining Denominationalism*, 82–84.

43. In the early decades of the twentieth century, at least three streams emerged: Scientific Management by Frederick Taylor (1911); Administrative Management by Henri Fayol (1919), and Bureaucracy by Max Weber (1924).

44. Frederick Taylor, *The Principles of Scientific Management* (New York: Harper and Brothers, 1911). Taylor focuses on bringing productivity and efficiency into the business organization. Businesses were to accomplish that by de-skilling tasks, organizing similar work activities into functional units, and building command and control systems through the establishment of a hierarchical bureaucracy—best illustrated by the Ford Motor Company's assembly line for manufacturing cars.

45. Shailer Matthews, *Scientific Management in the Churches* (Chicago: University of Chicago Press, 1912), 12–13.

boards and agencies. Championing this approach was the recently formed Federal Council of Churches.

Denominations continued to multiply and become more diverse in this period, along with their congregations, and these developments continued to reinforce some of the distinctive faith characteristics of the various regions of the country. But some changes were taking place within these regions. The Northern Baptists increasingly became more secularized as their membership became more wealthy, leading to a significant slowing of their growth.[46] The Methodists, in an effort to become more respectable, also became more secularized: they ended the circuit-rider system and began to require seminary-trained clergy. This led to their peaking in the late 1800s and their losing of their numerical dominance to the Baptists, especially the Southern Baptists in the Deep South.[47]

Denominational organizational capacity also grew as denominations developed their agencies' infrastructure. Refined methodologies for developing new congregations were developed by the latter part of the 1800s. This was especially true in both the West and in the growing cities: standardized plans for constructing church buildings were made available from national offices, such as the Akron Plan, which incorporated the growth of the Sunday school in its plan. Existing congregations also continued to adapt earlier approaches to ministry within the new conditions, as illustrated by the development of urban revivals that began springing up in the late 1800s under leaders such as Dwight Moody and Ira Sankey—not to mention Billy Sunday.[48]

There were several other major developments that had an impact on the system of denominations in the United States. One was the modernist/fundamentalist split that led to divisions within some denominations and the formation of new church bodies. This retrenchment among conservative Christians led many of them to become increasingly identified with fundamentalism, a movement that was supported by a growing system of Bible institutes and colleges. This movement was significantly facilitated by a group of ninety essays published in twelve volumes as *The Fundamentals* (between 1910 and 1915) by the Bible Institute of Los Ange-

---

46. Finke and Stark, *Churching of America*, 184–86.

47. Finke and Stark, *Churching of America*, 184–86 156–69, 186–89. A key difference contributing to these developments was the role played by seminaries. The Northern Baptists created independently run seminaries, while the Southern Baptists maintained denominational control of their seminaries.

48. Noll, *The Old World Religion*, 130–32; and Cox, *American Christianity*, 84–94.

les.[49] The 1925 Scopes Trial in Dayton, Tennessee, became the symbolic watershed of the fundamentalist voice's loss of credibility in the broader stream of American religious life, and that hastened the retrenchment of this movement for the next several decades.[50]

Another major development in the system of denominations was the rise of the Holiness movement in the latter half of the 1800s. This was especially prominent among the Methodists, from which several Holiness denominations emerged—for example, the Free Methodist, Wesleyan, and Nazarene denominations. They were soon joined by the Pentecostal movement, which emerged at the beginning of the twentieth century. These movements all placed an emphasis on revivalism, the supernatural gifts of the Holy Spirit being manifest, and the expectation of living in the end time.

The key leaders who helped launch the Pentecostal movement were Charles Parham, of Topeka, Kansas, and William J. Seymour, a black preacher who was trained by Parham. Seymour relocated to Los Angeles in the early 1900s, where he led the famous Azusa Street Revival, which helped give birth to what became a variety of denominations within the Pentecostal tradition.[51] Another key leader of this movement was Aimee Semple McPherson, founder of the Foursquare Church, whose work was also centered in Los Angeles in the 1920s and 1930s. Early on, foreign missions work became a hallmark of the Pentecostal churches, and in the twentieth century this movement became a worldwide phenomenon, generating especially huge growth in Latin American countries.[52]

---

49. R. A. Torrey and A. C. Dixon, *The Fundamentals: A Testimony to the Truth* (Grand Rapids: Baker Book House, repr. 1972).

These volumes argued for a traditional understanding of the faith in the face of the growing influence of evolution, the use of higher criticism to interpret the Bible, and the use of science and technology to fuel the engine of modernity.

50. Jeffrey P. Moran, *The Scopes Trial: A Brief Trial with Documents* (New York: Bedford/St. Martin's, 2002).

51. Some of these became doctrinally Trinitarian; others became anti-Trinitarian.

52. Because Latin America was predominantly Roman Catholic, the Protestant state churches of Europe and their related mission societies did not engage in mission in this context. This reflected the agreement reached in the Peace of Westphalia, where the European map was settled by "whose realm, whose religion." It is an irony of history that Pentecostal churches in the United States were growing and becoming involved in missions at the end of the modern missions movement. Latin America was the mission field that was most readily available to them, and they saw evangelizing Catholics there as part of their mission responsibility.

Developments Regarding the Discipline of Missiology

The progress made in missions work during this period continued to take place from the Western countries primarily within a world under colonial rule. This meant that the discipline of missiology continued to be developed primarily with regard to Western hegemony and control. It is important to bear in mind that the Protestant version of the modern missions movement in Europe had emerged largely outside the established, institutional church; rather, it grew through mission societies. In the United States, by contrast, it came to be conducted through a combination of mission societies, faith missions, and denominational mission boards. Here the recruitment of future missionaries was largely the work of voluntary associations of students who networked across the various theological schools—for example, the Student Volunteer Movement.[53]

The focus continued to be on developing efficient practices to support the training and sending of mission personnel to other parts of the world. The primary theology that continued to undergird these movements, following earlier precedents, was largely shaped by an understanding of a church-centric view of the necessity to obey Christ in seeking to fulfill the Great Commission (Matt. 28:18–20). It would not be until later, in the mid-twentieth century, that a theological alternative for framing an understanding of mission would emerge.

This all took place within the political and economic reality of colonialism, which encompassed 95 percent of the global South by the beginning of the twentieth century. The missionaries and their supporting churches worked, for the most part, under the protection of the colonial governments, even while they protested the excesses of these systems in abusing the native populations.[54]

It is important to note that this was also the period when the system of American missionaries increasingly included the involvement of women—the wives of male missionaries and, increasingly, single women—many of whom were sent out by the independent mission societies. Interestingly, by 1900 missionary women outnumbered their male counterparts by a ratio of 4 to 1.[55]

---

53. Michael Parker, *The Kingdom of Character: The Student Volunteer Movement for Foreign Missions (1886–1926)* (Pasadena: William Carey Library, 2008).

54. Hutchison, *Errand to the World*, 91–124.

55. For a full treatment of this important development, see Dana Robert, *American Women in Mission: A Social History of Their Thought and Practice* (Macon, GA: Mercer University Press, 1997), 125–316.

This formative period in the development of the discipline of missiology, however, paid little attention to congregations, either theologically or theoretically, whether at home or abroad—a problem that continues to this day. Congregations at home were assumed to be the primary constituents for supporting the work of foreign missions. Congregations on the mission field were, for the most part, the byproduct of the primary work of evangelism that focused on winning converts to the faith. The ethos of colonialism led most missionaries to assume the superiority and necessity of using Western forms and practices. Therefore, they simply transposed predominantly Western forms of congregational life onto the various mission fields—strategies that only later came to be deeply challenged.[56]

What is crucial to note is that the Protestant *foreign* mission societies focused primarily on one thing: taking the gospel to other parts of the world.[57] It is worth noting that the peaking of this movement, which only later became evident, came at the World Missionary Conference convened at Edinburgh in 1910. More than 1,200 delegates from Western churches and mission societies gathered at that time to plan the final advance to complete the challenge of the Student Volunteer Movement's watchword—"the evangelization of the world in our generation."[58] That world missionary conference clearly marked a time of transition, serving more as a culmination point for the success of the nineteenth century's foreign missions enterprise than as a staging area—as it had planned—for a major final initiative. This was primarily due to World War I, which dramatically disrupted these optimistic plans.

The devastation of World War I, which was experienced primarily in western Europe, contributed significantly to the decline of the modern missions movement and to the gradual dismantling of the vast colonial system over the next several decades. This brought substantial changes to the enterprise of foreign missions. Ironically, at the same time that these changes were being introduced, the theological academy in America was just beginning to expand courses as well as the number of teaching positions for the newly emerging discipline of missiology. The following examples are illustrative of this development:

56. Few voices offered a critique at that time, even as international mission conferences began to be convened in the West. The earliest of the international missions conferences were held in Liverpool in 1860, London in 1888, and New York in 1900, all sponsored and attended by Western churches and mission societies.

57. Accompanying their work, as secondary efforts, were ministries of benevolent causes such as schools, hospitals, and orphanages.

58. David J. Bosch, *Transforming Mission* (Maryknoll, NY: Orbis, 1991), 323; see also Hutchinson, *Errand to the World*, 135–36.

- *Gustav Warnack.* The appointment of Gustav Warnack in 1896 to a chair of missionary science at the University of Halle was the first official chair in missiology on the European continent. He held this chair until 1908, and it served as an important precedent for later developments in the United States.
- *Missions Courses.* In 1910 about half of the theological schools in the United States offered courses in missions, though most of these were elective offerings.
- *Missions Professors.* In 1910 there were three full professors of missions in theological schools: Southern Baptist Seminary in Louisville, Episcopal Seminary in Cambridge, Massachusetts, and Yale Divinity School in New Haven, Connecticut.
- *Missions Programs.* Significant expansion of the discipline of missiology occurred with the development of missions programs and professorships at Union Theological Seminary in New York in 1914; at Princeton Theological Seminary in 1914; and with the merger of the Kennedy School of Missions into Hartford Seminary in 1913.
- *Theological Schools.* By 1934 the vast majority of theological schools offered at least some courses in missions, with about half of them requiring such courses; in addition, significant numbers of these schools created at least one chair in the field of missions.

Meanwhile, the very validity of the foreign missions enterprise was increasingly being called into question, as illustrated in the report edited by W. E. Hocking in 1932 that challenged the notion of the uniqueness of Christianity.[59] The discipline of missiology had to deal with two challenges in the midst of this reality. First, most of the advocacy for including a chair in missiology within seminaries had come primarily from denominational agencies and volunteer student associations; its inclusion in the curriculum was somewhat suspect among the more established theological disciplines. Second, missiology continued to focus primarily on the practice of foreign missions, while the academy was turning its attention to either ecumenism or world religions.

There was a move in the West toward trying to define more clearly the relationship of the church to mission. This conversation began within

---

59. William Ernest Hocking and Laymen's Foreign Missions Inquiry, *Re-Thinking Missions: A Laymen's Inquiry after One Hundred Years*, ed. Commission of Appraisal (New York: Harper, 1932). Hocking challenged the notion of the uniqueness of Christianity and called instead for the world religions to collaborate in facing the common enemy, secularism.

three new organizations, all of which grew out of the work of the Edinburgh Conference.[60] A whole series of conferences were set into motion by these streams that largely shaped the missiological discussion in the twentieth century.[61] They all wrestled with the same question: How should church and mission be related? It was increasingly recognized that a theological framing more robust than the Great Commission obligation would be required to answer this question. Just as the discipline of missiology was gaining viability in the academy, the whole climate related to foreign missions was shifting. The very validity of the foreign missions enterprise was soon called into question, resulting in the phenomenon of the discipline of missiology within theological education being increasingly *marginalized* at the very time it was becoming increasingly *institutionalized*.

Developments were also taking place within the Catholic Church with regard to refocusing attention on missions and the field of missiology. An important work, entitled *Catholic Mission History*, was published in 1933 by Joseph Schmidlin, a professor of missiology at the University of Muenster.[62] This book paralleled the emerging Protestant practice of telling the story of missions by carefully mapping the two centuries of Catholic mission work, and in formulating a mission theology. Also important to the development of Catholic missionary thinking were the five papal "mission encyclicals" that were published between 1919 and 1959.[63]

Public Missiologies in the Church during the City Period

The earlier public missiologies developed by the church in its engagement with culture continued to morph during the turn-of-the-century era. They interacted with the themes and events noted above, with most becoming deeply embedded by design or by default within the social imaginary of American exceptionalism and manifest destiny.

60. These were the International Missionary Council (IMC), formed in 1921, the Life and Work Movement (1925), and the Faith and Order Movement (1927).

61. See the Appendix for a chart and summary definitions related to the twentieth- and twenty-first-century ecumenical and evangelical mission conferences.

62. Joseph Schmidlin, *Catholic Mission History*, trans. Matthias Braun (1919; Techny, IL: Mission Press, 1933).

63. James Kroeger, "Papal Mission Wisdom: Five Mission Encyclicals, 1919–1959," in *A Century of Catholic Mission: Roman Catholic Missiology 1910 to the Present*, ed. Stephen B. Bevans, Regnum Edinburgh Centenary Series (Cornwall, UK: Regnum Books, 2013), 93–100.

Table 5.1 Public Missiologies of the Church in the City Period

Missiology Strain	Colonial Period	Frontier Period	Urban Growth Period	Suburban Success Period	Strategies for Success Period
Focus on Nation	Conquest to Civilize and Christianize -Established -Religious Freedom	Protestant Nation-building	Protestant America as Destiny		
Focus on Tradition	Maintain Traditional Faith -Immigrants	Maintain Traditional Faith -Immigrants	Maintain Traditional Faith -Immigrants -Withdrawal		
Focus on Engaging in Missions or Mission	Native American Missions	Foreign Missions	Expanded Foreign Missions		
Focus on Social Reform	"True" Christian Society	Social Reform -Morality -Slavery	Social Gospel -Urban Poverty -Temperance		
Focus on Justice and Liberation	Pursuing Freedom from Margins -Slavery	Pursuing Freedom from Margins -Slavery	Protest and Liberation -Jim Crow Blacks -Reservation Native Am.		
Focus on Revival and Renewal	Revival and Renewal -Great Awakening	Expanded Revival and Renewal -Second Great Awakening	Urban Evangelistic Revivals		
Unique Focus					

The prior missiology of Protestant nation-building had now evolved into what can be described as an *expanded missiology of a Protestant America destiny,* as the earlier Protestant empire evolved into a sense of national destiny for the United States within the larger global order. During this period, the United States was generally on the ascendancy regarding its influence in world affairs, largely because of its increased immigrant population, its rapidly expanding industrial sector—with the accompanying wealth— its substantial technological developments, and its growing national identity. But it was the Spanish-American War, in particular, that provided the occasion for the United States to take on the role of a world power by acquiring the territories of Cuba and the Philippines. This expanded role for the United States led it to join the European colonial powers in intervening around the globe in the midst of political crises. The ideology of the day viewed this as America's Manifest Destiny, and most church leaders readily supported this expansion of America's role in the world.

The pursuit of a *missiology of maintaining the traditional faith* increased in importance during this period, largely as a result of the significant numbers of newly arrived immigrants. Many came from Roman Catholic countries, and the Catholic Church continued to develop its practice of building an extensive system of institutions to serve them, enfold them, and keep them within the faith. Other immigrant groups pursuing this missiology (focusing on the traditional faith) included the diverse Lutheran ethnic groups, who settled in the expanding frontier. But this missiological approach was also used by those who were opposed to the Social Gospel, the theory of evolution, and the practice of using higher criticism to study and interpret the Bible. These groups often used the strategy of withdrawing from their parent body and forming another denomination.

The modernist/fundamentalist controversy deepened the divide between two highly contested worldviews, with the fundamentalists seeking to resist change and preserve tradition. Caught up in the divide was the foreign missions enterprise. Many of those who continued to champion foreign missions tended to side with the fundamentalist, or conservative, view, as illustrated by the formation of the Interdenominational Foreign Missions Association in 1917. The missiology of trying to maintain the traditional faith contributed greatly to the dichotomy developing between evangelism and social concerns at home and on the mission field.

The expanded political and economic role of the United States in the world created a kind of holding environment for the dramatic increase in foreign mission activity by mission societies and denominations in the last decades of the nineteenth century, during the height of the expansion of the colonial system. The student volunteer movement greatly stimulated interest in foreign missions. Thousands, including many single women, were sent out as missionaries by independent mission societies and denominational agencies to spread the gospel, a gospel that was, of course, largely clothed within the cultural forms and ethos of the West. This *missiology of expanded foreign missions* functioned well within a cultural understanding of Manifest Destiny and played a major role in strengthening American interests in the larger world. This was especially true of the mission field in China, which became a uniquely American field for mainline denominations; it also was true of Central and South America for the conservative denominations, especially the Pentecostals, who grew rapidly there after the turn of the century.

Various cultural strains from previous periods now evolved somewhat as they interacted with these demographic shifts. The earlier emphasis on social reform now evolved into a more comprehensive effort to transform society from the perspective of the Social Gospel, especially in light of the gains made through scientific discoveries and technological advancements. The earlier social imaginary of Yankeedom, with its focus on building a better society and pursuing human perfectibility, now seemed to be within the grasp of human effort. Many churches became deeply inspired by this vision and caught up in this effort. This led to the earlier missiology of social reform morphing into a *missiology of the Social Gospel*, in which significant energy was invested by churches to address social ills, especially poverty.[64] Society's challenges increasingly came to be seen as structural in nature and in need of systemic solutions beyond promoting individual morality. This view aligned theologically with the ideals expressed in the kingdom of God, which many felt was being realized in their day—a postmillennial understanding. Accompanying this broader focus on reforming society was the continued focus on Temperance as a signature issue of the Protestant churches. Their efforts eventually led to the enactment of Prohibition with the passage of the Eighteenth Amendment in 1920.

A missiology that was very much a part of this period involved the African American community, where the *missiology of protest and liberation* continued as an aspiration for most of the black population (increasingly, it also became the aspiration of the Native American peoples, who were restricted to living on reservations). The church gradually took on a more holistic role in shaping the lives of those living in black communities, especially in the growing segregated neighborhoods in Northern cities. It developed an understanding of the gospel that incorporated personal salvation with an engagement in social concerns and an involvement in political issues. This was a vibrant time for the development of a more publicly visible and culturally engaged black community, especially in the North, and the churches were deeply involved in these changes. The church on the reservations, for the most part, continued being complicit with the government in promoting reservation schools. But the Native American response to this work led increasingly to a renewal of native religion, as well as the commingling of native religion with Christianity.

There continued to be an emphasis during this time on revival and

---

64. Ronald C. White Jr. and C. Howard Hopkins, *The Social Gospel: Religion and Reform in Changing America* (Philadelphia: Temple University Press, 1976).

renewal, with previous patterns of conducting annual revivals continuing in the village churches that served small towns and rural areas, especially in the South. But this was complemented by the rise of evangelists working in the growing cities of the North, such as Dwight Moody and Billy Sunday, who helped pioneer a *missiology of urban evangelistic revival.* Their work gave birth to a whole set of practices that became associated with the work of evangelists: the preparatory choir; a message that focused on personal salvation and a changed life; and the call forward to the altar, with evangelists prepared to counsel those who responded. The growing Pentecostal movement, under the leadership of evangelists such as William Seymour and Aimee McPherson, also contributed greatly to this missiological strain during this period: a focus on rejecting the social norms of the day, such as segregation, and allowing women to speak and to lead.

Theological Education and Leadership Formation

Theological education and the formation of leaders continued to develop during this period within the framework of viewing missions as only one activity among many for the church or as something to be pursued by independent organizations. Missiology was still largely ancillary to the theological curriculum, a curriculum that was preoccupied with a significant shift in theological education, as higher criticism was gaining ground in the seminaries and divinity schools. This had an impact on the formation of church leaders: it shifted the focus to one of training them to be scholars as well as pastors.[65] This, in turn, had an impact on how they provided leadership for congregations to engage in pursuing various public missiologies. The shock wave set in motion by the incorporation of higher criticism into biblical study increasingly took hold, and it began to produce casualties by the late 1800s, when some seminary professorships began to be challenged and several professors were dismissed.[66]

This influence of higher criticism on seminary education, by the first decades of the twentieth century, contributed to the modernist/fundamentalist split and the formation of alternative schools with more conserva-

---

65. Leadership in most Protestant denominations and access to theological education during this period was limited to males.

66. Glenn T. Miller, *Piety and Profession: American Protestant Theological Education* (Grand Rapids: Eerdmans, 2007), 92–97, 104–8. Examples include Prof. Crawford Toy, of Southern Seminary in the late 1870s, and Prof. Charles Briggs, of Union Seminary, in 1893.

tive pastoral leadership.[67] A reaction to the Social Gospel and the rising influence of dispensational theology among many of the more conservative Christians also led to the founding of numerous Bible schools, many of which later developed their own seminaries or became seminaries themselves.[68] Some of the immigrant population who were settling into the central and upper Midwest states brought with them strong confessional identities. They soon established denominations and founded schools to reinforce their theological and confessional traditions. This followed the earlier nineteenth-century pattern of building confessionally oriented seminaries.[69]

There was also a significant expansion in the number and size of colleges and universities following the Civil War, and all the way into the first decades of the twentieth century. Led by the land-grant universities that resulted from the 1862 Morrill Act, other state colleges and universities were also founded.[70] These were complemented by an expansion of private colleges and universities, for example, Vanderbilt (1873), Johns Hopkins (1876), Clark (1889), Stanford (1891), and The University of Chicago (1892). Joining these were many previously established church colleges and universities that were becoming increasingly nonsectarian. With the huge increase in the number of schools, with their expanded enrollments, seminaries and schools of theology began to be pushed to the margins within the larger educational arena.

Organizational changes were also taking place within the system of seminaries and schools of theology. The rise of the corporate denomination influenced developments that led to the increased professionalization

---

67. This impacted especially the Northern Presbyterians, with the formation of the Orthodox Presbyterian Church, and the Northern Baptists, with the formation of the General Association of Regular Baptists.

68. Examples include now Biola University (1908) with Talbot School of Theology (1952) in southern California; now Columbia International University (1921) with CIU Seminary and School of Missions (1936); and Evangelical Theological College (1924), which became Dallas Theological Seminary (1936).

69. Examples of such denominations and their schools include: the German Lutherans who formed the Missouri Synod Lutheran Church in 1847, but who had already started Concordia Seminary in St. Louis in 1839; the Dutch Calvinists, who formed the Christian Reformed Church in 1857 and Calvin Theological Seminary in 1876; and the numerous Scandinavian Lutheran church bodies and seminaries formed across the upper Midwest in the late 1800s and early 1900s.

70. Robert J. Sternberg, *The Modern Land Grant University* (Lafayette, IN: Purdue University Press, 2014), 3–14.

of ministry and the emergence of what might be called the *churchly pastor*. New standards were being developed for what constituted *professional* ordained ministry, with educational requirements directly impacting both the number of persons seeking theological education and the educational process they encountered in doing so.[71]

The development of the research graduate school also influenced theological education, with seminaries patterning themselves after Johns Hopkins University (founded in 1876), where faculty members were expected to engage in generating original research.[72] Seminaries and schools of theology that adopted this approach by the latter part of the 1800s and into the early 1900s included: Harvard, Yale, Union (NY), Chicago, Drew, Perkins, Duke, Bright, Candler, Vanderbilt, and Iliff. This development fostered increased emphasis on specialized disciplines as well as the theological guilds. The theological curriculum increasingly came to reflect the values of research and scholarship as a driving force, competing with the earlier emphasis on confessional and doctrinal approaches for the formation of pastors.

Significant changes were taking place within the curriculum, as well as increased pressures to create standards and achieve some consolidation within the system of seminaries. An extensive survey of seminaries was sponsored by the Interchurch World Movement in 1920.[73] This study noted that the curriculum had shifted in most seminaries to include more social-science perspectives, and also to have a more direct engagement with the world, including increased field work requirements. One of the biggest challenges facing most seminaries, however, was the lack of any agreed-upon standards or criteria for what constituted professional theological education. There began to be a push for establishing such standards, which followed the pattern of other professional graduate schools at that time.[74]

---

71. Miller, *Piety and Profession*, 271. Also accompanying this organizational revolution in theological education was the rise of "a new type of president" as "the executive officer of the management of the business of the seminary." Academic deans would join this new organizational complexity by midcentury.

72. This approach was patterned after the University of Berlin (founded in the early 1800s), where faculty were expected to engage in generating original research.

73. Miller, *Piety and Profession*, 341. This survey was conducted by Robert Kelly and O. D. Foster.

74. Miller, *Piety and Profession*, 339. Another survey was published in 1934: Mark Arthur May, William Adams Brown, and Frank K. Shuttleworth, *The Education of American Ministers* (New York: Institute of Social and Religious Research, 1934). This led to the creation of the American Association of Theological Schools (AATS) in 1936, where standards for

Accompanying the lack of standards was the unwieldy character of a system of seminaries that had grown up piecemeal, and too many of the schools were simply underresourced.

Roman Catholic theological education during this period also underwent development along some of these same lines. Catholic seminaries had continued to expand in number during the 1800s, especially after the 1880s, with the increased immigration from southern European countries. There was a need to bring some standardization to their methodologies and curricula. This was accomplished at the Third Plenary Council of Baltimore in 1884, where the church developed a "thorough systematic structure and course of studies that lasted into the early 1960s."[75] One important development for Catholics that paralleled Protestant practice was the founding of the Catholic University of America in 1889, which helped promote graduate theological education. Other Catholic universities pursued this same pattern by the 1920s.[76]

Time of Transition

Several significant shifts were taking place in the early decades of the twentieth century that fundamentally changed the outlook of the church in America, and their fuller implications became clearer by the 1930s and early 1940s. World War I represented the beginning of the end for the system of colonialism: this system eventually was dismantled by midcentury and replaced by the formation of independent nation-states. This independence movement was accompanied by the resurgence of other religious faiths around the world, as well as the growth of indigenous churches in the Global South. These realities all occurred within the rise of an increased secularism in the West, which further eroded the confidence of the Western church in the aftermath of the war, especially in Europe—but also in the United States.

The momentum of the modern missions movement began to falter in the midst of these changes, which was typified by the experience of the

judging academic quality were adopted. The first list of accredited schools was published in 1938. This Association was incorporated in 1956, when it secured a full-time staff; today it is known as the Association of Theological Schools (ATS).

75. Patrick W. Carey and Earl C. Muller, SJ, *Theological Education in the Catholic Tradition: Contemporary Challenges* (New York: Crossroad, 1997), 1.

76. Carey and Muller, *Theological Education*, 29.

Student Volunteer Movement: it reached its peak in recruiting in 1921, but by the late 1930s it was struggling to continue to exist.[77] Representative of the debate generated about missions in the midst of this transition was the one taking place between W. E. Hocking and Hendrik Kraemer during the 1930s over the question of the continuity or discontinuity of Christianity with other faiths.[78]

Accompanying these significant shifts in the church were the hardships brought on by the economic depression of the 1930s. Church construction came to a screeching halt, and the halting of construction lasted until the end of World War II. The churches also lacked the resources to respond adequately to the overwhelming needs of society. The social programs of the New Deal filled this void and displaced much of the role of the church. The prestige of Protestant denominations started to decline as their role in shaping society began to diminish.

In many ways, World War II put addressing these shifts on hold for most churches, as they became caught up in supporting the war effort. Patriotism was reborn with a growing awareness of the necessity for the United States to accept an international role in world affairs.[79] By the end of the war, it was becoming increasingly clear that a bipolar world was emerging: the forces of democracy, led by the United States, were being challenged by the forces of communism, led by the Soviet Union. The dividing up of Germany into East and West Germany—indeed, the division of the city of Berlin into a bipolar entity—quickly came to symbolize the growing confrontation between these world powers.

All these shifts represented massive changes in the key narratives shaping the social imaginary in the United States, as well as significant challenges for the church in trying to relate the gospel through its public

77. Michael Parker, *The Kingdom of Character*.

78. W. E. Hocking, a professor at Harvard, provided leadership for the Laymen's Foreign Missionary Inquiry, which published its report in 1932 as *Re-thinking Missions: A Laymen's Inquiry after One Hundred Years* (New York: Harper and Brothers Publishers, 1932). This report advocated the position that it was time for Christianity to join hands with those of other faiths to work on confronting the greater problem of secularism rather than compete with it. It was Hendrik Kraemer who argued for discontinuity in 1938, in "The Christian Message in a Non-Christian World," written at the request of the International Missionary Council and presented at its Madras/Tambaram Conference that same year.

79. Unfortunately, this patriotism also manifested itself racially in the internment of approximately 120,000 people of Japanese ancestry following the attack on Pearl Harbor; they were relocated into camps across the western United States even though 62 percent of those internees were US citizens.

missiologies to these changing cultural realities. The key questions facing denominations and their congregations in the aftermath of the Great Depression and World War II were: (1) How do we best go about expanding our systems of congregations now that resources are becoming available? and (2) How is the gospel to be understood and lived with respect to a world about to decolonize, with the global influence of the United States rising within an emerging bipolar world?

CHAPTER 6

The Suburban Success, Mid-1940s to Mid-1970s

The Church in the Suburban Success Period

The church in the suburban success period is known primarily by the housing and construction boom that followed World War II, when an explosive growth of automobile suburbs emerged beyond the edges of the older city neighborhoods that were served by streetcars. At least six other significant changes took place (which we will explore in this chapter), and all of these changes greatly contributed to reshaping the public missiologies in which the church engaged.

First, we need to note the suburban growth and its impact on the church in a bit more detail. The Depression and World War II had delayed almost all church building for over fifteen years. But now a surging postwar economy, the mass-produced automobile, the development of large acreage plats where mass-produced housing could be built, and thousands of returning GIs marrying and beginning to raise a growing "baby-boom" population helped account for the rapid growth of a new kind of housing development—the automobile suburb. Church denominations were quick to respond to this new opportunity: they started up thousands of new congregations in these communities, which were quickly filled by young families who were moving out of the older cities and those who were relocating to these new suburbs from rural areas.

Second, during this period the church experienced a major move toward ecumenism that promoted church unity and cooperation. Several major church organizations were formed to give expression to this development. The World Council of Churches (WCC) was organized in 1948, building on the Faith and Order and the Life and Work movements of earlier decades. The older Federal Council of Churches in the United States joined the WCC and soon evolved into the National Council of Churches (NCC) in 1950, with thirty-eight member church bodies.

Third, the evangelical churches, in an effort to move beyond the old modernist/fundamentalist split, also engaged in the growing cooperation among church denominations and formed the National Association of Evangelicals (NEA) in 1942. This reflected a renewed evangelical faith that had begun to grow by midcentury, and this growth included the founding of a number of new seminaries. The member denominations of the NEA soon began to coordinate their missions efforts with the formation of the Evangelical Foreign Missions Association (EFMA) in 1945, which would soon begin, in turn, to coordinate missions efforts with the Interdenominational Foreign Missions Association (IFMA), formed in 1917 by faith missions organizations and fundamentalist denominations.

Fourth, the foreign missions enterprise of the church denominations experienced a major transition as it was redefined in the wake of the dismantling of the colonial systems throughout the world. Newly organized independent countries also formed organized national churches. This greatly impacted the church in the United States: much mission work shifted to serving the national churches; missiology was dropped from the curriculum of many mainline seminaries; evangelicals increasingly picked up the foreign missions banner; and a major debate took place within missiology as to what constituted a theology of mission.

Fifth, after World War II there was a second Great Migration of African Americans out of the South and into the Northern cities. During this period the African American churches made major advances in the centuries-long struggle by blacks to achieve justice and equal standing under the law. These churches were at the center of the nonviolent civil rights movement, led especially by Martin Luther King Jr., who blended biblical themes with constitutional rights. This resulted in the passage of major legislation guaranteeing voting rights and open housing.

Sixth, the Roman Catholic Church experienced massive change during this period as a result of the efforts of Vatican II to bring the church into the modern age. These changes included such innovations as allowing liturgy in the vernacular, encouraging the laity to read the Bible, and the church itself opening up to the larger world and beginning to work more directly with Protestants. The Catholic Church also began to participate actively in the larger ecumenical movement.

Seventh, a significant disruption took place within society that had an impact on the church at all levels, with massive changes working their way through the social and political order. This resulted in movements of protest and conflict, as well as calls for renewal, including: the civil-rights movement; the counterculture of the baby boomers; the Vietnam War and the antiwar movement; the sexual revolution and feminism; the urban riots; the political assassinations of King and John and Bobby Kennedy; and the green movement. In the midst of these challenges, voices calling for the church to change and engage in renewal became more frequent.

Key Themes, Events, and Population Shifts

New Realities and New National Narratives Following World War II

World War II ended with the Allies defeating Germany and Italy in Europe in the spring of 1945, and then Japan in Asia in August of that year. However, even before the war ended, a new bipolar political world was already beginning to form around the two emergent superpowers, the United States and the Union of Soviet Socialist Republics (USSR). What became known as the Cold War quickly settled into place with the political division of Europe into spheres of East and West; a peacetime standoff was soon playing itself out around the world as a contest between democracy and communism.[1] There was a resurgence in patriotism supporting democratic ideals that most of the churches readily supported.

The end of World War II saw the total unraveling, over the next two decades, of the colonial empires built up by European nations over the previous several hundred years. A new word entered the public vocabulary—"postcolonial." Scores of new nations came into existence as these former colonies became independent nations. The United Nations, which was formed in 1945 by fifty-one nations, soon added scores of other nations to its membership, and most of these were located in the Global South. The World Council of Churches (1948) was a development in the churches that was parallel to the organization of the United Nations.

The leadership for both movements initially came largely from Western nations, but this gradually shifted to include leaders from the Global South during the following decades. The formation of both organizations

---

1. John Lewis Gaddis, *The Cold War: A New History* (New York: Penguin, 2006).

had huge implications for foreign missions. Churches in the newly formed nations quickly organized their own national churches as well as independent church bodies. This raised two questions: How were these former mission churches, now independent, going to interrelate with the Western mission structures? What would be the actual role of these mission societies and denominational agencies going forward?

An ever-escalating contest ensued between the United States and the USSR in the years following the end of World War II, as these two superpowers competed for military superiority, as well as their political and economic influence on smaller nations around the globe. Armed conflict between competing forces backed by the United States and the USSR, along with its new ally China in 1949, became the pattern. The Korean War (1950–1953) was the first example of this; the pattern spread to other former colonies that were seeking their independence throughout southeast Asia and also Africa.[2] The United States became involved in Vietnam by the 1960s, a war that initially received support from most churches for pursuing a limited military intervention to defend democracy. However, that quickly changed for a growing number of churches as US military involvement escalated.

The Western nations solidified their economic influence in the world through the Bretton Woods Agreement, hammered out by representatives of forty-four allied nations in 1944.[3] This agreement stabilized the postwar economy by tying the monetary exchange rate to the US dollar. All too soon, many of the new nations became debtors to these new institutions, especially with respect to what became known as the "decade of development," which was the policy pursued by the United Nations in the 1960s.[4] This influence by the United States was accompanied in the world through its effort to try to control the number of nations that were able to develop a nuclear capacity.

2. The French tried to hold on to their former colony of Vietnam in the 1950s, but withdrew in 1954. By the 1960s, a divided Vietnam became a war zone where the United States took a major stand in an effort to defeat the forces of communism.

3. The exchange rate for the dollar was backed by the price of gold, set at $35 an ounce, which gave the United States disproportionate economic power in controlling the world economy via the newly formed institutions of the World Bank, the International Monetary Fund (IMF), and the International Bank for Reconstruction and Development (IBRD).

4. Shahid Yusuf, *Development Economics through the Decades: A Critical Look at Thirty Years of the World Development Report* (District of Columbia: World Bank Publications, 2008).

In the United States an emphasis on democracy, the American way of life, and God's providential blessing coalesced to become a new narrative in the 1950s and 1960s that became known as "civil religion."[5] This was a quasi-religious faith that incorporated the legacy of the Judeo-Christian faith with key sacred symbols of the national story. Representative of this emphasis was the inclusion in 1954 of the words "under God" in the US pledge of allegiance. The pledge became both a patriotic oath and a public prayer as it epitomized the ethos of civil religion. This effort was led by the Roman Catholic fraternal organization Knights of Columbus.[6]

All of this was reinforced in the 1950s by an expanding economy, increased prosperity, a growing middle class, the expansion of access to higher education, and an expectation of upward mobility for succeeding generations. Feeding much of this shift was the birth of what became known as the baby-boom generation, those born between 1946 and 1964. The development of what increasingly became the expectation and realization of the "American Dream" was well under way. It was a dream that had roots back in the 1920s, but after World War II came to be largely limited to the white population.[7]

Population Shifts

The population of the United States, which stood at over 131 million in 1940, increased to over 203 million by 1970. This remarkable growth came largely as a result of higher than normal birthrates during much of this time.[8] Furthermore, that growth in the US population was complemented by renewed immigration after the passage of the Hart-Cellar Act in 1965, which abol-

5. Robert N. Bellah, *The Broken Covenant: American Civil Religion in a Time of Trial* (New York: Seabury Press, 1975).

6. See Richard J. Ellis, *To the Flag: The Unlikely History of the Pledge of Allegiance* (Lawrence: University Press of Kansas, 2005), 129–39. This broader conception of an American religious faith was articulated regularly by then President Eisenhower, who often spoke about God and country, and who also convened an annual prayer breakfast in seeking to address what he considered a decline in American religious values.

7. James Truslow Adams, *The Epic of America* (1931; New York: Simon Publications, 2001).

8. Birthrates in 1955, at the height of the baby boom, stood at 25 live births for every 1,000 persons in the population; by 1985 that number had declined to 18 live births for every 1,000 persons. See Robert Wuthnow, *The Restructuring of American Religion* (Princeton: Princeton University Press, 1988), 14–34.

ished the old national-origins quotas from the Immigration Act of 1924 and opened immigration to countries outside western and central Europe. And though it set limits on first-time immigrants from other countries, it set no limit on what was known as "family reunification."[9]

This act greatly increased the immigration of people of color into the United States. By 1970, there were over nine million individuals of Hispanic origin in the population and over one and half million persons from Pacific Rim countries. These growing communities of color joined an African American population that had doubled between 1930 and 1970 to over twenty-two million, along with a Native American population now comprised of 792,000 in 1970, up from 334,000 in 1940. The United States was increasingly being forced to acknowledge more publicly its multiracial citizenry and its multicultural character.

White Population Growth

Further changes in farm technology continued the century-long erosion of the viability of the family farm; many people who were displaced from farms migrated to the urban areas. The rural percentage of the population declined from over 43 percent in 1940 to about 25 percent in 1970. There was also significant migration from east to west. This had begun during World War II, when new military bases were formed up and down the West Coast, and the necessary industries were put into place to support them. Many of these migrants came from the Midwest: as they were displaced from farming, they sought new economic opportunities as well as a more moderate climate.[10] They brought their Midwestern faith practices with them: many congregations re-created their ethno-religious culture and became locked within it—living as islands of Midwestern culture up and down the West Coast.

But it was particularly in the cities that a profound transformation was taking place in urban life. This was the rise of what became known as the "family suburb," a planned community of similarly styled houses that were mass-produced and affordably priced. This approach was pioneered

9. David A. Gerber, *American Immigration: A Very Short Introduction* (New York: Oxford University Press, 2011).

10. Gerald A. Nash, *The American West Transformed* (Bloomington: Indiana University Press, 1985).

in the construction of Levittown on Long Island, NewYork, between 1947 and 1951 by Levitt and Sons.[11] The growth of suburbs was initially a white phenomenon that was fed substantially by returning GIs and their families. African Americans were systematically excluded from most suburban neighborhoods and the government benefits that gave rise to them. Contributing to this growth was an expanding white middle class that benefited from: increasing levels of education; the mass-produced automobile; three-dollar-a-barrel oil being imported from the Middle East; a newly expanding interstate highway system; and the creation of the FHA and VA thirty-year fixed-rate mortgages. The suburbs became the new location of choice for white migrants from both the central cities and the rural areas.[12]

The religious landscape had been changing over the previous decades. This included a shift from the United States as a primarily Protestant Christian domain to becoming a more diverse society representing a Judeo-Christian heritage that included Catholics and Jews along with Protestants. In 1955, Will Herberg captured this shift decisively in his book entitled *Protestant, Catholic, Jew*, finally naming what had become an increasing reality since the early decades of the twentieth century.[13] The election of John Kennedy as president in 1960 marked a real turning point for bringing Catholics into mainstream American life. This was further broadened and deepened ecumenically as a result of the changes in the church introduced by Vatican II.

All of the religious communities benefited significantly from the high birthrates that were occurring between the mid-1940s and the mid-1960s. But while the mainline Protestant denominations began to peak in numbers by the mid-1960s, due to the slowing down of their birthrates, the Roman Catholic Church continued to grow. This was largely because of the increased immigration of Hispanics into the United States following the changed immigration laws. The Catholic Church reached its peak—in terms of its proportional representation in the overall population—in the early 1970s at about 25 percent of the US population, and has basically re-

11. Barbara M. Kelly, *Expanding the American Dream: Building and Rebuilding Levittown* (New York: State University of New York Press, 1993).

12. David Halberstam, *The Fifties* (New York: Villard Books, 1993), 131–43. Halberstam captures the dynamics of this new suburban growth well as he discusses the beginning of mass-produced suburban housing that was developed at Levittown, NY.

13. Will Herberg, *Protestant, Catholic, Jew: An Essay in American Religious Sociology* (New York: Doubleday, 1955).

mained at that level since that time.[14] The Jewish population showed modest gains, increasing from about 4.75 million in 1940 to 5.5 million in 1970.[15]

There was a tremendous expansion in the postwar economy that fed a corresponding expansion of the middle class. This generation experienced greater opportunities in education: a college education was increasingly within reach—indeed becoming the norm—largely as a result of the GI Bill, which made college affordable to the returning veterans.[16] The children of the baby boom began to enter college in the early 1960s, which resulted in more than a doubling of college and university enrollment during that decade—an increase from 3.6 million in 1960 to 8.6 million in 1970.[17] Many of the white youth who were part of the baby-boom generation were experiencing a different lifestyle from that of their predecessors, one of affluence and a level of upward mobility as they were raised in a new kind of housing community.

Mainline suburban churches grew substantially during the postwar period, largely as a result of the large numbers of children being raised in the suburbs. But this growth was also the result of people relocating there from city neighborhoods and rural areas. As of 1945, three-quarters of all Protestant congregations were still located in rural areas, but with the population migrating out in the decades after the war, many of these congregations were simply not viable as the rural population declined.[18] Thousands of the older village congregations in the rural areas had to close during this period.

The starting of new churches was substantial: for example, the Congregational Church started up 400 new congregations, mostly suburban, between 1945 and 1948.[19] The Southern Baptist Convention paralleled this expansion by founding 500 new congregations between 1946 and 1949—at

14. http://www.reuters.com/article/idUSN0945928720080410 (accessed June 21, 2016).

15. http://www.jewishvirtuallibrary.org/jsource/US-Israel/usjewpop1.html (accessed June 21, 2016).

16. The race to space, which the USSR won in 1957 with its successful launch of Sputnik, also spurred the United States to support higher education more aggressively. President Kennedy's pledge in 1961 to land a man on the moon and return him safely to earth by the end of the decade helped lead to the passage of the 1965 Higher Education Act under President Johnson, which for the first time provided federal funding for student aid. See United States Office of Education, *The Higher Education Act of 1965*, vol. 1: *Some Questions and Answers* (The University of California Libraries, 2012).

17. Robert Wuthnow, *Restructuring of American Religion* (Princeton: Princeton University Press, 1988), 155.

18. Wuthnow, *Restructuring of American Religion*, 27–28.

19. Wuthnow, *Restructuring of American Religion*, 27.

a cost of $95 million.[20] The national denominational church bodies rapidly expanded their staff and programming to meet this challenge, and the full flowering of the corporate denomination began to be realized.

All this growth and expansion contributed to a culture of rising expectations, both for the new baby-boom generation that was coming of age and for the black population, which had not previously had full access to the economic and political life of the United States. The civil rights movement became the arena for addressing the rising expectations of the black population, which we will discuss below. What became known as the "counterculture" became the equivalent arena for addressing the rising expectations of the youth movement. This counterculture had gradually progressed from the beatniks of the late 1950s to the hippies of the mid- to late 1960s and the yippies of the late 1960s and early 1970s.[21] Their mantra of the day became "Never trust anyone over thirty," and they were successful in creating their own youth culture.[22]

This counterculture became deeply intertwined with the Vietnam War and antiwar protests by the mid-1960s, which heightened its anti-institutional stance. Christianity became intertwined in it with the emergence of the Jesus Movement in the late 1960s. This movement built on the decade-old charismatic movement, which had swept across most denominations.[23] All of this mixed together to help generate a whole series of new movements seeking change, for example, feminism and equal rights for women, along with ecological concerns and the first Earth Day in 1970.

Some proposed at the time that we were seeing what was called "the greening of America" and the rise of a "consciousness three" that would take us beyond the old politics of democratic competition and create a

20. Wuthnow, *Restructuring of American Religion*, 36.

21. The yippies became the colloquial name for the movement started by the Youth International Party. It was an offshoot of the free speech movement and became a more radical version of the counterculture that sought revolutionary change.

22. This phrase is attributed to Jack Weinberg who coined it during the Free Speech Movement at the University of California, Berkeley, in October 1964. This generation came of age listening to the music of Elvis Presley in the 1950s and the Beatles in the 1960s and turned to hard rock by the 1970s. They also created their own clothing style (e.g., tie-dyed t-shirts and bell-bottom jeans), gave birth to their own language (e.g., "bummer," "cool," "be real," "drop out," etc.), practiced an anti-institutional stance, and challenged the sexual mores of their day as the birth control pill became available.

23. Richard A. Bustraan, *The Jesus People Movement: A Story of Spiritual Revolution among the Hippies* (Eugene, OR: Pickwick Publications, 2014).

more egalitarian society.[24] But the reality experienced by many was one of conflict that was evident in the antiwar protests, the urban riots in black communities in the mid-1960s, the assassinations of Martin Luther King Jr. and Robert Kennedy in 1968, the radical-militant politics of the early-to-mid-1970s, and the killings of students on the university campuses of Kent State and Jackson State. In the midst of this substantial cultural upheaval, the church also became increasingly fractured and divided.

Mainline Protestant denominations increasingly became a house divided, in which many of the more conservative and evangelical churches began to pick up disenchanted members of mainline churches who were exiting, a trend that would continue into the decades that followed.[25] In the midst of this, there was a resurgence of evangelical churches, a movement that began to come of age after World War II. The city crusades conducted by Billy Graham across the country were a major contributor to this resurgence, as well as the new Christian organizations and schools that were formed to help build and guide it.[26]

Complicating the problem for mainline churches was that they had peaked in membership growth nationally in the mid-1960s. This can be attributed largely to the fact that the baby-boom generation had left the church in the 1960s and '70s in greater numbers than young adults had in any previous generation—and had returned in fewer numbers over the next several decades.[27] The calls for renewal became more frequent. In response, what became known as a "church renewal movement" emerged in the 1960s and 1970s. It included various dimensions, including the beginning of the lay renewal movement and a focus on worship renewal.[28] The intention of

24. Charles A. Reich, *The Greening of America* (New York: Bantam, 1971).

25. The issues that created divisions in the church were multiple: the civil rights movement, women in office, the authority of Scripture, the ecumenical movement, support for and opposition to the war, the charismatic movement, the support of radical movements by the national church, and so on.

26. The first major crusade conducted by Billy Graham took place in Los Angeles in 1949, and it served to launch his career as an evangelist. Organizations that were formed include the National Association of Evangelicals (1942) and the Evangelical Foreign Missions Association (1945), and the new schools included Fuller Theological Seminary, Conservative Baptist Theological Seminary, and Biblical Seminary.

27. Dean R. Hoge, Benton Johnson, and Donald A. Luidens, *Vanishing Boundaries: The Religion of Mainline Protestant Baby Boomers* (Louisville: Westminster John Knox, 1994).

28. Early contributors to the lay renewal movement were Keith Miller and Bruce Larson, who emphasized developing right relationships as the key ingredient. Another contributor was the work of Laity Lodge, which started in 1961 in the hill country of Texas. The

all these initiatives was to make the church more relevant to a new generation in the midst of a changing culture. It is worth noting the emergence of the small-group movement, which also took place during this period as part of the renewal emphasis.[29]

African American Population

Those who had been part of the earlier Great Migration at the beginning of the twentieth century were now joined in a second phase of this migration out of the South to the North in the post–World War II years. Conditions for many of these migrants, however, did not improve all that much; they ended up having to locate within the restricted housing areas of the Northern cities. But some progress had been made with regard to race relations following the war years, when President Harry Truman in 1948 signed an executive order requiring equality of treatment and opportunity for all persons in the military.

But the landmark case that helped launch the civil rights movement was *Brown v. The Board of Education of Topeka, Kansas* in 1954.[30] The civil rights movement gained momentum in 1956, when Rosa Parks refused to move to the back of a city bus in Montgomery, Alabama, and the boycott that ensued brought Martin Luther King Jr. to prominence. His focus was on setting in motion a movement that was nonviolent, though the participants were regularly treated with great violence. Sit-ins, marches, protests, and voter registration drives became the strategies for change. The black churches across the country were at the center of this movement, and they were joined by numerous white church leaders, which often created controversies within their church bodies.

The police overreaction in violently stopping the Selma march by

---

worship renewal of the 1950s and 1960s was heavily influenced by the charismatic movement and the music associated with it.

29. Robert Coleman was the author of the often reprinted and widely read book *The Master Plan of Evangelism* (Westwood, NJ: Fleming H. Revell Company, 1964). The renewal movement leadership included: Sam Shoemaker (founder of Faith at Work), Elton Trueblood (founder of Yokefellows), and John Crosby and Elizabeth O'Connor (Church of the Savior in Washington, DC).

30. In that case, the Warren Supreme Court unanimously approved a decision that separate educational facilities were inherently unequal, thus overturning the Supreme Court's *Plessy v. Ferguson* decision of 1896.

blacks to Montgomery in 1965 finally forced Congress to act and pass the landmark legislation of the Voting Rights Act of 1965. Later, King's opposition to the war in Vietnam placed him at odds with President Johnson. The civil rights coalition was by this time beginning to fracture, especially with the emergence of the black power movement and the redirection of its focus to economic and political issues. The race riots in the mid-1960s in various cities across the country sought to redress the problem of redlining and restricted housing regulations. The Fair Housing Act, finally passed in 1968, had profound implications—as well as some unintended consequences— for demographic patterns within many cities.[31] Within a few years, there was the beginning of massive population shifts in neighborhoods, as blacks moved out of their restricted housing spaces into formerly white urban neighborhoods, which typically hastened white relocation to the suburbs. Along with this, hundreds of white city-neighborhood church buildings across the country were sold to black congregations.

Native American Population

World War II marked a significant change for Native Americans in the United States. Over 44,000 of them served in the military; this was the first time that large numbers of Indians had left the reservations to mix with whites in the general population, and it led to profound changes in Native American culture. The US Indian Commissioner in 1945 said, "The war caused the greatest disruption of Native life since the beginning of the reservation era."[32] Besides entering into military service, many Indians left the reservations for urban areas to take well-paying jobs that were available due to wartime conditions, especially on the West Coast, with its massive defense industry buildup. The beginning of migration from the reservations to the urban areas was now under way for Native Americans, a pattern that would continue to the present day.

The activism of the civil rights movement within the United States, as well as the numerous movements of the 1960s, also spilled over into Native American life. There were increased calls for the adjudication of previous

31. United States Congress House of Representatives, *Protesting the American Dream (Part I): A Look at the Fair Housing Act* (District of Columbia: BiblioGov, 2010).

32. Alison R. Bernstein, *American Indians and World War II: Toward a New Era in Indian Affairs* (Norman: University of Oklahoma Press, 1999), 131.

injustices associated with the historical treaties imposed by the federal government. By the late 1960s, Native Americans had achieved several strategic takeovers of properties.[33] That led to a reorganization of the movement in 1972: a coalition of eight indigenous organizations formed the American Indian Movement (AIM) concerning what they called the "Trail of Broken Treaties."[34]

This activism also had an impact on the work on the reservations by church missions and the sponsorship of local churches by white denominations. Native leaders increased their calls for white denominations to turn over leadership roles to Native people and to change restrictive policies. In addition, white churches and mission organizations were asked to begin to account for their earlier complicity in how federal government policies were carried out. A renewed emphasis by American Indians on returning to Native spirituality and practices forced churches to rethink and retheologize their approach to working in partnership with Native American churches.

Hispanic Population

According to the US census, the white percentage of the total population had exceeded 80 percent for most of the nation's history, reaching a high of 89.9 percent in the 1930s and 1940s; as of 1960, it still stood at 86.6 percent. The vast majority of the remaining people of color were African Americans. But the change that came with the passage of the Hart-Cellar Act in 1965 began to change the proportion of the population that was Hispanic. A guest-worker program, the Bracero Program, had been established in 1942 to help out the agriculture sector of the US economy by providing an ad-

33. This included the takeover events of Alcatraz Island in 1969, an abandoned naval air station near Minneapolis in 1970, and a dam in Wisconsin the same year that had flooded reservation land. See Lara Waterman Wittstock and Elaine J. Salinas, "A Brief History of the American Indian Movement," http://www.aimovement.org/ggc/history.html (accessed June 24, 2016).

34. Roxanne Dunbar-Ortiz, *An Indigenous Peoples' History of the United States* (Boston: Beacon, 2014), 185. AIM developed a "20-Point Position Paper that focused on the federal government's responsibility to implement Indigenous treaties and sovereignty." But its activism came to a head in the seventy-one-day occupation of the Wounded Knee site in South Dakota in 1973, when it forcefully engaged in battle with US armed forces. It was an event that marked the movement's identity over the next several decades.

equate number of laborers.[35] The Hispanic community doubled between 1960 and 1980, expanding from a small, regionally concentrated population of fewer than 6 million in 1960 (just 3.24 percent of the US population at that time), to more than 14.6 million in 1980 (representing 6.4 percent of the population).

Part of this growth resulted from Hispanics entering the United States at that time from several other countries. Puerto Ricans had migrated to the continental United States as citizens since 1922, when the Supreme Court had granted them full citizenship. This migration settled primarily along the East Coast, especially in New York. The Cuban crisis of the early 1960s also led to an influx of more Hispanics, in this case Cuban immigrants who were given access to US citizenship and who settled primarily in south Florida. The vast majority of these immigrants from Mexico and Cuba, as well as the migrants from Puerto Rico, were Catholic, and the Roman Catholic Church readily took steps to serve the needs of its Hispanic people. This influx of new Catholic members took place at the same time that birthrates in the United States in general began to decline, thus making it possible for the Catholic Church to hold its own. But Protestant churches, especially Pentecostals and other evangelical groups, also began to engage in mission work in these newly settled communities.

Asian Population

Immigration from Asian countries had been significantly curtailed in the late 1800s to early 1900s, and then was completely excluded with the passage of the Immigration Act of 1924. It was not until forty-one years later that the Hart-Cellar Act opened the doors somewhat to immigration from Asia. This small stream of immigrants increased during the Vietnam War, when the United States took increased numbers of Vietnamese, as well as people—such as the Hmong in Laos—who supported US policies in Southeast Asia. The family reunification provision in the legislation soon expanded the number of people entering the United States as legal immigrants. Many

---

35. National Park Service, US Department of the Interior, "American Latino Theme Study," https://www.nps.gov/heritageinitiatives/latino/latinothemestudy/immigration.htm (accessed June 24, 2016). About 70,000 farm laborers from Mexico were involved during the war, but after the war it gradually expanded so that by the 1960s it involved more than 400,000 immigrants. This program helped pave the way for many Mexican citizens to immigrate legally to the United States.

white churches sponsored such families during this period; few of those immigrants, however, ended up joining these churches.

System of Congregations

As we have discussed above, there were numerous factors that explain the rapid growth of the suburbs in urban America after World War II. But two of the most important were the push-and-pull factors of central cities and the rural areas. The expansion of cities had been placed on hold during the Great Depression, due to the collapsed economy, which continued through the war because construction materials were unavailable. This resulted in a buildup of population density for over fifteen years in the city neighborhoods. This constituted a pull factor for the growth of suburbs, as young families, especially, left the crowded space of city-neighborhood life and relocated to the spacious suburbs. The rural areas represented a push factor as the size of farms grew, crowding out small family farms, and a generation of young adults were also displaced that way, mostly to the suburbs. By the 1950s, the patterns were clearly evident: both city-neighborhood churches and rural churches were in decline, which is a crisis that continues to the present time.

The churchly denominations that took shape during the first decades of the twentieth century, having been thwarted by the Depression and World War II, were poised for expansion following the war. They were especially well positioned to take advantage of the expanding economy and the rapidly growing suburbanization of the cities, and they began doing so already by late 1945, which led to a remarkable increase in congregations and represented the fourth major expansion of the system in the United States. The phenomenal success following World War II of the *family-suburban congregation* as a new type of congregation led to this expansion and is now a matter of record.[36] Continued high levels of denominational loyalty during this period allowed for the rapid growth of suburban congregations by almost all denominations; in 1955 only one person in twenty-five would leave his or her faith tradition as an adult.[37]

---

36. Halberstam, *The Fifties*, 131–43.

37. A Gallup poll in 1955 found that only 1 in 25 persons switched from their childhood faith as an adult, whereas by 1985, 1 in 3 persons were found to have switched, as reported by Wuthnow, *The Restructuring of American Religion*, 88.

The profound success of the family-suburban congregation between 1945 and 1975 took the logic of the denominational church—with its organizational self-understanding around a purposive intent—to a new level. The logic of the city-neighborhood congregation had been a mixture of intergenerational relationships deeply integrated socially and economically within cohesive neighborhoods. In the suburban congregation, relationships became largely functional amid high rates of mobility. Membership in community was cultivated in suburban congregations through shared participation in denominationally sponsored programs, which were administered under a committee structure, organized around ministry functions, and managed by a professional minister.[38] The organizational, programmatic development of the congregation within corporate denominationalism was now in full bloom.

Development of the Denominational, Organizational Church

Numerous changes were taking place in denominational church life in the United States in the years following World War II. The ecumenical movement made significant organizational achievements and became what Finke and Stark call the "Mainline Cartel."[39] This was the heyday of church life for mainline denominations, with their large-scale organizational changes leading to the expansion of national offices. The Inter-Church Center was built in New York City in the late 1950s to house the national offices of member denominations, and nonmember denominations also expanded their national offices or built new ones. Vatican II led to the establishment of ecumenical ties between the Roman Catholic Church and the mainline Protestant churches. All of this took place as denominations experienced continued membership growth into the 1960s. But by the mid-1960s, mainline churches had peaked in membership numbers, largely due to the decline of the baby boom and the growing obsolescence of the geographic-neighborhood church that was becoming evident.

38. Gibson Winter, *The Suburban Captivity of the Churches: An Analysis of Protestant Responsibility in the Expanding Metropolis* (New York: Macmillan, 1962), 96–101.

39. Finke and Stark, *The Churching of America, 1776–2005: Winners and Losers in Our Religious Economy* (New Brunswick, NJ: Rutgers University Press, 2005), 216–18. This included the creation of the World Council of Churches (WCC) in 1948, followed by the creation in the United States of the National Council of Churches (NCC) in 1950, whose predecessor was the Federal Council of Churches.

But a resurgence in the growth of the evangelical movement now occurred. Some of it was stimulated by their suspicions surrounding the formation of the WCC and NCC, which evangelicals viewed as having inadequate theological foundations for supporting a robust Christian faith. Some of it was stimulated by evangelicals picking up the slack as mainline Protestants began to withdraw from engaging in foreign missions in the postcolonial environment. Another aspect of this shift was a new generation of leaders who were making a fresh intellectual defense of the faith as they shook off the aftermath of what had been a fundamentalism symbolized by the Scopes Trial, in which the earlier fundamentalists won the battle but lost the war.

This period saw the emergence of an evolved denominational type for both mainline and evangelical churches—beyond the earlier churchly denomination to what became known as the fully developed *corporate denomination*.[40] Its development paralleled the growth of a corporate culture that was taking place throughout the broader society. The structure of the business community changed significantly in the 1940s into the 1950s, as numerous local and regional businesses were reorganized or merged into national entities. By the 1960s, many of these companies had extended their reach—as multinational corporations—to international markets.[41]

In the midst of these developments, denominations increasingly became complex organizational systems with multiple boards and agencies—at both the national and regional levels. The system of organizing and managing ministry around various functions became the norm and was overseen by managerial command and control structures at all levels—local, regional, and national. The national church had the lead in developing program initiatives and providing resources because loyalty to the system continued to be strong throughout most denominations. Members of congregations willingly offered their financial resources so that the larger church body could wage the campaign for church expansion on their behalf.

The dramatic success of the fully developed corporate denomination, however, began to change in the mid- to late 1960s and early 1970s, as a cultural upheaval shook the institutions of American society to their

---

40. Russell E. Richey, "Denominations and Denominationalism: An American Morphology," in *Reimagining Denominationalism: Interpretive Essays,* ed. Robert Bruce Mullin and Russell E. Richey (New York: Oxford University Press, 1994).

41. Business life, as well as church life, was becoming increasingly corporate and bureaucratic, perhaps best symbolized in the book by William H. Whyte Jr., *The Organization Man* (New York: Simon and Schuster, 1956).

very core.[42] This was accompanied by a significant decline in birthrates, which contributed to most mainline denominations' peaking in membership growth during the mid-1960s—after more than 150 years of sustained increases. In reality, they had peaked decades earlier in proportional representation within the total population. In addition, the social fragmentation brought on by the countercultural upheaval entered the internal life of the churches, with dividing lines between groups of constituents within denominations becoming pronounced.[43]

Developments Regarding the Discipline of Missiology

The discipline of missiology underwent significant changes during this period, with regard to both the theory and practice of mission, as well as the theology used to justify the church's participation in it. These changes were taking place as the colonial systems that had served as a holding environment for the modern missions movement were fully dismantled between the end of World War II and the end of the 1960s. It was a twenty-five-year period that experienced a change from Western colonial rule over 95 percent of people outside of the West to the complete dismantling of that system.[44] This incredible shift in the political and economic ordering of the nations also introduced tremendous changes into the mission enterprise—both in their complex organizational structures and operations on foreign mission fields and in the teaching of missiology in Western seminaries and related training institutions.

With regard to the teaching of missiology, R. Pierce Beaver led the way in 1950 in America for the formation of the Association of Professors of Mission (APM) to help address these changes. This effort built on an earlier association that had been developed on the Eastern Seaboard among persons teaching missiology at key theological seminaries. Beaver intended

---

42. Kenneth Leech, *Youthquake: The Growth of a Counter-Culture through Two Decades* (Totowa, NJ: Littlefield, Adams, 1977).

43. Dean R. Hoge, *Division in the Protestant House: The Basic Reasons behind Intra-Church Conflicts* (Philadelphia: Westminster, 1976).

44. Ralph D. Winter, *The Twenty-Five Unbelievable Years, 1945-1969* (Pasadena: William Carey Library, 1970). The process began with the independence of India in 1947, picked up pace with China's independence under the People's Republic of China in 1949, and continued apace into the early 1960s, when African countries and other Asian countries also became independent in the final wave of the dismantling.

the APM to serve not as an expression of the old missionary triumphalism but as an attempt to build a lifeboat for floundering brothers and sisters.

This new association faced challenges that were indicative of the problems that the discipline of missiology was also encountering in the academy by midcentury. There was clearly a need to reconceive the discipline—that is, beyond preparing individuals to participate in foreign missions. Less evident, but more substantial, there was a need to develop a more substantive theological foundation for the discipline. Significant changes taking place during this phase in the development of the discipline of missiology include the following:

- *Association of Professors of Mission (APM).* The formation of a professional society in the United States in 1950 by professors of mission in the midst of the eclipse of a missiology of foreign missions.
- *Willingen 1952.* It was at this International Mission Council (IMC) conference that a proposal for a Trinitarian basis for mission was made, which later came to be identified as the *missio Dei* (the "mission of God").
- *The IMC becomes CWME in WCC.* The merger of the former IMC into the World Council of Churches (WCC), and becoming the Commission on World Mission and Evangelism (CWME) in 1961, which led many Western evangelicals to become further disaffected with that movement, even as majority-world evangelical ecumenicals began to participate.
- *Ending Mission Programs.* Many former mainline and flagship seminaries ended their mission programs during the late 1960s and early 1970s, or changed their former chairs of missiology to interreligious studies or ecumenism (note, e.g., the termination of the missiology programs at Hartford, Union, and Yale, and the changing of the program at Princeton to ecumenism).
- *American Society of Missiology.* The ASM was formed in 1973 and was made up of missiologists from Roman Catholic, evangelical, and ecumenical streams, whose aim was to help to reconceive missiology as a discipline.
- *Evangelical Resurgence and LCWE.* The reorganization of evangelical missions in the 1960s and 1970s through the influence of IFMA and EFMA, and especially the Billy Graham Evangelistic Association, led to the formation of the Lausanne Committee on World Evangelization following the Lausanne 1974 conference.

The IMC Becomes the CWME within the WCC (1961)

We should note an important structural change within the WCC during this period, which will help us appreciate the theological developments that were taking place. It was becoming increasingly clear by the mid- to late 1950s that the category of so-called younger churches was obsolete. Many were now becoming organized as national churches within newly formed independent nations; they were no longer satisfied to relate to the larger world church movement through the various mission society structures. A change took place in 1961, when the IMC ceased to exist, but was reorganized as the Commission on World Mission and Evangelism (CWME) within the WCC.[45]

It is worth noting that Lesslie Newbigin was serving as the general secretary of the IMC at the time of this integration and became the first director of the newly formed CWME. Unfortunately, many evangelicals in the former IMC felt that they had lost their theological as well as organizational home. The seedbed for a new movement of evangelicals was planted by way of several conferences in the 1960s.[46] The major conference that took place in Lausanne in 1974 led to the formation of the Lausanne Committee for World Evangelization (LCWE), an organization that continues to serve as the major clearing house for evangelical mission activities around the world. The "Lausanne Covenant," produced by that conference, became a document around which evangelicals found agreement for working in cooperation with other denominations and mission organizations over the next several decades.

From a Theology of Mission to Mission Theology

A significant contribution toward a theological reframing of missiology took place at the meeting of the IMC at Willingen in 1952. The concept

---

45. Increasing pressure was being placed on the IMC to address this situation. By the time of the Ghana meeting in 1958, it was clear that an integration needed to take place between the IMC and the WCC. This was effected at the New Delhi assembly of the WCC. The CWME was originally named as the "Department" of World Mission and Evangelism (DWME), but this was later changed to "Commission."

46. One was sponsored by the Interdenominational Foreign Mission Association (IFMA) and the Evangelical Foreign Mission Association (EFMA) at Wheaton College (Wheaton, IL) in 1966, which gave rise to the Wheaton Declaration, and another by the Graham Evangelistic Association in Berlin the same year, with the theme "One Race, One Gospel, One Task."

of a Trinitarian understanding of mission was discussed during this meeting; this later became known as the *missio Dei*.[47] It represented a shift from viewing missions as the work of the church, being the primary agent (based on a high Christology and the obligation of churches to obey the Great Commission), to an understanding that a Trinitarian God is involved in mission in the world and the church participates in that mission. Instead of viewing the church as having a mission, the understanding was that God's mission has a church. This conception of the *missio Dei* proved to be a Copernican revolution within the discipline of missiology, though not without controversy.[48] Unfortunately, another shift took place by the late 1960s that diverted the attention and energy of this emerging connection between missiology and ecclesiology with respect to congregations.

This shift, with an increased focus on secularization, led some to begin to conceive of the church as needing to give up its life for the sake of the world.[49] One problem with this emphasis was that it failed to keep an ecclesiology clearly connected to the missiology of *missio Dei*. Another problem was the diminished emphasis it seemed to place on the redemptive dimensions of the kingdom of God being dynamically connected to the *missio Dei*, resulting in the work of God in the world being conceived largely in social and political terms.[50] This suspicion was compounded by the increased

---

47. This language was used by Georg F. Vicedom in 1958 to summarize the work done at Willingen. See Vicedom, *The Mission of God: An Introduction to a Theology of Mission*, trans. Gilbert A. Thiele and Dennis Hilgendorf (St. Louis: Concordia, 1965). See also the discussion of the emergence of the *missio Dei* concept in John G. Flett, *The Witness of God: The Trinity, Missio Dei, Karl Barth, and the Nature of Christian Community* (Grand Rapids: Eerdmans, 2010).

48. Craig Van Gelder, "How Missiology Can Help Inform the Conversation about the Missional Church in Context," in *The Missional Church in Context: Helping Congregations Develop Contextual Ministry*, ed. Craig Van Gelder (Grand Rapids: Eerdmans, 2006), 12–43. The literature representative of this work among ecumenical Protestants includes Johannes Blauw, *The Missionary Nature of the Church: A Survey of the Biblical Theology of Mission*, 1st ed., Foundations of the Christian Mission (New York: McGraw-Hill, 1962); Johannes Christiaan Hoekendijk, *The Church Inside Out* (Philadelphia: Westminster, 1966); Hendrik Kraemer, *A Theology of the Laity* (Philadelphia: Westminster, 1958); World Council of Churches; Dept. on Studies in Evangelism; Western European Working Group; World Council of Churches, Dept. on Studies in Evangelism; North American Working Group, *The Church for Others, and the Church for the World; A Quest for Structure for Missionary Congregations, Final Report of the Western European Working Group and North American Working Group of the Department on Studies in Evangelism* (Geneva, 1967).

49. See, e.g., Hoekendijk, *The Church Inside Out*.

50. This emphasis came to a peak at the 1968 WCC meeting in Uppsala, and at the

influence of liberation theology, which came primarily from Latin American Roman Catholic theologians, who were calling for a proactive stance on social and political action.[51] Many evangelicals viewed this movement as discontinuous with the historical understanding of missions.[52]

An alternative to this emerging mission theology developed from the work of Donald McGavran in the 1970s, in what became known as "church growth." The debate regarding the shift toward a more secular understanding of the *missio Dei* in the 1960s came to a head leading up to the Uppsala assembly of the WCC in 1968, where McGavran laid down a critical challenge by asking, "Will Uppsala betray the two billion?"[53] What became known as the "church-growth movement" sought to recapture, in many ways, the spirit of Edinburgh 1910, and it also largely drew on the theological framework of the Great Commission that was operative at that time.[54]

It is important to note that biblical and theological developments during this period began to coalesce into a vibrant mission theology that led many in the field of missiology to reshape the conversation about church and missions/mission as well as to reframe the relationship between ecclesiology and missiology. Symbolic of this shift was the dropping of the "s" from "missions" in the title of the IRM journal in 1969: instead, it became *The International Review of Mission*. This conversation, on the one hand, led to a significant amount of convergence among participants from diverse faith traditions. But in the midst of this convergence came another movement toward divergence, which is part of the next phase of the story.

1972–1973 meeting of the CWME in Bangkok, and led many evangelicals to question whether it was a helpful framework for the discipline of missiology, or even if it was biblical. See Peter Beyerhaus, *Shaken Foundations: Theological Foundations for Mission* (Grand Rapids: Zondervan, 1972), 34–48.

51. Gerald H. Anderson and Thomas F. Stransky, *Liberation Theologies in North America and Europe*, Mission Trends No. 4 (New York: Paulist Press, 1979).

52. See, e.g., David J. Hesselgrave, ed., *Theology and Mission: Papers Given at the Trinity Consultation No. 1* (Grand Rapids: Baker, 1978).

53. Donald McGavran, "Will Uppsala Betray the Two Billion?," *Church Growth Bulletin: Institute of Church Growth* 7, no. 6 (July 1971).

54. The church-growth movement was centered in the School of World Mission at Fuller Seminary, where McGavran took up teaching in the late 1960s. It was very influential for several decades among evangelicals involved in foreign missions, and it also had a significant impact on churches in the United States that were engaging in mission, which we discuss in the following chapter.

Public Missiologies in the Suburban Success Period

The public missiologies from previous periods significantly evolved during this period, in the midst of the massive changes taking place both in the world at large and also in the United States. The expressions that were developed are displayed in Table 6.1.

Table 6.1 Public Missiologies of the Church in the Suburban Success Period

Missiology Strain	Colonial Period	Frontier Period	Urban Growth Period	Suburban Success Period	Strategies for Success Period
Focus on Nation	Conquest to Civilize and Christianize -Established -Religious Freedom	Protestant Nation-building	Protestant America as Destiny	Civil Religion -American Dream	
Focus on Tradition	Maintain Traditional Faith -Immigrants	Maintain Traditional Faith -Immigrants	Maintain Traditional Faith -Immigrants -Withdrawal	Maintain Traditional Faith -Withdrawal	
Focus on Engaging in Missions or Mission	Native American Missions	Foreign Missions	Expanded Foreign Missions	Postcolonial Mission Evangelical Foreign Missions	
Focus on Social Reform	"True" Christian Society	Social Reform -Morality -Slavery	Social Gospel -Urban Poverty -Temperance	Social Justice Liberation -Social/Political -Economic	
Focus on Justice and Liberation	Pursuing Freedom from Margins -Slavery	Pursuing Freedom from Margins -Slavery	Protest and Liberation -Jim Crow Blacks -Reservation Native Am	Civil Rights/ Liberation -Responding to AIM	
Focus on Revival and Renewal	Revival and Renewal -Great Awakening	Expanded Revival and Renewal -Second Great Awakening	Urban Evangelistic Revivals	Evangelistic Revivals Charismatic Renewal	
Unique Focus					

A cultural narrative that sought to blend national interests with religious purposes continued to manifest itself during this period and significantly influenced the engagement of gospel and culture with respect to missiologies. Earlier, the missiology of Protestant nation-building had morphed into an expanded missiology of Protestant American destiny. Coming out of World War II, the sense of national pride being tied to God's favor in connection with the Judeo-Christian heritage was strengthened in the bipolar world of the competing ideologies of democracy and communism. This led to what is best described as a *missiology of civil religion*, which was championed by many churches as the key to standing strong in the face of communism, the totalitarian enemy. This contributed to a coalescing of God and country, symbolized in the addition of the words "under God" to the Pledge of Allegiance in 1954.

A subset of this missiological strain emerged with the rising education and affluence, especially in the white population. It made up what might be labeled the *missiology of the American dream*. This strain was developed primarily among the expanding white middle class, which was the first to experience the full expression of the good life of the American dream as it was packaged and commodified into the suburban ideal and made operational through the family-suburban congregation.[55] The American dream, reinforced by Christian values, became an ideal to which millions aspired. But it was an ideal that was largely closed off to minority populations, especially the black community. This represented something of the problematic side of this suburban success, which was, in 1962, prophetically named by Gibson Winter a "suburban captivity."[56]

The strain of missiology from the previous period that focused on living out the traditional faith also continued during this period. There was a shift in the practice of promoting a *missiology of maintaining the traditional faith*. Now it became the strategy of a conservative coalition within a denomination who felt that the denomination was moving too far to the left theologically.[57] The pattern all too typically became one where those seeking to maintain traditional theological views also tended to continue traditional practices of mission and evangelism long after those practices had begun to become obsolete in the mission field.

---

55. Halberstam, *The Fifties*, 131–43.

56. Winter, *The Suburban Captivity*. These newly formed communities cut themselves off from identity-forming traditions and extended-family systems even as they pursued conspicuous consumption as a way to fill the void that was left.

57. An example of this was the movement within the Presbyterian Church USA to form the Presbyterian Church in America in 1973. Similarly, the opposite pattern of expelling the progressives took place in the Missouri Synod Lutheran Church. Those who were going to be purged formed a seminary-in-exile, called Seminex, and they established Evangelical Lutherans in Mission as a new denomination. See Frederick William Danker, *No Room in the Brotherhood: The Preus-Otten Purge of Missouri* (St. Louis: Clayton, 1977).

The missiological strain dealing with foreign missions also morphed significantly during the 1960s and 1970s because of dramatic changes in the world at large. The formal structures of the Western colonial systems that were imposed on the majority world during the nineteenth century were dismantled between the late 1940s and the mid-1960s. This often resulted in armed conflicts taking place. Many Western churches, especially the mainline denominations, along with some parachurch mission organizations, increasingly reoriented their previous missiology of foreign missions into a *missiology of the postcolonial mission*. This involved shifting their mission work away from evangelism and church planting toward teaching and providing a supporting infrastructure to national or independent churches in the previous mission fields.[58] Western mission agencies associated with the CWME of the WCC would no longer have the lead in initiating cross-cultural missions, and increasingly they were required to shift their roles to supporting the local leadership of the emerging national churches.

The more conservative churches, however, were slow to warm up to this new reality and continued much of the earlier missiology of foreign missions for several more decades. Many evangelical denominations and mission organizations continued to promote a *missiology of foreign missions*, sending mission personnel who engaged in evangelism and church planting directly. In 1965, the Wheaton Declaration clearly reflected the traditional mindset and approach to missions that had been operative for over a hundred years. Evangelical views matured somewhat at the Lausanne Conference of 1974, where 2,500 representatives from around the world gathered to discuss mission and plan strategy. This conference shifted the focus of foreign missions primarily to unreached people groups.[59]

Critical developments took place during this time with regard to the earlier missiology of protest and liberation within the black community, which emerged as a *missiology of civil rights and liberation* and sought to bring an end to the Jim Crow laws that blanketed the daily life of African Americans. Black church leaders such as Martin Luther King Jr. drew

---

58. The changed *mission* part of this postcolonial missiology was clearly reflected at the CWME meeting in Mexico City in 1963 where world missions was reframed as being an enterprise that involved missions from six-to-six (continents)—the whole church taking the whole gospel to the whole world.

59. This focus was proposed at the first LCWE congress in 1974 and since that time has been picked up by numerous mission organizations. It morphed over the next decade to focus on what became known as the 10/40 window, where the vast majority of unreached people groups live. See p. 208 n. 45, below, for more on the 10/40 window.

deeply on the long tradition of spiritual and political resistance to racism that had been manifest in the black church and tied this to US constitutional commitments in calling America to account to honor its espoused ideals of freedom and equality for all. It was also increasingly influenced over time by the rise of liberation theology in Latin America among the Roman Catholics that promoted God's "preferential option for the poor."[60] Accompanying this focus on civil rights, a new generation of leaders in the Native American community, the American Indian Movement (AIM), began to espouse many of its central tenets in demanding change in federal policies dealing with Indians. Some churches working on Indian reservations began to revise their own practices, which included bringing an end to the reservation schools that sought to diminish Indian culture among the children.

There had been earlier missiologies that sought to redress social injustices, for example, the missiology of social reform and the missiology of the Social Gospel. Influenced substantially by the civil rights movement and the values expressed by the emerging counterculture, the focus now broadened to the whole of society, and a political agenda was developed that enacted some key federal legislation: for example, the War on Poverty in 1964, the Voter Rights Act in 1965, and the Fair Housing Act of 1968. This represented a *missiology of social justice and liberation*. This growing social consciousness in the nation sought to lift people out of poverty, primarily through providing equal opportunity, and focused its strategies especially on education. It is notable that a new generation of evangelicals also joined in the call for social justice, symbolized most prominently at that time in the Chicago Declaration of 1973.[61]

The missiological strain associated with renewal and revival took on two new expressions during this time. The first was a *missiology of evangelistic revival*, which emerged from among evangelicals with the rise of Billy Graham and the evangelistic crusades he organized across America and around the world. A substantial infrastructure was put into place for these events: this required up to a year of lead-time in planning for them and extensive follow-up afterwards. The second was a *missiology of charismatic renewal*, which swept across Protestant denominations and the Roman Cath-

---

60. Gerald S. Twomey, *The "Preferential Option for the Poor" in Catholic Social Thought from John XXIII to John Paul II* (Lewiston, NY: Edwin Mellen, 2005).

61. Ronald J. Sider, ed., *The Chicago Declaration* (Carol Stream, IL: Creation House, 1974).

olic Church in the 1960s through 1970s. It put emphasis on experiencing the second blessing of the Spirit in being able to speak or pray in tongues. Significant networks of persons experienced this gift and began to meet in interdenominational gatherings. In many ways, this missiology reflected the rapid growth of the Pentecostal church taking place around the world.

Theological Education and Leadership Formation

Theological education underwent a major change at this time regarding the formation of leaders for the church: mainline seminaries reduced their missiology curriculum, while evangelicals started new seminaries, many with a missions focus. Coming out of World War II, there were 144 seminaries and schools of theology that were members of the AATS; Princeton and Southern seminaries were the only two that were moderately conservative.[62] Evangelicalism, however, was on the resurgence: the NAE was formed, and fifty Bible schools started up their own accrediting associations by 1949. The influence of these resurgent evangelicals began to be felt throughout the larger church system by the 1950s, and Billy Graham's crusades put a public face on it. These evangelicals of the Billy Graham persuasion founded numerous new seminaries.[63]

Leadership formation within the larger church also saw the rapid expansion of parachurch organizations, with their alternative leadership-formation processes. Significant college campus organizations were begun or expanded their operations.[64] Hundreds of men and women entered active ministry via the informal leadership formation processes practiced by such organizations. These movements coalesced with the expanding youth culture of the time and became for many a vehicle for effecting change in

---

62. Glenn T. Miller, *Piety and Profession: American Protestant Theological Education* (Grand Rapids: Eerdmans, 2007), 620.

63. The most significant was Fuller Theological Seminary (1947), but others included schools such as George Fox Evangelical Seminary (1947), Conservative Baptist Theological Seminary (1950), Gordon-Conwell Theological Seminary (merger 1969), and Biblical Seminary (1971). There were also increasing fractures within some denominations that led to the formation of alternative denominational seminaries that were more conservative, such as Reformed Theological Seminary.

64. These included Campus Crusade (formed in 1951) as a new organization and the expanding operations of existing groups, such as InterVarsity (formed in 1941) and the Navigators (formed in 1933).

the church and the world—for example, the Jesus Movement.[65] Increasing numbers of these leaders entered seminary as young adults, but they tended to enroll in the more evangelical/conservative seminaries.[66]

Protestant seminaries and schools of theology nearly doubled their enrollments following World War II, as many returning troops took advantage of the GI bill, which covered educational costs; in the same period, Catholic schools experienced a 30 percent increase.[67] The expanding suburban system of congregations readily absorbed this increased supply of ministerial personnel. From the mid-1960s until the early 1970s, enrollments in seminaries continued to expand. These were driven in part by students seeking to receive a ministerial deferment in order to avoid the draft that was feeding young men into the military conflict of the Vietnam War.

The delivery of theological education underwent a significant change in light of an AATS study of its member schools in the mid-1950s; this study was funded by Carnegie and led by H. Richard Niebuhr, Daniel Day Williams, and James Gustafson.[68] It focused on what was theological about theological education, which was identified as "extending the love of God and love of neighbor in the world."[69] Seminaries were to serve as the intellectual centers for their respective denominations in preparing professional *pastoral directors* who could administratively lead the expanding system of suburban congregations with their increased denominational programming. Graduate theological education was now becoming the norm for pastoral leadership, and seminaries were seen to need to pay of attention to the matters of governance, funding, and faculty development.[70]

The curriculum of theological education underwent significant development as new courses were added that placed increased emphasis on utilizing the social sciences for developing ministry skills. Educational theory began to reshape the pedagogy, as well as to place an increased emphasis on

---

65. Bustraan, *The Jesus People Movement.*

66. The places often chosen included schools such as Dallas Theological Seminary, Fuller Theological Seminary, and Asbury Theological Seminary.

67. See Wuthnow, *The Restructuring of American Religion,* 36. Protestant seminary enrollment in 1950 was nearly double that of prewar numbers, and Catholic seminary enrollment was up 30 percent.

68. H. Richard Niebuhr, Daniel Day Williams, and James Gustafson, *The Purpose of the Church and Its Ministry* (New York: Harper and Row, 1956); Niebuhr et al., *The Advancement of Theological Education* (New York: Harper, 1957).

69. Niebuhr et al., *The Purpose of the Church,* 27–39.

70. Miller, *Piety and Profession,* 669–99.

students gaining some field experience during their course of training. Finally, clinical pastoral education was also introduced into the curriculum of many schools, its genesis being the T-Group and sensitivity training models of the 1960s.[71]

Changes in Catholic theological education paralleled those of the Protestant churches and their seminaries, and became more evident in the aftermath of Vatican II in the early 1960s. The Catholic theological education system reached its peak during this period: 169 theologates enrolled 8,916 students, though over two-thirds of these institutions had fewer than fifty students.[72] Vatican II envisioned renewal of theological education, and in 1969 the Catholic Church published *A Basic Plan for Priestly Formation* in an attempt to standardize the work of the seminaries.[73] Two important new schools also came into existence as a result of the consolidation of smaller schools: Catholic Theological Union in Chicago in 1968 and Washington Theological Union in 1969. Another development took place in Berkeley, California, in those years, when several Catholic schools joined other Protestant denominational seminaries to form the Graduate Theological Union.

Time of Transition

Challenges to the social order became pervasive in the late 1960s to mid-1970s. The calls for social change tore at the very fabric of the society concerning what it meant to be an American. These upheavals greatly disrupted all of society, and that included many of the denominations and their congregations: young members left the institutional churches in disproportionately high numbers, and challenges to traditional practices increased. The social consciousness of the dominant culture was deeply challenged—and forever changed. The youth movement and counterculture paralleled the earlier civil rights movement in reshaping society, but it did so primarily in the arena of challenging prevailing cultural values, especially any notion of expected institutional authority. Perhaps the music of that period best rep-

71. Robert T. Golembiewski, *Sensitivity Training and the Laboratory Approach* (Itasca, IL: F. E. Peacock, 1973).

72. Robert J. Wister, "Theological Education in Seminaries," in *Theological Education in the Catholic Tradition,* ed. Patrick W. Carey and Earl C. Muller, SJ (New York: Crossroad, 1997), 155.

73. Wister, "Theological Education in Seminaries," 155.

resented the spirit of the times, and the most prominent musicians, taken as a social bellwether, were the Beatles.[74]

The countercultural revolution quickly diversified into other movements. What became known as the second wave of the feminist movement took place during this period, stimulated initially by Betty Friedan's book *The Feminine Mystique* (1963).[75] A whole new generation was challenged by the issues of inequality that faced most women; many took up this cause in print as well as in the streets. Another movement came to life seeking to address the increasing crisis in the environment. The ecological movement coalesced around the hosting of the first Earth Day in 1970, an event that continues to be convened annually.[76] These various movements were all deeply interrelated with the protests over the Vietnam War, where a whole generation of students became politically active in seeking to subvert governmental authority even as they attempted to change public policy concerning the war.

This disruption was also evident in the economy when President Nixon free-floated the value of the dollar in 1972, thus ending the Bretton Woods agreement, which had been in place for twenty-five years. Compounding that situation was the action taken by the Organization of Petroleum Exporting Countries (OPEC) to take control of domestic production in 1973 and enforce an oil embargo, which led to significant inflation and long lines at the gas pump.

Some churches responded to these profound changes by reframing pastoral identity primarily around pastoral care, introducing what became known as the *therapeutic pastor*. This concept relied heavily on psychological models, especially the work of Carl Rogers.[77] It was not particularly theological, and thus it received an uneasy welcome within theological education. Accompanying this change in pastoral leadership was a fundamental shift in what could be called the DNA of forming new congregations. By the early 1970s, traditional church planting of new geographic-neighborhood

---

74. Their 1967 release of *Sgt. Pepper's Lonely Hearts Club Band*, which symbolized their rebirth in Eastern religion and the drug culture, also symbolized the substantial cultural shifts that were taking place. See Olivier Julien, *Sgt. Pepper and the Beatles: It Was Forty Years Ago Today* (New York: Routledge, 2009).

75. Betty Friedan, *The Feminine Mystique* (New York: Norton, 1963).

76. Adam Rome, *The Genius of Earth Day: How a 1970 Teach-In Unexpectedly Made the First Green Generation* (New York: Hill and Wang, 2014).

77. Carl Rogers, *Carl Rogers on Personal Power: Inner Strength and Its Revolutionary Impact* (Philadelphia: Trans-Atlantic Publications, 1978).

congregations came to an abrupt end; what emerged in its place was an alternative that would become known as "lifestyle congregations." In these congregations, people would make choices to participate based on personal preference related to characteristics of the congregation; this was especially evident in the choices of music and worship styles.

This period is sometimes referred to as the third disestablishment of the church in the United States: the increasing marginalization of the church and the privatization of the faith.[78] Mainline denominations, after decades of continued numerical growth, simply quit growing amid all these changes and began what has become decades of decline. On the opposite side of the Protestant ledger, many conservative and evangelical denominations were beginning to have increasing influence as their membership rolls continued to show significant growth. An ongoing and continuing controversy surrounding this phenomenon was set in motion by Dean Kelley's book *Why Conservative Churches Are Growing* (1972). He argued that conservative churches were growing because they made serious demands on people in terms of doctrine and behavior.[79] Kelley's book was readily critiqued, and numerous alternative explanations have been proposed that continue the debate to this day.

By the mid-1970s, the United States was beginning to turn back to the right both politically and religiously. Politically, this shift was a response, in part, to the perceived excesses of the countercultural movement that began to peak out in the early 1970s. It was nurtured especially by the bicentennial celebration in 1976, which reclaimed the ethos of the nation's constitutional beginnings. Religiously, the election of Jimmy Carter, a self-professed born-again Christian, as President that same year was a contributing factor to this shift as well as the rapidly expanding media churches and television evangelists who took to the airwaves in the mid-to-late 1970s.

78. Wade Clark Roof and William McKinney, *American Mainline Religion: Its Changing Shape and Future* (New Brunswick, NJ: Rutgers University Press, 1987), 11–39.

79. Dean M. Kelley, *Why Conservative Churches Are Growing: A Study in Sociology of Religion* (San Francisco: HarperCollins, 1972).

CHAPTER 7

Late-Modern Success Strategies, Mid-1970s to Early 2000s

The Church in the Late-Modern Success-Strategies Period

The church underwent major changes during this period as a result of some significant developments. There was a substantial increase in immigration, particularly people of color from the Global South, many of whom were Christians already. A remarkable expansion of personal choices provided individuals with more freedom than ever before, largely as a result of technological innovations. National borders became less consequential economically as the deepening effects of globalization set in. The modern project was also increasingly being realized by using rational strategies and organizational designs as predominant means to accomplish intentional goals. Yet all this took place even as many of the core assumptions that supported the modern project were challenged and deconstructed by postmodernity. As a result, the public missiologies of the church continued to evolve as the church was shaped by, and responded to, these realities.

The biggest change for the church was the shift from the centuries-long pattern of starting denominational, geographic-neighborhood congregations to the development of congregations around attractional-lifestyle choices. With this shift, a congregation's location was no longer tied to a specific neighborhood, and its identity was no longer necessarily tied to a larger institution. A whole range of new forms of congregations emerged, most of them designed to serve a particular generation. These congregations primarily used strategy and emphasized organizational leadership in helping the church redesign itself to engage a changing culture. This was facilitated by the rise of the church-growth movement, which later further evolved into the church effectiveness/health movement. The majority of these new congregations were started by evangelicals, while the mainline denominations struggled to redefine themselves in the midst of their continued membership decline.

This membership decline, along with declining finances, led the ecumenical movement in its various organizational expressions to undergo significant change, both in downsizing operations and in reconceiving its role. Alongside this change, the church experienced the continued growth of the evangelical movement and the rise of the Christian Right, as evangelicals became more politically active while America was becoming more conservative in the aftermath of the counterculture phase. Feeding this shift was the innovative use of television by a whole series of evangelists and pastors of megachurches. This also contributed to the earlier Pentecostal movement's becoming more mainstream in the form of a charismatic movement that swept across mainline denominations and some parts of the Roman Catholic Church.

The church's involvement in missions continued to diversify as global partnerships with national churches and a practice of accompaniment became the modus operandi of most mainline denominations' involvement in missions. This occurred as immigrant churches continued to increase within the United States, as a result of both Christians who had immigrated and new congregations being started in these ethnic communities. Evangelicals, for the most part, continued to expand their operations by sending personnel to engage in foreign missions. They increasingly used focused strategies to accomplish this; several of these movements made efforts to reclaim the vision and energy of the Edinburgh 1910 conference. In the midst of these developments, there was a concerted effort to develop a more robust theology of mission, to include missiologists from Roman Catholic, Orthodox, ecumenical, and evangelical faith traditions.

Key Themes, Events, and Population Shifts

Population Shifts

The population of the United States grew from 205 million in 1970 to over 282 million by 2000, and to 308 million by 2010. The largest proportional gains during this forty-year window occurred in communities of color. This was partly a result of higher birthrates in those communities than in white communities and partly a result of further changes in immigration policy. The Immigration Reform and Control Act of 1986 attempted, for the first time, to address the growing issue of illegal immigration by offering amnesty to many undocumented persons. This especially helped those who had come from Mexico and Central and South America. The Immigration Act of 1990 (IMMACT) raised the total number of yearly immigrants allowed into the United States to approximately 675,000, and it retained family reunification as a primary criterion.[1]

These policy changes led to an increase in the Hispanic population—from 9 million in 1970 to over 35 million in 2000—and that helped the Catholic Church's continued growth because many of these Latino immigrants were Roman Catholic.[2] But the largest proportional increase came from Asian and Pacific Rim countries, where the 1965 family reunification clause facilitated an increase of immigrants: from 1.5 million in 1970 to 11.8 million by 2000. These dramatic increases in residents of color joined the growing African American community, which rose from 22.5 million in 1970 to 36.4 million in 2000, and the American Indian population, which stood at 4.1 million in 2000. The issue of illegal immigration increasingly became a major political issue in the first two decades of the twenty-first century. Several political initiatives sought to address this by way of some kind of comprehensive immigration reform; but all efforts have failed. Underneath the political struggles over immigration lie the deeper questions of American identity and multiculturalism.

The white proportion of the population also declined by 20 percent during this half century: from more than 85 percent in 1960 to only 65 percent in 2010. It is anticipated that over the next roughly thirty years this proportion will decline by another 20+ percent points, dropping it to about 42 percent by 2050. The last several presidential elections have made it evident that we are now experiencing the beginning of the end of the historical majority exercised by the white population in national elections. The sig-

1. By the mid-1990s, however, stricter laws were passed to deal with immigrants involved in criminal activity, which led to several million individuals being deported over the next decade and a half. These laws included the Antiterrorism and Effective Death Penalty Act (AEDPA) and the Illegal Immigration Reform and Immigrant Responsibility Act (IIRIRA), both passed in 1996: https://secure.ssa.gov/poms.nsf/lnx/0500501440 (accessed July 3, 2016); and http://www.uscis.gov/ilink/docView/PUBLAW/HTML/PUBLAW/0-0-0-2593.html (accessed July 3, 2016).

2. Roger Finke and Rodney Stark, *The Churching of America, 1776–2005: Winners and Losers in Our Religious Economy* (New Brunswick, NJ: Rutgers University Press, 2005), 267.

nificant increases in population within the communities of color are now beginning to realign the traditional patterns of decision-making within all aspects of public life in the United States. This includes the church.

Most of the white denominational churches and congregations in America are aware that this change is taking place, and many have responded with various efforts and strategies to become more multicultural and inclusive. But these strategies still appear to be working largely within the assumptions of the white majority of those denominations. Increasing the proportion of minorities in their midst falls short of addressing the systemic shift now taking place and the reality of learning to live within a multicultural society.

New Realities at the Beginning of the Last Half of the Twentieth Century

The tumult taking place in American society during the late 1960s and early 1970s began to settle down by the mid-1970s, The reason for this was, in part, that the Vietnam War had begun to wind down: the Paris Peace Accord was signed in January 1973, calling for a ceasefire in place of all military action, and US troops began to be withdrawn. The few remaining troops had only an advisory role when the war finally came to an end in April 1975. By that time, President Nixon had been forced to resign the presidency (August 1974) as a result of the Watergate scandal and investigation, and Vice President Gerald Ford had become President. The winding down of the war saw a parallel decline in the antiwar protests and urban unrest that had rocked the nation for over a decade. Contributing to this change was the fact that the early baby boomers who had participated in the battle on university campuses and in the streets had moved on into the work force.

Rise of the Christian Right

The mood of the country began to shift to a more conservative posture by the mid-1970s. A clear indicator of this shift was the Equal Rights Amendment, which sought to provide equality for women. It had passed both houses of Congress in 1972, and by 1977 it had acquired thirty-five of the thirty-eight states required for it to be ratified and become law. But its full approval stalled in the next several years, and the clock ran out in 1979, reflecting a political turn to the right that was taking place across the country.

Contributing to this turn was the bicentennial celebration in 1976, which caused many people to reflect on and reclaim the roots of American democracy. The 1976 election to the presidency of Jimmy Carter, a self-professed born-again Christian—specifically a Southern Baptist from Georgia—also symbolized this cultural shift.[3]

Further enhancing this turn was an increasing number of prominent conservative evangelists and megachurch pastors who emerged with weekly television programs in the mid- to late 1970s. They built on the pioneering TV work introduced by Pentecostal Oral Roberts and the Roman Catholic Bishop Fulton Sheen in the 1950s and 1960s. The newcomers in the 1970s were media savvy in their use of the power of the medium to reach large audiences of conservative-minded Christians. These new "televangelists" included Jerry Falwell, Jimmy Swaggart, Jim Bakker, Rex Humbard, James Kennedy, Pat Robertson, and Charles Stanley.[4] The work of these televangelists was complemented by the periodic televising of Billy Graham crusades from around the world.

This more conservative understanding of the faith, which focused on "family values," did much to contribute to the formation of what became known as the "Christian Right."[5] A major player in this movement was the Moral Majority, founded by Jerry Falwell, a Baptist minister and founder of Liberty University. His organization, among others, did not hesitate to enter into political discussions and quickly took stands on various social issues. This coalition, in turn, became instrumental in helping to elect Ronald Reagan to the presidency in 1980, and were joined in the early 1980s by the Family Research Council, founded by James Dobson, as an increasingly broad-based coalition gained a national voice for conservative Christians.

This coalition advocated for a number of issues, such as prayer in public schools and the teaching of creationism, and opposed other issues, such as pornography, the rights of homosexuals, and especially abortion.

---

3. Mark A. Noll, *The Old World Religion in a New World* (Grand Rapids: Eerdmans, 2002), 169–70.

4. Noll, *The Old World Religion*, 171–72. The high-profile scandals of a significant number of these TV evangelists, resulting in their eventual disappearance in the next decade, also created problems of credibility for this movement as a whole. But by the late 1990s and early 2000s, this earlier phase of media evangelists morphed into the TV broadcasting of worship services from some of the more prominent megachurches, such as those of Rick Warren at the Saddleback Church and Joel Osteen at the Lakewood Church in Houston, TX.

5. Daniel K. Williams, *God's Own Party: The Making of the Christian Right* (New York: Oxford University Press, repr. ed., 2012).

The earlier "right-to-life" movement, which had been promoted primarily by the Catholic Church after the *Roe v. Wade* decision by the Supreme Court in 1973, now gained momentum across the country and joined forces with this evangelical coalition. In many ways, this cause became—and still serves as—the signature issue of what are now known as the "Christian social conservatives," who represent the Christian Right.[6] This coalition has become substantially associated with the Republican Party, whose political fortunes have relied heavily on the white Christian vote in recent decades to win elections. Yet, white Christians in the electorate have steadily declined, from 73 percent in 1992 to 55 percent in 2015.[7]

The Reagan Revolution and Polarized Politics

Ronald Reagan's election in 1980 symbolized the substance of the shift that had taken place in the country during the second half of the previous decade. The "Reagan revolution" of the 1980s brought numerous changes to the country, not the least of which was the massive military buildup, an effort to stay ahead in the Cold War. Much of this buildup was accomplished by cutting or eliminating social-welfare programs, some of which had been in place since Franklin Roosevelt's New Deal and others that had been mandated under Lyndon Johnson's War on Poverty. The decline of the social-welfare system was also significant for the church because, as numerous programs were curtailed or eliminated, the church struggled to respond to the increasing numbers of people needing assistance. By the end of the 1980s, the Cold War had ended and the Soviet Union broke up—due primarily to internal struggles.[8]

A polarization between the political parties continued to develop in the two decades that followed, largely because of differences over social issues, initially the issue of abortion and later human sexuality. The influence of the Christian Right within the Republican Party led to the development of yet another version of a *missiology of a Christian America*. The civil religion of the

---

6. Williams, *God's Own Party*; see also Jim Wallis, *Christians, Liberals, and the Fight for America's Future* (Grand Rapids: Brazos, 2013).

7. Robert P. Jones, *The End of White Christian America* (New York: Simon and Schuster, 2016), 106.

8. Gil Troy, *The Reagan Revolution: A Very Short Introduction* (New York: Oxford University Press, 2009). The question of whether the US military buildup contributed to the winning of the Cold War is a matter of debate that continues to the present day.

1950s and '60s now took a turn to the right, as efforts were pursued to restore the nation back to its founding roots. The resurgence of evangelicalism in the second half of the twentieth century helped feed this cause. It was played out politically in the 1990s during the Clinton presidency, when congressional Republicans came up with the "Contract with America."[9]

This polarization in America experienced a truce for a short time because of the events of September 11, 2001, when terrorists used hijacked airplanes to take down the twin towers of the World Trade Center in New York City and to badly damage the Pentagon in Washington, DC. But the subsequent wars in Afghanistan and Iraq under the George W. Bush administration soon divided the country politically once again. The election of Barack Obama as the first African American president in 2008 and his introduction of health-care reform during the first years of his administration deepened the divide of the political polarization in the United States.

The metaphor of "red states and blue states" became a regular focus in the media, and it all played out within the churches and denominations primarily in terms of their positions on social issues. It is worth noting that the earlier settlement patterns of the United States, as Colin Woodard discusses in his book *American Nations,* helps us understand the electoral map of these red and blue states. Red states are made up largely of the Tidewater area, the Deep South, Greater Appalachia, the western part of the Midlands, and the Far West (except for the Pacific coastal areas). Christian social conservatives are disproportionately represented in these areas. Blue States are made up largely of Yankeedom, New Netherlands, the West Coast, some of El Norte, the eastern part of the Midlands, and the state of Florida.[10] These areas are disproportionately underchurched compared to the overall population, though many Roman Catholics live in these "blue" areas.

Globalization and the Economy

A major shift also took place during this time in the world economy with the free-floating of the value of the US dollar in 1973. Capital now flowed beyond the control of any national borders to places where the profit margin

9. Republican National Committee, *Contract with America* (New York: Three Rivers Press, 1994). All but two members of the congressional Republican caucus signed this document six weeks before the congressional elections.

10. Colin Woodard, *American Nations: A History of the Eleven Rival Regional Cultures of North America* (New York: Penguin, 2011).

could be maximized. By the 1980s, the globalization of the world economic order was well under way. In an effort to lower costs, businesses relocated to cheaper labor markets around the world. The decline of the steel industry in the North and the textile industry in the South were initial examples of the structural changes taking place in the economy. This structural change was further accelerated with the development of the tech industry in the 1990s and afterwards: the United States increasingly experienced a two-tier economy, a low-wage service industry and a high-wage professional and skilled sector.

These changes also had an impact on the distribution and location of the population. In the 1970s and '80s, the new metaphors of the "rust belt" and "sun belt" were introduced to describe the new reality. The cities located in the older industrial areas of the North experienced massive dis-investment in their manufacturing industries, accompanied by population losses, while cities on the coasts and across the South experienced signif-icant growth. Included in this relocation of population to the South were many of the children of those African Americans who had participated in the second phase of the Great Migration north after World War II. Many now returned to a South that had changed because of the gains made via the civil rights movement.

The globalization of the economy and its attendant economic restruc-turing continued to play itself out politically in various debates over ap-proving free-trade agreements with other countries in the world.[11] This glo-balization also greatly impacted the church: many congregations declined or died in the large cities, especially in the manufacturing sector, where there was a significant disruption of the economy. Denominations that ear-lier had invested heavily in starting up city-neighborhood and suburban churches were the hardest hit.

Corporate Success

The major restructuring that took place in the economy helped generate a period when mergers and acquisitions were a booming business in them-selves. Churches began to pay attention to the corporate culture during

---

11. This began with the North American Free Trade Agreement (NAFTA), which was introduced by then President George H. W. Bush in 1992 and approved by Congress in 1993 under President Clinton; it continued through the election of Donald Trump in 2016.

this period because of the challenge of blending diverse cultures. They also focused more intentionally on strategic planning in order to achieve success.[12] Managing an organization by clarifying its core values, identifying its purpose/mission, and formulating a clear vision for the future became the order of the day. This required focused attention on finding the right leaders to implement this approach. All of this was reinforced by the values of efficiency and productivity that became part of the effort to realize the modern project: the increasing rational management of the social order. Denominations, as well as parachurch organizations, offered numerous systems for strategic planning and congregational development; the churches' health and effectiveness movement was the result. Its impact lasted into the beginning of the new century, but by that time other changes began to disrupt these success-driven strategies.

Generational differences also became evident in the 1980s, as the younger brothers and sisters of the early boomers (born between 1955 and 1964) came of age. They adopted a set of values that were very different from those of the early boomers. The previous generation produced the *hippies*, who were at the center of the counterculture and whose focus was on changing the world; the emerging generation became known as the *yuppies*, and their focus was on corporate success and owning their piece of the world. The late boomers were the same generation that helped give birth to the market-driven church, where the equation of "what meets my needs" became the underlying logic of personal decision-making about church.

Technology Changes and the Rise of Social Media

Alvin Toffler's book *Future Shock* (1970), plus his later work *Third Wave* (1980), captured well what was happening in the economy. The former book identified the condition of information overload: technological and cultural changes required a fundamental reorientation of one's worldview—at an ever-increasing speed. The latter book described the revolution that was taking place in our society because of the process of mass production.[13] It predicted the changes that would occur as a result of the invention of the

---

12. One of the first books to promote this approach for businesses was George A. Steiner, *Strategic Planning: What Every Manager Must Know* (New York: Free Press, 1971).

13. Alvin Toffler, *Future Shock* (New York: Random House, 1970); see also Alvin Toffler, *Third Wave* (New York: Bantam Books, 1980).

microchip, which soon led to the development of the personal computer and the further compression of time required to reorient one's worldview.

Enhancing the value of the personal computer was the development of the Internet in the late 1980s and early 1990s. It had its roots back in the 1960s, when projects were funded by the federal government, but its use was initially limited to the technology of large mainframe computers. It was the creation of the personal computer—and its linkage to the Internet— that gave anyone with a computer access to a massive amount of public-domain information that keeps multiplying to this day. By the mid-1990s, the Internet began to become a worldwide phenomenon, and today it has over 3.5 billion users.[14] Access to this growing body of information greatly increased with the introduction of Internet search engines, such as Google, in the early 2000s.

This interconnectivity took on increased importance with the development of social media, which allowed people to connect and network virtually. The rapid growth of Facebook, introduced in 2004, is but one example. Further enhancing the connectivity was the creation of the smartphone in the late 2000s, which literally gives persons access anytime and anywhere to the global web and the ability to connect—in real time as well—with anyone who has a similar device. The fuller implications of this networked virtual world and its implications for the church are still being explored, and we will take them up with respect to the church in later chapters.

Truth, the Postmodern, and the Individual

These systemic changes in society brought on by technological changes were paralleled by intellectual and social changes. The first arguments began to be made in academic and public circles in America during the 1970s that the Enlightenment foundations that underegirded the modern project were themselves problematic. The "postmodern" condition (as it came to be called) began to be discussed in relation to almost every dimension of life, including, for example, architecture, history, the social sciences, art, music, and literature.[15] This movement critiqued and deconstructed all claims of

14. This statistic reported at: http://www.internetworldstats.com/stats.htm (accessed July 3, 2016).

15. Steven Best and Douglas Kellner, *The Postmodern Turn* (New York: Guilford Press, 1997). The more extreme postmodern position moved in the direction of a complete relativism that paralleled the earlier European development of nihilism at the turn of the previous

objectivity and the use of universal metanarratives to interpret reality; it made a turn toward the local, the particular, and the differing narratives. Interpretation began to be understood as being multiperspectival: that is, there is a certain relativity to all knowing, and everyone has to work out his or her own social construction of reality.[16]

This combination of technological innovations that multiplied personal choices and the move away from the necessity of external authorities to shape one's values and decisions increasingly placed the focus on the individual. The only referent a person now had for making decisions was him- or herself, with the focus shifting toward pursuing personally meaningful experiences. The result was that people began to tribalize in order to secure some form of community.

System of Congregations

The church experienced a fifth expansion in the number of congregations during this period. The historical review of church life we presented in the preceding chapters makes it clear that denominations and their congregations have had to evolve continuously in order to respond to the changing population trends, demographic shifts, and changed cultural contexts. The geographic-neighborhood congregation, in all four of its historical expressions—ethnic-immigrant, village, city-neighborhood, and suburban—was able to rely on geographic proximity for its membership; but this approach became obsolete by the late 1970s.

Church participation in relation to geographic proximity largely evaporated in the face of increased mobility, lifestyle preferences, and multiple options. Although most former geographic-neighborhood congregations still had a symbolic presence in a particular location because of their facilities, the logic of congregational identity dramatically shifted from geographic proximity to associational networks and members' lifestyle preferences. This led historical-geographic congregations to engage more and more in niche marketing to target populations in order to reach new members. They were joined in this by scores of newly founded congregations.

The fifth period of the expansion of the system of congregations—from

---

century. But the majority of those making a postmodern argument focused on the social construction of all meaning-making.

16. John R. Searle, *The Construction of Social Reality* (New York: Free Press, 1997).

the mid-1970s to mid-2000s—introduced a "change of kind" and gave rise to a form of church that might be called the "attractional-lifestyle congregation," with two characteristics tending to define them: first, the majority of these new congregations have been either independent of or quasi-independent of historical denominational systems, as well as formal theological education processes; second, there has been an increase in the number of different types of lifestyle congregations that started up during this period.

Most were the result of new congregations being planted with regard to a clearly defined purpose and vision—and using target or niche marketing. A substantial technology for such church planting emerged during the 1980s and 1990s, when proponents used a variety of strategies.[17] However, the basic life cycle and viability of each appears to have shortened to roughly ten to fifteen years because they targeted a specific generation. The fuller impact of these two shifts is still being sorted out in the life of the American church, but it is clear that the traditional patterns of denominational church life are undergoing massive changes and realignment as they face the great unraveling.

Movements Giving Birth to the Fifth Period of Expansion

During the second half of the twentieth century, several new initiatives were introduced that sought to help the church respond to these changing conditions. (These built on the work that had been introduced by the earlier church-renewal movement, which we discussed in chapter 6.) The first new initiative was the church growth movement of the 1970s and early 1980s, which placed an emphasis on evangelism and focused largely on utilizing social science and pragmatic techniques to enhance organizational effectiveness. The original work of Donald McGavran, which focused on foreign missions, began to be applied to congregations in the United States in the early 1970s by church-growth advocates such as Winn Arn, Peter Wagner, Virgil Gerber, Elmer Towns, and Carl George.[18]

17. A leader who is representative of this movement is Bob Logan, who developed extensive resources for coaching and mentoring church planters: http://www.coachnet.org/en/ (accessed July 3, 2016).

18. The key volume that introduced the church-growth movement was Donald McGavran, *Understanding Church Growth* (Grand Rapids: Eerdmans, 1970; fully revised ed., 1980). All of the advocates listed, along with McGavran and many others, contributed important books to the church-growth movement in the 1970s and 1980s.

This approach focused on helping congregations utilize social science research methods to reach unchurched persons with the gospel by stressing the necessity of obeying the Great Commission and by developing strategies and techniques to engage in this task. This movement largely lost its credibility in the academy by the early 1980s, as Wilbert Shenk documented in *Exploring Church Growth* (1983).[19] But a version of it evolved into the congregational life of the church in America as the next generation of church leaders adapted its emphasis to a more holistic understanding of ministry that moved beyond church growth.[20]

Many of these leaders were part of a second initiative for engaging in organizational success, which was the *church effectiveness movement*. It surfaced in the 1980s and continued well into the 1990s, focused on the theme of organizational effectiveness. It moved beyond the narrow focus of church growth by incorporating a wider range of social-science and organizational perspectives for managing and leading congregations through renewal and growth in the midst of change.[21] Numerous programmatic initiatives became available, for example, the use of strategies such as Purpose-Driven and Alpha.[22] Such initiatives soon evolved further into what became the *church health movement*, which borrowed a medical image for understanding congregational life. The best known of the several "health" methodologies that emerged was Natural Church Development, marketed by Christian Schwarz.[23] Parallel to this is the emphasis that emerged in the 2000s concerning the theme of pastoral excellence.[24]

19. Wilbert R. Shenk, ed., *Exploring Church Growth* (Grand Rapids: Eerdmans, 1983).

20. Bob Logan, *Beyond Church Growth: Action Plans for Developing a Dynamic Church* (Grand Rapids: Revell, 1990); see also Craig Van Gelder, "Gospel and Our Culture View," in *Evaluating the Church Growth Movement: 5 Views,* ed. Gary L. McIntosh (Grand Rapids: Zondervan, 2004), 80–81.

21. Craig Van Gelder, "Understanding the Church in North America," in *Missional Church: A Vision for the Sending of the Church in North America*, ed. Darrell Guder (Grand Rapids: Eerdmans, 1998), 72–73. In particular, there was a fuller appreciation of the congregation as an organizational system where the interrelatedness of every dimension of congregation life needed to be understood and addressed.

22. For Purpose Driven, see: http://www.saddleback.com/ (accessed July 3, 2016); for Alpha, see: http://alphausa.org/Groups/1000065342/Alt_Home_page.aspx (accessed July 3, 2016).

23. Many denominations have adopted this approach by using the program of Christian A. Schwarz, *Natural Church Development: A Guide to Eight Essential Qualities of Healthy Churches* (St. Charles, IL: ChurchSmart Resources, 1996).

24. Grants being made available over the past decade by the Lilly Endowment, Inc., for developing and sustaining pastoral excellence are illustrative of this.

The Attractional-Lifestyle Churches

There have been at least six types of attractional-lifestyle churches that have emerged over the past forty years.[25] The first began to appear in large numbers in the mid-1970s. Subsequent versions have continued to come on the scene as new generations create new types and as new technologies are used.

1. Regional Church Ministry Centers

Increased mobility of the population, especially in cities, took place by the late 1960s, as the interstate highway system was coming to completion. Locating a church near a major interstate interchange became a strategy for growing churches to serve a regional area. These churches often became quite large. The key to the regional church is that it was able to break through the limitations of the earlier geographic-neighborhood church while maintaining its denominational identity. Many denominations either planted or used an existing, well-located church to create a regional church that served as a ministry center.

2. Megachurch/Teaching Church

This type of church in many ways was an extension of the regional church. These churches used the tools of marketing to target and reach unchurched persons. They were market-driven.[26] An early practitioner was Robert Schuller, who started his evangelism ministry in a drive-in theater in southern California and eventually built the Crystal Cathedral. His annual Institute for Successful Church Leadership introduced hundreds of pastors to his approach.[27] Representatives of the emerging generation of

25. A seventh type of an attractional-lifestyle congregation is the Social Media/Virtual Church that is discussed in later chapters as part of the transition that is now taking place.

26. Most of these churches were started over the past decades as being either seeker-sensitive or seeker-driven, meaning that they worked to remove the barriers keeping those outside the church from being engaged. They typically have used contemporary music, offered very practical teaching sermons, engaged in very intentional programming, and used small groups to cultivate relationship and promote formation.

27. Robert H. Schuller, *2005 Robert H. Schuller Institute for Successful Church Lead-*

leaders in the church effectiveness movement, such as Bill Hybels and Rick Warren, regularly spoke at this annual conference. "Megachurches" emerged from this, and many of them also became "teaching churches" as they shared their approach with other leaders who were starting up additional churches. The typical definition used to define megachurches is an average weekly attendance in all their services of over 2,000 persons. There were only ten such churches in the United States in 1970; by 2010 it was estimated that there were more than 1,500, of which more than ninety averaged a weekly attendance of at least 10,000.[28] Many of these churches are independent or nondenominational, but examples of megachurches exist that cover the whole spectrum of denominations. The typical individual in the leadership role of this type of church has the style of an entrepreneurial pastor.[29]

3. Emerging Church

The generation known as the "busters" (or "Gen-X") began to come of age in the late 1980s and 1990s, and they brought a different set of values to cultivating church life. They were not attracted to the megachurch; instead, they introduced what became known as the "emerging church." The emphasis was on a participatory style of worship, often with a liturgy that was crafted by a local worship team. This type of church incorporated into its worship space many of the symbols of the faith that the megachurch movement had removed in its effort to become seeker-sensitive. The cross and baptismal font reappeared in prominent places, along with incense, icons, and other elements of Christianity from the early church. Leadership was provided by a participatory pastor; sermons were often delivered in a dialogical style. This approach to church life appears to have peaked in the early 2000s, as yet another generation emerged.[30]

---

ership, Dr. Schuller's "Classic Lectures" from the early 1970's (Los Angeles: Crystal Cathedral Ministries, 2005).

28. The primary source of information for megachurches is made available by the Hartford Institute, which can be accessed at: http://hirr.hartsem.edu/megachurch/database .html (accessed July 3, 2016).

29. See, e.g., Walt Kallestad et al., *Entrepreneurial Faith: Launching Bold Initiatives to Expand God's Kingdom* (New York: WaterBrook Press, 2004).

30. See, e.g., Eddie Gibbs and Ryan Bolger, *Emerging Churches: Creating Christian Communities in Postmodern Cultures* (Grand Rapids: Baker, 2006); see also Doug Padgitt,

4. Multicongregational and Multisite Churches

Up until the 1980s, the term "multicongregational church" typically referred to churches that had more than one congregation of differing ethnicities worshiping in the same facility. This began to change by the 1990s, when more churches offered diversely styled worship services to serve their diverse memberships. This often led, at least functionally, to multiple congregations within the same church. By the early 2000s, technological changes made it also possible for congregations to meet simultaneously in multiple locations. Typically, these multisite services made it possible for people at other locations to experience the same message via a simulcast on screens.[31]

5. Cell-Groups and Network Churches

Also emerging in the late 1990s and early 2000s were churches made up of multiple cells. The small-group church, often known as a "house church," has been part of the historical Christian movement from its earliest beginnings. What is different about these churches is their ability to use technology to link multiple house churches together organizationally under a common leadership. Some of these cell-structured churches have grown to be quite large.

6. Immigrant Churches

Accompanying these congregations with multiple expressions of lifestyle was a dramatic increase in the number of congregations related to newly arriving immigrants—especially from the Pacific Rim, Central and South America, and Africa. This, in turn, led to the rebirth of an older type of congregation—the ethnic-immigrant congregation. Their formation over the past several decades followed the same pattern of the earlier European immigration, with whole or partial faith communities immigrating

---

Church Re-Imagined: The Spiritual Formation of People in Communities of Faith (Grand Rapids: Zondervan, 2005).

31. An example of this approach is Community Christian Church in the Chicago area, which currently has thirteen campuses: http://communitychristian.org/ (accessed July 6, 2016).

and becoming organized congregations in the American context.[32] Some of these congregations joined existing denominations, while others organized under their own ethnic leadership as new denominations or as independent congregations.[33] These congregations are attractional in that they often draw their members from across a large geographic area since their building location is typically not contingent on the location of their members.

Thousands of congregations representing these six types of attractional-lifestyle styles have been started up over the past forty years. They have multiplied even as the geographic-neighborhood congregations have either plateaued or declined. Most remaining village congregations continued to decline as a result of the loss of population in rural areas; those who have remained consist of a high percentage of older adults. Many of the former white city-neighborhood congregations either struggled on with declining numbers of members who drove in from the suburbs, or they merged, relocated, or closed; when they did, they often sold their properties to congregations of color. Most family-suburban congregations now owned extensive facilities that were underused in the aftermath of the bust of the baby boom. Furthermore, many members drove back to the old neighborhood from distant suburbs where they had relocated.

It is noteworthy that significant numbers of the people serving as ministerial leaders in these new streams of church planting are not seminary trained. Many received their leadership formation from informal processes for theological education that have increasingly become available through web-based strategies, as well as from the megachurches that serve as teaching churches. In addition, extensive networks for forming leaders and providing them with the necessary resources emerged to fill the theological education void.[34]

---

32. Noll, *The Old World Religion*, 174–76; Finke and Stark, *Churching of America*, 140–41.

33. Michael W. Foley and Dean R. Hoge, *Religion and the New Immigrants: How Faith Communities Form Our Newest Citizens* (New York: Oxford University Press, 2007).

34. The Willow Creek Association has over 12,000 churches in thirty-five countries; and the Purpose Driven Network of Saddleback Church has trained over 400,000 pastors from 162 countries in Rick Warren's model of church: https://www.willowcreek.com//membership/index.asp (accessed July 3, 2016); and https://www.mnnonline.org/mission_groups/purpose-driven-ministries/ (accessed July 3, 2016).

Development of the Denominational, Organizational Church

Important shifts continue to take place within the system of denominations during the last several decades of the twentieth century. One change was a dramatic decline in loyalty among constituents to institutional Christianity, which in turn led to a decline in funding to regional and national structures. Another change was the dramatic decline in membership in all mainline denominations, which peaked in the mid-1960s for many reasons. One important reason was that church leaders had become disconnected from the beliefs of the people and the troubles of the local congregation.[35] This has recently also been the experience of many evangelical denominations: the slowing of growth—even the beginning of a decline.

Deep divisions within both American Christianity and American political life had become evident by the 1990s, usually tied to differing views of key theological issues. The formation of political coalitions within mainline denominations increasingly became the primary politics for internal decision-making regarding matters of theological policy. Much of the shift noted above can be accounted for by internal theological debates within denominations over such issues as abortion, women in church office (beginning in the 1970s and continuing to the present), and human sexuality, which came to the fore in the first two decades of the twenty-first century.[36]

There were approximately 1,200 denominations in the United States (using a broad definition) by the end of the twentieth century; if one uses a more standard definition, the number is approximately 200; only about 100 denominations have any substantial membership.[37] In the midst of the dramatic cultural changes and the struggle to recontextualize, many congregations chose to invest more resources in their local ministries: expanding programming, hiring staff, or adding facilities. Alongside a general decline in revenues at the local level, they sent less funding to their national church bodies. This has led to the continued downsizing of the national agencies and of the regional judicatories of many denominations, a pattern that continues apace.[38]

35. Finke and Stark, *Churching of America*, 275.

36. Dean Hoge, *Division in the Protestant House: The Basic Reasons behind Intra-Church Conflicts* (Philadelphia: Westminster, 1976).

37. Robert Wuthnow, *The Restructuring of American Religion* (Princeton: Princeton University Press, 1988), 108; see also Noll, *The Old World Religion*, 282–86.

38. The Evangelical Lutheran Church in America, newly formed in 1987, is a case study of the continuing pattern of denominational downsizing at the national level as revenues for

Previous chapters have shown how the denominational organizational church continued to evolve and adjust over time. Denominations have responded to these changes during the past forty years with a series of organizational initiatives, all designed to bring the denomination back to what it had been. Thus, we have seen the emergence of the *re-denomination*.[39] These initiatives include: (1) efforts toward re-vision—trying to coalesce energy around a shared vision; (2) efforts to revitalize—trying to cultivate effective ministry by engaging in strategic planning or introducing a programmatic approach to vitalization; (3) efforts to regulate—seeking to secure compliance by passing new regulations; and (4) efforts to restructure—changing the organizational design as a way to either improve governance or save money. By the early 2000s, denominations were beginning to realize that these initiatives were largely a cul-de-sac with regard to trying to restore their fortunes.

Developments Regarding the Discipline of Missiology

It was during the last third of the twentieth century that earlier biblical and theological developments began to coalesce into a vibrant mission theology that led to a reshaping by missiologists of the conversation about church and missions/mission as well as to a reframing of the relationship between ecclesiology and missiology. This conversation, on the one hand, led to a significant amount of convergence in thought among participants from diverse faith traditions; on the other hand, it also generated a significant organizational divergence.

Convergence

Biblical and theological developments taking place in the 1970s led to the development of a "mission theology" that used the mission of God as a hermeneutical lens by which to read the whole of Scripture. Substantive documents that drew on many of the same biblical and theological con-

---

churchwide programs continue to decline. Most other mainline denominations are following a similar trend.

39. Russell E. Richey, "Denominations and Denominationalism: An American Morphology," in *Reimagining Denominationalism: Interpretive Essays*, ed. Robert Bruce Mullin and Russell E. Richey (New York: Oxford University Press, 1994), 89.

cepts were produced within different faith traditions, and those documents were later used to inform the missional church conversation.[40] A key focus within all these documents was an effort to bring together evangelism and social concerns as part and parcel of the same holistic gospel. Three streams contributed to this conversation.

The first stream was the Roman Catholic Church, which further developed its mission theology through the CELAM conferences. These conferences influenced the work of Pope Paul VI in his apostolic exhortation, *Evangelii Nuntiandi* (1975), in which he gave expression to the growing theological consensus that linked evangelization with concerns for peace, justice, and development.[41] The second stream was the ecumenical movement. In 1982, through the work of the CWME, the Catholic Church contributed its version of the growing consensus in mission theology in the document *Mission and Evangelism: An Ecumenical Affirmation.*[42] This document was greatly influenced by voices from the Two-Thirds World who were both evangelical and ecumenical; it integrated classical evangelical themes of mission within the larger framework of the mission of God and the announcement of the reign of God by Jesus.

The third stream involved evangelicals in the Lausanne Committee on World Evangelization movement. This organization worked toward affirming the growing consensus in mission theology in a consultation held in Grand Rapids in 1982, which sought to clarify further the affirmations of the Lausanne Covenant adopted in 1974.[43] There the reign-of-God theology was used in an attempt to build a bridge between evangelism and social involvements. These representative developments, in addition to numerous other initiatives within the larger world church community, demonstrated an amazing convergence of thinking that was emerging about mission and mission theology in relation to the concepts of the *missio Dei* and the reign (kingdom) of God.[44]

40. These various concepts are referred to as a "missiological consensus" by Darrell Guder in the introduction to *Missional Church: A Vision for the Sending of the Church in North America*, ed. Darrell L. Guder (Grand Rapids: Eerdmans, 1998), 8.

41. See the discussion of this document in Norman E. Thomas, ed., *Classic Texts in Mission and World Christianity* (Maryknoll, NY: Orbis, 1995), 143–44.

42. Emilio Castro, ed., "Mission and Evangelism: An Ecumenical Affirmation," *International Review of Mission* 71, no. 284 (October 1982): 427–51.

43. Lausanne Committee for World Evangelization and the World Evangelical Fellowship, Lausanne Occasional Paper 21: "Evangelism and Social Responsibility: An Evangelical Commitment," available at: http://www.lausanne.org/all-documents/lop-21.html (accessed July 3, 2016).

44. See David Jacobus Bosch, *Transforming Mission: Paradigm Shifts in the Theol-*

Divergence

On the other hand, there continued to be deep concerns among many evangelicals in the United States regarding the ecumenical movement. The gains made within the CWME toward a growing consensus regarding mission theology were not sufficient to overcome long-standing evangelical suspicions of the National Council of Churches in the United States, as well as the larger body of the WCC. Unfortunately, the growing consensus for a mission theology failed to sufficiently bridge the differences between ecumenicals and evangelicals and resulted in a growing divergence taking place organizationally between these movements.

Illustrative of this divergence was the formation in 1976 of the US Center for World Missions by Ralph Winter, who sought to reclaim the mantle of Edinburgh 1910 by arguing for the need to continue cross-cultural missions. That organization's journal, *Mission Frontiers*, was soon promoting the evangelization of unreached groups of people, especially with regard to what has become known as the "10/40 window."[45] Further illustration of this growing divergence was the gradual withdrawal of numerous evangelical missiologists from the American Society of Missiology (ASM) during the early 1980s.[46] They left to join the Evangelical Missiological Society,

---

ogy of Mission, American Society of Missiology Series, No. 16 (Maryknoll, NY: Orbis, 1991); James A. Scherer, *Gospel, Church, and Kingdom: Comparative Studies in World Mission Theology* (Minneapolis: Augsburg, 1987). In the midst of this increasing convergence of thinking, a growing number of people from the Two-Thirds World viewed themselves as evangelical ecumenicals. They found value in associating with both streams of the multiple conferences and congresses sponsored by the Commission on World Mission and Evangelism of the WCC and the Lausanne Committee on World Evangelization (LCWE). Included were Emilio Castro, a Methodist from Peru who was director during this time, as well as Orlando Costas from Latin America, David Gitari from Africa, and Samuel Escobar from Peru.

45. Most of the people groups still unreached by the gospel live in places stretching across the maps of northern Africa and Asia. Christian missions strategist Luis Bush started calling this rectangular area or band "the 10/40 window." He used that easy-to-remember name because it lies across Africa and Asia from 10 degrees latitude north of the equator to 40 degrees latitude south of the equator: of the fifty-five least evangelized countries, 97 percent of their population lives within the 10/40 window (world evangelism statistics). See: http://home.snu.edu/~HCULBERT/1040.htm (accessed October 4, 2013). Hundreds of missionary personnel, both short-term and long-term, continue to access the resources of this organization.

46. The ASM was formed in 1973 to give expression to the growing convergence among evangelicals, ecumenicals, and Roman Catholics. The author recalls that professors from various Southern Baptist seminaries withdrew from active participation in the

which had been reorganized in 1990 out of the former Association of Evangelical Professors of Missions.[47]

These alternative ecumenical and evangelical missiologies are still very much at work within the church today, where there continues to be significant suspicion expressed by each movement toward the other.[48]

The discipline of missiology went through several major shifts during this period:

- *Curricular Revision*: Some mainline schools used the missiological concept of the *missio Dei* to shape their whole curriculum, among them Catholic Theological Union in the 1970s, the Lutheran School of Theology at Chicago in the early 1980s, and Luther Seminary (St. Paul) in the early 1990s.[49]
- *Evangelical Resurgence*: Many evangelical seminaries and educational institutions expanded their departments of missiology in reclaiming a more traditional understanding of mission (note, for example, the start-up of the School of World Mission and Institute of Church Growth at Fuller Theological Seminary (1969); later the E. Stanley Jones (ESJ) School of World Mission and Evangelism at Asbury Theological Seminary (1983).
- *Gospel and Culture Discussions*: Lesslie Newbigin brought to the fore the conversation between the gospel and culture on his retirement from mission in India and return to England in the 1970s. By the 1980s, his publications led to the formation in England of the Gospel and Culture Programme; this theme was picked up in the United States in the 1980s by the Gospel and Culture Network.

---

early 1980s, when that denomination took a more conservative turn theologically. It is worth noting that the evangelical participation in the ASM has experienced resurgence over the past several decades and now constitutes approximately 60 percent of the total membership.

47. For information on the formation of the EMS, see: https://www.emsweb.org/about (accessed March 30, 2017).

48. The ecumenical approach seeks to attend primarily to a larger theological understanding of mission, especially the mission of the triune God, leaving many evangelicals concerned that evangelism is being diluted or lost. The evangelical approach seeks to attend primarily to obeying the Great Commission and thus focuses especially on Christology and human agency; this, in turn, leaves many ecumenicals concerned that a holistic gospel is being compromised.

49. James A. Scherer, "Future of Missiology as Academic Discipline in Seminary Education: Attempt at Reinterpretation and Clarification," *Missiology* 13, no. 4 (1985): 445–60.

- The Publication of *Missional Church*: That book, jointly authored by six missiologists and published in 1998, introduced the conversation about a missiological ecclesiology that focused on the sending of congregations in North America.
- *Intercultural Studies*: In the early 2000s, several evangelical seminaries, such as Fuller and Asbury, that were known for their missions programs changed the names of their programs to "Intercultural Studies."

Congregations, both at home and abroad, began to be viewed in new ways during this period. What had been the former foreign mission fields were now reconceived as both sending and receiving locations, with indigenous churches and their congregations assuming a more active role in contributing to this work.[50] Church-growth strategies in the United States brought an intense focus on congregations engaging in mission within their local communities. But the formal discipline of missiology initially struggled in its attempts to refocus its efforts in supporting these strategic changes with regard to congregations in America.

Significant progress was made toward that goal, however, with the introduction of "the gospel and our culture" conversation in the early to mid-1990s and the "missional church" conversation in the late 1990s. Congregations in all contexts were beginning to be taken seriously by missiologists and the discipline of missiology, and that helped to displace the legacy of the modern missions movement, with the emphasis on foreign missions that had shaped the discipline for decades.[51] Unfortunately, many of those joining this conversation turned the missional discussion back into a con-

50. Robert O. Latham and World Council of Churches Commission on World Mission and Evangelism, *God for All Men; the Meeting of the Commission on World Mission and Evangelism of the World Council of Churches at Mexico City, December 8th to 19th, 1963* (London: Edinburgh House Press, 1964); Ronald K. Orchard and World Council of Churches Commission on World Mission and Evangelism, *Witness in Six Continents; Records of the Meeting of the Commission on World Mission and Evangelism of the World Council of Churches Held in Mexico City, December 8th to 19th, 1963* (London: Published for the Division of World Mission and Evangelism of the World Council of Churches by Edinburgh House Press, 1964).

51. A Gospel and Our Culture Programme was initiated in England by Lesslie Newbigin in the early 1980s; a Gospel and Our Culture Network was formed in the United States by the mid-1980s. The latter helped bring about the birth of the missional church conversation with the publication in 1998 of *Missional Church*. See: http://www.gocn.org/ (accessed July 6, 2016).

versation about church and culture—that is, how to change the church to reengage a changing culture.

The focus of much of the missiology discipline during the latter half of the twentieth century and the beginning of the twenty-first century has been devoted primarily to the development of mission theology and the reconception of the church in the midst of world Christianity. But within the United States, the underlying ethos of church growth and church health/ effectiveness is still very much present and represents the functional missiology of many congregations, especially evangelical congregations.[52] However, the inadequacies of such success-oriented approaches are becoming clearer in the midst of the great unraveling.

Mission Theology and the Renewal of Missiology

Mission theology began to come into its own in the 1990s, building in some ways on efforts that had begun in the 1960s. The earlier work of missiologists like Lesslie Newbigin was instrumental: in particular, his book *The Open Secret: Sketches for a Missionary Theology* (1976) provided an explicit argument for a mission theology that was grounded in an understanding of the triune God as a sending God.[53] Another key figure who contributed to the renewal in missiology in the 1980s and 1990s was David Bosch, whose seminal work *Transforming Mission* (1991) brought together the primary themes of mission theology emerging from the theological consensus discussed above. A key contribution of his work was his use of what came to be called a "missional hermeneutic" to read both Scripture and church history.[54]

Unfortunately, Bosch did not proceed to use his missional hermeneutic to reframe and integrate the concepts of "church" and "mission," though his own work offered the tools for doing so. He continued, to a large extent, to work within the dichotomized concept of the organizational expressions of the church; therefore, he was unable to move the discussion forward to-

52. Craig Van Gelder, "The Gospel and Our Culture Views of Church Growth," 73–102.

53. Lesslie Newbigin, *The Open Secret: Sketches for a Missionary Theology* (Grand Rapids: Eerdmans, 1976); see also *Foolishness to the Greeks: The Gospel and Western Culture* (Grand Rapids: Eerdmans, 1986); *The Gospel in a Pluralist Society* (Grand Rapids: Eerdmans, 1989).

54. See, e.g., Christopher J. T. Wright, *The Mission of God: Unlocking the Bible's Grand Narrative* (Downers Grove, IL: IVP Academic, 2006).

ward the development of an explicit missiological ecclesiology (missional church). A later Catholic contribution that moved in the direction of developing an explicit mission theology is the work of Stephen Bevans and Roger Schroeder, *Constants in Context* (2004), which focuses on prophetic dialogue.[55]

The Introduction of *Missional Church*

Missiology, for the most part, has never taken the actual lives of congregations in the United States as being at the core of its focus and work. While it has focused extensively on the planting of congregations, especially overseas, it has not developed an explicit congregationally focused missiology that deals substantively with the challenges of congregations living in particular contexts. Because of this, it has not paid adequate attention to the fundamental relationship of missiology and ecclesiology, although there was some movement in that direction in the 1960s, as we have noted above. However, this issue was picked up again in the 1990s in the work of the Gospel and Our Culture Network in North America. This conversation eventually led to the multiauthored volume *Missional Church*.

Drawing primarily on an understanding of the sending Trinity, this work built on earlier publications that had engaged Newbigin's question regarding the relationship between gospel and culture. *Missional Church* collapsed the dichotomy of the church and mission categories by developing a missiological ecclesiology that focused on congregations as the primary location of God's work in the world. Numerous other volumes were published during the next decade and a half that further nuanced this argument about a missiological ecclesiology—"missional church" in shorthand.[56] It is clear that missional theology and an understanding of missional church began to resonate deeply within the church at the beginning of the twenty-first century.

The vast majority of this literature, however, focuses on the relationship of church and culture and on the necessity of the church reconnecting

---

55. Stephen B. Bevans and Roger P. Schroeder, *Constants in Context: A Theology of Mission for Today* (Maryknoll, NY: Orbis, 2004).

56. Craig Van Gelder, *The Essence of the Church: A Community Created by the Spirit* (Grand Rapids: Baker, 2000); see also Van Gelder and Zscheile, *The Missional Church in Perspective: Mapping Trends and Shaping the Conversation* (Grand Rapids: Baker Academic, 2011), for a thorough mapping and discussion of this published literature.

with a changing context.[57] This provides a useful contribution for helping congregations take more seriously the relationship of a changing church to a changing cultural context. But what clearly has gotten lost in this part of the missional church conversation is the core question in Newbigin's original challenge regarding the relationship between gospel and culture: "Can the West be converted?"[58]

What is required for us to address this question with regard to the American church is for the church to engage in a substantive critique of the deep cultural narratives that frame our existence and shape our lives. This critique should use the lens of a theological missiology that is shaped by a robust Trinitarian theology. Such a theology allows for reconnecting missiology and ecclesiology into a missiological ecclesiology—in shorthand, a missional church.[59]

Public Missiologies in the Late-Modern Success Strategies Period

The public missiologies continued to evolve in this period in relation to the massive changes taking place in the United States. In addition, there was a new approach that emerged as a unique missiological engagement: organizational success.

57. Early works that framed this conversation were: Ed Stetzer, *Planting Missional Churches* (Nashville: Broadman and Holman Academic, 2006); Alan Hirsch, *The Forgotten Ways: Reactivating the Missional Church* (Grand Rapids: Brazos, 2009); Reggie McNeal, *Missional Renaissance: Changing the Scorecard for the Church* (San Francisco: Jossey-Bass, 2009); Milfred Minatrea, *Shaped by God's Heart: The Passion and Practices of Missional Churches* (San Francisco: Jossey-Bass, 2004). Additional contributions to this literature frame the reconnection with different metaphors, such as: Rick Rusaw and Eric Swanson, *The Externally Focused Church* (Grand Rapids: Group Publishing, 2004); Dave Browning, *Hybrid Church: The Fusion of Intimacy and Impact* (San Francisco: Jossey-Bass, 2011); Neil Cole, *Organic Church: Growing Faith Where Life Happens* (San Francisco: Jossey-Bass, 2005); Neil Cole, *Church 3.0: Upgrades for the Future of the Church* (San Francisco: Jossey-Bass, 2010); Jim Belcher, *Deep Church: A Third Way beyond Emerging and Traditional* (Downers Grove, IL: IVP Books, 2009); Mark Dever, *The Deliberate Church: Building Your Ministry on the Gospel* (Wheaton, IL: Crossway, 2005); Tim Chester and Steve Timmis, *Total Church: A Radical Reshaping around Gospel and Community* (Wheaton, IL: Crossway, 2008).

58. Lesslie Newbigin, "Can the West Be Converted?," *International Bulletin of Missionary Research* 11, no. 1 (January 1987): 2–7.

59. Van Gelder, *The Essence of the Church.*

Table 7.1 Public Missiologies of the Church in the Late-Modern Success Strategies Period

Missiology Strain	Colonial Period	Frontier Period	Urban Growth Period	Suburban Success Period	Strategies for Success Period
Focus on Nation	Conquest to Civilize and Christianize -Established -Religious Freedom	Protestant Nation-building	Protestant America as Destiny	Civil Religion -American Dream	Christian America
Focus on Tradition	Maintain Traditional Faith -Immigrants	Maintain Traditional Faith -Immigrants	Maintain Traditional Faith -Immigrants -Withdrawal	Maintain Traditional Faith -Withdrawal	Maintain Traditional Faith -Withdrawal -Immigrants
Focus on Engaging in Missions or Mission	Native American Missions	Foreign Missions	Expanded Foreign Missions	Postcolonial Mission Evangelical Foreign Missions	Global Mission -Short-Term Mission Trips Foreign Missions Frontier Missions
Focus on Social Reform	"True" Christian Society	Social Reform -Morality -Slavery	Social Gospel -Urban Poverty -Temperance	Social Justice Liberation -Social/Political -Economic	Peace and Justice -Environment
Focus on Justice and Liberation	Pursuing Freedom from Margins -Slavery	Pursuing Freedom from Margins -Slavery	Protest and Liberation -Jim Crow Blacks -Reservation Native Am	Civil Rights/ Liberation -Responding to AIM	Human Rights -Women -Human Sexuality
Focus on Revival and Renewal	Revival and Renewal -Great Awakening	Expanded Revival and Renewal -Second Great Awakening	Urban Evangelistic Revivals	Evangelistic Revivals Charismatic Renewal	Pentecostal and Charismatic Renewal
Unique Focus					Organizational Success

It is noteworthy that the missiology of civil religion from the previous period now morphed back into a more specific earlier strain that was championed by the Religious Right (Christian social conservatives), a re-energized cultural strain that supports the notion that the United States was founded on Christian principles and that tightly melds the concepts of God and country. It has come to expression over the past forty years as a *missiology of a Christian America*, and in many ways it is a throwback to the earlier missiologies of Protestant nation-building and Protestant American destiny, with regular appeals to participants to restore the intentions of the "Founding Fathers."[60] This strain of civil religion also emphasizes the need to engage in a literal interpretation of the Constitution. This strain of missiology continues to contribute substantially to a growing divide today between conservatives and progressives in the church, as it does between Republicans and Democrats in politics.

The strain of missiology from the previous period that focuses on living out the traditional faith continued into this period as well: a *missiology of maintaining the traditional faith*. The expansion of immigration over the past forty years has opened up the United States to immigrants from all over the world. Many of these indiviuals are immigrating as Christians and are bringing their faith traditions with them. It is the first generation, similar to patterns in the past, who tend to practice a more traditional form of the faith. There is also a continued pattern of withdrawal similar to what occurred in the suburban period. It is a strategy usually exercised by a conservative coalition within a denomination to split off from their denomination once they believe that it has moved too far to the left theologically.[61]

The strain of missiology that deals with foreign missions continued to develop during this time in several forms. One strain sought to modify its narrative to some extent to move beyond the postcolonial missiology prevalent in the previous period into what has become a more nuanced *missiology of global mission*. There were several important developments that influenced this shift. First, there has been an increase in the number of partner relationships between American church bodies and corresponding church bodies in the Global South. Second, there has been the substantial increase of short-term mission trips sponsored by denominations, as well as by congregations. Third, there has been the continued rise of the majority church in the Global South, which began to outpace the Western churches in size, spiritual energy, and missionary focus, as noted in the first chapter.[62]

---

60. The majority are thought to have been professing Christians, though some, like Thomas Jefferson, were acknowledged Deists.

61. An example of this in the past two decades is the Lutheran Congregations in Mission for Christ (LCMC), which left the Evangelical Lutheran Church in America (ELCA) in the late 2000s and early 2010s. A further example of this has been the recent moving away of more conservative congregations from the Presbyterian Church (USA) for the same reasons. The presenting reason for the exodus has been the human sexuality debate: i.e., the decision by the main church body to allow for gay and lesbian marriage and to ordain gays and lesbians to the clergy.

62. Philip Jenkins captures this shift well in *The Next Christendom: The Coming of Global Christianity* (New York: Oxford University Press, 2002).

And fourth, there continues to be an increasing number of cross-cultural missionary personnel being sent around the globe by the majority-world churches in the South. This has supplanted the dominant role that Western missions occupied for several centuries. Furthermore, their missionaries are also coming to the shores of the United States, many as part of ethnic-immigrant communities. This has helped the churches in the United States realize that this country is also now increasingly a mission field.[63]

Another strain of this missiology continued to develop somewhat with regard to the cultural narrative of the assumed dominance of the United States within the larger global scene. This is a *missiology of foreign missions,* which continues largely to be the posture of evangelical denominations and mission organizations. There is a substrain within this mix, however, that needs to be noted. It was initiated primarily through the work of Ralph Winter and the US Center for World Missions in an effort to reclaim the mantle of the nineteenth-century modern missions movement and the heritage of Edinburgh 1910. It can best be identified as a *missiology of frontier missions.*[64] This approach continues to be used by numerous Western mission agencies, especially the more evangelical and conservative agencies that are engaged in sending Western personnel as cross-cultural missionaries into countries that are located in the 10/40 window.[65]

The earlier missiology of social justice, which had focused largely on addressing injustices within American society, evolved during this period into a *missiology of peace and justice* and continued to be influenced by earlier themes associated with *liberation theology.* It sought to address issues of injustice both within the United States and throughout the world, while also engaging in economic and community development. A key focus of this missiological strain has been on dealing with the abuses to the environment, and it has also been known as "creation care." Significant numbers of agencies have formed for this purpose, in addition to other justice issues, both within denominations and independently. Many of them have continued to pay attention to issues of relief in the midst of crises; but the

---

63. A book that helpfully named this reality for many in the 1990s is *The Church between Gospel and Culture: The Emerging Mission in North America,* ed. George Hunsberger and Craig Van Gelder (Grand Rapids: Eerdmans, 1996).

64. Originally known as the Center for World Mission, this organization has changed its name to Frontier Ventures: https://www.frontierventures.org/ (accessed August 5, 2016).

65. http://www.joshuaproject.net/10-40-window.php (accessed August 5, 2016).

majority of these agencies have increasingly shifted their primary focus to addressing longer-term matters of development.[66]

The earlier missiology of civil rights and liberation continued into this period, but broadened significantly in terms of its focus—and of its constituencies. It has become a *missiology of human rights*. The issue of women's rights within human rights has become a major tenet of the more liberal churches, where all of the offices have been opened up to women. Likewise, in the first decades of the twenty-first century, we are seeing the emergence and acceptance of gay rights—both in the national culture and in the more liberal churches.

The rise of the Global South as the majority church in the world continues to influence missiology in the United States. The *missiology of Pentecostal and charismatic renewal* continues to become mainstream as the immigrant churches become more pervasive and the earlier charismatic revival matures within Protestant denominations and the Roman Catholic Church.[67]

A new missiological strain emerged in the United States during this period as the result of the shift from the geographic-neighborhood church to the attractional-lifestyle church. The dramatic developments taking place over the last several decades of the twentieth century have required congregations in the United States to change in order to survive. Numerous initiatives emerged under the influence of the organizational and management sciences that placed an emphasis on shaping an organization around core values, a common purpose, and a shared vision in order to reengage with a changing cultural context. They represent what might be called a *missiology of organizational success*. Various phases of this approach emerged between the 1960s and the early 2000s, which included some aspects of the church-renewal movement; but it was especially the emphasis of the church-growth movement and the church effectiveness/health movement. Though different in focus, all three movements shared the same basic logic of using a functional approach of technique in an effort to help the church engage a changed culture and context in order to be successful.

---

66. An agency that typifies this pattern is World Vision International: http://www.wvi.org/ (accessed July 6, 2016).

67. Noll, *The Old World Religion*, 179–85.

Theological Education and Leadership Formation

Theological education during this period began to experience a crisis, as it became increasingly professionalized and specialized and, at the same time, increasingly disconnected from actual congregations. This crisis had huge implications for the formation of pastoral leaders, especially with respect to the deficit in cultivating a missiological imagination. David Kelsey focused in on the question clearly when he asked, in 1992, "What is theological about a theological school?"[68] This emerged within a vibrant discussion about theological education that took place from the early 1980s into the 1990s. What was at stake was the very purpose—and the practices—of forming leadership for the church. That discussion was effective in highlighting the issues that needed to be addressed in confronting the problem; but it stopped short of answering it.

Ed Farley kicked off this conversation in 1983 with his book *Theologia*.[69] Others quickly weighed in as the key question became: What is theological about theological education? Critical analysis was brought to bear in identifying key issues in theological education: (1) the overreliance on the school model; (2) the lack of integration within a fourfold division of the curriculum reinforced by theological guilds; (3) the split between theory and practice; and (4) whether theological education should be more about gaining knowledge (*Wissenschaft*) or forming character (*paideia*). Unfortunately, this conversation wound down in the late 1990s, before meaningful resolution was achieved in most of these issues.[70]

The enrollment patterns in seminaries and schools of theology experienced significant change during this period. As more and more mainline denominations were ordaining women, their seminaries were naturally experiencing increasing enrollments of women preparing for pastoral ministry. This led to a dramatic increase in the 1980s and 1990s of second-career students, many of whom were women, enrolling in theological schools. This resulted in an older profile of student bodies for a time, but this was a trend that peaked by the late 1990s, as the backlog was absorbed and an increasing number of younger students brought the average age down again.

68. David H. Kelsey, *To Love God Truly: What's Theological about a Theological School?* (Louisville: Westminster John Knox, 1992).

69. Edward Farley, *Theologia: The Fragmentation and Unity of Theological Education* (Philadelphia: Fortress, 1983).

70. We pick this discussion up in chapter 10, where we engage it from the perspective of a theological missiology.

Another interesting change in theological education during this period was the shift in the makeup of the schools accredited by the Association of Theological Schools (ATS). As we noted above, the resurgence of evangelicals in the 1950s and 1960s led to the formation of many new Bible colleges and seminaries, and a number of these schools sought, and received, accreditation in the 1980s and 1990s. This took place at the same time that some consolidation was occurring among seminaries and schools of theology associated with mainline denominations. The increase in the number of accredited seminaries and schools of theology associated with conservative/evangelical denominations has now changed the makeup of ATS.[71]

There was also a dramatic increase in nonformal educational opportunities designed to help form pastoral leadership. Many of these were put into place in conjunction with the practice of congregations starting up other congregations. Theological education no longer was seen as being value-added or a necessary requirement for many of the leaders who were emerging as pastors of new congregations. Many of them were trained and mentored in formation processes established by the larger teaching congregations. Others took advantage of theological education resources available online, such as those available from BILD International, which promotes church-based theological education in the United States and around the world.[72]

New kinds of pastoral leaders, as we discussed earlier in relation to attractional-lifestyle congregations, surfaced with these changes—for example, *entrepreneurial leader, participatory leader, networking leader,* and so on. Mainline seminaries and schools of theology—and even many on the evangelical side—have had a difficult time adjusting to these changing realities or warming up to these approaches, believing that they lack sufficient theological integrity. But in the midst of this general discomfort, there appears to be a recognition that more attention needs to be paid, both theologically and organizationally, to the issue of leadership.

Catholic schools during this time continued to experience a decline that had begun earlier: between 1965 and 1995, enrollment figures for Catholic seminarians in theological studies dropped more than 60 percent.[73]

---

71. The executive director of ATS reported in a conversation (in February 2007) that the makeup of member schools and leadership in the association was continuing to shift to those schools that are more conservative and evangelical in their emphasis.

72. http://www.bild.org/ (accessed July 3, 2016).

73. Patrick W. Carey and Earl C. Muller, SJ, eds., *Theological Education in the Catholic Tradition* (New York: Crossroad, 1997), 151.

By 1995, there were only 2,781 students enrolled in the remaining schools. This led to the closing of many schools, and to the consolidation of others: there were twenty-five freestanding Catholic schools, ten university-related schools, and another ten collaborative schools as of the mid-1990s. Another major change was the increase in the number of women and laypersons teaching in Catholic theological programs, including graduate theological education. A further change was the increase of programs, especially an expansion of MA degrees.

Time of Transition

The challenge of trying to read what is happening in one's own time is always fraught with complexity, so we approach an interpretation of what is happening in the first decades of the twenty-first century with some caution. Nevertheless, as we argued in chapter 1, there do appear to be some significant patterns of change—both within the United States and on the global scene—indicating that the United States is now going through another significant period of transition. As we argued in chapter 2, the church would be well served by using a theological missiology to engage these changes.[74] It is helpful to review the basic outlines of that argument.

If the church hopes to be able to address the future we are beginning to live into, with the great unraveling now under way, it is essential to go beyond yet another attempt to reframe the purposive intent of the church. The focus on trying to change the church in order to be able to respond to a changed context has run its course. We need to move beyond this and focus on developing further the very identity of the church with respect to mission theology; and mission theology invites a return to the crucial issue of the relationship of the gospel and culture. A key question to be answered deals with the matter of agency: Is missiology primarily a study about exploring the church's mission in various contexts? Or is it primarily about

---

74. Authors who have helped establish the first point are Phyllis Tickle, *The Great Emergence: How Christianity Is Changing and Why* (Grand Rapids: Baker, 2008); and Diana Butler Bass, *Christianity after Religion* (San Francisco: HarperOne, 2013). Someone who has helped establish the second point is Alan Roxburgh, whose books include *Joining God, Remaking Church, Changing the World: The New Shape of the Church in Our Time* (New York: Morehouse Publishing, 2015) and *Structured for Mission: Renewing the Culture of the Church* (Downers Grove, IL: IVP Books, 2015).

discovering the intended participation of the church in God's mission—God's agency in the world?

God is a missionary God. Instead of the church having a mission on God's behalf in the world, God's mission has a church. The church is created and led by the Spirit—meaning that the church is missionary by nature. The argument we develop in this book follows this logic: the core of this argument is that it is crucial to pay careful attention to the Spirit of God's agency in the world as we develop a Trinitarian missiological approach and seek to understand the relationship of missiology to ecclesiology. This leads to the necessity of offering a deep critique of both contemporary American culture and the public missiologies that have emerged, as well as the necessity of developing a theological missiology for America. We examine these issues in the following chapters.

PART 3

Engaging the Challenge

The second part of this book explored the variety of public missiologies that the church in the United States has used over time to engage its own context missiologically. We argued that these diverse approaches during each period were highly contextual: specific to their time and place and bearing particular cultural and theological assumptions. Christian mission always plays out in the particulars of the concrete world, as disciples seek to relate to their neighbors in witness and service. Such encounters—as ambiguous and complicated as they may be—unfold amid cultural themes and historical events that necessarily define their shape. As we argued in Part 1, the church is an incarnate reality, always culturally and socially embodied. That is its power and promise, as well as its challenge, in a world of ever-changing cultures and contexts.

In this third and final part of the book, we turn our attention to the contemporary American situation. In chapter 8 we trace the basic contours of contemporary American culture through a critical missiological lens. This chapter probes in more depth some of the reasons for the unraveling of Christian participation and practice introduced in chapter 1 and further developed in chapter 7. It examines these questions: What does it mean for the church to inhabit and seek to engage this moment in American history? What are the realities that affect the formation of identity, meaning, and community?

Chapter 9 then turns to a theological, missiological engagement with these cultural currents in light of the legacy missiologies named in the five chapters of Part 2. Chapter 9 begins by providing a substantive critique of the various strains of public missiologies that have evolved over time from period to period. This serves as a background for the development of a theological missiology, one that seeks to rediscover how the triune God's life and love for the world can ground a faithful and adequate participation by the church in God's mission in the American context in our day.

Chapter 10 builds on this Trinitarian missiology to address the church's life in the important areas of church organization and leadership formation. We explore implications of the contemporary cultural environment for the formation of Christian communities, the shaping of denominations, and the forming of leaders for the church. In the conclusion we offer some reflections on faithfully going forward into the culture in which the church in America finds itself today.

CHAPTER 8

A Missiological Interpretation
of the Contemporary Cultural Environment

Understanding the Great Unraveling

Today's American religious context is marked by pluralism, fluidity, hybridity, and fragmentation. We turn now to trace some of its major contours: the rise of the unaffiliated; the disorganization or deinstitutionalization of American religion; the privatization of faith; and the emergence of do-it-yourself (DIY) spirituality. We live in a nation of innumerable personal "sacred stories" and a great diversity of "spiritual tribes" (to use Nancy Ammerman's terminology), in which religion and spirituality are in many ways thriving, but also profoundly challenged.[1]

Surveying the Landscape

Surveys of American religious affiliation and sentiment paint a picture of both enduring faith and commitment among many who are already religious, but also of significant generational disconnections from religiosity. The percentage of Americans who describe themselves as religiously affiliated dropped from 83 percent to 77 percent between 2007 and 2014, while the portion that claims no affiliation rose to nearly a quarter of the populace (23 percent).[2] The unaffiliated

1. Nancy Tatom Ammerman, *Sacred Stories, Spiritual Tribes: Finding Religion in Everyday Life* (New York: Oxford University Press, 2013).

2. "U.S. Becoming Less Religious" (Washington, DC: Pew Research Center, November 2015).

are the fastest-growing and second-largest religious category—after Catholics.[3] While some of this drop in religious affiliation may reflect a willingness of nominal believers to acknowledge their disengagement more openly than in previous eras, this still marks a dramatic increase from the 1950s and '60s, when only 2 percent were unaffiliated, or even from the late 1980s, when 9 percent were. When broken down by generational cohort, the trend toward disaffiliation among younger generations becomes especially pronounced. Millennials (especially younger Millennials, those born between 1990 and 1996) are far less religious than their elders. For instance, only 27 percent of them say that they attend religious services on a weekly basis, compared with 51 percent of the "Silent" generation (born between 1928 and 1945). Only about half of Millennials say that they believe in God with absolute certainty, compared to 70 percent of Americans in the "Silent" and "Baby Boom" cohorts.[4]

This generational shift is worth unpacking more deeply. Sociologists have long charted a generational pattern to religious participation: people tend to become more religiously affiliated and active when they get married and start a family, as well as toward the end of life.[5] Religious congregations in America continue to serve the populations of young families with children and the elderly most prevalently. In 1970, 40 percent of US households consisted of a married couple with children under eighteen; however, by 2012, that percentage had dropped by half, to under 20 percent.[6] Younger generations are far more likely to have grown up in households of divorce, which are less likely to be active in congregations. They are also more likely to have been raised by parents who rejected religion than were earlier generations. With little religious formation, what is "normal" for many of them is no religious engagement at all. It should come as no surprise that a generation that has been told by parents and society to go their own way spiritually is doing precisely that.

Moreover, in a trend that Robert Wuthnow calls "coming of age at 40," younger people today are postponing such threshold experiences as finishing school, leaving home, getting married, and having children.[7] If people

3. James Emery White, *The Rise of the Nones* (Grand Rapids: Baker, 2014), 17.

4. Pew Research Center, "U.S. Becoming Less Religious," 7.

5. Robert D. Putnam and David E. Campbell, *American Grace: How Religion Divides and Unites Us* (New York: Simon and Schuster, 2010), 72.

6. Jonathan Vespa, Jamie M. Lewis, and Rose M. Kreider, "America's Families and Living Arrangements: 2012" (Washington, DC: US Census Bureau, August 2013).

7. Robert Wuthnow, *After the Baby Boomers: How Twenty- and Thirty-Somethings Are Shaping the Future of American Religion* (Princeton: Princeton University Press, 2007), 9.

tend to engage in religious communities when they marry and settle down, that engagement is happening much later—if at all. Mary Eberstadt argues that the changing shape of the family in Western societies constitutes a major factor in decreasing religiosity. Families in advanced industrial nations, such as Europe and the United States, are smaller than before, more scattered, and less likely to be bound by marriage. Fewer people are having children or sustaining two-parent homes intact for the children to grow up in.[8] Given the correlation between family cohesiveness and religious participation, this represents a significant shift.

Research among youth and young adults in America over the past decade reveals that, for many of them, religion just isn't all that important in their lives.[9] While many teenagers tend to mirror their parents' religious affiliations in describing themselves, they struggle to articulate their beliefs in the language and categories of those traditions.[10] Religious belief and participation seem to have been reduced to an extracurricular activity like sports or music: a good, well-rounded thing to do, but ultimately unnecessary for an integrated life.[11] Religion is understood to be primarily about helping people to make good choices and to behave well; but once young people learn the basics of morality, there is no real need to continue to be involved in religious communities.[12] The predominant belief of young adults in America, according to the researchers in the National Study of Youth and Religion, is "Moralistic Therapeutic Deism," a lowest-common-denominator faith that denies major differences between religions. God is there to make you feel better about yourself and become a better person morally, but asks little in return. All morally "good" people go to heaven when they die.[13] If this is what religion consists of, no wonder leaving congregations is easy for young people, especially in a culture that emphasizes keeping options open rather than committing to something.

8. Mary Eberstadt, *How the West Really Lost God* (West Conshohocken, PA: Templeton Press, 2013), 169. For further discussion on changing family patterns in American society, see Andrew J. Cherlin, *The Marriage-Go-Round: The State of Marriage and the Family in America Today* (New York: Alfred A. Knopf, 2009).

9. Kenda Creasy Dean, *Almost Christian: What the Faith of Our Teenagers Is Telling the American Church* (New York: Oxford University Press, 2010), 17.

10. Christian Smith and Melinda Lundquist Denton, *Soul Searching: The Religious and Spiritual Lives of American Teenagers* (New York: Oxford University Press, 2005).

11. Dean, *Almost Christian*, 6.

12. Christian Smith and Patricia Snell, *Souls in Transition: The Religious and Spiritual Lives of Emerging Adults* (New York: Oxford University Press, 2009), 286.

13. Smith and Denton, *Soul Searching*, 148.

Spiritual Tribes

Amidst these shifts, many Americans continue to embrace religious belief and practice. Not only is belief in God—among those who identify as religious—consistent over the past several years, but there are some signs of an increase in religious observance among that group.[14] Nancy Ammerman's research on the spiritual lives of ordinary Americans offers an insightful framework for mapping the diversity of approaches to spirituality that exists today. She describes three primary categories of spiritualities: theistic, extra-theistic, and ethical.[15] Theistic spiritualities focus on God and engage in practices that are intended to develop a relationship with God. In Ammerman's study, they were most common among Christians (Protestant and Catholic) and Mormons, and less common among Jews and the unaffiliated. Extra-theistic spiritualities focus on transcendence without reference to God, often through experiences of beauty, life philosophies crafted by an individual seeking meaning, and an inner core of individual self-worth. They are most prevalent among neo-pagans, the unaffiliated, and Jews, along with slight majorities of mainline Protestants and Catholics. Finally, ethical spirituality constitutes a common denominator across spiritual tribes in America: everyone agrees that real spirituality is about living a virtuous life characterized by helping others. Mainline Protestants are most prone to this notion of spirituality, but it is broadly shared.

What is particularly notable in Ammerman's framing is the overlap between these spiritualities. When one asks Americans to describe their spiritual lives, there is a good deal of hybridity. Ammerman notes that, "for the large majority of people who make some claim to a religious sensibility or connection, the nature of their religiousness does not come in a neat package."[16] Yet she discovered a strong correlation between high spiritual saliency, individual practices, and organized activities in congregations.[17] In other words, *spiritual lives require spiritual communities*: attendance, participation, and involvement clearly do matter for shaping spiritual and religious practice.

---

14. Pew Research Center, "U.S. Becoming Less Religious," 6.
15. Ammerman, *Sacred Stories, Spiritual Tribes*, 28–46.
16. Ammerman, *Sacred Stories, Spiritual Tribes*, 289.
17. Ammerman, *Sacred Stories, Spiritual Tribes*, 101.

The "Dones"

This is a finding that is particularly important, given the current trends of organizational decline among religious communities. Participation in organized faith communities is integral to the shaping of faith; yet we are in the midst of a major generational abandonment of congregational affiliation. There are a variety of reasons for this. One of them is the shift away from external authorities and structures toward individualism (which we will explore below). We are living in an age of "loose connections" to institutions, organizations, and communities.[18] Religious institutions and their leaders do not, by and large, hold the same kind of cultural authority they once did in most American communities.[19] Many denominational franchise congregations were built or reshaped in the post–World War II period by the most civic-minded generation in American history, a generation that trusted, built, and sacrificially supported institutions (religious and otherwise). However, many of the children and grandchildren of that generation do not share their levels of institutional trust, loyalty, or commitment.

Research among the "dones"—those who have left the church—reveals an erosion of institutional trust. This has been exacerbated by clergy abuse scandals in the past generation, as well as the sense that churches are ultimately not concerned with the day-to-day realities that their members face.[20] Many people experience congregations as being so caught up in their own organizational, political, or theological agendas that they have little space for people to participate in more deeply or to engage in genuine conversation about things that matter to them. Robert Wuthnow's research on middle-class churches corroborates this: these churches' own members experience them as disconnected and disengaged from the primary challenges in daily life that their members are facing.[21] The hunger for community remains, but people leave the church in part because the church isn't addressing it.

This research has important implications for congregations of all

---

18. Robert Wuthnow, *Loose Connections: Joining Together in America's Fragmented Communities* (Cambridge, MA: Harvard University Press, 1998).

19. The historically black church and immigrant communities constitute exceptions to this trend in many ways.

20. Josh Packard and Ashleigh Hope, *Church Refugees: Sociologists Reveal Why People Are Done with Church but Not with Faith* (Loveland, CO: Group Publishing, 2015), 18.

21. Robert Wuthnow, *The Crisis in the Churches: Spiritual Malaise, Fiscal Woe* (New York: Oxford University Press, 1997).

kinds. Established congregations designed around a professional model of ministry, in which the clergy and staff provide religious goods and services—and perform the Christian faith *for* people—are failing to connect with this hunger for conversation and mutual meaning-making. It is simply not sufficient for the conversation to be monopolized by the top few or for the church's time and energy to be dominated by leaders' agendas without cultivating deeper listening and mutual engagement among the whole people of God. There is a major opportunity for churches to provide what few spaces or communities in American society are providing: generative spaces for conversation across lines of social difference and interpretation of the longings and losses that define human life. Unlike other organizations, the church can do this in the context of prayer, discernment, and making connections with the stories of the gospel.

A variety of cultural critics and sociologists have argued that mainline Protestant churches, in particular, have struggled to retain their members because they haven't distinguished themselves from the wider culture clearly in the past half-century. N. Jay Demerath observed two decades ago that, as the liberal values of tolerance, critical inquiry, freedom, pluralism, and relativism triumphed in the wider society, the rationale for the organizational existence of liberal congregations and denominations that espoused those values diminished. Their cultural victory brought organizational defeat.[22] Who needs to join a church to be a freethinker anymore? The inheritors of mainline Protestantism have tended to secularize the Social Gospel legacy of such thinkers as Walter Rauschenbusch. Jesus disappears from an agenda that is focused on teaching people knowledge of social oppression, with the assumption that if people feel differently about it, it will go away.[23]

As mainline Protestantism's accommodation to liberal cultural values deepened in the second half of the twentieth century, evangelicalism took a different path. Unlike fundamentalists, who vehemently rejected and tried to isolate themselves from the cultural changes taking place around them, evangelicals sought to stay culturally relevant without capitulating to the secular culture. They fostered a "subcultural identity" that emphasized the distinctiveness of Christian belief and belonging, expressed through

22. N. J. Demerath, "Cultural Victory and Organizational Defeat in the Paradoxical Decline of Liberal Protestantism," *Journal for the Scientific Study of Religion* 34, no. 4 (1995): 458–69.

23. Joseph Bottum, *An Anxious Age: The Post-Protestant Ethic and the Spirit of America* (New York: Image Books, 2014), 68–70.

the more rigorous practices of discipleship and higher expectations for membership and participation in church life than the mainliners observed. Evangelicalism has thrived on distinction, engagement, tension, conflict, and threat with the wider pluralistic culture.[24] The broader trends of institutional disengagement are affecting evangelical churches nonetheless, and the growth that characterized the second half of the twentieth century has now shifted toward decline.

Spiritual but Not Religious

Research among those who are "spiritual but not religious" puts the formative impact of late-modern culture into sharp relief.[25] This subset of the US population assumes that faith is a matter of individual choice for everyone, and that the self holds ultimate authority. Indeed, the self is thus sacralized (68–73). When all truth is thought to be relative, all religions are understood to be essentially the same at their core; therefore, no one religion gets it all right (81). Amidst hybridity and syncretism, these Americans tend to regard Jesus, Buddha, and other religious figures as "realized masters"—role models for spiritual growth (103). Such spiritual growth begins with the assumption of the inherent goodness of human nature and views the self as traveling on a trajectory of self-actualization that spans this life and subsequent ones—thus the popularity of belief in karma and reincarnation. Reincarnation seems most plausible and fair in a worldview that emphasizes personal choice and assumes evolutionary consciousness and self-determination (107). We are perpetually working on ourselves—never quite arriving.

Linda Mercadante summarizes what she has discovered in her research among those who self-identify as "spiritual but not religious":

God is transposed from transcendent actuality into sacred or divine self. Sovereignty or freedom of God becomes instead readily accessible, even impersonal divine energy to be used by the individual as he or she

24. Christian Smith, *American Evangelicalism: Embattled and Thriving* (Chicago: University of Chicago Press, 1998), 89.

25. See Linda Mercadante, *Belief without Borders: Inside the Minds of the Spiritual but Not Religious* (New York: Oxford University Press, 2014). Hereafter, page references to this work appear in parentheses within the text. See also Elizabeth Drescher, *Choosing Our Religion* (New York: Oxford University Press, 2016).

sees fit, with progress nearly guaranteed. Spirit becomes less an agent of God than self-generating personal intuition. Instead of a savior figure or prophet, there may be multiple guides or gurus to provide help so the individual can heal him- or herself. (232)

Encountering nature is the focus today of much spiritual experience, with community receding into an optional and instrumental dimension. As one interviewee remarked, "I am my own church. I am my own congregation" (165). For many of those who hold organized faith communities in harsh judgment, *not* belonging is a point of righteousness.

The "spiritual but not religious" tend to stand in an ambiguous relationship with religion, neither completely in nor out. They draw on elements of religious traditions, narratives, and practices, though largely in "detraditioned" form—shorn of community, organizational participation, deeper coherence, or commitment. Underneath all of this, Mercadante observes, is a reaction to the larger forces of life in modernity: "Their affirmation of personal identity seems less like overwhelming self-focus and more like a defensive tactic in a bureaucratic, transient, mobile world where many people feel anonymous and unimportant" (236).

Privatized, Immanent, and Intimate Faith

The public dimension of faith is eclipsed in all of this. Spirituality is a private journey of the self—not a shared, communal endeavor. This reflects modernity's privatization of faith, which Americans largely embrace. A survey as far back as 1999 found that 72 percent of Americans agreed that "my religious beliefs are very personal and private"; meanwhile, 70 percent agreed that "my spirituality does not depend on being involved in a religious organization."[26] These trends have likely sharpened since then. This has become the default position; those claiming a communal and public dimension to their faith are exceptions. No wonder religious organizations are experiencing declining participation.

Diana Butler Bass celebrates these shifts in her most recent books, which reflect the expressive individualism of our age. She proposes that a renewed "Christianity after religion" will shed the dying, hierarchical, for-

26. Robert Wuthnow, *American Mythos: Why Our Best Efforts to Be a Better Nation Fall Short* (Princeton: Princeton University Press, 2006).

mal, institutional structures in favor of self-driven personal narratives and practices.[27] Embracing the natural religion of Romanticism and its American variant, Transcendentalism, Butler Bass calls for a turn toward a God of immanence. She implicitly links this to the contemporary turn toward individual originality: "In every arena, we customize and personalize our lives, creating material environments to make meaning, express a sense of uniqueness, and engage causes that matter to us and the world. It makes perfect sense that we are making our spiritual lives as well, crafting a new theology."[28]

Thus we find ourselves in an age of do-it-yourself religion—individualized, customized, self-made. Elizabeth Drescher's research on the religiously unaffiliated within contemporary American society has found that the boundaries between the affiliated and unaffiliated are remarkably porous. Most "nones" do believe in God or a higher power, and most share the basic values of their religiously affiliated neighbors. When Drescher asked a broad sample of Americans to rank a variety of elements according to their spiritual meaningfulness, family, friends, food, and pets topped the list, followed by prayer. Practices in organized religious institutions were at the bottom of the list. Families, friends, and food are spiritually meaningful because they offer relational intimacy not experienced in institutional religion.[29]

These researchers paint a paradoxical picture. On the one hand, many Americans are abandoning participation in or affiliation with organized religious communities. They are seeking spiritual meaning elsewhere and seem to be finding it. On the other hand, as Nancy Ammerman's research confirms, spiritual or religious vitality is correlated with participation in communities of faith practice. She argues that those who place spirituality and religion in opposition are themselves neither very spiritual nor religious.[30] While the boundaries of religious identities in contemporary America are permeable, "sacred consciousness is neither confined to individual minds nor to self-contained religious institutions, but it is still social."[31]

---

27. Diana Butler Bass, *Christianity after Religion: The End of Church and the Birth of a New Spiritual Awakening* (San Francisco: HarperOne, 2012).

28. Diana Butler Bass, *Grounded: Finding God in the World* (New York: HarperOne, 2015), 21.

29. Drescher, *Choosing Our Religion*.

30. Ammerman, *Sacred Stories, Spiritual Tribes*, 289.

31. Ammerman, *Sacred Stories, Spiritual Tribes*, 300.

The ways in which existing congregations and other religious bodies express their faith traditions have become disconnected from increasing numbers of people in American society today. The emerging trend seems to be toward hyperprivatization and personalization, where it is up to each individual to make up her or his own spiritual story and path. However, this is in many ways a false premise, not to mention a dead end. Many congregations have attempted to stay relevant in the past few decades by embracing cultural shifts toward individualism, self-expression, pluralism, and choice. Attractional-lifestyle or affinity-based congregations have often played right into this by offering an individualistic gospel. Yet the trajectory of this kind of individualism ultimately leads people out of church altogether. Established neighborhood-based congregations have been wondering why people are not looking to join a church anymore. The idea that one would join a church to find meaning and purpose would not even occur to many of their neighbors, who see themselves on a more personalized, individualized journey of self-discovery. It is worth pausing to explore more deeply the roots of some of these shifts in the larger transformations taking place in American society and culture.

An Insecure Age

The dawn of the twenty-first century ushered in an increasingly insecure world for the United States on multiple fronts. Geopolitically, America's post–Cold War hegemony was challenged by terrorism and the rise of a newly polycentric world; economically, Americans experienced deepening displacement and inequality amidst globalization; and environmentally, climate change emerged as an apocalyptic threat. While nuclear holocaust was a lurking threat in the second half of the twentieth century, the world was divided into a clear Cold War dichotomy from which the United States emerged victorious.

Ambiguity and Uncertainty

Many Americans assumed the twenty-first century would bring peace and prosperity to the globe under the umbrella of American values. That is not how things are playing out. A variety of shifting cultural factors has rendered everyday life fluid, uncertain, and anxious for many Americans.[32] For an America that saw its strength and self-confidence peak in the mid- to late twentieth century, the twenty-first century seems far more ambiguous.

The Promise of Modernity

Modernity promised the inevitable universal triumph of the Western liberal values of democracy, individual autonomy, equality, and human rights. The rise of institutions such as the United Nations, the International Monetary Fund, the World Bank, and the European Union in the postwar period of the last century heralded an internationalist order, with the United States at the center. This narrative continues to unravel in a fragmented world of resurgent ideological, religious, racial, and ethnic polarization and conflict. The rise of Islamic extremism and terrorism, embodied in the 9/11 terror attacks—and more recently by the emergence of the Islamic State—offers perhaps the most acute challenge, with the extremists' dramatic rejection of modern Western values and their attempts to establish a medieval-style caliphate. The fact that many of those joining these radical groups are young people who have grown up in the capitals of modernity (Paris, London, Brussels, Boston, Los Angeles, New York) attests to the fraying of the universalist modern narrative.

The peace and equality toward which humanity is supposed to move under the guidance of strong centralized institutions such as the nation-state and the global market seems less and less within reach. The Arab Spring, which took place between late 2010 and 2012 promised liberation and democracy; but it quickly devolved into sectarian conflict, religious radicalism, continued authoritarian rule, and in some places, anarchy. The European Union is fracturing amidst a populist revolt among some of its member nations in the direction of national autonomy and a rejection of multiculturalism and migration. From the 2003 Iraq War onward, America's sense that it can remake the world in its image has been profoundly called into question. The political establishments in the West face a crisis of trust and credibility.[33] The deep modern narratives of peace and prosperity

32. For a multifaceted treatment, see Hugh Gusterson and Catherine Besteman, eds., *The Insecure American: How We Got Here and What We Should Do about It* (Berkeley: University of California Press, 2010).

33. See Zygmunt Bauman and Carlo Bordoni, *State of Crisis* (Malden, MA: Polity Press, 2014).

through a globalized, pluralist world are being challenged and rejected by those who feel displaced by them.

Even though actual terrorist attacks on US soil have been rare, post-9/11 America remains an anxious America. Surveillance of citizens has proliferated. Incidents of mass gun violence against strangers, including children, have tragically become almost routine. Public places have become spaces shadowed by fear and vulnerability. Schoolchildren rehearse lockdowns of their campuses. Parents are hypervigilant about letting their children out of their sight. Strangers are seen as threats. Violence continues to plague inner-city neighborhoods, disproportionately affecting people of color.

Insecurity has, of course, long been a fact of life for many communities of color and other minorities. Attempts to inculcate tolerance and sensitivity in schools and across the society have led to greater familiarity with ethnic, cultural, religious, and sexual diversity, especially among younger generations in America. Yet deeper reconciliation across differences often remains elusive. Zygmunt Bauman writes:

> When mutual tolerance is coupled with indifference, communal cultures may live alongside each other, but they seldom talk to each other, and if they do, they tend to use the barrel of a gun for a telephone. In a world of "multiculturalism," cultures may coexist but it is hard for them to benefit from a shared life.[34]

Underneath the veneer of tolerance and inclusivity lie enduring enmities, divisions, and injustices that surface in flashpoints of violence or protest. Meanwhile, the capacity for deeper conversation across differences has become tenuous at best in a fragmented media culture. Many working- and middle-class whites feel estranged from an increasingly multicultural society, particularly as the economic opportunities that provided security for their families have been eroded by globalization.[35] Donald Trump tapped into this deep sense of alienation in the 2016 election, which marked a watershed moment in a new struggle for America's identity.

---

34. Zygmunt Bauman, *Community: Seeking Safety in an Insecure World* (Malden, MA: Polity Press, 2001), 135.

35. See Arlie Russell Hochschild, *Strangers in Their Own Land: Anger and Mourning on the American Right* (New York: New Press, 2016).

Globalization and the Diminished Middle Class

Globalization has connected the world in a complex web of interdependence as never before, remaking the American economy along the way. The emergence of China, India, Brazil, and Russia alongside Europe as economic powerhouses has created a polycentric twenty-first-century world. Globalization has also meant economic dislocation for generations of American workers. This first took place massively with manufacturing and blue-collar jobs in the second half of the twentieth century. Today it is increasingly the professional and service jobs that are being moved overseas. Not only are blue-collar Americans seeing their jobs disappear as labor is displaced to cheaper global locations, but so are highly educated white-collar workers, such as lawyers and radiologists, as their work migrates to India and Bangladesh.

Globalization provides efficiencies and opportunities for a global elite who have the education, skills, opportunities, and capacity to adapt, as well as some workers in developing countries who have recently been rising out of poverty (China is one example). Even those thriving economically in America today find themselves scrambling to keep up with the pace of change. They bear the stress of continually having to reinvent their jobs as whole industries are remade within the span of a few years. The concept of a "career"—for which one could train and then settle into for a whole lifetime—has become increasingly tenuous. More common is a whole series of short-term positions, which place high demands on workers, who then need to retool and seek out new opportunities, largely on their own. Companies are bought, sold, merged, restructured, downsized, spun off, or simply fail—at a rapid pace. Many workers are expected to be connected electronically at all hours to their place of work, placing new burdens of stress on an already overworked culture. When there have been income gains for the average American family in the past generation, they have come at the expense of huge increases in the number of hours worked.[36] In the new entrepreneurial economy, some flourish, but many remain stagnant or flounder.

It is little wonder that many people have too little energy to join and participate in church programs and activities today. Many congregations continue to perpetuate patterns of volunteer activity that originated in the

---

36. The average American family increased its income by 16 percent between 1973 and 2005 by working an extra 533 hours a year per family, compared to the previous generation (Gusterson and Besteman, eds., *The Insecure American*, 5).

early twentieth-century urbanization, when churches served as natural centers of community life. For middle-class people in particular, the church was a hub of cradle-to-grave education, recreation, moral improvement, and connection—much of it sustained by extensive volunteerism. However, fewer and fewer people have the extra time and energy to dedicate to sustaining this paradigm of church.

The twentieth-century expansion in American security, influence, and prosperity coincided with a post–World War II strengthening of the middle class. But the past forty years have witnessed the erosion of the middle class.[37] Labor participation and personal health have fallen for a generation of working-class people (men in particular) who see no place for their gifts or skills in the contemporary economy.[38] Businesses that offered the security of stable lifetime employment and generous benefits packages (including defined-benefit pensions) in the last century have been forced, due to heightened domestic and global competition, to reduce or eliminate such provisions. Unions have lost much of their influence in the economy, taking with them security and protection for many workers. Workers now shoulder more of the cost of health care, retirement, and other support systems.

The new economy is much more entrepreneurial and fluid, demanding high skills and education for those who would prosper. For many who find such opportunities beyond their reach, the alternatives are low-wage positions that offer little promise of economic security or growth. The result is an America increasingly divided into two trajectories by class: the well-educated elite who are able to survive and thrive in a highly competitive globalized economy, and the working-class people who fall further behind and face barriers to rising out of that eroded class that their parents and grandparents did not face.[39] Robert Putnam charts this division in his book *Our Kids*, noting how different the opportunities are for those growing up in households and communities of privilege from those without those opportunities. From a low point in the 1950s, barriers to socioeconomic advancement in America have steadily risen.[40] Now many middle-class

37. "The American Middle Class Is Losing Ground" (Washington, DC: Pew Research Center, December 2015).

38. Andrew J. Cherlin, *Labor's Love Lost: The Rise and Fall of the Working-Class Family in America* (New York: Russell Sage Foundation, 2014).

39. See Charles A. Murray, *Coming Apart: The State of White America, 1960–2010* (New York: Crown Forum, 2012).

40. Robert D. Putnam, *Our Kids: The American Dream in Crisis* (New York: Simon and Schuster, 2015).

Americans are haunted by the very real prospect of dropping out of the middle class. People turn to unsustainable levels of debt to maintain a certain level of lifestyle or to finance expensive college educations, which are deemed a necessity for economic progress in the twenty-first century—but don't always yield good jobs.

Looking Back, Looking Ahead

A strongly nostalgic impulse has surfaced in the United States today— particularly among older white Americans—for a mid-twentieth-century moment that provided robust middle-class prosperity, social cohesion, and security. However, that moment was in many ways anomalous in American history—and hardly that secure for minorities and women. Immigration was at a low point. Big government collaborated with big industrial business and big labor to create favorable conditions for the middle class. The trajectory of increasing individualism, diversity, dynamism, and liberalization that was unleashed in the late 1960s may have come at the cost of dwindling solidarity, cohesion, authority, and social order, as Yuval Levin observes. But it cannot be reversed.[41]

America remains a land of promise and opportunity for immigrants. Thousands risk their lives to enter the United States illegally every year, or seek with patience and persistence a legal route to citizenship. Immigrants' energy and skills enrich the American economy, even though they are subject to scapegoating by established citizens whose economic opportunities have diminished because of globalization. Throughout the centuries, immigrants have been at the core of the identity and cultural dynamism of America (as we have seen in the preceding chapters). That continues today, even though some Americans, of course, struggle to accept them.

One of the major sources of insecurity in the twenty-first century is environmental. Americans have known for a few generations that their collective consumption of the earth's resources is unsustainable, and the emergence of climate change as a looming challenge has taken on apocalyptic overtones. While the assumption of many previous environmental crises has been that technology would resolve them, climate change is so global and complex that no easy fix seems likely (even as its very existence is con-

41. Yuval Levin, *The Fractured Republic: Renewing America's Social Contract in the Age of Individualism* (New York: Basic Books, 2016), 2.

tested by some conservative lawmakers and citizens). Climate change functions as a kind of ominous, overwhelming, slowly unfolding catastrophe for those sensitized to it and seeking to address it. The end of the world as we know it via nuclear war may seem less likely today than it was a couple of generations ago, but climate change has replaced it as an apocalyptic threat.

There is an emerging awareness in all these developments around the world and across the neighborhood—spanning lines of social, cultural, religious, economic, and ethnic difference—that we are all yoked together, ultimately sharing a fate in a shrinking world. Yet American society also feels increasingly divided, fragmented, privatized, and disconnected. We are increasingly being linked together, even as we increasingly live our lives in isolation from one another.

The Loss of Common Spaces

The sense of fragmentation is due in part to changes in the built environment of American communities. Political polarization stems in part from a "Big Sort" of Americans into like-minded enclaves who tend to share their social class, culture, political leanings, and theological commitments.[42] American neighborhoods and towns have always had varying degrees of cultural, economic, and racial segregation, and today's divisions often have deep historic roots. At the same time, common spaces such as schools, voluntary organizations, clubs, and congregations in many American communities served to bridge populations—particularly by culture and class, if not by race. In today's America of fluidity, mobility, and choice, people often self-select into communities of those most like them. Of course, many who are on the lower income scale have little choice about where to live due to economic and social constraints; nonetheless, they find themselves surrounded by neighbors who share those constraints.

Polarization

This sorting corresponds with the erosion of the middle class, as well as the erosion of a shared culture shaped by a variety of public institutions,

---

42. Bill Bishop and Robert G. Cushing, *The Big Sort: Why the Clustering of Like-Minded America Is Tearing Us Apart* (Boston: Houghton Mifflin, 2008).

such as daily newspapers and broadcast media. For decades those print and television/radio media brought a common interpretation of the world into American homes. The rise of digital media has allowed people to choose from an endless array of cultural "channels," including participating in creating their own media products. This new media culture is highly cocreative and participatory, decentering traditional brokers of power and influence and allowing for remarkable collaboration.[43] Americans who would have been isolated in previous eras can now find community online. In this sense, it is a welcome means of connection. The downside of the social media is that they foster cultural segregation and the disintegration of common spaces and stories. Views are reinforced rather than challenged; it is easy to demonize those who are different; and we increasingly talk past each other rather than with each other. The result is a new microtribalism.

This has created a deeply polarized political environment in which what was once a robust center has shifted toward the extremes.[44] Americans now hold more strident ideological views than they did in recent decades, and they also inhabit differing geographies. Conservatives prefer to live in communities with more space between homes, for instance, while liberals like to cluster tightly together in walkable urban settings. Many American communities now reflect distinct subcultures that are disconnected from each other—not only in "red" and "blue" states, but in regions, towns, and neighborhoods whose residents conform to shared political, cultural, and ideological assumptions. The common spaces in which people of differing views, outlooks, and commitments intermixed and engaged one another are collapsing. Congregations once served this purpose in many communities, but today they can easily reflect ideological and socioeconomic homogeneity. Mediating institutions such as churches, clubs, and unions, which once connected people in society, are continuing to disintegrate, as people find themselves caught between the individual self and big forces of government and corporations.[45]

43. See, e.g., Clay Shirky, *Here Comes Everybody: The Power of Organizing without Organizations* (New York: Penguin, 2008); Yochai Benkler, *The Wealth of Networks: How Social Production Transforms Markets and Freedom* (New Haven: Yale University Press, 2006).

44. "Political Polarization in the American Public" (Washington, DC: Pew Research Center, June 2014).

45. Levin, *Fractured Republic*, 89.

Anonymous Neighbors

Mark Dunkelman describes this shift as the "vanishing neighbor."[46] Americans today spend more time with their intimates (immediate family and closest friends) as well as in an outer ring of loose social ties facilitated by social media and the Internet around specific interests. What is disappearing is the middle ring—traditionally the city neighborhood, village, or township—where voluntary organizations like congregations exist. Expectations for neighborliness have changed, from block parties and potlucks, sharing tools and child care, to keeping to oneself and not interfering in one's neighbor's business. Adults involved in intensive parenting spend more hours with their children, while these overscheduled children spend fewer hours roaming the neighborhood with their peers. Americans retreat to their messaging devices to connect with people on social media who may be geographically far removed, ignoring the people immediately around them on the bus, street, or at the playground. People can now largely avoid relationships with those of differing views.[47]

This represents a significant transformation of everyday life for American communities. The institutions that offered the common spaces for people to connect with strangers and neighbors—such as clubs, service organizations, adult sports leagues, and congregations—are all facing marginalization and organizational decline.[48] People are not present to one another in public in ways they were a generation ago, particularly due to the rise of digital devices. On the one hand, social media allows for connections unimaginable a generation ago, in which geography no longer serves as a constraint. The world of digital media is profoundly collaborative, creative, and participatory. At the same time, contemporary America is a place of constant digital interruption, continuously fragmented attention, and multitasking. The result is an erosion of people's capacity to be present for one another or to have face-to-face conversations. Empathy among college students has decreased 40 percent over the past two decades.[49] Children fight for the attention of digitally distracted parents. Conflicts are negoti-

---

46. Marc J. Dunkelman, *The Vanishing Neighbor: The Transformation of American Community* (New York: W. W. Norton, 2014).

47. Dunkelman, *The Vanishing Neighbor*, 111.

48. This was classically documented in Robert D. Putnam, *Bowling Alone: The Collapse and Revival of American Community* (New York: Simon and Schuster, 2000).

49. Sherry Turkle, *Reclaiming Conversation: The Power of Talk in a Digital Age* (New York: Penguin, 2015), 21.

ated through "texting" and "chatting" rather than in person. A woman in her fifties from Portland, Maine, remarked in an interview conducted by Sherry Turkle: "No one is where they are. They're talking to someone miles away. I miss them."[50] The paradox of a technologically interlinked society is increasing aloneness.

These shifts in the sociology of American community life are both disrupting long-established patterns of congregational engagement and being reflected in contemporary American church life. Many geographical neighborhood congregations find themselves disconnected from their immediate neighbors. The churches once functioned as connective centers for the surrounding area, but people no longer look to them in the same way. As the geographical neighborhood paradigm for ministry broke down starting in the 1970s, the attractional-lifestyle or affinity-based congregation arose to replace it. But those churches often played into the larger patterns of atomization in American community. They attracted those who shared cultural or ideological affinities rather than offering ways to build bridges between them. In this way, many congregations ceased to serve a mediating function in their locales.

Absolute Pluralism

Amidst all this, awareness of difference has become a hallmark of contemporary American life. There has always been significant cultural diversity in America, going back to precolonial days. As we noted in chapters 3 and 4, deep regional subcultures endure in America: they are rival "American nations" that have never really seen eye to eye and always construed such constitutive shared values and concepts as "freedom" differently.[51] Some of the diversity of missiologies in American history stems from these regional subcultures and their varying assumptions about human nature, purpose, and community. Such cultural differences are often overlooked in the analyses of contemporary cultural and political divisions. Historically, what it has meant to be American has always been contested: it depends on social and cultural location.

---

50. Sherry Turkle, *Alone Together: Why We Expect More from Technology and Less from Each Other* (New York: Basic Books, 2011), 277.

51. Colin Woodard, *American Nations: A History of the Eleven Rival Regional Cultures of North America* (New York: Penguin, 2011).

In the past decades, though, there has been a new emphasis on pluralism and difference that coincides with a rising anxiety and incoherence about what national and communal identity is and ought to be in America.[52] The cultural revolutions starting in the 1960s unleashed a new dynamism and diversity in American life, but they disrupted conformist patterns and were experienced by many Americans as oppressive. This brought liberation and new possibilities, despite the resulting culture wars that continue to the present day. The questions of unity and coherence haunt American life.

Plurality and Pluralism

Lesslie Newbigin argued that the fact of plurality must be distinguished from an ideology of pluralism.[53] There is no denying the great diversity of cultures, religions, experiences, and perspectives present in American communities today: that is the fact of plurality. Many, if not most, Americans would celebrate the dynamism and diversity that has arisen. At the same time, there is in late modernity an ideology of pluralism that governs public discourse, and it has evolved into a kind of absolute force both in privatizing religious faith and fostering an increasing fragmentation and disengagement from shared spaces, stories, and practices. Postmodernism challenged the premise that there can be any kind of shared metanarrative; every story is conditioned by perspective and power. However, the rejection of metanarratives is itself a metanarrative, one that has gained considerable power in shaping American life.

In describing pragmatism as a philosophical approach, William James once used the metaphor of a corridor with many rooms opening off of it. Pragmatism recognizes that there may be truth in all of these rooms, and they are thus worth exploring. However, in today's America, there is a new relativism that insists that we dwell in the corridor rather than in any one room.[54] Pluralism has been absolutized, rendering the individual self the ultimate authority and eroding the moral or spiritual cohesion of shared, external authorities. And the digital media have multiplied the impact of this phenomenon.

52. Todd Gitlin, *The Twilight of Common Dreams: Why America Is Wracked by Culture Wars* (New York: Metropolitan Books, 1995), 41.

53. Lesslie Newbigin, *The Gospel in a Pluralist Society* (Grand Rapids: Eerdmans, 1989), 14.

54. Bottum, *An Anxious Age*, 76.

The rise of identity politics in the late 1980s asserted categorical differences based on race, class, gender, and sexuality. But today's pluralism has gone one step further: identity is increasingly a matter of self-construction; we are expected to write our own stories based on how we feel. For instance, racial categorization has always been an ambiguous and problematic construct in American history, but it is now being contested in new ways. While some African Americans have long "passed" as whites in a racist society, can a white person choose to self-identify as black?[55] Who gets to decide? Sexual orientation and gender identity are now culturally assumed to be matters of discernment and self-discovery for many Americans. Traditional categories of gender identity are being revised to embrace greater ambiguity and hybridity. Culture wars are being waged over transgender bathrooms.

The Search for Identity

This is all taking place as established structures that traditionally defined personal identity are eroding. The family—not just the nuclear family but the extended relatives—once located people within relatively stable relationships that were not matters of discretion: you spent time with relatives because these were the social ties that were most proximate, cohesive, and significant. Your family's congregation or denomination was your congregation or denomination by inheritance. Your parents' farm or business was often the vocational legacy into which you would step. Their social location was largely your location. You were born into a neighborhood, township, or village in which you were known to neighbors. To a large degree, identity was defined by this web of ties (as oppressive and confining as they may have been).

These structures are disintegrating in today's America. Family has become a fluid and fragile thing due to decreased and delayed marriages, high divorce rates, and greater mobility. People are far less likely to live in a place surrounded by immediate or extended family, as they once were. The assumption is not that people will follow in their parents' footsteps vocationally, but rather that each generation will chart a new path, often in opposition to what they have known. Religion has shifted from being

55. Greg Botelho, "White NAACP Leader Rachel Dolezal: 'I Identify as Black,'" CNN .com, June 17, 2015, http://www.cnn.com/2015/06/16/us/washington-rachel-dolezal-naacp/.

your identity, which you pass on to your children (either by intention or more or less by default) to something you encourage your children to explore and decide for themselves. Furthermore, neighborhoods do not contain the same kind of relational connections they once did for many Americans.

This represents a profound disembedding of American life from traditional structures for forming identity, meaning, and community. Individuals are assumed to be largely on their own, which brings a whole new level of insecurity to daily life. Rather than receiving their identity from established structures, people must shoulder the burden of making their own way, choosing between a seemingly endless array of possibilities, and constructing their own sense of self, purpose, and belonging. Whereas identity was once defined by roles, now identity has shifted to the individual self, understood often in terms of emancipation from socially imposed roles. However, when internalized authority becomes the ultimate arbiter of social life and practical decision-making, there are no grounds for mutual recognition and unity.[56]

All of this represents something of a crisis of community in twenty-first-century America. The United States has always contained significant diversity and has struggled to live up to its own ideals of equality, democracy, and freedom. Minority populations have too often been oppressed, which remains the case today; and most Americans have no desire to recover the conformity and homogeneity of the 1950s. Yet there seems to be a deeper fragmentation and disintegration of the commons taking place now. Institutions like the US Congress, which are predicated on the existence of trust and collegiality, are breaking down. People are becoming disconnected from shared stories and structures that once gave life coherence, at least for many Americans. What has emerged instead is an "anxious tribalism" of exclusionary identities chosen and cultivated over against other groups.[57] How people will come together to seek and discover community and shared purpose is not at all clear in today's world, partly because the roots of this fluidity and uncertainty lie deeper in modernity.

---

56. See Adam Seligman, *Modernity's Wager: Authority, the Self, and Transcendence* (Princeton: Princeton University Press, 2000), 121–22.

57. Robert Hunt, "Public Missiology and Anxious Tribalism," *Missiology* 44, no. 2 (2016).

Searching for the Self

Charles Taylor and others have noted that modernity brought a new sense of priority on the individual self, understood in terms of freedom and expression.[58] In an "Age of Authenticity," the locus of identity and meaning has moved from established social roles to inner depths that must be explored, discovered, and expressed in order to realize self-fulfillment. Being true to ourselves means being true to our own originality—something we can only discover and articulate on our own.[59] Rooted in the Romantic period of the late eighteenth century, such a conception prioritizes self-determination through individual choice. Rather than settling into timeworn structures and patterns of community in order to have a fulfilling life, the individual is expected to discover her- or himself on a journey of experiences chosen from a range of options. All options are assumed to be equally worthy, because they are freely chosen, and it is choice that confers worth.[60] Authenticity means originality, which requires the rejection of convention.

This inward shift toward individual autonomy offered a new sense of freedom and possibility to those whose lives were defined by external structures over which they had little power. This is especially true of women and other members of society who were socially disenfranchised. The Copernican revolution toward individual authority and autonomy has been taken to an extreme trajectory, however, in recent years. Inherited roles and structures that once provided continuity, stability, and connection have been supplanted by a new emphasis on choice.

The Individual Self as Ultimate Authority

Consumer culture offers a seemingly limitless array of possibilities from which to choose, but this fosters a new kind of paralysis: infinite choice leads to the inability to commit long to anything or anyone, as we seek perfection somewhere other than where we are.[61] Fear of missing out due

---

58. See Charles Taylor, *A Secular Age* (Cambridge, MA: Belknap Press of Harvard University Press, 2007); see also Anthony Giddens, *Modernity and Self-Identity* (Stanford, CA: Stanford University Press, 1991).

59. Charles Taylor, *The Ethics of Authenticity* (Cambridge, MA: Harvard University Press, 1991), 29.

60. Taylor, *Ethics of Authenticity*, 37.

61. Turkle, *Reclaiming Conversation*, 183.

to the endless distraction of better options renders us restless and discontent—all the better for marketers seeking to feed an insatiable hunger for more. "Optionality" has replaced enduring commitment: "Haunted by the possibility of buyer's remorse, we dawdle on the brink, trying this, trying that."[62] The digital media environment heightens this effect, as the online self is driven by a desire to keep moving, to connect and disconnect, seeking momentary harbor in online "places," but these are rarely enduring or stable.[63] The online world becomes a space to try out identities—which can naturally be endlessly revised. Of course, options are not unlimited for anyone, and those who are economically and socially disenfranchised find their choices severely limited, despite the endless promises of "freedom" that the culture makes.

Rationality becomes instrumentalized in modernity, as the world is reconceived in terms of "resources" (natural, human, or otherwise) that can be manipulated and exploited for various ends. This leads to relationships becoming instrumentalized: people become a means for one's individual self-fulfillment.[64] Should a relationship no longer feel fulfilling, it can (should) be exchanged for another. In all this, *emotions* are primary. How do we make these choices that define our identities, our relationships, our lives? Largely through feelings.[65] The ultimate criterion for ethics, lifestyles, behaviors, commitments (such as they are) is how it *feels* to the individual. Late modernity has turned the reference points for meaning, authority, purpose, and community from external sources (God, a shared idea of the good, traditional communal norms and structures) to the individual self. Authority and ultimate meaning lie within each of us individually—there to be extracted.[66]

This makes the self a focus of insecurity and striving: "Because the modern world expects of each adult the capacity for personal autonomy and authority, the self is not only a laborer, it is an arena of labor (we 'work on ourselves'). The self becomes a project."[67] Such work requires strenuous

---

62. Thomas De Zengotita, *Mediated: How the Media Shapes Your World and the Way You Live in It* (New York: Bloomsbury, 2005), 80.

63. Rachel Wagner, *Godwired: Religion, Ritual, and Virtual Reality* (New York: Routledge, 2012), 127–28.

64. Anthony Giddens, *The Transformation of Intimacy: Sexuality, Love, and Eroticism in Modern Societies* (Stanford, CA: Stanford University Press, 1992), 49–64.

65. Taylor, *Ethics of Authenticity*, 38.

66. Taylor, *Ethics of Authenticity*, 26.

67. Robert Kegan, *In Over Our Heads: The Mental Demands of Modern Life* (Cambridge, MA: Harvard University Press, 1994), 234.

discipline, as reflected in the ascetic demands of dieting and fitness regimes, which promise a kind of sanctification. Social media profiles demand constant curation as a self is performed representationally to the public. The "selfie" has become the iconic gesture in a reflexive twenty-first-century era.

Consumer marketing has stepped in to fill the void, as traditional structures of identity, meaning, purpose, and community become increasingly tenuous. Within the last few decades, marketers shifted from trying to convince consumers of a product's superiority to trying to sell something far more profound: spiritual aspirations of meaning and belonging.[68] Brands have become markers of personal and tribal identity. Consider, for instance, Nike advertisements, which hardly need linger on the shoes or sports equipment they are ostensibly selling; the real promise is self-transcendence, tribal identity, performance, or heroic glory. Amidst the erosion of larger narratives that once shaped human purpose and community, people look to product choices to express identity. Brands promise wholeness, love, community, redemption, and even ecstasy, addressing deep emotional and spiritual longings.

Experiential Satisfaction

Miroslav Volf argues that in recent decades human flourishing in Western societies has been reduced to "experiential satisfaction."[69] As we have noted above, the eighteenth century brought an anthropocentric turn away from a transcendent God toward a new focus on the individual self and mundane affairs. This ethos retained a moral obligation to love the neighbor, an ethical universalism rooted in Judaism and Christianity that offered a framework for beneficence that spanned tribal and national boundaries. Yet, beginning in the late twentieth century, that framework began to be replaced by something far more self-referential: the idea that human life consists primarily in a series of self-gratifying experiences, shorn of any larger framework of universal human solidarity. Other people matter mainly insofar as they serve an individual's experience of satisfaction. This even applies to God, who exists to glorify the individual self (a remarkable inversion of

---

68. "The Persuaders," PBS *Frontline*, November 9, 2004, http://www.pbs.org/wgbh/frontline/film/showspersuaders/.

69. Miroslav Volf, *A Public Faith: How Followers of Christ Should Serve the Common Good* (Grand Rapids: Brazos, 2011), 59–60.

the premodern Christian idea that humanity exists to glorify God).[70] The result is a reduction of human purpose and meaning to aesthetics, shaped by a consumerist culture of endless desire.[71]

Life in the Immanent Frame

These cultural shifts are being expressed in varying ways and to varying degrees among different communities in American society. They are possible because of a much more basic transformation that has taken place over the past few centuries in how people in Western societies experience daily life in the world. Charles Taylor says that people in the modern West have generally come to live within an "immanent frame" as individuals buffered or insulated from what in previous eras (or in many other cultures today) would be a universe of cosmic spiritual forces.[72] Instead of depths outside us that we must contend with (think in biblical terms of demon possession or the "fear of the Lord"), the depths we contend with are assumed to lie inside us. Rather than praying for deliverance from adverse spiritual forces, as Christians in much of the majority world commonly do, people look to psychology or self-help to address their "inner demons." The sense that external, transcendent spiritual agency affects daily life becomes difficult to comprehend and recedes into implausibility. Sin is now sickness, and tolerance becomes the only remaining shared virtue.[73]

Social orders are seen as based in individual human preferences—rendering them fluid and negotiable—rather than grounded in some transcendent cosmic framework. Society can be continually "reformed" according to human choices, without disturbing a deeper sacred architecture that is given from beyond. This makes all patterns and structures of human life and community open for revision, deconstruction, and reconstruction. Legitimacy is ultimately grounded in the individual self. Self-empowered individuals are understood to be the primary agents of reshaping social orders, though, in reality, powerful external forces such

70. This is expressed notably in the Westminster Shorter Catechism, 1.

71. See James K. A. Smith, *Desiring the Kingdom: Worship, Worldview, and Cultural Formation* (Grand Rapids: Baker Academic, 2009); Graham S. Ward, *The Politics of Discipleship: Becoming Postmaterial Citizens* (Grand Rapids: Baker Academic, 2009).

72. Taylor, *A Secular Age*, 539–40.

73. For a concise exploration of these shifts, see James K. A. Smith, *How (Not) to Be Secular: Reading Charles Taylor* (Grand Rapids: Eerdmans, 2014).

as corporations, government, and the media actually condition and colonize life in society.

The Place of Religion

It is in this kind of shared experience of the world ("social imaginary," in Taylor's parlance) that the belief in God or the practice of religion becomes just one option among countless others for expressing oneself, discovering meaning, constructing an identity, or finding purpose or community. There is a "supernova" of possibilities from which to choose, and no one of them can claim priority.[74] There is nothing to keep us from trying one after another, in any order in which we choose, for however long seems to suit us. The immanent frame does not preclude the notion that some people would choose to believe in God and seek to order their lives accordingly. But it does make it difficult to imagine God acting as the primary force shaping human life in the world. If so, the culture forms us to look inward first, to our emotions, to sense God's presence. This inner emotional turn is a hallmark of both modern liberal Protestantism (e.g., Schleiermacher's "feeling of absolute dependence"[75]) and pietism, with its conservative evangelical and charismatic expressions.[76] Rituals and structures once understood as necessary mediators of sacred presence become optional add-ons for what is basically an interiorized reality.

We thus see approaches to worship in contemporary evangelicalism designed primarily to bring individuals into an experience of emotional intimacy with God. Congregations affirm the glorification of the self and emphasize personal choice, all in the name of a "personal relationship with Jesus"—a framing that assumes modernity's individualism. Liberal Protestant churches have absorbed these cultural currents just as deeply when they embrace pluralism and relativism and encourage their members to chart their own way and pick and choose what to believe. Their engagement with social justice often has little imagination for God's agency in the world. Instead, it is up to the church to "build the kingdom of God" (something

---

74. Taylor, *A Secular Age*, 300.

75. Friedrich Schleiermacher, *On Religion: Speeches to Its Cultured Despisers*, trans. John Oman (Louisville: Westminster John Knox, 1994).

76. For a treatment of contemporary evangelicalism that highlights this emotional dimension, see T. M. Luhrmann, *When God Talks Back: Understanding the American Evangelical Relationship with God* (New York: Alfred A. Knopf, 2012).

Jesus never tells his followers to do), as if it were a grand engineering project.[77] Congregations position themselves to attract a niche market of those who share cultural, socioeconomic, political, and ideological affiliations. In this way, they are just one more option within the supernova of endless consumer choices, tailored for various microtribes.

Searching for Meaning

We should note that this turn toward immanence and individual self-empowerment has a genuinely freeing dimension, particularly given the fact that the rituals and mediating structures of religious transcendence have historically been in patriarchal hands. But the downside is that everyday life can seem disenchanted, drained of transcendent reference points, and emptied of intrinsic cosmic meaning in the immanent frame.[78] Meaning must then be constructed; but since this is assumed to be an essentially individualized process, common stories no longer exercise their holding power over communities in ways they once did. We are each, individually, on our own to compose meaning, and our attempts to solemnize moments of passage in our lives can come to feel flat. Meaning is a fragile thing. Douglas Porpora argues that, as the cosmos of Judaism and Christianity has been abandoned in American life without replacement, not only has belief in cosmic meaning withered, but even concern for cosmic meaning has withered.[79] Popular morality is full of negative strictures (e.g., "don't judge others," "don't be intolerant," and "don't treat others unfairly")—but offers no larger positive vision for human purpose.[80]

The malaise of material existence that people feel can propel them toward transcendence, but it just as often leads people to look within immanence for a solution.[81] One option is environmentalism, which, for some, takes the place of religion by offering overarching narratives and frameworks for understanding the world (evolution, ecology, climate science, and so on) and disciplines of ascetic practice (conservation, recycling, political

---

77. Darrell L. Guder, ed., *Missional Church: A Vision for the Sending of the Church in North America* (Grand Rapids: Eerdmans, 1998), 93.

78. Taylor, *A Secular Age*, 309.

79. Douglas Porpora, *Landscapes of the Soul: The Loss of Moral Meaning in American Life* (New York: Oxford University Press, 2001), 78.

80. Porpora, *Landscapes of the Soul*, 4–9.

81. Smith, *How (Not) to Be Secular*, 69.

advocacy, veganism, "green" lifestyles, and so on) that promise a form of sanctification. The search for purity is reworked from transcendent to immanent terms, with just as strong a sense of morality (perhaps even stronger). Or consider the popularity of CrossFit and Soul Cycle (particularly among those of the Millennial generation), networks of fitness clubs that offer intensive community, practices for personal transformation (rigorous exercise routines), accountability, and mutual support. Options abound in the immanent frame, yet few seem to hold transcendence and immanence in dynamic and life-giving balance.

Conclusion

What might the Spirit of God be up to in the cultural shifts that are taking place? On the one hand, many people find themselves inhabiting a twenty-first-century America in which they are fundamentally isolated, forced to invent a sense of self, purpose, and belonging. Everything seems fluid and fragile, as if no fixed anchor points remain. There is great "freedom" to exercise personal choice and self-determination; yet there is also the bondage of endless self-construction. The search for identity, security, and community—in other words, to find deep connection and a place to flourish—becomes a lifelong struggle.

Even as many established structures for identity, connection, security, meaning, and coherence seem to be disintegrating, the emergence of a participatory culture has a strong positive dimension. In some ways, this represents the outworking of one of modernity's deep impulses, which is toward communicative reason and democratic authority.[82] Grass-roots people are empowered to engage one another without traditional elite power brokers. Endless new expressions of creativity, connection, and collaboration are emerging. Populations that have long been marginalized and disempowered in American society have found new voices and authority, even as discrimination and injustice stubbornly persist.

There are huge opportunities for Christian churches to speak into the search for identity, purpose, meaning, and community that many Americans experience today. The divisions in the United States and the world, which seem bitterly enduring, call out for healing and reconciliation. In a

---

82. See esp. Jürgen Habermas, *The Theory of Communicative Action*, 2 vols. (Boston: Beacon, 1984).

country where people seem increasingly turned away from one another and separated into tribes who are too ready to point fingers or guns at one another—or to simply coexist without connection—the church has a powerful vocation to bring people together. In a moment in which many have lost a sense of hope or larger purpose, there is need for an alternative story that promises a different future.

But the assumption that people will look to established institutional religious structures to meet these needs and formally affiliate with them as in previous generations does not seem to be holding for many people today. Many who were once affiliated are abandoning these structures (whether through diminished participation or departure), and formally joining is an increasingly countercultural proposition for younger generations accustomed to very different ways of participating. Unless churches provide new ways of connecting with people where they are and of bringing them together meaningfully, they will continue to struggle and decline.

Contemporary America is a profoundly diverse, dynamic, and networked place, even as it is fragmented, disconnected, and fraught with conflict. The patterns of connection have shifted in many ways—from geographical neighborhoods and civic organizations to social media. The face of the United States continues to reflect more of the world through immigration, which brings a dazzling cultural richness into many American communities, even though some established citizens struggle to receive that richness. There is great opportunity for self-expression and autonomy, which can be profoundly empowering, especially to those socially disenfranchised. Yet this has been accompanied by a larger disintegration of social roles, structures, and norms. Much that was formerly taken for granted seems to be up for grabs in contemporary America.

Reflecting on what the Spirit of God might be up to with respect to these cultural transformations involves deep, reflective discernment by the church. That is crucial if the church wants to be able to sort through what to let go of from its past while courageously engaging the future that is emerging. (We return to this important question in the conclusion to this book.) In the next chapter we turn to an exploration of how the gospel of Christ might speak to this moment.

CHAPTER 9

Participating in the Triune God's Mission

Toward an Emerging Missiology for the United States

This book has so far explored the historical engagement of the church with its changing context and the insecurity and fragmentation of contemporary American life. The question now is: How might Christian communities faithfully participate in God's mission in America today? American churches (like churches everywhere) have struggled over the centuries to contextualize the gospel faithfully. Some moments have seen undercontextualization, the failure to incarnate the gospel deeply enough in diverse local cultures; other moments have seen overcontextualization, the accommodation of the gospel to culture in such a way that it loses its distinctiveness and critical engagement of culture. The great unraveling now taking place within late-modern culture creates challenges but also presents opportunities for us to once again recontextualize the gospel. The unraveling occurring in the church bodies that were shaped by Euro-tribal Christianity requires them to engage in systemic change with respect to their ecclesiologies, polities, and practices in order to participate in God's mission more fully.

Diverse Missiological Strains

It is important to bear in mind two things that we discussed in chapter 2: (1) the church is missionary by its very nature; (2) the gospel is multidimensional. The first one means that, on the one hand, it is the very identity of the church to pursue a missiological engagement with each context. Such a missiological engagement is deeply formed and given expression to in relation to the particular issues and power dynamics at work within the context. It is the ongoing responsibility of the church, through the leading of the Spirit, to discern how to steward its missionary nature with respect to its engagements within a particular context. On the other hand, the gospel—in relation to any context—is always multidimensional in that it has the inherent capacity to relate the mission of God to a variety of issues and struggles that may be present. Different contexts will lead the church to pursue different dimensions of the gospel as it shapes a missiological engagement. In addition, diverse churches within the same context will often pursue different missiological engagements depending on their social locations. It is always the responsibility of the church, through the leading of the Spirit, to discern how to steward the presentation of the good news of the gospel in relevant ways within a particular context.

In light of these two realities, participation by the church in God's mission in today's America would be served by critically reflecting on the legacy missiologies that the church implemented in the past. A summary of these legacy missiologies (discussed in chapters 3–7 above) is summed up in table 9.1. This table identifies six primary strains of the church's missiological engagement, all of which were expressions of its missionary nature. It also identifies how these engagements morphed over time in relation to the various phases of church life in the American story. The extent to which there were direct, or only indirect, connections within these missiological strains varies from phase to phase. What is important to note is that all the strains appeared in some form of missiological engagement within each of the phases. It is also worth noting that there appears to be one missiological engagement that had a unique focus in the most recent phase of church life: organizational success.

Table 9.1 Public Missiologies of the US Church over Time

Missiology Strain	Colonial Period	Frontier Period	Urban Growth Period	Suburban Success Period	Strategies for Success Period
Focus on Nation	Conquest to Civilize and Christianize -Established -Religious Freedom	Protestant Nation-building	Protestant America as Destiny	Civil Religion -American Dream	Christian America

Missiology Strain	Colonial Period	Frontier Period	Urban Growth Period	Suburban Success Period	Strategies for Success Period
Focus on Tradition	Maintain Traditional Faith -Immigrants	Maintain Traditional Faith -Immigrants	Maintain Traditional Faith -Immigrants -Withdrawal	Maintain Traditional Faith -Withdrawal	Maintain Traditional Faith -Withdrawal -Immigrants
Focus on Engaging in Missions or Mission	Native American Missions	Foreign Missions	Expanded Foreign Missions	Postcolonial Mission Evangelical Foreign Missions	Global Mission -Short-Term Mission Trips Foreign Missions Frontier Missions
Focus on Social Reform	"True" Christian Society	Social Reform -Morality -Slavery	Social Gospel -Urban Poverty -Temperance	Social Justice Liberation -Social/Political -Economic	Peace and Justice -Environment
Focus on Justice and Liberation	Pursuing Freedom from Margins -Slavery	Pursuing Freedom from Margins -Slavery	Protest and Liberation -Jim Crow Blacks -Reservation Native Am	Civil Rights/Liberation -Responding to AIM	Human Rights -Women -Human Sexuality
Focus on Revival and Renewal	Revival and Renewal -Great Awakening	Expanded Revival and Renewal -Second Great Awakening	Urban Evangelistic Revivals	Evangelistic Revivals Charismatic Renewal	Pentecostal and Charismatic Renewal
Unique Focus					Organizational Success

Often these legacy missiologies carried embedded assumptions that were quite different from the cultural contexts that the church was encountering. This often led to the problem of significant overcontextualization or undercontextualization. For example, some were marred by deeply problematic histories of colonialism and coercion; others supported too readily the nationalist agendas of the day; still others were used to try to stave off inevitable cultural changes that were affecting the church. On the one hand, awareness of this missiological history has led some churches to abandon attempts to steward a missiological engagement with the culture. On the other hand, a lack of awareness of this history continues, unfortunately, to lead some churches to pursue a legacy missiology that does not adequately take into consideration the changed cultural situation.

It is important to bear in mind three things as we pursue a critique of these legacy missiologies. First, it is important to appreciate the multiple creative ways that the Spirit has used the gospel through the church to address issues of the day. Second, we need to pay attention in order to

assess whether an adequate biblical and theological framing was operative in bringing clarity and focus to each missiological strain within each
phase of the story. Third, we need to pay attention in order to assess the
extent to which any missiological strain adequately addressed particular
issues within the cultural context without becoming captive to it. These
three dimensions bring us back to the issues of undercontextualizing and
overcontextualizing.

A Critique of the Missiological Strains

Focus on Nation

This missiological strain evolved over time, but there was consistently some
kind of expression of it that focused on the church's support of the national
agenda as it was being privileged by the state. This was probably inevitable
in light of the influence of the state-church tradition in Europe that was
carried into the formation of the church in the United States. The nation's
founders came to realize, however, that some kind of wall needed to be built
between the church and the state; so they approved the First Amendment
to the Bill of Rights, which prohibits the establishment of any religion as
the state religion while also guaranteeing the free exercise of religion. In
light of this separation, the United States developed what might be called a
"churched culture," which was in many ways a variation of European Christendom that continued to privilege the church within the broader culture.
This evolved by way of a number of expressions over time, but the basic
relationship of the church and nation was always assumed to be comple-
mentary. The dominant culture supported the role of the church in society,
while the church championed the role of the nation as serving the purposes
of God. Times of war, in particular, have enhanced this relationship, weaving together very closely the themes of God and country.

The great unraveling of both late-modern culture and the Euro-tribal
churches that is going on at the present time is leading to a changed situation. The last gasp of the battle for a throwback version of a Christian
America is presently being waged—primarily by Christian social conservatives. Given the trajectory of this missiological strain over time, it is likely
to fail. But there appears to be a continued appetite for some to make a direct association between God and country, probably best illustrated by the
almost ubiquitous functional benediction at the end of political speeches:

"God bless the United States of America." This symbolic rhetoric is intentionally ambiguous, leaving it up to the hearer to construe precisely what such a blessing entails.

We are coming to a new place in our history, a place where it will be both necessary and advantageous to develop a different missiological perspective of how the gospel is to be understood in relation to the nation. The church in the United States would be served by learning from the majority church in the Global South, where many of the churches have learned to live as minority faiths within their own national cultures. There has also been a long stream of American Christianity (largely Anabaptist) that has prophetically challenged the church's accommodation to empire and nation. It is long past time in the United States to biblically and theologically rethink the relationship between the church and any nationalist agenda. It is also long past time to discontinue the practice of tying together "God and country" and talking in terms of a "Christian America."

Focus on Tradition

There is always a close interrelationship between a church's identity and the practices and customs that become embedded in its life. While theology certainly plays a role in helping to shape identity, it is important to also understand the formative influence that these practices and customs provide in shaping a church's self-understanding. As new immigrants continued to enter the colonies (and later states), it was common for them to form faith communities that reflected the practices and customs they were familiar with in their home countries. This was especially true of first-generation immigrants, most of whom were just learning to speak English. In light of this language barrier, they typically built language-specific, ethnic congregations and continued to practice their faith in ways that reflected the traditions of their homeland. Focusing on tradition also became a missiological approach for those seeking to preserve their homeland practices and customs over time in the new land, where, in effect, they became a distinct subculture. This was the most common missiological approach used in the first phases of the American story, but it has continued throughout all the phases, especially with respect to new immigrants.

Another pattern became particularly prominent in the late 1800s, when a portion of the church withdrew from an existing denomination to form what they considered a more faithful church that was true to its heritage. There were some earlier examples of this pattern in the first phases of the story. But this strategy became especially prominent in the latter part of the nineteenth century, when different approaches to biblical interpretation led to the modernist/fundamentalist controversy: numerous congregations, or groups within congregations, withdrew to form new—more conservative—denominations. The twentieth-century story of the church in America has been filled with examples of the use of this missiological strategy. The rationale given was usually theologically framed: the mother denomination had departed from the true faith. But underneath many such withdrawals often lay a cultural conservatism on social issues that was reinforced by a theological conservatism to justify the withdrawal.

The first application of the missiological approach used by immigrants will likely continue into the future. Within socially and culturally marginalized communities that are forced to navigate the dominant culture during the week, maintaining a distinct cultural space on Sunday can be crucially life-giving. But perhaps there is an opportunity to have a different conversation with regard to the second application—withdrawing. The great unraveling of both late-modern culture and the current institutional expressions of Euro-tribal churches presents an opportunity to discuss anew how a church's heritage should continue to form its identity. The conversation needs to take place at a much deeper level with regard to a church's confessional heritage and organizational polity.

This conversation needs to explore to what extent these were initially shaped within the assumptions of a worldview of a particular cultural context that is quite different from the one we live in now, for example, medieval or Reformation Europe versus late modernity. Having this kind of conversation also relates to the "made in America" churches that came out of the Restoration and free-church traditions. They typically use a particular biblical understanding of organization to guide their life, but this interpretation was also shaped by the cultural worldview operative at the time each was formed. These conversations will be difficult to have, but they are increasingly essential if the church in America is to continue both to form and reform itself within its dramatically changed cultural context.

Focus on Engaging in Missions or Mission

Historically, the church has always sought to share the Christian faith with others, and the church in America was no exception. Many of the charters of the original colonies stated that one of their purposes was to evangelize the Native Americans; unfortunately, they usually put this into practice by trying to Europeanize the natives culturally. But the concept of the church engaging in missions took on new expressions after the Revolutionary War, when the modern Protestant missions movement gained momentum and mission societies began to be formed. This effort was expanded as the newly formed denominations created internal boards and agencies to carry out the same work. They paid some attention to engaging in what became known as "home missions." But it was at this time that the predominant emphases came to be placed on foreign missions, which also led to the unfortunate separation of church and missions; missions typically came to mean an activity conducted somewhere else in the world.

The primary theology that undergirded the development of the modern missions movement in the United States arose out of the Great Commission—Matthew 28:18–20. It was based on a high Christology and the *obligation* of the church to engage in this work. The inadequacy of the biblical basis of this understanding for the church to engage in missions in relation to God's mission has been noted by various biblical scholars and missiologists.[1] Foreign missions continued to expand well into the twentieth century, when a more substantive theological basis was developed with respect to a Trinitarian understanding of God's mission. As we discussed in chapter 7, it was during the 1970s and 1980s that there was a convergence in mission theology; unfortunately, there was at the same time a divergence organizationally between evangelicals and ecumenicals. This divergence continues to the present time: each of these traditions wrestles in its own way with the changed global church.

In recent decades, short-term mission trips have arisen as a primary way for congregations to pursue mission in contexts removed from their own.[2] While framed as "mission" trips, the great majority are in fact primarily cross-cultural partnerships or service projects.[3] Their transformational effect on participants and their benefit to the communities that re-

---

1. See, e.g., David Bosch, *Transforming Mission: Paradigm Shifts in Theology of Mission* (Maryknoll, NY: Orbis, 1991), 6, 65–68.

2. It has been conservatively estimated that over 1.6 million Americans participate in these trips each year, many of them youth. See Robert Priest, Terry Dischinger, Steve Rasmussen, and C. M. Brown, "Researching the Short-Term Mission Movement," *Missiology: An International Review* 34, no. 4 (2006): 431–50

3. Michael Goheen, *Introducing Christian Mission Today* (Downers Grove, IL: IVP Academic, 2014), 432.

ceive them are ambiguous. They can readily fall into the trap of a kind of "service tourism."[4]

The changed situation with the two great unravelings presents an opportunity to have a different conversation, one that moves beyond the typical categories of "church" and "mission/missions"—as if these were two different things. We need to reenter the conversation in the 1960s about the church being missionary by nature (a conversation that ended too soon) and continue the conversation initiated in the 1990s about the missional church, where the focus was on God's mission having a church. This will, first of all, help churches in America take seriously their own contexts as mission locations. Second, it will help bring to an end the incessant effort to fix the church, and will instead focus on trying to understand the content and meaning of the gospel in all of its dimensions within a particular cultural context.

Focus on Changing the Social Order

There is a missiological strain in the gospel that causes the church to seek to remake the social order in some way in order to reflect more fully what the Bible teaches. The Puritans pursued this missiological engagement by initially seeking to bring about the perfectibility of believers in their efforts to construct a Christian society. By the early 1800s, this evolved into addressing social issues, such as Christians living moral lives on the rugged and often lawless frontier. But the signature issue of the time that called for a change in the social order was the abolition of slavery. By the late 1800s, this focus coalesced around a social gospel that used a postmillennial eschatology to promote the scientific and technological progress of the era as the realization of the kingdom of God on earth. During that same phase there was another focus that was more specific, building on previous efforts: it was the Temperance movement, which eventually led to the passage of a Prohibition amendment, where Protestant white churches won the battle but lost the war in terms of being able to actually manage the broader culture. By the middle of the twentieth century, the focus had shifted to addressing issues of economic justice within the social order, often coalescing with themes in the civil rights movement.

4. Miriam Adeney, "Shalom Tourist: Loving Your Neighbor While Using Her," *Missiology: An International Review* 34, no. 4 (2006): 463-76.

By the late twentieth century, the focus shifted again—to issues related to the environment.

The changing agenda for this missiological strain illustrates the contextuality and translatability of the gospel. Issues emerge and change over time, and the church's instinct in living out the gospel is to take up these issues and seek to address them as they evolve. It is crucial to note the capacity of the church to respond to issues of injustice, both within the church and within the broader society. But the downside of focusing on one particular issue too narrowly is a failure to pursue it in relationship with other strains that are inherent within the gospel.

Focus on Justice and Liberation

The gospel also has a strain within it that works from the margins to challenge and seek to change the social order. This is parallel to the focus on changing the social order but different in terms of the social location of the church that is pursuing it. When churches seek change in the social order, they often have ready access to the existing system to pursue the desired change, for example, passing laws. When churches are oppressed or excluded by the existing system from making desired changes, they need to pursue a different kind of missiological engagement. This was especially true with respect to the enslavement of the black population and the government's use of armed conflict as the policy of choice in controlling the Native American population. In both examples, change had to be initiated from the margins, which usually required great courage and which also was usually fiercely resisted by the dominant cultural and political system, including much of the white church.

This missiological strain is evident within every phase of the story of the church in the United States. However, the focus of what was being challenged changed over time. For example, the African American experience moved from a system of legalized slavery to legalized sharecropping and then to a Jim Crow system of limited access to political and economic power. But the process was always the same: the African American church had to challenge and confront the dominant cultural system in order to change it. The biblical and theological challenge was how to pursue this strategy nonviolently in the face of violence being forcefully used by white America. A theological theme that came to prominence in the mid-twentieth century that supported this effort was *liberation theology*. The strategy pursued by the early civil rights movement reflected well the biblical motifs of a suffering servant and cruciform discipleship, embodied in nonviolent protest and calling on America to live up to its own ideals.

The church in the United States in recent years has experienced a number of challenges from groups of people who have been marginalized. One of these groups has been women, who have sought full access to the institutional life of the church; another one has been the LGBT community. The legitimacy of both struggles is usually disputed in the church, and whether one is using a biblical hermeneutic or a cultural hermeneutic is hotly debated. These debates bring the issue of the relationship of gospel and culture front and center.

What is interesting in the midst of the great unravelings now taking place is that white churches are increasingly experiencing a process of being themselves marginalized within the broader culture. We have already critiqued the missiological strain of trying to go back to recapture some kind of churched culture, identifying that as a cul-de-sac. What would be interesting for these churches to pursue is a missiological discussion of what it means to live as a minority community that conducts a faithful—and yet prophetic—life.

Focus on Revival and Renewal

Throughout its history the church has at times experienced fresh movements of the Spirit that we have come to refer to as times of renewal or revival. This was clearly evident in the early phases of American church history, when the church experienced the Great Awakening and the Second Great Awakening. There were other times when the Spirit appeared to be doing a new thing, such as the Azusa Street Revival and the numerous crusades that took place in the 1950s and 1960s. Typically, each new expression of what appeared to be the Spirit moving in a fresh way created controversy and conflict in the church. For example, Presbyterians divided into the Old Side and New Side parties in light of the Great Awakening; and into the Old School and New School parties in light of the Second Awakening as new evangelistic measures were adopted on the frontier. More recently, the charismatic renewal movement of the 1960s and 1970s often resulted in congregations experiencing internal division.

It is always a challenge for the church to discern fully and accurately such movements of the Spirit as they begin to take place. One piece of evidence appears to be that new spiritual energy is released into the life of the church. At times, such as the revival at Azusa, social divisions are overcome. Those participating in and supporting such a movement typically want to make their experience normative for everyone, which usually heightens controversy about the movement within the rest of the church community. In addition, these movements all too often become institutionalized into standardized programs that rely on technique to continue trying to re-create the experience of what took place originally—for example, the church that schedules an annual revival each year in the third week of August. On the one hand, the church needs to develop the capacity to allow space for such movements to emerge without too quickly moving to judge or condemn them. On the other hand, those involved in such movements would be well served not to judge or condemn those who choose not to participate.

Focus on Organizational Success

There appears to have been a unique missiological engagement that emerged for the church in the second half of the twentieth century. This occurred as the normative pattern of the geographic-denominational congregation was displaced by the attractional-lifestyle congregation. Denominations had previously had to adjust to geographical shifts taking place in the population; but they usually had several decades to do so, even as they continued to enjoy fairly high levels of denominational loyalty. But what had been increasingly and reasonably predictable for denominations to plan for in previous decades quickly came to an end. The rapidly changing culture that began to emerge in the midst of the social upheaval of the late 1960s to mid-1970s set into motion the need for a different missiological engagement of the church in relation to culture. This was a strategy for pursuing success by changing the church in order to engage a changing culture, and it became the dominant approach for the newly emerging attractional-lifestyle churches as well as for the existing geographic-denominational churches.

The church in America has continually defaulted into focusing on the church rather than realizing that it must engage more substantively the question raised by Lesslie Newbigin several decades ago: What would a missionary engagement between the gospel and modern Western culture look like?[5] The issue to be addressed is not *church and culture* but the *gos-*

5. Newbigin, *Foolishness to the Greeks: The Gospel and Western Culture* (Grand Rapids: Eerdmans, 1986).

pel and culture. As Alan Roxburgh points out, even the missional church conversation, which was inspired by Newbigin, has tended toward an ec-clesial default of focusing on the church and how to do church differently.[6] In many respects, it is easier to have a conversation about church renewal or church growth than it is to confront the ambiguities of contemporary culture.

The church needs to develop a missiological engagement with the culture of twenty-first-century America that moves beyond the impulse to find yet another way to fix the church in order to be successful. As we have noted above, what is required is a different set of questions about how the church is gifted and called to participate in God's mission in its time and place. This begins by recognizing the church's missionary nature. It requires paying critical attention to the cultural context and the faithful translation of the gospel to speak meaningfully in the vernacular of that context. It in-volves ongoing discernment of the Spirit's leadership as the church contex-tualizes its ministry all over again in its relationship with its neighbors. This calls for the development of a theological missiology that deeply informs our understanding of the church.

The Need for a More Holistic Narrative

We believe that churches should neither abandon nor diminish their mis-siological engagements within the United States; rather, they should re-new, deepen, and enrich those engagements through the use of a robust theological missiology. The most fruitful place to turn for developing such an approach is the triune God's mission as narrated in Scripture and the Christian theological tradition. God is a missionary God; God's mission has a church. Focusing primarily on the church's mission without a larger dis-cernment of the church's identity with respect to God's mission will get us nowhere. Instead, we need to place God's mission as lived out with respect to a holistic gospel into dialogue with the realities of contemporary cul-ture. This has the promise of yielding new paths for imagining the church's participation in God's life and love for the world, while also helping us to reclaim what is usable from the past.

6. Alan J. Roxburgh, *Missional: Joining God in the Neighborhood* (Grand Rapids: Baker, 2011), 31–55.

Rediscovering the Triune God's Mission

Renewing the church's identity begins with recovering the story of the triune God's life and love for the world—in other words, God's mission (*missio Dei*). That mission is about the forming and restoring of community through creation; the calling of Israel; the life, death, and resurrection of Jesus; and the church's witness to the new creation—God's ultimate restoration and consummation of all things. There is not space in this chapter to explore that mission in its full depth.[7] However, our intention here is to examine key themes that speak missiologically to the contemporary American cultural situation. Similarly, no one emerging missiology can address the full complexity of theological traditions and cultural contexts in America today. We offer this with the aim of contributing to a larger missiological conversation from many social locations, church traditions, and theological perspectives. We believe that a more expansive, more intentional, more diverse, and deeper missiological dialogue about faithful Christian witness and service in contemporary America is vital for churches in the twenty-first century.

In offering this constructive missiology, we draw from a variety of sources. Two of these sources warrant highlighting: (1) the renewal of Trinitarian theology that has taken place over the past several decades, providing a rich basis for reimagining God's life and mission;[8] and (2) the missional church conversation spawned by Lesslie Newbigin and cultivated initially by the Gospel and Our Culture Network in the United States, which has since expanded to include many contributors.[9] These conversations have

7. For fuller explorations, see Christopher J. H. Wright, *The Mission of God: Unlocking the Bible's Grand Narrative* (Downers Grove, IL: IVP Academic, 2006); David J. Bosch, *Transforming Mission* (Maryknoll, NY: Orbis, 1991); Stephen B. Bevans and Roger Schroeder, *Constants in Context: A Theology of Mission for Today* (Maryknoll, NY: Orbis, 2004). For a shorter treatment, see Goheen, *Introducing Christian Mission Today*, 35–113.

8. See Catherine Mowry LaCugna, *God for Us: The Trinity and Christian Life* (San Francisco: HarperSanFrancisco, 1991); Jürgen Moltmann, *The Trinity and the Kingdom: The Doctrine of God* ((Minneapolis: Fortress, 1993); John D. Zizioulas, *Being as Communion: Studies in Personhood and the Church* (Crestwood, NY: St. Vladimir's Seminary Press, 1985); Colin E. Gunton, *The Promise of Trinitarian Theology* (Edinburgh: T. & T. Clark, 1991).

9. See esp. the seminal book edited by Darrell Guder, *Missional Church: A Vision for the Sending of the Church in North America* (Grand Rapids: Eerdmans, 1998). We map and explore the missional conversation in Craig Van Gelder and Dwight Zscheile, *The Missional Church in Perspective: Mapping Trends and Shaping the Conversation* (Grand Rapids: Baker Academic, 2011).

been particularly generative in shaping our imaginations for how the gospel might speak to today's America.

A God of Communion

In John's Gospel, Jesus prays: "As you, Father, are in me and I am in you, may they also be in us, so that the world may believe that you have sent me" (John 17:21b). The Christian confession of a triune God (Father, Son, and Holy Spirit in traditional terms) emerged from the church's reflection on the God of Israel, Jesus the Messiah, and the Spirit that they experienced together in community. To say that God is triune is to assert a provocative thing: ultimate reality consists of communion, the shared, interdependent life of a community of persons united in love (2 Cor. 13:13). Jesus demonstrates this reality in his ministry through his deep and intimate relationship with the one he called "Father" (*abba*) and through the ongoing leadership of the Spirit.[10] God is not a solitary monad or impersonal force but constituted in God's very self by relationality. This relationality is predicated on difference: Father, Son, and Spirit are not the same, yet also not divided.[11] Their identities depend on their relationships with each other. This is classically referred to as perichoresis, the mutual indwelling and dynamic reciprocity of the three persons of the Trinity.[12]

God's life of communion is not a closed, inward one; rather, it is *ecstatic*— outward-reaching, generative, and creative. God creates the universe in love to share in right relationships of ordered difference and communion. Communion describes not just the inner life of God, but also God's vision for the fabric of creation. As the creation narratives in Genesis declare, God creates all that is and blesses it as intrinsically good: that is, possessing its own integrity and value for what it is, not just how it can be used (Gen. 1). This flies in the face of the modern instrumental view of the world as a collection of "resources" to be exploited. Modernity has formed people to see themselves as independent actors detached from their environment and free to manipulate the earth as they see fit. This way of seeing has led to both amazing technological advances and great environmental devastation. Contemporary environmentalism is correct

---

10. See esp. Matt. 17:1–8; 28:19–20; Mark 1:9–11; Luke 4:14–21; John 1:1–5, 14–17.

11. See John D. Zizioulas, *Communion and Otherness: Further Studies in Personhood and the Church* (New York: T. & T. Clark, 2007).

12. See Jürgen Moltmann, "Perichoresis: An Old Magic Word for a New Trinitarian Theology," in *Trinity, Community and Power: Mapping Trajectories in Wesleyan Theology*, ed. M. Douglas Meeks (Nashville: Kingswood Books, 2000).

in protesting the modernist picture of the world as a machine to be manipulated, and to insist, instead, on a holistic ecology of interdependence.

Humanity is created with a particular vocation: to cultivate creation collaboratively with God (Gen. 1:28). This includes naming, taking care of other creatures, and seeking the flourishing of the whole in relationship with God's ongoing creative work. The Fall is a description of humanity turned from trusting dependence on God toward isolation, self-centeredness, and estrangement. This leads to suffering, domination, and distortion of relationships (Gen. 3). God's mission begins with creation but unfolds biblically in large measure as a response to this predicament of broken communion. In a culture that has fragmented into absolute pluralism and hyperindividualism, the Christian story speaks of deep belonging as the bedrock of reality. Humans are created in a world of vast and delightful diversity to enjoy relationships of mutual flourishing (*shalom* in Hebrew) with their Creator and all that is. Our tendency is to violate that world by going it alone and using difference as a pretext for division.

The Christian vision of communion as ultimate reality is good news in a contemporary America that faces fractured community. A Trinitarian understanding of personhood affirms difference as the basis of relationships, rather than insisting on uniformity as the precondition of unity. Difference need not lead to division, as it so often does in today's world. Community, rather than isolated individualism, is the ground of being and the future of humanity. This is why the Bible depicts heaven as a city, flourishing in right relationships of mercy and justice (Rev. 21:10–14). The Christian vision for human life in the image of a triune God embraces created diversity reconciled together, that is, breaking down the "dividing walls" of social and cultural division (Eph. 2:14). The challenge of unity and reconciliation across difference is central amid today's pluralism and anxious tribalism.

A Community of Promise

God's mission of restoration in response to human mistrust and estrangement unfolds alongside God's ongoing mission of creation. This mission begins with ordinary, unlikely people who receive God's promise and embark on an adventure in response to God's call. Abraham and Sarah have seemingly been passed over and forsaken—old and barren, with no future to hope in—when God blesses them so that they might be a blessing to all (Gen. 12:2). God's mission through Abraham and Sarah begins with the command to leave what is familiar and join God on a journey of trust and patience that takes nearly a quarter century before the promised child arrives. It is a story laughable in its absurdity, but a story that stubbornly insists that no human situation is beyond redemption. The call of Abraham and Sarah sets a pattern for God's mission through the Bible: that is, God works through the particular for the sake of the universal, choosing a few for the sake of the many.[13] Those whom God chooses are neither perfect nor well qualified; typically, they are reluctant, unclear on the stakes of what God is accomplishing through them, and prone to errors—even big ones.

The people of Israel, formed as a community of promise out of the legacy of Abraham and Sarah and a motley assembly of freed slaves, receives the Mosaic Law as a way to define its life in distinction to its neighbors. Its identity as a people led by and dependent on God rather than idols is expressed through a calling to worship faithfully, to live justly, to provide for the widow, alien, and orphan, and to seek the flourishing of all (Deut. 10). Like the patriarchs before them, Israel demonstrates in its own history the ambiguity of what it means to be a people of covenant and promise by succumbing to idolatry and oppression just as the surrounding nations have done. God bears with them in love, pledging unconditional faithfulness (*hesed*) in the face of repeated betrayals, as God, via the prophets, calls them back to right living. Throughout this narrative God seeks restoration by working through a particular people to show forth an alternative human future to the world.

There is in this dimension of God's mission a provocative embrace of the local, particular, and ordinary. It is good news to affirm that God chooses regular, imperfect, and even unlikely people in a contemporary world in which many people feel caught in depersonalized and dehumanizing political, economic, and social systems and structures. Against powerful forces of empire, God claims and calls the forsaken—enslaved, vulnerable, and seemingly unqualified—to be agents of God's liberating mission. No matter how society categorizes or assigns value, in God's mission anyone can play a critical role. God's steadfast love overcomes our failures.

Entering the Local

Amidst Israel's oppression under a global empire, God joins humanity in the ordinary and local in the incarnation of Jesus. The incarnation rep-

---

13. Lesslie Newbigin, *The Open Secret: An Introduction to the Theology of Mission*, rev. ed. (Grand Rapids: Eerdmans, 1995), 68.

resents a turning point in God's mission to restore humanity to communion with God and all of creation. God participates with us, where we are, in the very ambiguity and complexity of daily life, under seemingly inauspicious circumstances, within a particular local culture, in the neighborhood. Jesus embodies humanity reborn, renewed, and recapitulated (Eph. 2:15): the cosmic order of the universe (*Logos*) present in a particular human life (John 1). In him the image of God is restored.

The narrative of the incarnation is not only a "stumbling block to Jews and foolishness to Gentiles" (1 Cor. 1:23). It also goes against the grain of modernity, which sought to locate truth in abstraction away from the local in a universal, "objective" realm. This is reflected in the built environment of many American communities today, where so much is made to look the same, in their standardized, homogeneous chain stores and homes. Technology has also transformed the contemporary sense of place through social media, both fostering participatory, democratized cultural creations and shifting many people's primary relational connections from the geographically proximate to the remote. Yet the incarnation speaks of God's life and truth becoming enfleshed in the specific, unique, and local. By embracing the particularity of one culture (e.g., first-century Palestinian Judaism), God proclaims all cultures capable of receiving (and distorting) God's life and truth while rendering moot any attempt to elevate one culture above any others.

Jesus comes to invite people to follow him as disciples, to abide with him in deep relationship, like branches rooted in a vine (John 15:4–5). Through this relationship with Jesus and in his presence, abundant life breaks forth (John 10:10). Participation in Jesus is participation in God's Trinitarian community of self-giving love, not for disciples' sakes alone, but so that they may witness to the reality of that love to the world (John 17:22–23). To be a disciple is to be a witness; following Jesus means being sent to show forth God's love to those who do not know it, in the power of the Spirit (John 20:21–23).

Incarnation is translation: it is the Word becoming flesh as a prelude to repeated acts of translating that message into every culture in every time and place.[14] The process of translation is integral both to the incarnation and to Christian mission historically. It is a dynamic, reciprocal engagement in which new insights into the gospel are surfaced as the Bible and

---

14. Andrew Walls, *The Missionary Movement in Christian History: Studies in the Transmission of Faith* (Maryknoll, NY: Orbis, 1996), 27.

the church's life and witness are translated into new vernaculars.[15] The essentially vernacular character of Christianity has not always been claimed deeply or faithfully in American mission history. One legacy of cultural establishment is the confusion between the gospel and a particular cultural expression of it, which compromises the church's vitality and witness as the cultural and social context changes. One of the central challenges for American churches today is to translate their life and witness into the cultures of their neighborhoods, which are often different from the legacy cultures of the congregation or the cultures of their own members.

Some recent missiological literature has sought to return the local to its primary place as a focus for congregations. These voices are calling for a fruitful turn toward the engagement of ordinary disciples in neighborhood life rather than trying to attract people from far and wide to drive to big-box-style megachurches or focus their mission efforts on distant places.[16] It is in the local and concrete, not the abstract, where we join up with what God is doing to restore community in Christ in the power of the Spirit. Such a neighborhood focus plays out not so much in organized church activities or programs, but through abiding and accompanying—cultivating relationships, hearing stories, and discerning God's presence and movement among the lives of neighbors. Out of these relationships and practices come opportunities for witness and service.

As we noted, however, in the preceding chapter, neighborhood is no longer a meaningful place of connection for many Americans today; or, if it is, it has become an increasingly homogeneous zone rather than one where social differences might be bridged. The twentieth-century organizational church paradigm, in which Christian discipleship was focused on staffing and participating in formal church programs, activities, and projects, is becoming exhausted. The shape of contemporary American life, with its incessant time demands, overwork, mobility, and constant connectivity, conspires against it. Simultaneously, those pressures also make being present to local neighbors difficult. Practicing incarnational presence in the neighborhood has become a countercultural act that runs against the grain of twenty-first-century American life. For some, going local reflects a craft

15. See Lamin Sanneh, *Translating the Message: The Missionary Impact on Culture* (Maryknoll, NY: Orbis, 1989).

16. See, e.g., Paul Sparks, Tim Soerens, and Dwight J. Friesen, *The New Parish: How Neighborhood Churches Are Transforming Mission, Discipleship and Community* (Downers Grove, IL: InterVarsity, 2014); Alan J. Roxburgh, *Joining God, Remaking Church, Changing the World: The New Shape of the Church in Our Time* (New York: Morehouse, 2015).

lifestyle of eschewing chain stores, shopping at farmers' markets, knitting their own sweaters, and brewing their own beer. For others, these are not economically or culturally viable—or even attractive—options. They experience their lives as constrained by powerful social and economic forces that leave them with little time, energy, or freedom to "go local" in this sense.

This tension is important to note in reflecting on incarnational mission. Turning toward the local and particular is at the heart of God's engagement with us in Christ and the church's engagement (as the body of Christ) with our neighbors. At the same time, it would be easy to turn this expression of "missional" into a lifestyle niche for a narrow subgroup of people who have already chosen to repattern their lives around the local and particular. The sociological forces that run against this incarnational approach should not be underestimated. When you add in the layer of social media, which both embraces particularity and can lead people to be much less present to their physical neighbors, engaging the local in incarnational mission seems complex.

The key question becomes one of discernment, echoing the lawyer's question to Jesus in Luke 10:29: "Who is my neighbor?" With whom are we called to be in relationships of witness and service? Our immediate geographical neighbors? Our neighbors on the other side of town who may differ socioeconomically or culturally? People across the globe with whom we are linked through technology, social media, or globalization? God begins with us where we are in the incarnation, and discernment also begins where we are. There are simply no easy answers to these questions; instead, practices of faithful attention to God's Word, to prayer, to one another, and to our neighbors are necessary for us to hear the Spirit's leading.

In a time when the late-stage capitalist narratives of standardization, homogeneity, and consumption are being challenged by a new focus on the local, the particular, and the "craft-made," the incarnation affirms God's indwelling in ordinary spaces and practices. The exhaustion of the consumerist-program paradigm of church offers a welcome opportunity to reclaim the incarnation and reenter the spaces of neighborhood life in simpler ways. The church does not need to compete with the entertainment and shopping industries on their terms. Ordinary disciples can indwell local relationships and spaces as Jesus did, and by doing so they can help American communities rediscover their connectedness.

The church as a covenant people who practice baptism, Eucharist, mutual listening, forgiveness, reconciliation, hospitality, simplicity, Sabbath, and service has a powerful vocation in restoring community life in American neighborhoods. Practices of community life are being lost in many places in American life today. Americans are turning away from each other, without the practices or spaces for shared life, especially across social and cultural differences. Americans' capacity to listen to one another seems to be eroding. There is little space and less time for being present to one another, for abiding together. The church has an opportunity to deepen its own engagement in Jesus's Way by focusing on such core practices and sharing them with the neighborhood.

The Leadership of the Spirit

Disciples in the New Testament are often surprised to discover that the Spirit of God is out ahead of them in mission, already at work in the lives of the neighbors to whom they are sent. Peter is challenged to discover that the Spirit is present in the household of Cornelius, a Gentile, forcing him to reinterpret his understanding of the sacred and profane (Acts 10). Paul, Barnabas, Timothy, and others are guided by the Spirit in their cross-cultural missionary journeys. Jesus even affirms the exorcisms done by someone outside his circle of followers: "Whoever is not against you is for you" (Luke 9:50).

It is in the power of the Spirit that we participate in God's mission. The Spirit is the Christian way of talking about God's presence and agency in the here and now. Many churches in Western cultural contexts have lost an imagination for the Spirit due to the effects of modernity.[17] They struggle to imagine God acting in their midst or in the world around them. Or if they recognize the Spirit at all, it is in a primarily interiorized sense—that is, within the heart of the believer. The Spirit does indeed work there. However, biblically speaking, the Spirit also works *in between* people in public, forming and restoring community in patterns of justice and mercy. This public dimension of the Spirit recurs throughout the biblical narrative, from the Spirit's activity in creation, through the raising up of leaders in Judges, to the call and empowerment of the prophets. Jesus is a concrete bearer of the Spirit. The church is animated by the Spirit from Pentecost onward as it witnesses to God's ultimate future of restoration and communion.[18]

---

17. See Michael Welker, *God the Spirit* (Minneapolis: Fortress, 1994), 1–49.

18. See Anthony C. Thiselton, *The Holy Spirit—in Biblical Teaching, through the Centuries, and Today* (Grand Rapids: Eerdmans, 2013), 3–94.

The Holy Spirit is the key to interpreting God's expansive ongoing work of creating and reconciling in the church and world. The Spirit moves within the church and also beyond it. Joining God's incarnational movement into the neighborhood begins with discerning the Spirit's gifts and the Spirit's call for each disciple personally—and for Christian communities corporately. The Spirit brings energy, lifts people beyond themselves, unifies communities that are caught in doubt, despair, and anxiety, and opens up new relationships of flourishing characterized by forgiveness and restoration. In the Spirit, the socially marginalized are empowered and given voice (Joel 2:28–29).

God's Reign of Reconciliation

God joins us in Jesus to participate with us in ordinary life and to announce God's kingdom or reign. Unpacking the reign of God is crucial for an emerging missiology, especially in a nation whose history includes various explicit or implicit conflations of national identity with God's kingdom. God's reign is "good news" (Mark 1:15) that brings a call to repentance, renewal, and trust. It is about restoring relationships through healing, forgiveness, mercy, justice, and grace, as Jesus demonstrates in his own ministry. The sick and disabled, who were cursed and ostracized in Jesus's day, are restored to community (Matt. 8–9, Luke 5, John 9). Outsiders (cultural and religious foreigners, prostitutes, tax collectors, and sinners) are included rather than rejected. The disempowered find a new voice and place. The lost are found, enmities healed.

The kingdom, or reign, of God lies at the heart of Jesus's teaching and work, for it points to a different order for human life and community. To confess God's reign is to recognize that powerful corporate and government forces that affect human life are relative. At the opposite extreme, the individual self need not be the ultimate authority. There is an anchor for human identity and community that transcends us, for in God's reign we belong to God and one another as participants in God's unfolding restoration of the fabric of humanity.

The kingdom of God remains a contested missiological concept in American life today, as it has been historically. Behind this lies the Constantinian legacy of cultural, social, and political establishment of the church in America. Deep in the founding myths of the United States is the idea that America was a promised land that was exempt from the sinful complications of European history, a place where human community could be perfected and the kingdom of God realized on earth. This began as an explicit theological narrative for the Puritans, but it morphed into various iterations over time, including the Social Gospel, which combined progressive socialist economics and politics with postmillennial eschatology. As the twentieth century unfolded, what began as a kingdom-focused Social Gospel gradually lost awareness of the king and became secularized: it looked primarily to the government to bring about justice and peace. Alternatively, a counterstream of premillennial eschatology has understood the kingdom as a heavenly reality that people are inducted into through faith in Christ, with little hope of the kingdom becoming manifest on earth until the apocalyptic end times. Such a missiology has naturally tended to focus on otherworldly concerns rather than on efforts to ameliorate society.

The search for a more holistic view of the kingdom of God has led a younger generation of progressive evangelicals to embrace social justice as the primary lens through which to interpret God's reign. Like mainline Protestant and Roman Catholic liberals before them, these evangelicals construe the good deeds that foster the common good of society in terms of kingdom work. On the one hand, recognizing the social dimension of the gospel is vital, as God's reign is not just over individuals, but over the whole of the cosmos. The danger, of course, is the secularization of the kingdom. What distinguishes a church's missionary efforts for social justice, equality, or peace from that of any other nonprofit voluntary organization in society—or even government, for that matter?

The result (as has been acutely true in the liberal mainline churches) can be a loss of ecclesial identity. The church is legitimated on the instrumental terms of modernity as an organization that contributes to the common good by doing good works, offering moral uplift to its members, and producing or passing on an artistic and cultural heritage.[19] However, the larger narrative of God as the ultimate authority in heaven and earth and of God's rule being brought into history in order to restore all of creation, is lost. It is easy to bypass church entirely when there are countless nonprofit organizations offering opportunities to do good.

The conservative-evangelical wing of American Christianity has also been captive in many ways to modernity through its own instrumental ec-

---

19. Sociologist Mark Chaves argues that the primary activity of American congregations is to perpetuate cultural traditions of worship and the arts. See Chaves, *Congregations in America* (Cambridge, MA: Harvard University Press, 2004).

clesiologies and tendency to disregard tradition in favor of techniques to grow the church. The presumption that the early church can be re-created through the correct strategies is a deeply modern one. The kingdom of God can similarly default into a project for human effort and ingenuity, accomplished through the latest program, marketing strategy, or charismatic leader. Political mobilization to return America to a presumed historic Christian national identity has been part of this impulse.

American Christianity remains deeply captive to Constantinian conceptions of the kingdom, both in progressive social justice and Religious Right versions, which function as mirror images of each other.[20] Both assume on some level that the United States should be an essentially Christian society, or that the kingdom of God should be coterminous with the nation. The primary alternative has been an anti-Constantinian (largely Anabaptist) identification of the kingdom with the church.[21] This stream, influenced particularly by John Howard Yoder, has made an important contribution by reclaiming a sense of the church's distinct identity as a community practicing radical discipleship that resists captivity to the forces of empire.[22] It remains one of the most cogent protests against the nationalist missiological stream, whose roots lie deep in American history.

Emphasizing the distinctive practices of Christian community is crucial (something we will explore later in this book as we reflect on steps the churches might take to discover a faithful future). At the same time, when the reign of God is identified primarily with the church, it is easy to idealize the local church and its members. Beautiful theological ideas of the church embodying the kingdom can be difficult to square with the far more complicated reality that sociological studies reveal of the empirical church as a body of people holding and practicing far more ambiguous, hybrid, and diffuse faith practices and beliefs. God's rule over all of creation—and the Spirit's movement in the broader world—can also be eclipsed from view.

The relationship between God's reign, the church, and the world might be construed within two overlapping biblical themes: *abiding*, which is central to John's writings, and *participation*, which appears particularly

---

20. James Davison Hunter, *To Change the World: The Irony, Tragedy, and Possibility of Christianity in the Late Modern World* (New York: Oxford University Press, 2010).

21. Examples include Stanley Hauerwas and William H. Willimon, *Resident Aliens: Life in the Christian Colony* (Nashville: Abingdon, 1989); Scot McKnight, *Kingdom Conspiracy: Returning to the Radical Mission of the Local Church* (Grand Rapids: Brazos, 2014).

22. John Howard Yoder, *The Politics of Jesus* (Grand Rapids: Eerdmans, 1972).

in Paul's writings.[23] The church as the body of Christ abides through the Spirit in God's life in Jesus, an abiding that is expressed through practices of discipleship and witness (John 15–20). To be a disciple is to live in—and to share—the light (John 3:16–21; 8:12). The church as the body of Christ is incarnationally present in the world, dwelling in and among the neighborhood (John 1:14), participating in life there, but possessing a distinct identity through its rootedness in Jesus. It is in—but not of—the world (John 17:16).

Paul similarly talks about being "in Christ" (Rom. 6:3; 8:1–2; 2 Cor. 5:17), a new identity through the power of the Spirit that frees us to live differently from the world. In Christ, God shares in our life and suffering, redeeming us by the cross and making us new creations (Rom. 6:3–8; 2 Cor. 5:17). This sharing in Christ (koinonia: participation or communion) is integral to both discipleship and witness. Even as Christians participate in the lives of their neighbors, their rootedness and sharing in God's life frees them to live and love as bearers of God's peace. The church participates both in God's life and in the life of the neighborhood, neither absorbed by the world nor isolated from it; its missionary vocation is grounded in this deep sharing or abiding.

Integral to the coming reality of the kingdom is reconciliation—the restoration to right relationships of those estranged—and the redemption of the whole of life. Reconciliation is a vital missiological theme in a fragmented and divided America that is full of diversity and long legacies of oppression and violence. Paul describes his ministry as being an ambassador for the God who reconciles us and makes us new creations in Christ (2 Cor. 5:16–20). Reconciliation, as Emmanuel Katongole and Chris Rice describe it, is a journey of pilgrimage, relocation, and confession. It means being willing to follow and search, like Abraham and Sarah, to slow down long enough to hear the cry of suffering, and to seek God's forgiveness and grace. It displaces people from centers of privilege and demands that they unlearn speed, distance, and innocence in order to be restored to right relationships with each other.[24]

Modernity promised that the market and the nation-state would provide security and prosperity for all. In the twentieth century, this coalesced

---

23. See Michael J. Gorman, *Becoming the Gospel: Paul, Participation, and Mission* (Grand Rapids: Eerdmans, 2015).

24. Emmanuel Katongole and Chris Rice, *Reconciling All Things: A Christian Vision for Justice, Race, and Healing* (Downers Grove, IL: InterVarsity, 2008), 77–91.

as the American middle-class dream. Yet these promises are unraveling. To reenter the biblical narratives of the reign of God is to discover a different orientation for human community and authority. God's rule or reign is not coterminous with governments and empires, as Jesus's refusal to conform to his own people's messianic expectations reveals. It is instead a dynamic force through which God works to gather and govern a people for an alternative future. The reign is manifest in small things and surprising places; it is hidden and partially revealed; it unfolds in the midst of the ordinary.

Cruciform Mission

Reconciliation is possible only because God has stepped into the very midst of human enmity, violence, mistrust, and betrayal and has absorbed those forces in his own body on the cross without passing them on. God goes where no one wants to go in the crucifixion—the most depraved, shameful, humiliating places of human existence—in order to join us there and break the cycles of violence and retribution, restoring us to community with God. It is only because of this restoration to community with God that reconciliation with others becomes possible (Rom. 5:1–11).

The cross is about a dramatic decentering of power in order to empower the powerless. God comes in vulnerability and passivity, succumbing to human sin, so that humans might no longer be bound by that sin (2 Cor. 5:21). How ironic it is, then, that American Christians have used power to coerce others in the name of the gospel. Christian mission must be cruciform or it does not reflect Christ. The cross takes the incarnation to another level of depth in understanding the character of the triune God's mission and the church's participation in that mission. Mission patterned in the way of the cross requires a new humility and willingness to share power, in which space is opened up for neighbors to be heard and embraced. The church's establishment posture often focused on getting people to join the church on its terms, in its spaces. In that paradigm, the church retains power and privilege. But on the cross, Jesus goes to Golgotha, the place of the godforsaken, and he joins with those who are outcast and suffering there.[25] If we want to find Jesus in our neighborhoods, the seemingly godforsaken places are where we should begin.

25. See Jürgen Moltmann, *The Crucified God: The Cross of Christ as the Foundation and Criticism of Christian Theology* (Minneapolis: Fortress, 1993).

In a secular age, it is easy for American Christians to forget that reconciliation is not a human work, that is, as if humanity just needed an inspiring example of self-sacrifice or a pedagogical lesson on how to treat our neighbors. Reconciliation is not a program, strategy, or project. The powers of mistrust, alienation, self-centeredness, and estrangement lie too deep within us, personally and communally, for anything other than God's deliverance to free us from them (Rom. 3:23–24; 1 John 1:8). In reducing sin to sickness or ignorance, modernity has assumed that humans can create a perfect, peaceful world on their own. Some liberal churches have operated missiologically as if educating people into the correct beautiful ideas about a pluralistic, inclusive human community is enough to somehow inspire people to bring about such a world. As necessary and vital as education is, it is not sufficient to accomplish that. On the other hand, some conservative churches have taught a premillennial dispensationalist eschatology that tries to save people out of the world rather than affirming God's redemption of the whole cosmos, which begins in the here and now.

To confess the crucified God is to name clearly the deep brokenness in the human condition and in human community. There is no need for superficial self-affirmation that denies the estrangement that lies within and between us. Yet God joins us precisely there—on the cross—in the worst of human circumstances. God does not abandon us to work it out on our own, but steps into human suffering and violence to absorb and transform it. Being joined to the Christ who suffers with us means sharing in the new creation he offers as a gift to us and all people.

Resurrection Hope

The incarnation and cross mean little without the resurrection. Jesus is raised from the dead in the power of the Spirit as a tangible sign of our future restoration to community with God and with all who share in that promise (1 Cor. 15). The resurrection is a demonstration of God's power over the forces of evil, estrangement, violence, torture, and sin. It is about the healing of human relationships with God and others.

Resurrection hope is about a promised future that differs markedly from contemporary American culture's sense of time. The modern myth of progress, by which humanity will become increasingly perfected through the use of reason and technology and thereby escape the powers of sin, death, and suffering, has become less and less plausible in a world torn by violence and division. The eschatological promises of modernity, where the whole world will be joined under universal (Western) values of equality, democracy, and self-determination—thereby ending war forever—are collapsing. But late-modern secular culture offers no alternative. People face nihilism as these deep narratives of progress run aground.

Resurrection hope that passes through the cross paints a very different picture, one that honestly names the brokenness of the human condition but offers a path forward that does not depend on human self-construction or striving. Ultimately, resurrection hope is about *gift*, the coming from beyond us of a power to deliver and restore that does not depend on our own strength to accomplish it. Indeed, such a gift comes precisely into our weakness and vulnerability (2 Cor. 4).

Grace (or gift) is a strange concept in a culture of self-justification and self-authorship. Contemporary America tends to construe the self as an object of constant self-improvement and striving, a kind of project that we never cease to work on. Central to this project is the construction of identity, meaning, purpose, and community—attributes that are no longer provided by established structures in American life as they once were. To assert grace as ultimate reality is to confess that our worth is a free gift: all people are immeasurably valuable in God's eyes, and there is nothing we can do to earn or lose that value. Our identities in Christ are not based on personal striving or on the markers of culture, gender, and class that are used to categorize and rank people in society's hierarchies. We are adopted as a gift into a new human family made up of people from every tribe, nation, and class, where creaturely identities are penultimate to sharing new life in the Spirit (Gal. 3:28; Eph. 2:11–22).

Americans are strangely obsessed with purity and sanctification, especially for a culture that has embraced modernity's "liberation" from tradition and constraint, which we can see in various ascetic regimes that focus on the body (dieting, fitness, veganism, "purges," organic food, and so on), on the environment (conservation, recycling, alternative energy), and on technology (campaigns to expose the secrets of corporations, governments, or public figures, social media shaming, and "transparency"). People struggle to feel at home with the world and with themselves. Within this secularized, immanent view, there is little basis for forgiveness and no grace. There are few resources for reconciliation or restoration; instead, there is much moralizing, judgment, and self-righteousness.

It is easy, in this framework, for people to turn against one another in judgment, or for society to fracture into competing cultural tribes. Coexistence underwritten by tolerance becomes the primary goal, with no stories, spaces, or practices for learning deeper reconciliation and shared life from one another. Resurrection says that our future belongs together on very different terms: God's claiming and calling of people from every tribe and nation into a new community (Rev. 7:9). Sanctification is not something we can earn or achieve; rather, it is a free gift, a different way of seeing and being seen that changes how we relate to each other.

Community of Promise

The gospel of grace and the hope of resurrection are known through the local and particular, the ordinary, concrete, imperfect gatherings of disciples known as Christian community, the body of Christ. The heart of Jesus's legacy is a community of promise—the church. If the contemporary American church finds itself in something of an identity crisis with the collapse of Christendom and cultural establishment, clarifying who the church is and why it exists is vital to a renewed missiology.[26]

Understanding the church requires reentering the biblical narrative of Acts, where the Holy Spirit, who led Jesus in his earthly ministry, forms and leads the Christian community into witness.[27] The coming of the Spirit that occurs at Pentecost signifies a polyvocal, multicultural testimony to God's reconciliation of humanity in Christ (Acts 2). Ordinary people (the apostles) are empowered to shape a new story that builds on God's long faithfulness to Israel. That story of humanity restored in Christ is expressed not only in words comprehensible in multiple languages, but also in spiritual experiences of power and healing. It is accompanied by the sharing of possessions, prayer, communal study, and devotion (Acts 2).

As persecution and resistance unfold, the early Christian community is dispersed from Jerusalem across cultural barriers in the Mediterranean world. The Spirit leads in translating the good news into new cultural vernaculars. This process is more improvisational than planned out on the part of the apostles (see, e.g., Acts 16:6–10). It is characterized by ongoing communal discernment about the Spirit's call and gifts. Such gifts, as Paul's

---

26. See Cheryl M. Peterson, *Who Is the Church? An Ecclesiology for the Twenty-First Century* (Minneapolis: Fortress, 2013).

27. For a fuller discussion, see Amos Yong, *Who Is the Holy Spirit? A Walk with the Apostles* (Brewster, MA: Paraclete Press, 2011).

letters detail, are integral to the participation of ordinary disciples in God's mission.

The church is a product of God's mission, as well as a participant in that ongoing mission. It exists as the body of Christ animated by the Spirit to continue Jesus's ministry of restoration and reconciliation in every cultural context. Central to that ministry is the witness of baptism, by which new believers are incorporated into the promises of new community in Christ. The Eucharist embodies God's grace, healing, and provision as local bodies of believers share in a foretaste of the heavenly banquet. The Spirit's presence transforms the ordinary things of daily life (water, bread, wine) into visible signs of the new creation—to cleanse and nourish us. These sacramental practices point toward the restoration of community in Christ that is at the heart of the church's identity. Such practices of the gathered community are integral to the participation of the dispersed body of Christ in God's mission, for they are the things that make disciples who they are, the means by which Christians participate in God's love, grace, and reconciliation, and the hermeneutical keys for interpreting what God might be up to in the wider world.

Christians have answered the question of the church's identity in various ways over the past several centuries in American mission history. The church's identity did not require a lot of attention during the period of cultural and social establishment or privilege; it was assumed that everyone knew what the church was and what it did. It stood at the center of society as a force for moral and spiritual uplift and a shaper of culture. Its reach was assumed to be broad, reflecting the cultural power it held. This reflects the establishment ecclesiological legacy carried over from Europe, particularly by the Euro-tribal state churches.

The advent of denominations in America brought a new organizational identity as a corporate body focused on a purposive intent—in other words, a primarily *functional* identity. The church existed as an organization in civil society alongside others that accomplished certain goods for its members and the public. In the twentieth century this paradigm was explicitly embraced by churches that construed their identities in instrumental terms. For instance, Willow Creek Community Church's mission statement is: "To turn irreligious people into fully devoted followers of Jesus Christ."[28] Churches across the spectrum went through exercises of strate-

28. http://www.willowcreek.org/en/about/beliefs-and-values (accessed March 30, 2017).

gic planning to formulate mission statements as a way of clarifying their organizational identity. These were often legitimated within the dominant cultural narratives of secular modernity.

The danger of this approach is that in a secular age, the church's deeper identity of participation in the triune God's mission is easily eclipsed. The church understands itself as a nonprofit voluntary association of individuals who enter into a social contract in order to meet their self-identified needs or to do some good in society. The kind of theological discernment that shapes the church's life and witness in the New Testament falls to the background or is lost entirely. Human agency replaces the leadership of divine agency, rather than recognizing God's primary leadership and human participation. When the church reduces its identity to those terms, it becomes easy for people to shift their allegiances to another community that promises to meet their needs better ("church shopping") or to abandon engagement completely. The larger narrative of the triune God's life and love for the world becomes instrumentalized and colonized into the culture's predominant stories.

Recovering a life-giving and faithful identity for the church today lies in reentering the Bible's narrative witness to God's ongoing mission of creation and restoration. It is God's mission that has a church as witness to that mission. Identity is deepened through dwelling more deeply in the stories and practices of God's mission, through which we discover ourselves anew in a new community. This must be carried out in the ordinary, the concrete, and the local—among regular disciples where they are in daily life. Rather than focusing on defining organizational mission and goals, many local churches would be better served by shifting their attention to helping their ordinary members live more deeply into the Christian story and basic Christian practices (such as prayer, Scripture study, discernment, service, reconciliation, hospitality, Sabbath, and generosity).[29] If the era of the organizational church offering programs and projects for people to consume in their free time has exhausted itself, recovering an identity for the church as a community gathered and formed around the gospel and practicing the Way of Jesus (Acts 9:2; 18:25–26; 19:9) in the Spirit's power in the neighborhood offers a hopeful way forward.

---

29. See Dorothy C. Bass, *Practicing Our Faith: A Way of Life for a Searching People* (San Francisco: Jossey-Bass, 1997).

Holistic Mission: Being, Doing, Saying

It is out of being the church in this way that more holistic approaches to participating in God's mission emerge. American missiology has struggled in the modern period with a deep bifurcation between the verbal witness concerning Jesus and acts of justice and mercy for the neighbor. This is reflected in the mission history explored in the chapters above, where mainline Protestant and Roman Catholic missiology embraced an emphasis on justice and liberation in the second half of the twentieth century, while evangelicals emphasized conversion and church growth. Such divisions reflect the bifurcations of modernity, in which public "facts" are distinguished from private "values."

Of course, the biblical witness knows no conflict between these two dimensions of witness, nor do most Christians in other cultural contexts throughout history. In the twenty-first century, more American Christians are seeking to embrace a holistic approach to mission. Dean Flemming helpfully frames God's mission in the Bible as having three dimensions: being, doing, and telling.[30] Being the church involves practicing a way of life as a community that shows forth an alternative narrative and an alternative future to the dominant cultural narratives. The church embodies something by nature of who it is, which is expressed in how it practices its life together. Its life is anchored in God's ongoing reconciliation of the world in Christ.

That identity is, in turn, expressed by doing things in relationship with neighbors—acts of mercy, compassion, justice, and service. Such actions are not simply "ethical spirituality" or "Golden-Rule Christianity"—things that "good" moral people do in society. Instead, they reflect the deeper reality of God's reconciling the world in Christ. Because we have received compassion and grace, we are freed to share that compassion with our neighbors. God seeks justice for all and is bringing about God's reign on God's own time and through God's own agency (the kingdom of God is not a project for the church to undertake). The Christian community participates in God's work of reconciliation and justice in the power of the Spirit, which is integral to its identity.

The church must tell its story to neighbors in ways that are faithful to God and intelligible to those neighbors. Embodiment and actions without interpretation fall short. Saying—or verbal witness—is a vital and necessary

---

30. Dean E. Flemming, *Recovering the Full Mission of God: A Biblical Perspective on Being, Doing, and Telling* (Downers Grove, IL: IVP Academic, 2013).

dimension of Christian mission. Such witness must be grounded in deep listening to neighbors, in the demonstrations of love and concern, in relationships over time. To be an effective witness requires credibility, and one gains that in part by being and doing.

All three of these dimensions belong together. Now is a time for churches in the American context to cultivate a holistic and integrated approach to mission that, above all, recognizes God's mission as primary. For many churches, this means learning habits and practices that have grown unfamiliar. Churches that are oriented around social justice must learn to tell the story of Jesus. Churches that are focused on verbal witness must embody the grace of the gospel, as they point toward an alternative kingdom, in addressing structures and systems that keep people oppressed and estranged. In many places, this seems to be happening. Liberal churches are realizing that, without Jesus and a life-changing gospel at the heart of their life, they have no future. Conservative churches are embracing ministries of compassion and social engagement with new intentionality. Many recognize that the integrity of the church's mission must be grounded deeply in a distinct way of life and witness to the triune God.

Conclusion

Missiological engagement with contemporary American culture invites the church deep into its own biblical and theological narratives and embodied practices of discipleship. Biblically speaking, discipleship involves a deep and abiding participation in God's love through the power of the Spirit. That witness today must be holistic, speaking to God's rule over the whole of life, both personal and communal. This rule is cruciform, shaped by meeting humanity in the depths of its suffering. It offers the promise of hope in a cultural moment in which many alternatives seem exhausted and the need for reconciliation, forgiveness, purity, and the restoration of community remain strong. In the next chapter we turn to an examination of how the church might organize its life and leadership formation in service to participation in God's mission in a changing context.

CHAPTER 10

Church Organization and Leadership Formation for a New Missionary Age

The Contextual Nature of Church Organization

This book has traced the shape of church organization in the United States as it reflects the varying historical circumstances in which the church has found itself. This fits with the incarnational nature of the body of Christ. Christians have always borrowed, adapted, and transformed organizational and leadership patterns and structures from their surrounding cultures. This began in the New Testament period, when the church modified leadership structures from contemporaneous synagogues.[1] It has continued ever since.

In Part 2 we identified some of the historical patterns of church organization that emerged in the American context in each era. Many of these patterns were brought from Europe by settlers and adapted to the American environment. For instance, ethnic-immigrant congregations in the colonial period were organized along the lines of European state churches. Religious diversity in the colonies led to the formation of the denominational-organizational church as a voluntary association. Missions such as those established in the Southwest by the Spanish and the Praying Towns of John Eliot required Native Americans to live within colonial structures. Mission organizations such as the Society for the Propagation of the Gospel and Society for the Promotion of Christian Knowledge helped to spread the gospel throughout the colonies. Under slavery and after Emancipation, African

---

1. James Tunstead Burtchaell, *From Synagogue to Church: Public Services and Offices in the Earliest Christian Communities* (New York: Cambridge University Press, 1992).

Americans developed their own congregations and associations because they were excluded by white churches.

As America grew and continued to diversify in population, village congregations came into prominence as churches were founded across the frontier. Americans created the denominational form of the church to organize the growing systems of congregations. They also developed voluntary associations and parachurch structures for mission and social service, such as home mission societies and Sunday school unions. The geographic-neighborhood church, which had served so well for centuries, began to become obsolete in the latter part of the twentieth century, spawning diverse types of attractional-lifestyle churches (including megachurches) and their training networks as alternatives. Some of these were within established denominations, but many more were outside of them. New waves of immigrants have created vibrant storefront ministries and house church networks. In recent decades, experiments in the contextualization of congregational life in postmodern cultures have appeared.

The United States has been a hotbed of creativity and innovation in church organization throughout its history, and that process is very much alive today. This chapter reflects on the present period of massive change and displacement that is taking place among established church structures, which is impacting both congregational and denominational organization and leadership formation. In chapter 8 we traced how the many structures that once meaningfully connected Americans together and provided a sense of security, meaning, purpose, and community are now being disrupted or are disintegrating. In this chapter we reflect on what some of these cultural shifts might mean for how churches are organized and leaders formed.

The Rise and Fall of the Denominational-Organizational Church

As we traced in the historical discussion, denominations have gone through successive periods of development since the Revolutionary War as the American context has evolved. When America was predominantly rural, the village congregation served as the primary expression of Christian community for most Americans. As the United States urbanized and industrialized during the nineteenth century and into the twentieth, the city-neighborhood congregation took on greater prominence as the population began to move to cities and shift away from rural areas. After World War II, the suburban boom led to yet another phase of development as the church recontextualized itself in the growing suburbs. In each of these phases, changes to the population makeup and location had a major impact on the church. The dramatic movement toward urban and suburban population centers that came with mechanized farming put the system of rural-village congregations under stress. Its declining and increasingly obsolete structures remain across rural America as a legacy of an earlier period. Urban congregations experienced their own diminishment in the mid-twentieth century as parishioners moved to the suburbs; many of those congregations remain shadows of their former selves, even with the wave of reurbanization that has taken place in recent years.

What these various phases had in common was a geographic-neighborhood focus for ministry. By the late 1970s, church participation in relation to geographic proximity had largely come undone in the face of increased mobility, lifestyle preferences, decline in institutional loyalty, and multiple options from which to choose. Although most former geographic-neighborhood congregations still had a symbolic presence in a particular location because of their facilities, the logic of congregational identity shifted from geographic proximity to associational networks and members' cultural affinities and lifestyle preferences. This led historical-geographic congregations to engage more and more in targeted niche marketing in order to reach new members. They were joined in this by a plethora of newly founded congregations that sought to free the church from established denominational baggage; they, in turn, marketed themselves, for instance, as "community churches."

The Assumptions Underlying Denominational Organization

It is worth probing more deeply the basic organizational assumptions that have shaped the legacy system of denominational churches, as well as the newer attractional-lifestyle congregations that arose in the past few generations. As we noted in chapter 5, the organizational-denominational form of church emerged out of the earlier forms of the ethnic voluntary association and neighborhood congregations. Beginning in the early twentieth century, these congregations adopted an increasingly uniform denominational "brand" identity and offered a relatively consistent and predictable form of worship and programming provided by centralized denominational bureaucracies. Denominational adherents could visit a local church of their denomination in other neighborhoods or regions and find themselves right at home, with little change in the look and feel of what they experienced.

This model tended to assume a dedicated building, a seminary-educated and salaried clergyperson (in many traditions and contexts, though not all), a Sunday school using denominational curricula, a small staff, and denominationally sourced hymnals and worship resources. These practices became the norm of the "institutional" form of local church that emerged in the late nineteenth and early twentieth centuries. Rather than being locally educated and deployed, as was the case in many earlier paradigms, clergypersons were formed in denominational seminaries according to denomination-wide standards (often certified through uniform ordination examinations). Like interchangeable parts in a machine, they were understood to be capable of serving in any franchise outpost of the denomination. In the postwar suburban-church boom, there were even standard architectural designs for church buildings available off the shelf from denominational offices. In all this, the emphasis was on efficiency and standardization, fitting the "modernization" taking place in the culture at the time.

This model of church was underwritten by a business plan that was dependent on the tithes and offerings from members of a congregation who formally affiliated with and joined the denomination. While expressing the practice of Christian stewardship, this model also resembled the dues members would pay to a local chapter of the Rotary, the VFW, a union hall, or a garden club. The church provided a vital community gathering space for civic connection. Programming was sustained through volunteerism, particularly by women, who, after World War II, found themselves with greater time due to innovations in domestic technology. Pastors had a clear identity and role as religious professionals: they presided administratively over this operation and marked life transitions (birth, marriage, death) in their members' and communities' lives.

The majority of denominational congregations in the United States are still essentially organized according to this paradigm of church, which remains meaningful for some people, especially older generations, and in some pockets retains its vitality. Yet the cultural forces we described in chapter 8 are undercutting its foundations. The turn toward expressive individualism, the rise of social media, and the collapse of the neighborhood have diminished community institutions of all kinds. Many people no longer seek them as places of connection, as they once did. Spare time to volunteer or participate in church programs and activities has vanished for many people. Joining and committing financially to institutions as a formal member makes much less cultural sense to emerging generations than it did to earlier ones. The paradigm of a professionalized religious program presented by credentialed experts for people to consume stands at odds with a new participatory age, where co-creation and collaboration are highly valued. Many people seek to have a voice instead of just listening to a professional speak.

Obsolescence of the Denominational Franchise Church

For all these reasons, the denominational franchise church finds itself organized for a world that is quickly disappearing, and many denominations have seen their numbers and membership plummet in the past fifty years. During this period, the membership of mainline denominations—proportional to the larger US population—has dropped by between half (American Baptist, United Methodist) and as much as two-thirds (Evangelical Lutheran Church in America, Presbyterian Church USA, Episcopal, United Church of Christ, and Christian Church [Disciples of Christ]).[2] The members who have remained in these denominational churches are older and whiter than the mean of the US population. The religious groups in America with the greatest diversity have also been some of the fastest growing: Seventh-Day Adventists, Jehovah's Witnesses, and various Pentecostal denominations cluster high on the list; mainline denominations are among the least diverse and are, again, the most rapidly declining.[3] Yet the high growth rate of Pentecostal and evangelical denominations has also slowed recently, particularly among the white population. Despite aggressive church-planting efforts, the Southern Baptist Convention lost 800,000 members in the decade between 2003 (when its membership peaked) and 2014.[4] What Protestant growth there is comes increasingly from new immigrants, especially Latinos.[5] Like Protestants, millions of

---

2. See table 1.1.

3. Michael Lipka, "The Most and Least Diverse U.S. Religious Groups" (Washington, DC: Pew Research Center, July 27, 2015).

4. Bob Smietana, "As Church Plants Grow, Southern Baptists Disappear," *Christianity Today,* June 12, 2015.

5. Robert P. Jones, *The End of White Christian America* (New York: Simon and Schuster, 2016).

Roman Catholics have left the church in the past generation; but their overall numbers have been sustained, largely because of the religiosity of new immigrants.

Within a decade or so, as the older generation that currently sustains many of these congregations passes from the scene, there will likely be wholesale closures of congregations—and at an unprecedented level. In many denominational systems, a majority of congregations are already in crisis mode, struggling to survive. Even in places where greater numbers and momentum remain, participation is diminishing and leaders find themselves having to make do with fewer resources and reduced expectations for involvement. Recruiting people to staff volunteer committees and boards is more and more difficult, and the fall pledge campaign is a harder sell.

At the judicatory and denominational level, this has presented a huge crisis over the past fifty years for church systems organized to oversee and resource these franchise outposts. Waves of retrenchment have come one after another, and denominational and judicatory executives struggle to sustain the familiar old structures and patterns. Denominational church life has evolved into its fifth phase of becoming the "re-denomination" over the last fifty years. Many are consumed with reacting to crises in local congregations, with little ability to bring about renewal. Round after round of strategic planning, reorganization, church-planting initiatives, and attempts to hold leaders accountable to growth measures fail to make much of a difference to the broader situation. Meeting the expectations of older members, who recall times when this model of church flourished, becomes increasingly difficult as younger generations seek to participate and connect differently. Finding established expressions of the church inhospitable, many are simply walking away.

It is important to note that the challenges these church systems face to translate their life and witness in order to connect with new generations and populations lie much deeper in their DNA, transplanted from the established-church ethos of Europe. The Euro-tribal denominations were birthed out of the state churches of Europe, and they assumed a geographic-neighborhood logic to ministry in a cultural context that privileges and supports Christian faith and practice. Their polities are predicated on the principle of geographical domain, where the church exercises authority over its social and cultural space. Governance and leadership are enshrined in formal hierarchies, and the church's life is dependent on a caste of professional Christians who perform ministry for the people. Architecturally, the church stands at the center of community life, its steeple the tallest structure around. The made-in-America denominations drew largely from Scripture in trying to re-create the New Testament church, but their reading of Scripture was substantially shaped by the individualism and revivalism prevalent on the frontier in their time.

This basic organizational DNA was reshaped in the American context by religious pluralism and the voluntary principle. Yet many of the underlying assumptions by which these churches have operated are deeply at odds with the context in which they find themselves. The shift toward individual choice as the basic factor in religious affiliation has now gone to another level. It is no surprise that denominational churches that tried to overlay attractional-lifestyle strategies on their establishment DNA have not addressed the deeper crisis. Churches birthed in the attractional-lifestyle mode are also equally vulnerable to the fickle tastes and fluid preferences of generations formed deeply by a consumer culture. A fundamentally different imagination is required in order to contextualize the gospel faithfully in twenty-first-century America, an imagination that must rethink deeper cultural and theological assumptions.

Alternatives to the Denominational-Organizational Church

A variety of alternatives to the denominational-organizational church have emerged over the past few generations. These have been largely shaped by the attractional-lifestyle paradigm of seeking to market the church to various generational or cultural niches. They include new immigrant churches, regional ministry centers, megachurches, emerging churches, multisite and multicongregational churches, cell groups and network churches, and social media/virtual churches. Still others take the form of house churches, missional communities, and experimental expressions of church life (café churches, neomonastic communities, and so on). These alternatives to the established denominational church represent creative attempts to recontextualize ministry within the diversity of American society and culture today. It is worth reflecting on the promise and challenges of some of these expressions.

New Immigrant Congregations

American Christianity has thrived from its very beginnings on immigrants who came and brought their churches with them. This has brought people, resources, energy, and cultural and theological richness and diversity. A commonly neglected but vital organizational expression of the church in America today is the new immigrant congregations. Since the expansion of US immigration policy in the mid-1960s, immigrants have brought an array of African, Asian, and Latin American cultural expressions that reflect the vitality of Christianity as the predominant majority-world religion that it is today.

Unlike the establishment legacy that has shaped many native-born American churches, many new immigrant faith communities have different expectations for institutional life. Many do not expect to own a dedicated building, pay the full-time salaries to professional clergypersons and staff, and support an elaborate committee and program structure. These immigrants often work long hours, attend school, and are struggling to adapt to American life. They do not have the time or resources to support an elaborate institutional church.

Instead, their focus is often on creating a powerful weekly worship experience (often lasting a few hours), fellowship, and cultivating communal connections that allow for the preservation of cultural traditions and the sharing of social and economic support. The consumer expectations that have come to shape many established Americans' experience of church do not necessarily function in the same way in these churches. Clergy may work full time elsewhere; their role is less focused on institutional administration than on theological and liturgical leadership and providing social services to those newly arrived in the United States. Bible studies and other groups often meet in homes. These Christian communities claim a subcultural identity and sustain their witness in a leaner organizational form. Some of them have adopted a missionary posture toward their new neighborhoods as they realize that the country that they expected to be Christian is only tenuously so.[6]

---

6. See, e.g., Jehu Hanciles, *Beyond Christendom: Globalization, African Migration, and the Transformation of the West* (Maryknoll, NY: Orbis, 2008); see also Harvey Kwiyani, *Sent Forth: African Missionary Work in the West* (Maryknoll, NY: Orbis, 2014).

Megachurches

Among the attractional-lifestyle forms of congregational life that have become more prominent in the past several decades are megachurches (typically defined as congregations with 2,000 or more weekly worship attendees).[7] Megachurches have grown to occupy a significant place in the American religious landscape—even as they face challenges of their own. In 1970, there were fewer than ten congregations in the United States that met this definition; today there are more than 1,600, with several hundred having over 5,000 in weekly worship.[8] In 2015, about one in ten Protestant churchgoers on a typical weekend was at a megachurch.[9] Megachurches represent a contextualization of Christianity in late-modern consumer and entertainment culture.

If the denominational franchise church emerged as the religious equivalent of a Walgreens lunch counter or an A&P store in the 1950s, megachurches are the Walmart, Home Depot, or multiplex movie theaters of many American communities today. Megachurches have embraced high production values in trying to out-compete rock concerts, motivational speakers, and shopping malls in their attractiveness. Food courts, Starbucks cafes, video-game consoles for youth, and multimillion-dollar campuses that resemble corporate office parks, shopping centers, or even sports stadiums surround stages where celebrity preachers and professional musicians perform, sometimes beamed virtually to multisite locations on huge video screens.

The rise of megachurches over the past forty years was initially driven by baby boomers who had become estranged from the traditional churches of their childhood experience. Indeed, much of the megachurch growth has come from traditional congregations that were failing to engage their members in meaningful ways. Megachurches have offered a contextualized form of Christianity that is far more culturally accessible than that of many traditional churches. Their institutional success has come in part at the cost of traditional churches, though many megachurch attendees would likely not have church affiliations anywhere if megachurches did not exist.

---

7. See Scott Thumma and Dave Travis, *Beyond Megachurch Myths: What We Can Learn from America's Largest Churches* (San Francisco: Jossey-Bass, 2007).

8. See the megachurch database developed by the Hartford Institute: http://hirr.hart sem.edu/megachurch/database.html (accessed August 20, 2016).

9. Cathy Lynn Grossman, "The Megachurch Boom Rolls on, but Concerns Are Rising Too," *Religion News Service*, December 2, 2015.

Megachurches represent the modern, established, professionalized version of Christianity taken toward another trajectory. Just as late-modern capitalism has harnessed technology to squeeze out every possible efficiency from supply chains (think Walmart) or has offered emporiums of seemingly endless choices (megamalls, mammoth big-box stores, Amazon), megachurches promise a culturally appropriate religious experience for every age cohort and musical preference, often simultaneously in multiple worship venues. Like other attractional-lifestyle churches, many megachurches are oriented around meeting people's needs. Many, to their credit, call for high levels of commitment and accountability in discipleship, which is practiced especially through their small-group ministries. But there are others who preach a prosperity gospel and wholeheartedly embrace the culture of expressive individualism.

Yet megachurches are not immune to the broader cultural trends, even as they have sought to embrace many of them. They are experiencing patterns of disengagement from younger generations that are similar to what denominational-franchise churches have seen. For instance, engagement in megachurches by Millennials has flattened out since 2010; and the participation of Gen-X members (those born between 1965 and 1981) was down 18 percent from 2010 to 2015.[10] Many younger Americans are suspicious of the consumer-entertainment version of Christianity that many megachurches offer. Just like people who avoid big-box and chain stores and prefer local shops and restaurants, some react negatively to the Walmarts and megamalls of American religion. Some people can feel lost in them, even as their relative anonymity is attractive to others. For the increasingly large numbers of Americans with no connection to church to begin with, megachurches can be just as irrelevant as traditional churches. The megachurch paradigm was initially designed around the assumption that people are seeking God but are turned off by traditional forms of church. However, many of the unaffiliated are not seeking to join any religious community, no matter what form it takes. Increasing numbers of Americans have no traditional church background to rebel against.

Emerging Churches

It was initially Generation-X youth pastors within a variety of denominational and independent churches (especially megachurches) that chal-

10. Grossman, "The Megachurch Boom."

lenged the cultural and theological assumptions of their elders in giving birth to the emerging-church movement in the early 2000s. They called into question both the foundationalism of modern evangelical theology and the embrace of corporate business strategy and entertainment culture being practiced by many churches. The roots of the emerging church lie in alternative worship experiences in the United Kingdom and the United States that sought to reach younger generations who had little taste for the soft-rock Christian music and styles that have come to characterize so much contemporary worship.[11]

It wasn't long before these younger leaders formed networks and began to launch worshiping communities that sought to reflect the postmodern cultural assumptions of their own generation. They adopted traditional liturgical and spiritual practices and aesthetic expressions from earlier periods that the seeker-sensitive baby-boomer generation had rejected. The Christian publishing industry seized upon the emerging church as the next latest thing, and books and blogs proliferated. Yet as the basic logic of the attractional-lifestyle congregation has defined the emerging church, many of its creative expressions have struggled to survive institutionally. The same publishing houses that had seized on the emerging church stopped publishing titles associated with the movement by 2005. An older generation of evangelicals committed to foundationalism rejected the philosophical and theological turn made by the emerging churches, and many established churches have proven unwilling to subsidize emerging worship services and congregations over the long term. Some emerging churches continue to reach their intended cultural audience, but many more have disappeared. It is not clear what kind of institutional and organizational future this movement will have.

House Churches and Other Alternative Expressions

House churches in various forms have been part of the world Christian movement in many contexts, from the early church to base communities in Latin America to contemporary China. They began to flourish in the United States especially within mostly evangelical circles from the 1970s on. Some of these churches continue, while this form of church also of-

---

11. See Eddie Gibbs and Ryan K. Bolger, *Emerging Churches: Creating Christian Community in Postmodern Cultures* (Grand Rapids: Baker Academic, 2005).

fers a compelling alternative expression to younger Christians who have walked away from organized congregations.[12] Institutionally light, with low overhead and strong grass-roots empowerment, house churches and the networks that connect them can be nimble and highly responsive to their members' callings and neighborhoods. They are typically unburdened by legacy expectations and structures. At the same time, they are less public and thus can be more inaccessible than other forms of church.

Countless experiments have arisen within the past few decades of congregational life that don't fit into the boxes of the establishment church. These include pub churches, café churches, missional communities, and neomonasticism.[13] They typically share a highly participatory approach to Christian life and leadership as they seek to be contextualized among populations that are not being reached by most established forms of church. There is often an intentional focus on forming relationships with local neighbors and focusing community life on simple practices rather than extensive activities, programs, and committees. Many of these communities are experimental in nature and have yet to navigate transitions beyond their founding generation of leaders. They do offer concrete examples of vibrant forms of church life among people otherwise not connected to the church. One of the challenges for these expressions is that they don't fit into the existing categories of denominational polities. For instance, the Presbyterian Church (USA) has committed to starting a thousand new worshiping communities, and many of these are not expected to end up looking like established congregations.[14] But presbyteries (regional judicatories) within the denomination are struggling to know what to do with them. This is the case with many other established denominational systems that are trying to foster new expressions of church.

12. See Jervis David Payne, *Missional House Churches: Reaching Our Communities with the Gospel* (Colorado Springs, CO: Paternoster, 2008); see also Josh Packard and Ashleigh Hope, *Church Refugees: Sociologists Reveal Why People Are Done with Church but Not with Faith* (Loveland, CO: Group Publishing, 2015).

13. See, e.g., Reggie McNeal, *Missional Communities: The Rise of the Post-Congregational Church* (San Francisco: Jossey-Bass, 2011); see also Jonathan Wilson-Hartgrove, *New Monasticism: What It Has to Say to Today's Church* (Grand Rapids: Brazos, 2008).

14. https://www.presbyterianmission.org/ministries/1001-2/ (accessed December 26, 2016).

The Stories beneath the Structures

One of the great temptations in times of significant cultural change, disruption, and challenge is to focus on organizational reform as a primary response. Since the 1970s, when many church systems in America began to face precipitous decline, they made countless attempts to renew the church through reorganization and revitalization—what we call the "re-denomination." This has included the restructuring of denominational offices, the establishment of new policies and procedures, attempts to improve performance through accountability measurements, and various strategies for planting and renewing congregations. Huge amounts of time and energy have been invested in these efforts. Largely, though, they have failed to address the church's changed situation.

Understanding Defaults

There are good reasons for this, as Alan Roxburgh points out.[15] Beneath organizational structures lie cultural narratives that reflect shared assumptions about how the world works. Such narratives are embodied in practices and behaviors in communities—the very patterns by which we participate and belong. These narratives are often implicit; they form lenses through which people interpret reality. They are the "defaults" by which people go through their daily lives. Attempts to restructure without addressing these underlying narratives will inevitably fail. This is because defaults are too powerful: they operate at a much deeper level than do structure and organization, which are expressions, or embodiments, of their logic.

One powerful default shaping life in American churches is the establishment one (as we have explored above), the narratives reflected not only in the Euro-tribal denominations but also in conservative-evangelical churches focused on "making America Christian again."[16] These narratives assume cultural privilege and centrality for the church in society, and their presumption is that Christianity is normative in American society (or should be). Even as Christianity becomes increasingly marginalized or

---

15. Alan J. Roxburgh, *Structured for Mission: Renewing the Culture of the Church* (Downers Grove, IL: InterVarsity, 2015).

16. James Davison Hunter, *To Change the World: The Irony, Tragedy, and Possibility of Christianity in the Late Modern World* (New York: Oxford University Press, 2010), 111–31.

functionally co-opted in a pluralistic American culture, these narratives are difficult to dislodge. They have provided a sense of identity, purpose, and orientation for too many generations. The structures of church life reflect them too deeply.

Church polities also reflect these deep cultural narratives. They embody theological and cultural commitments that often emerged during very different contextual situations than the present moment. For instance, Calvin's Geneva implemented a church order that relied on the authority of the magistrates to enforce religious uniformity and control. It was an attempt to create a Reformed Christendom by turning 10,000 former Roman Catholic Christians into 10,000 Reformed Christians. Similarly, Lutherans in Germany turned to the use of prince-bishops, with both roles residing in the same person, to regularize church life and legitimate it within the social order. The Church of England followed the same pattern in largely accepting the structures and roles of medieval Catholicism in forming a national church. These polities and others were rooted in the worldview of the sixteenth-century cultural moment. All of them were hierarchical in authority and developed their view of church office out of a high Christology, which created a divide between clergy and laity, limiting the administration of the sacraments to clergy for the "sake of good order."[17]

The made-in-America denominations took a different approach in forming their polities. They sought to re-create what they believed to be *the* New Testament pattern of government and organization. This approach had two problems: first, these denominations tended to read the New Testament through a worldview lens that was operative in the nineteenth century, one that was rooted in Lockean social-contract theory and emphasized individualism and democratic egalitarianism; second, they failed to account for the diversity regarding offices and church order that is present in the New Testament.[18] This diversity became manifest in the various church systems they created. The church today, however, lives within a profoundly divergent context in America, one that does not correspond well with sixteenth-century Europe or nineteenth-century America.

Alan Roxburgh observes that a defining narrative or cultural default for many American churches in the twentieth century became the modern corporation.[19] In many ways, this made sense in the early years of the

---

17. This is the rationale given in the writings of the time.
18. For a mapping of that diversity, see Burtchaell, *From Synagogue to Church.*
19. Roxburgh, *Structured for Mission,* 80–81.

last century, when American society was being revolutionized by the triumph of large industrial companies, with their standardization, branded goods, efficiency, central coordination, bureaucracy, and hierarchy. American churches that adopted these patterns in structuring judicatory and denominational offices, for instance, were contextualizing their life to the environment in which they found themselves. It made sense to create elaborate hierarchical bureaucratic staffs, to standardize training for clergy, to develop extensive committee structures, to disseminate uniform programs and curricula from denominational centers to the franchise congregations, and to apply a managerial focus on efficiency throughout the system. Denominationally branded religious goods and services were retailed through local churches embedded in a centrally coordinated, hierarchical corporate structure. Leaders saw themselves as managers or executives, either of branch offices, regional centers, or headquarters. This all fit with traditional notions of polity from the establishment era.

The church struggled to adapt when the American economy started to shift away from industrial production toward an information economy in the second half of the twentieth century; this was because the corporation had become the legitimating narrative by which leaders framed and interpreted the church's situation. Like many businesses, their response to the cultural changes taking place in the wider society was to try to manage and control their way to a different outcome—a modern managerial response. Denominations shifted into regulatory mode and tried to be even more efficient in their use of diminishing resources. Challenges were framed primarily in technical terms of expert responses, dispersed from hierarchical centers out to local peripheries. These took the form of strategies, techniques, and programs for organizational renewal—the "re-" period of denominational life. Managerial rationality was the operative approach.

Ineffective Strategies

Embedded in this approach is the establishment default, where the church stands in a position of authority and power in its relationship with its neighborhood. Neighbors tend to become objects of marketing, recruitment, or benevolence. The waves of renewal efforts in the late twentieth century operated within this basic modern managerial narrative. For instance, the church-growth movement sought to use the culture's best techniques (advertising, marketing, entertainment, consumerism) to attract unchurched and dechurched people to come back through the doors and to keep them satisfied long enough to stay. Church effectiveness sought to identify the best practices to replicate across varying contexts. The modern managerial imagination formed people to seek the right technique or killer app that would secure a new future of prosperity and influence.

The megachurch boom, which also brought the rise of training networks such as the Willow Creek Association and Rick Warren's Purpose-Driven network, operates within this basic modern managerial paradigm. Many traditional churches were failing to reach people with outmoded and old-fashioned practices and cultural expressions, like so many mom-and-pop stores or old franchise outlets. So megachurches harnessed the power of technology, the latest marketing science, which they added to strategic programming and production. The training networks of successful megachurches disseminated these programs and techniques out to the periphery, where others could adopt them.

Needless to say, there is no killer app. There is no quick fix or easy remedy by which the church can recover its position of privilege in a society that is undergoing the kinds of huge cultural transformations that are rapidly and relentlessly unfolding today. These transformations fundamentally reframe the basic legitimating narratives of human life and community. What churches need in facing these kinds of disruptions are not further restructuring proposals and techniques; they need the time and space in which to learn to name new habits and practices, and to try them out—in a changed environment.[20] Experts don't have the answers, for the work is primarily adaptive, requiring new learning on the part of the people.[21] Rather than claiming managerial rationality, it would be more fruitful to claim participatory practices of deliberative communication and discernment, which have deep roots in Christian history as well as in modernity. We shall explore what this looks like in the conclusion to this book.

Another temptation of the traditional church as it tries to stay afloat in today's culture is to jettison established structures entirely: to liberate the church from existing organizational patterns and replace them with "organic church," or some kind of primitive expression of the early Jesus movement or presumed apostolic formula.[22] However, such approaches tend to

20. Roxburgh, *Structured for Mission*, 51.

21. See Ronald A. Heifetz and Martin Linsky, *Leadership on the Line: Staying Alive through the Dangers of Leading* (Boston: Harvard Business School Press, 2002).

22. Examples of this impulse include Neil Cole, *Organic Church: Growing Faith Where Life Happens* (San Francisco: Jossey-Bass, 2005); Alan Hirsch, *The Forgotten Ways: Reacti-*

be naïve about the necessity of structure for any human community to survive. Structures exist because they are a vital means of connection, security, and continuity in human life. These "organic church" proposals tend to reflect as much the expressive individualism of late modernity as they do the reclamation of Christian tradition. They assume that structure is inherently oppressive and confining, that it must be thrown off for the church to actualize itself. This denies two thousand years of the historical development of the church in varying global contexts, where structure has evolved and adapted in order to support the flourishing of Christian life and witness. It also sounds suspiciously like the larger contemporary Western cultural trend toward structural disintegration in favor of romantic individualism. This is not a helpful path forward.

Structure will always be with us in some form, but structures and patterns of community are always shaped by deep narratives embodied within them. Exploring in more detail the stories embedded in the cultural shifts taking place would be worthwhile. These new narratives stand at odds with many existing church structures and ways of life. No wonder the existing structures find themselves disconnected, under stress, and failing in many places. This is a moment that calls for a massive recontextualization of Christian life and witness in the American environment. What might the Spirit be up to in the midst of these changes?

Recontextualizing Church Organization in a Networked Age

Many legacy forms of church organization are hierarchical, shaped by cultural contexts in which hierarchies predominated households and society. The biblical world was a hierarchical one, even though Christianity disrupted and undercut many forms of hierarchy in favor of more inclusive, egalitarian, gifts-based leadership. As the church took root in Roman society, it embraced the hierarchical patterns of Roman life, becoming more patriarchal and establishing an ordered ministry (bishop, presbyter, deacon) that reflected the Roman imperial career ladder. In European Christendom, hierarchies endured, and the church took its place at the center of society and even conferred legitimacy on political rulers. Modern corporate bureaucracies use hierarchy to ensure uniformity, efficiency, and control from

---

vating the Missional Church (Grand Rapids: Brazos, 2006). See also Roxburgh, *Structured for Mission*, 42–46.

the top down. Experts are assumed to have the most knowledge, with work-ers carrying out their orders at the bottom of the organizational pyramid. This is an industrial economy approach.

The Rise of Networks

The past couple of decades have seen a major shift from hierarchies to net-works as a primary organizational paradigm.[23] This is embodied most pow-erfully in the rise of the Internet, which functions as a central metaphor for the twenty-first-century globalized world. Networks are decentralized, par-ticipatory, and self-organizing; and they are shaped by flows of information, typically in many different directions, from peer to peer. Unlike hierarchies, which concentrate power at the top, networks facilitate shared authority and collaboration at the grass roots.[24]

The emerging networked culture is characterized by rapid change, in part because networks empower participants at all levels to enact change and exercise influence. This radical redistribution of power opens space for previously unknown participants to gain global popularity overnight, for instance, through a viral video or meme. Millions of users share in pro-moting or adapting something through networks. Consider such massive collaborative projects as Wikipedia, with its countless contributors. Elites who once functioned as brokers of influence and authority in hierarchies can be easily bypassed.

One of the principal shifts that a network brings is the movement from a consumption-based media culture to a production-based one. The advent of radio and television in the twentieth century allowed for the mass dissemination of cultural products to millions from the production centers in Hollywood and New York, for instance. Creative people in these centers were responsible for coming up with cultural products that were then disseminated from the center out to end users. This still happens, but the Internet revolution complements and undercuts this with tools that allow any user anywhere to create and share content through platforms like YouTube. Peers can modify, add to, or spread cultural content cheaply

---

23. See Manuel Castells, *The Rise of the Network Society*, 2nd ed. (Malden, MA: Black-well, 2000).

24. Albert-Laszlo Barabasi, *Linked: How Everything Is Connected to Everything Else and What It Means for Business, Science, and Everyday Life* (New York: Plume, 2003).

and easily, which makes for a flattened and highly participatory cultural paradigm.[25]

Thinking Theologically about Networks

What does such a transformation mean for church organization, especially when legacy structures tend to be hierarchical? To begin with, we must reflect on the deeper theological narratives shaping church polity. Traditional hierarchical forms of church organization and leadership in the Western church have tended to operate out of Christology as the primary theological image. The bishop, priest, or pastor stands in the place of Christ in exercising authority over the church. This structure is typically complemented by assemblies of elders or other leaders, who are understood to function something like Jesus's apostles did. For this reason it has been difficult for many Christian traditions to expand their understanding of leadership to include women. The default tends to be solitary, hierarchical, and male.

There are helpful theological resources to draw from within God's Trinitarian life that move in a more inclusive, participatory, collaborative direction. Jesus's own identity is defined by his relationship with God the Creator and with the Holy Spirit. Together they function as a community of leaders, each acting uniquely but always in deep collaboration with each other. In the New Testament the Spirit creates and leads the Christian community in ways that empower the marginalized and voiceless (Joel 2; Acts 2) and relativize and reform inherited cultural patterns of leadership and authority. The Spirit is highly participatory, working among the grass roots and from the outside in. In fact, the Jerusalem apostles were the ones who learned from those engaged in ministry—at the edges in Antioch—about the culturally inclusive nature of the gospel. These biblical and theological narratives suggest a profoundly interdependent, shared understanding of leadership and authority, both within God's Trinitarian life and in the church, which resonates with what is emerging in contemporary American culture today.

Church members who stay in traditional congregations may continue to look to religious authorities (clergy or other professional staff) and

25. See Yochai Benkler, *The Wealth of Networks: How Social Production Transforms Markets and Freedom* (New Haven: Yale University Press, 2006); see also Clay Shirky, *Here Comes Everybody: The Power of Organizing without Organizations* (New York: Penguin, 2008).

formal structures for spiritual meaning, connection, and practice; but that simply doesn't make sense to increasing numbers of Americans. Nowadays authority is conferred in a network culture not by formal credentialing and office but by the "wisdom of crowds"—the approval of the highest number of fellow users.[26] Authority for religious organizations and their leaders is no longer automatically granted. It must be earned. This is a massively disconcerting shift for church systems that have for centuries invested in processes for credentialing clergy as religious professionals.

There are genuine dangers in shifting from hierarchies to networks. Hierarchies and formal credentialing of leaders (presumably) bring the benefits of high standards for knowledge of the tradition, accountability, and connectedness. Much wisdom is passed on through these structures, even though they can be restrictive. One cautionary example is how social media networks have disrupted professional journalism, leading to ominous effects for democracy when these networks disregard facts and spread distortions virally. It can be easy for the church, in a network world, to become unmoored from its anchors in tradition. Most networks are also managed today by corporate platforms (such as Facebook), which are underpinned by profit motives. They can be manipulated just as easily by the powerful globalized corporate interests that continue to shape contemporary life. Nonetheless, the transition from a hierarchical to a networked world is well under way.

Applying Network Thinking

Congregations, judicatories, and denominations remain organized for hierarchical participation. People are expected to become formal members, to join committees, and to volunteer. The most dedicated members might serve on the church board. This is how most voluntary organizations in society remain structured, including synagogues, which are facing the same cultural pressures that Christian congregations are.[27] However, these forms of participation simply do not make sense for increasing numbers of Americans, particularly those in younger generations, who have grown

---

26. James Surowiecki, *The Wisdom of Crowds: Why the Many Are Smarter Than the Few and How Collective Wisdom Shapes Business, Economies, Societies, and Nations* (New York: Doubleday, 2004).

27. See Hayim Herring, *Tomorrow's Synagogue Today: Creating Vibrant Centers of Jewish Life* (Herndon, VA: Alban Institute, 2012).

up in a world of participatory engagement through platforms rather than hierarchies. Platforms facilitate network connections, providing channels for people who share interests and passions to link up, collaborate, and contribute, all without hierarchical structures and formal membership—that is, beyond perhaps creating a login or user account.

Congregations that depend on pledging from members are beginning to find themselves caught in a culture moving in the direction of crowd funding. Crowd funding is participatory and driven by common interests and passions, not lasting membership in an organization. It is far more fluid, even as it can draw in people with no previous connection to the organization.[28] Joining a church formally as a member, volunteering, and pledging were culturally "normal" activities for older generations; but emerging generations are finding different ways of participating. They may be just as passionate about making a difference in the world, and just as eager to be connected; but the means of that connection is very different. The very premise of bounded-set membership that has been the assumed norm for congregational participation for so long doesn't fit with where many Americans are today. New ways of imagining participation are in the process of being developed.

Faith communities have largely only just begun to grapple with the implications of the shift from the hierarchical to a platform organization.[29] For now, American society exists in a transition period where both paradigms overlap, serving different populations, generations, and purposes in hybrid ways. For many churches, embracing platform structures will mean a huge transformation in expectations, practices, habits, and imagination, including the function of power. Platforms and networks are much harder to control than are hierarchies. Influence is less about position and more about communication and connection.[30]

These shifts invite churches in various locations to consider carefully the contextualization of their polity and organization. What assumptions are embedded in those systems of governance and patterns of organization that come from historical moments that are at odds with contemporary America? Which values and commitments are, in fact, gospel based, and

28. See Beth Kanter and Allison H. Fine, *The Networked Nonprofit: Connecting with Social Media to Drive Change* (San Francisco: Jossey-Bass, 2010).

29. See Hayim Herring and Terri Martinson Elton, *Leading Congregations and Nonprofits in a Connected World* (Lanham, MD: Rowman and Littlefield, 2016).

30. See Dwight Zscheile, "Social Networking and Church Systems," *Word and World* 30, no. 3 (Summer 2010).

which are historical and cultural from earlier eras that warrant revision? What alternative biblical and theological streams and sources can be mined for faithful recontextualization today? Many churches tend to assume that their inherited confessional and polity norms are ahistorical and thus above renegotiation, revision, or translation. However, the nature of church organization (like theology itself) needs to be contextual in order to embody and give witness to the gospel. This is the incarnational logic of the church.

A Post-Congregational, Post-Denominational Church?

These shifts away from institutional belonging and identification raise the question of what kind of future the basic unit of Christian community in American life—the congregation—has in a networked world. Christian faith is inherently communal; that is a nonnegotiable dimension of the gospel and Christian practice. Yet there are cultural forces under way that render the institutional congregation, with its formal structures and hierarchical leadership, vulnerable to collapse. What will happen when millennials, already the largest generation alive, come to predominance, and the faithful older generations that have sustained established institutional forms of congregational life move on? Who will underwrite the business model of institutional congregational life? Who will pay for buildings and salaries? It is not clear that Millennials will embrace the kinds of giving and participation patterns that preceding generations did. Either they will come to do so as deeply countercultural practices, or these structures will not survive in their existing form.

This is not to say that Christian faith will not be embodied in community. But if cultural trends hold, such communal forms may be institutionally light, fluid, and networked. They may well not become formal nonprofit organizations with budgets, staff, and buildings. This represents a major break with the historical legacy and embodied fabric of American Christianity. Such organizational expressions would face all kinds of challenges in sustaining their life and witness without the continuity and security that more formal institutions provide. They would also be freer to adapt, less focused on maintaining institutional structures, and able to share their resources more generously with neighbors in need.

Within many denominational systems today, a high percentage of established congregations face institutional collapse within the next few decades as their membership ages. For many of them, institutional survival in their present form is highly unlikely. Those congregations need to discover what Christian community and witness might look like without a building or paid staff. Many might embrace new forms of life as house churches or neighborhood missional communities. At the same time, within these same systems there are congregations that retain the institutional strength to continue and may serve as regional hubs within a networked church. The smaller house churches and missional communities might join them for important liturgical celebrations, theological education, equipping, and sharing of learnings. Those regional hubs can fulfill a role of gathering and oversight over the smaller communities within the network.

Likewise, denominations that have been organized to sustain congregations as their legacy forms face a highly uncertain future. Denominational identity and loyalty do not hold the same sway for younger Christians as they did for older generations in a hybrid and fluid world. There are some signs of convergence under way as Christians feel freer to borrow, adapt, and modify traditions from one another. For many engaged in these grass-roots experiments in Christian community, the existing denominational structures and divisions can feel largely irrelevant.

Denominational structures might reenvision themselves as networks of learning communities in mission rather than as hierarchical bureaucracies or regulatory agencies. They can link together grass-roots Christian communities that might take a range of forms for mutual learning, equipping, experimenting, and collaboration. This will require huge amounts of relearning on the part of denominational leaders who are consumed with trying to fix the present institutional church structure. They may reimagine their leadership as being cultivators of action-learning teams at the grass roots who do the primary work of discovering faithful new expressions of Christian community and witness. Rather than primarily managing an institutional system, they can exercise interpretive leadership as they help local disciples discern what the Spirit is up to in their midst and in their neighborhoods.

Leadership Formation for a New Missionary Age

The historical overview of the church in Part 2 of this book noted that the leadership of American churches evolved over time, depending on the era and the context. Primary paradigms of pastoral leadership have included the resident theologian (colonial period), the gentleman pastor (1780s to

1870s), the churchly pastor (1880s to 1940s), the pastoral director (1940s to 1960s), the therapeutic pastor and entrepreneurial pastor (1970s to 2000s). Alongside these have been a plethora of bivocational and nonprofessional models of leadership, such as the Baptist farmer-preacher and the Methodist circuit rider on the nineteenth-century frontier, as well as the leaders in the early black churches who were not allowed access to formal theological education. Leaders among new immigrant churches and in some economically marginalized communities have often held other employment by necessity.

The systems and practices of forming leaders for church ministry have varied contextually in American history alongside patterns of church organization. European models were adopted in the American context, giving birth to early colleges (William and Mary, Harvard, Yale, Princeton), whose initial purpose was primarily to educate ministers. Freestanding seminaries arose in the nineteenth century and were joined later in the century by divinity schools at colleges and universities. Throughout this history, there continued to be a long tradition of local tutoring and apprenticeship for ministry. During the twentieth century, the embrace of modern corporate forms of industrial education swept through many church systems, bringing standardization and a professionalized paradigm.

Changes in Theological Education

Established systems of theological education and leadership formation inherited from the twentieth century are experiencing the same challenges as their broader congregations, judicatories, and denominations are. The Association of Theological Schools notes a gradual decline in enrollment and in institutional health in general across the system of North American theological education in the past decade. While a small number of schools are growing, many more are declining. The decrease in enrollment in seminaries is most acute at mainline Protestant schools (23 percent from 2006 to 2014); the drop is 15 percent in Roman Catholic and Orthodox schools; and it is 4 percent at evangelical schools. Master of Divinity enrollment dropped by 10 percent across the system during this same period, while MA enrollment grew. Andover Newton, the first freestanding theological seminary in America, recently sold its campus and merged with Yale Divinity School. The number of students of color is increasing, reflecting the changing demographics of American society and the vitality of immigrant and African

American churches, but white student enrollment has declined. And the overall financial strength of theological schools has diminished in the past decade.[31]

Some of these trends may simply reflect reality: there are fewer paid professional positions in congregations that are available to seminary graduates. Mainline Protestant denominations that are experiencing the most severe decline in their institutions are also seeing the steepest drop in enrollment. Given the broader changes in the American religious environment, we can expect a further working out of these trends of decline in the years ahead. Changes in accreditation standards have allowed for greater curricular flexibility and reduced residency requirements, streamlining some MDiv and MA programs. Online learning and other forms of distributed education have become primary means of reducing the cost and increasing the accessibility of theological education.

The Changing Role of Clergy Leadership

The primary mental model that has defined the shape of theological education in the United States over the past century has been a professional one in service to an established church. The assumption operative in many systems has been one of providing full-time leaders for established congregations that can pay a salary and benefits. That assumption still holds in many places, but it is also eroding. Bivocational clergy are becoming more the norm in many church systems, as they have been in some communities all along.

The erosion of the established church has presented something of an identity crisis for clergy over the past few generations. When the church was reaching its mid-twentieth-century, postwar organizational peak, H. Richard Niebuhr defined ministerial identity in terms of the "pastoral director"—a manager of a complex nonprofit religious organization providing services to all ages.[32] The cultural crisis of the 1960s and 1970s saw some clergy adopt the paradigm of the therapist offering private spiritual counseling to individuals who wished to explore their inner lives. Others became

---

31. Stephen Graham and Daniel Aleshire, "ATS State of the Industry Webinar" (September 18, 2015).

32. H. Richard Niebuhr et al., *The Purpose of the Church and Its Ministry: Reflections on the Aims of Theological Education* (New York: Harper, 1956).

primarily community organizers and political advocates, concentrating on changing public policy. The late twentieth century brought entrepreneurship to the fore, where pastors embraced business strategies and techniques to launch new congregations and renew old ones. Needless to say, all of these identities are deeply indebted to modernity and tend to presume the existence of an established church.

Leaders have been groomed for generations to fill existing slots in the church system and to meet established members' needs and expectations. Training for church planters has tended to take place outside the seminary system, if at all. Formation concerned with maintaining existing structures and programs has been much more common than educating leaders to help their communities connect with those who are far from church. Students with passions and gifts for innovation and cultural translation of the church's life and witness have tended to be marginalized in many church systems. Ordination processes are often inhospitable to them, and by the time they finish seminary (if they do at all) they have been normed to the mindset, habits, and expectations of the established church.

Many megachurches have developed a system of theological education and leadership formation that is parallel to the established seminary system. Leaders are often identified and formed from within the congregation and may never attend seminary at all. Willow Creek, Saddleback, and other leading megachurches have also created training networks to disseminate their innovations and ministry programs around the world. These networks are meeting needs that established denominations have largely failed to address. However, they primarily operate in a web 1.0 paradigm, distributing information from experts and authorities out from a central hub to the periphery, rather than embracing a web 2.0 paradigm of distributed peer-to-peer learning, which is increasingly necessary when the primary challenges facing churches are adaptive, not technical, in character.

Looking to the Future

One of the hallmarks of the hierarchical, established church paradigm has been concentrating leadership in a solo pastor or priest. The emerging-church culture of the networked era is participatory, collaborative, and team-based. In such a cultural framework, it makes less sense to have one monarchical leader as the professional minister for the people than to have leadership shared according to gifts among the community. This reflects more closely the New Testament approach to leadership than the monarchical establishment model. Such an approach also helps address the financial sustainability questions of the professionalized paradigm of pastoral leadership. In emerging churches, contextualized within postmodern culture, this is called "leading as a body."[33] In many smaller congregations, often in rural areas, team-based models of pastoral leadership are providing an important alternative when the traditional solo-pastor approach is unavailable.[34] Inherited assumptions about ordained clergy as a separate professional religious class within the church beg to be examined and rethought in today's changing cultural context.

Many existing clergy and church staff were trained for a world that no longer exists. They struggle to respond to changing cultural conditions while negotiating the expectations of established members amid diminishing resources. One of the primary needs for theological education today is to help these leaders reimagine their roles, develop new capacities, and live into alternative ways of leading. This has largely not been the focus of most leaders' training. Many of these capacities and habits will need to be discovered and innovated through grass-roots experimentation. Spaces are needed for established leaders to come together alongside emerging ones to reflect on what is taking place in the culture, equip each other for experiments, and share learnings. There is an opportunity here for theological schools to help the church adapt: by providing spaces for connection; by offering deep knowledge of Christian traditions and wisdom from other fields of study; and by fostering experimentation. Yet most current continuing education programs offered by seminaries remain focused on addressing technical fixes.

Another major opportunity is a broader approach to theological education than just educating and certifying professional clergy and staff. In a platform church, every disciple is engaged in practicing the Way of Jesus, indwelling the biblical narrative, and trying out small experiments of Christian community, witness, and service with their neighbors. These disciples might be equipped and resourced for this work through forms of theological education that are lay-focused, accessible (through technology and other means), and participatory. This becomes less a matter of accredited degree programs than of accompanying ordinary disciples in their

33. Gibbs and Bolger, *Emerging Churches*, 191–215.

34. See, e.g., Stewart C. Zabriskie, *Total Ministry: Reclaiming the Ministry of All God's People* (Bethesda, MD: Alban Institute, 1995).

discipleship and missional participation—wherever they are. Theological schools might reimagine themselves as learning networks or platforms in this sense, rather than just professional schools.

Conclusion

This is a both/and moment in the life of American Christianity, where many inherited structures continue alongside emerging ones. Some of these legacy structures and patterns flourish in connecting people with God and each other and facilitating their participation in God's mission. Others no longer do so, and they find themselves at a loss about what to do next. Every context is different, and trends are playing out in varying ways across the American religious landscape among different populations and generations. This is a transition time: old paradigms and structures endure even as new ones struggle to be born. We can expect ambiguity, stress, and a certain amount of chaos for many churches and church systems as they seek to navigate these cultural shifts. But the Spirit is bringing forth new life and new expressions of Christian community and witness even amidst the collapse of the old.

Faithful navigation requires deeper reflection on the narratives that shape church life and structure with respect to the core stories of the Christian faith and a changing culture. It calls for an open-ended posture of learning and experimentation, which also requires vulnerability and risk-taking. The old maps that once promised clear paths forward no longer seem helpful. Like the biblical wilderness or exile, many churches find themselves in a sustained space of disruption and uncertainty—with no quick exit. As in those biblical moments, God's people face the opportunity to renew their identity as a community through the retelling of the stories of God's faithfulness, learning new practices and behaviors of discerning God's presence, and seeking the just and peaceful flourishing of the places to which God has sent them (Jer. 29:7). The church's organizational life and leadership formation must be reoriented for these purposes.

CHAPTER 11

Conclusion: Toward a Faithful Future

An Identity Crisis

The crisis facing the churches in the American context today is at root an identity crisis. What does it mean to be the church? What is its purpose and role within a pluralist, postestablishment America? For hundreds of years, American culture was assumed to be a largely Christian culture, dominated by Christian narratives, traditions, and institutions. Indeed, as we have explored in the historical sections of this book, many of the church's missiologies have been focused on fostering this identity or trying to reclaim it. In the America of today, both those cultural narratives and the institutions that supported them have been significantly weakened by the waves of cultural change.

Various responses to this crisis over the past few generations have stumbled in their capacity to offer a credible alternative to contrasting cultural narratives. Liberal churches have typically tried to accommodate themselves by embracing pluralism and secularism, which has diminished their theological distinctiveness. If what they have taught their children and grandchildren is moralistic therapeutic deism, it's no wonder so few find reasons to remain. Even as these churches aspire to racial and cultural diversity, they remain overwhelmingly white—because their central narratives are still so often defined by European culture and modernity.[1] Many

---

1. Liberal Protestant denominations such as the United Church of Christ, the Episcopal Church, the United Methodist Church, and the Evangelical Lutheran Church in America are 89–96 percent white. Lipka, "The Most and Least Diverse U.S. Religious Groups" (Washington, DC: Pew Research Center, July 27, 2015).

conservative churches have sought to reject modernity's pluralism and secularism, yet they remain deeply captive to modern narratives of foundationalism, corporate management, expressive individualism, and consumerism. Roman Catholic churches have in many places relied on ethnic identity and clerical hierarchies as key organizing principles, even as trust in those hierarchies has rapidly eroded, particularly due to the clergy-abuse crisis.

The answer to the church's identity crisis ultimately lies within the triune God's life and mission. It is there that the church discovers an alternative and hopeful future that does not depend on the support of cultural establishment or the metrics of organizational success. God's mission is ongoing in all of creation. The church has a particular vocation to bear witness to that mission as a sign, instrument, and foretaste of God's restoration of all things in Christ through the power of the Spirit.[2] God's promised future involves the healing of the nations, the reconciliation of what has been estranged, and the bringing together of what was once torn apart into patterns of just and merciful flourishing. Claiming these promises and sharing them meaningfully with neighbors in an America that desperately needs sources of hope and healing is the church's central work at this moment.

Discovering a Usable Past

As we have observed throughout this book, humans are shaped by deep narratives through which they interpret the world; these narratives are embodied in the patterns and structures of life. The present cultural and organizational crisis facing the church in America offers an opportunity to reclaim and practice biblical and theological narratives that have been submerged or sidelined in many churches' lives over recent generations. This involves reentering the story of God's mission in Scripture, indwelling practices of listening and learning in relationships with God and neighbors, and reflecting critically on the cultural assumptions currently shaping church life in order to recontextualize its witness.

The church in the twenty-first century must focus its life on reinterpreting the gospel and learning simple practices of participation in God's mission. As cultural support for church involvement in American society is being withdrawn, and established church structures continue to disinte-

2. Newbigin, *The Open Secret: An Introduction to the Theology of Mission* (Grand Rapids: Eerdmans, 1976), 110.

grate, it is tempting to concentrate on shoring up those structures or trying to change the surrounding culture. But it is more fruitful, first, for us to get clear about the story in which the church's identity lies. One of the legacies of cultural establishment is a certain ambiguity about the basic gospel narrative in many churches, which became organized around other narratives. Those alternative narratives might be functioning as a social club, a community service organization, or a cultural preservation society. Helping ordinary members live into a faithful and accessible interpretation of the gospel as a story that calls into question all other stories and reorients our view of the world is a good place to begin.

This involves reentering the biblical story imaginatively in participatory ways, ways in which all of God's people have spaces in which to interpret and relate it to their daily lives and struggles—without fear of being shamed. This carries forth modernity's rich tradition of deliberative democracy in today's participatory, collaborative culture. Organizing church life around engaging Scripture as a living narrative that provides a whole new orientation for making sense out of life and the world goes a long way toward deepening identity. The points of resonance and contrast with predominant narratives in society begin to surface. This requires many churches to develop new ways of shaping life together in a far more participatory fashion, where leaders cultivate and frame these spaces of engagement but do not dominate them. Such spaces for conversation and scriptural dwelling can take place anywhere—for example, in workplaces, in the neighborhood, and in homes—and do not require the use of a church building.

This begins with deep listening within the church. Leaders must find ways to invite people to name—authentically and together in community—the longings and losses that keep them up at night. The gospel is a response to these struggles and yearnings, but they must first be articulated and heard. Rather than leaders beginning with their own agendas, it is better to begin where people are with their daily challenges, hopes, fears, and dreams. Such deep listening to our lives opens up the possibility of deeper listening to Scripture and to the stories and wisdom of the Christian tradition.

Participatory engagement with Scripture helps to cultivate the simple practices of discipleship and discernment. This means inviting people to try on, adopt, or deepen their engagement with ancient Christian practices such as Sabbath, prayer, service, hospitality, and reconciliation, not as church programs or organized church ministries, but as a way of life in relationship with neighbors. Just as many churches have been unclear about what the gospel is for their members and their neighbors, they have also been fuzzy about the shape of the Way of Jesus (Acts 9:2; 18:25–26; 19:9, 23) and the simple practices that embody it. It is vital to have participatory, shame-free spaces in which disciples can experiment with these practices and come to indwell them more deeply in daily life.

Central to participating in the triune God's mission is the spiritual practice of discernment: working out how the Spirit has gifted and called us to join in God's healing of the world. The Spirit of God is always leading the church toward adapting its life and witness through joining with neighbors incarnationally in relationships of mutuality and openness. The Spirit of God is out ahead of the church in the world, not confined within the gathered assembly. Like the household of Cornelius in Acts 10, the households and neighborhoods of our world today are locations of the Spirit's movement to form and restore community. Like Peter, our call is to discern how the Spirit is leading us to connect with and receive from those neighbors, knowing that we also may be converted and changed along the way.

Discernment is a practice that involves entering the biblical narratives, learning the grammar of the Spirit, and listening closely to neighbors. It is for many congregations a new habit to adopt, and it requires intentional spaces of practice, experimentation, and conversation. Discernment unfolds through relationships within community, where we test the spirits with one another (1 John 4:1). It is about submitting to and being led by the Spirit. Discernment is not to be confused with the consumer choice of expressive individualism. Discernment must be profoundly participatory, for the Spirit works at the grass-roots level among the whole people of God, including those who are socially disenfranchised (Joel 2; Acts 2). But it is not the democracy of competing factions that characterizes political life and decision-making in many organizations (including church systems) today.

These ways of deepening the church's identity as a people claimed and called to share in God's mission are simple, concrete, ordinary, and thrive at the grass roots. They are what faithful Christians have done throughout history in various contexts. They require little in the way of an elaborate or expensive organizational church; in fact, such expressions can easily distract from them. These practices embody a key premise for opening up a more faithful future: going deeper into tradition in order to *reclaim a usable past*. Moments of revitalization and reform in Christian history have typically involved the recovery of deeper traditions, narratives, and practices that had been lost or distorted.

Abiding, Listening, and Accompanying

The spiritual renewal and deepening that begin within the gathered life of the church are essential for faithful participation in God's mission with respect to neighbors outside it. In a culture of distraction, superficiality, anxiety, fear, and division, disciples of Jesus must abide like branches of the true vine (John 15:4), rooted in God's love, in order to have anything unique to offer in witness. The abundant life Christians are called to share must be known experientially within Christian community first. This happens through spiritual practices—baptism, Eucharist, prayer, hospitality, reconciliation, Sabbath, simplicity, generosity, and so forth—that help make Christians what they are. It has become common today for churches to talk about being externally focused without first paying profound attention to internal spiritual grounding that makes meaningful witness possible.

This abiding in the triune God's communal life and love frees disciples of Jesus to attend and listen deeply to their neighbors. Such deep listening is learned within the gathered community of the church so that disciples grow in their ability to empathetically hear others' stories, struggles, and dreams. It proceeds from a posture of empathy that reflects Jesus's compassionate embrace of everyone, especially those socially shunned or far from God. Deep listening happens best in the context of relationships. It cannot be a technical fix that is aimed at meeting needs or recruiting people to church; it moves in an open-ended direction.

In this sense, such listening is a kind of *accompaniment*: it is literally the biblical "breaking of bread" with someone, that is, sharing life in a posture of mutuality, honoring the stranger as a guest, or being honored by a stranger when you are a guest yourself. Many of Jesus's most transformational moments come in the context of breaking bread: the feeding of the five thousand (Matt. 14:13–21; Mark 6:32–44; Luke 9:10–17; John 6:1–10); the Last Supper (Matt. 26:26–29; Mark 14:22–25; Luke 22:14–23), and the journey to Emmaus (Luke 24:13–35). To accompany is to walk with, to share life, to hear each other speak, and to recognize our mutual vulnerability and humanity.

In a society in which many people outside the church are suspicious of being proselytized, manipulated, or judged by Christians who have done little to hear their stories and earn their trust, deep listening and accompanying begin to create the space for a different kind of encounter. Jürgen Moltmann has said that "all life is community in communication."[3] This

---

3. Moltmann, "Perichoresis: An Old Magic Word for a New Trinitarian Theology," in

community in communication is rooted in God's life as Trinity and the love we participate in through the power of the Spirit. Joining neighbors where they are in order to be present for them, listening to their voices, and breaking bread together opens up the possibility of a deeper participation in God's movement to form and restore community in Christ. Communication of the gospel becomes possible in the context of compassionate community. Mission as abiding, participating, listening, and accompanying resists being boxed into projects or programs. It thrives in the adventure of ordinary disciples joining their neighbors in daily life, trusting the leadership of the Spirit.

A New Moment of Contextualization

The kind of renewed contextualization of Christian witness that is required in America today is not about abandoning tradition wholesale in order to embrace the latest cultural trend in the name of "relevance." Instead, it means tapping the roots of tradition in order to discern life-giving sources and stories for today. This involves distinguishing traditions from their present organizational expression, which many churches struggle to do. As one goes back into the history of most congregations or denominations, there are all kinds of stories of expressing Christian witness and practice in different historical moments and forms than what has come to predominate the present. For instance, most American churches developed a robust committee and program structure only in the early to mid-twentieth century, if at all. Prior to that, their lives were, organizationally, far simpler. Going back into history yields all kinds of moments in which the church adapted, risked itself in order to connect with neighbors, translated its life and language into new cultural vernaculars, or deepened its identity and discipleship.[4]

Many churches are struggling because they are no longer meaningfully contextualized within the changing cultures of their environments. It is important to note that this applies to both emerging generations and diverse populations of neighbors. Cultural vernaculars and forms of church

---

Trinity, Community and Power: Mapping Trajectories in Wesleyan Theology, ed. M. Douglas Meeks (Nashville: Kingswood Books, 2000), 113.

4. One fruitful tool for discovering this usable past is appreciative inquiry; see Mark Lau Branson, *Memories, Hopes and Conversations: Appreciative Inquiry and Congregational Change*, 2nd ed. (Lanham, MD: Rowman and Littlefield, 2016).

life and practice that made perfect sense to older generations are often foreign to younger ones. The wisdom embedded in those traditions must be translated into new cultural forms and practices. This is best done as a dynamic collaboration across groups, where established ways of doing things are honored, but power is shared. Otherwise, the gifts of those traditions will not be passed on.

Becoming Learners

The central identity for American Christians to recover and live more deeply into is perhaps the most basic of all: being disciples, or learners, or apprentices, or students of Jesus in the power of the Spirit. The posture of a learner contrasts with that of the establishment ethos of professionalized ministry, which was the providing of religious goods and services to consumers. The kinds of challenges facing the church today are those for which there is no quick fix, expert solution, or easy answer. In these situations, learning must emerge from among the people as they experiment with new behaviors and indwell new stories. Leaders provide the environments in which people can interpret their challenges, reflect on their guiding assumptions, and try small experiments in alternative ways of being together.[5] It is a matter of behaving our way into new thinking: we actually develop new beliefs and perspectives through behaving in new ways, which is the logic associated with action learning.[6]

Leading learning communities represents a new set of practices and a fresh use of imagination for many church leaders. They are accustomed to managing worship, programs, and pastoral care for an established membership. Their members often expect them to provide technical fixes for the church's challenges, when there is, in fact, no technical fix. Instead, new learning must emerge from the grass roots through processes of trial and experimentation, which will inherently involve some failure along the way. Many established congregations and denominations are not organized around this kind of learning; they are used to providing professional solu-

---

5. See Heifetz and Linsky, *Leadership on the Line: Staying Alive through the Dangers of Leading* (Boston: Harvard Business School Press, 2002); see also Alan J. Roxburgh and Fred Romanuk, *The Missional Leader: Equipping Your Church to Reach a Changing World* (San Francisco: Jossey-Bass, 2006).

6. See Chris Argyris, *Knowledge for Action: A Guide to Overcoming Barriers to Organizational Change* (San Francisco: Jossey-Bass, 1993).

tions, not mobilizing people for messy experimentation. Yet there is no other way for communities facing adaptive challenges to discover a better future than to engage ordinary people at the grass-roots level to try on new behaviors and learn together. Such experimentation is inherently open-ended, which contrasts to the managerial planning methods embraced by many church leaders (and expected by many church members).

No one knows what the future shape of American Christianity will look like, since there is no privileged place from which to view that future. As we noted in chapter 2, the Christian church operates within a dynamic polarity between *forming* and *reforming*. What seems clear at this point is that many established hierarchical forms of church are disintegrating in a fluid, autonomous, and participatory culture. If networks and platforms are the emerging cultural paradigms for organizations in the twenty-first-century environment, contextualizing requires the church to experiment with expressing its life and witness in these forms. The church's identity crisis will be addressed through deepened indwelling of biblical narratives and simple practices of discipleship, discernment, and participation in God's mission by all of God's people. This work unfolds in various kinds of gatherings of Christians, in daily life, and in the neighborhood. It is about *being* the church in ways that shape holistic witness, which is expressed in our doing and telling.

Complex, expensive church hierarchies, dedicated buildings, and professional clergy and staff are unnecessary to accomplish the above. This renewed focus thrives within lean, networked organizations. In this sense, the church can be understood as a *platform* for Christian discipleship and mission, whereby people sharing a story, traditions, and simple practices connect, equip one another, and learn to join God's life and love for the world more deeply. The equipping is multidirectional as participants across the network/community are empowered to have their own voice and influence. As in the early church, the gospel spreads through grass-roots relationships and networking. Deep historical roots for this expression of church are there to be rediscovered.

Platforms and networks are structures as much as hierarchies are, though with very different characteristics.[7] A church that is contextualized in this organizational form depends on cultivating a robust identity. It is

7. See Geoffrey Parker, Marshall Van Alstyne, and Sangeet Paul Choudary, *Platform Revolution: How Networked Markets Are Transforming the Economy and How to Make Them Work for You* (New York: Norton, 2016).

one that is shaped not by hierarchical regulation or top-down control, but via ongoing interpretation, conversation, practice, and engagement around core narratives. Such engagement must be cultivated intentionally. Those with knowledge of the traditions and practices of Christian faith have a vital role to play in mutual equipping, whether or not their authority is enshrined in formal credentialing or office.

Learning with Neighbors

A problem for many congregations today is that they don't know how to be in mission in partnership with their neighbors. The defaults of trying to attract neighbors into the church's established life or trying to meet people's needs as benefactors or providers of goods and services allow church members to avoid a deeper, more demanding task: learning how to form community with these neighbors on their cultural terms. If God is already active in the neighborhood, how do local churches discover and join in God's mission? Such learning involves relationships, deep listening, patience, and vulnerability. It requires going "without purse, bag, or sandals" into the neighborhood to offer God's peace and share in the neighborhood's life and concerns (Luke 10:1–12). Without deepened engagement in the biblical narrative and practices of discipleship and discernment, most church members are unlikely to feel willing or able to risk such a posture. Fundamentally, it undercuts the managerial narratives by which the church regards its neighbors as objects of mission. Instead, neighbors are subjects in God's good yet fallen world, and God is the primary acting subject of reconciliation and restoration. The church's calling is to learn how it is being led by the Spirit to join in this work.

Various forms of experimental Christian community and witness have already emerged in recent years, and their aim is to bring a usable past into this new missionary present. Many of these structures offer alternatives to established congregations that are leaner, lay-empowered, and far less expensive to sustain. They carry forward earlier traditions with a new focus on connecting with local neighbors for the sake of Christian witness and service. New immigrant Christian communities, whose contextualization of the gospel is not captive to the legacies of European modernity and cultural establishment, have much to offer to the wider American church as it navigates these challenges. Newer American Christians will also have to struggle with the faithful recontextualization of the gospel in this context, especially among their own younger generations. There is a great deal to learn from one another.

This is a moment in which many experiments are required, and no single form of church organization can be expected to suffice in all contexts. If the denominational-franchise church reflected the standardization of the twentieth-century economy, twenty-first-century American churches must embody the cultural diversity and complexity of today's environment. Some established churches will likely continue to thrive and connect meaningfully with their neighbors. But a wide array of experiments in forming Christian community will need to be undertaken—across church traditions and contexts—in order for congregations to learn and live into a faithful future. Rowan Williams's concept of a "mixed-economy church" is helpful here, because it recognizes the faithful legacy of established neighborhood churches alongside the need for new expressions of church that will connect with other neighbors where they are.[8]

Denominations and judicatories might shift the conceptualization of their role from being bureaucratic regulators of ministry to being learning networks for grass-roots discipleship and innovation. This presents deep challenges to forms of church polity that emerged out of European Christendom, where domain and control over geographical areas was assumed. Many of these historic polities will need to be systemically renegotiated, suspended, or made provisional to give space for new and better-contextualized patterns of governance and structure to emerge. There is an inherent ambiguity in the process of addressing this level of adaptive change, where the new future must be discovered at the grass-roots level rather than mandated from above.

The forms of Christian community, service, and witness that connect meaningfully with diverse populations and generations in American life today and in the future will emerge largely through local experimentation. Stories and what is learned from those experiments must be shared across contexts, not for replication of a single formula or strategy, but to spark imagination—like the parables. There will likely be large amounts of failure along the way. It would be tragic if what is learned from those failures were never harvested more broadly.[9] Of course, learning through trial and

8. Rowan Williams, "Traditional and Emerging Church," address to General Synod of the Anglican Church, York, UK, July 14, 2003.

9. For a further discussion, see Dwight J. Zscheile, *The Agile Church: Spirit-Led Innovation in an Uncertain Age* (New York: Morehouse Publishing, 2014).

error is nothing new in a biblical perspective. This is how God's people have always participated in God's mission: not in having the correct strategies and plans to follow, but improvisationally discerning the Spirit's leadership. Mistakes and failures certainly didn't prevent Abraham, Sarah, Moses, David, or the disciples from playing their role in God's mission.

Changing the Questions

For too long the church in America has been consumed with its own internal life, without paying sufficient attention either to the cultural changes taking place around it or to discerning what God is in fact doing amid those changes. In some respects, it is easier to devise new strategies and programs for church renewal than to confront the deeper and more bewildering shifts in identity, meaning, community, and participation unfolding in American society today. Established church members tend to expect leaders to keep things the way they are, not to reorient congregational life around innovation. It is especially challenging when that innovation involves new theological imagination, new practices, and new behaviors. Given the pace and magnitude of change in American society today, and the loss that accompanies it, established church members can hardly be blamed if they look to the church as an unchanging refuge in an insecure world.[10]

Yet the very nature of the church has the inherent ability to adapt and change in order to participate faithfully in what the Spirit of God is bringing forth in the world. That change does not represent a wholesale uprooting from familiar traditions, but rather the fruit of new growth that comes from tapping and translating the rich life within the roots of tradition. A plant can bring forth new growth only when it is deeply rooted in the sources of its nourishment. For the church, those sources are not just the ways of faithful ancestors, but the energy and leadership of the living God through the Spirit as the church continues to be formed in new cultural contexts.

Rather than jumping to a new focus on how to revitalize the church, or even how to plant new churches, it would be better to linger on the questions of what God might be up to in the midst of all this change and transformation. As in the biblical times of wilderness and exile, or when the new Christian community crossed cultural barriers from Jerusalem into

---

10. Reggie McNeal, *Kingdom Come: Why We Must Give Up Our Obsession over Fixing the Church and What We Should Do Instead* (Carol Stream, IL: Tyndale Momentum, 2015).

the gentile world, something new is emerging amid disorientation and loss. The temptation is to hurry through such a moment in order to escape its inevitable pain. However, the people of Israel spent a generation in the wilderness, and God made clear in Jeremiah's letter to the exiles in Babylon that there was to be no quick deliverance from the displacement they were experiencing (Jer. 29). It is not at all clear what forms of church will emerge in order to faithfully and fruitfully bear witness to neighbors in today's America. But if the historical discussion in this book teaches us anything, it is that the church has undergone dramatic adaptation before. That is its nature.

Joining the Spirit's Movement

What might the Spirit of God be up to in this moment of profound dislocation and transformation in American society and culture? As we have seen, the history of American Christianity has been marked by continuous changes and challenges as churches have struggled to engage in meaningful witness with their neighbors in this context. The temptation in recent years has been to identify the next big thing and jump on board. But this narrative is itself captive in many ways to late-modern consumer capitalism, which continually seeks to replace what is old with the latest product or fad. This planned obsolescence accustoms us never to linger for very long in any one place or to abide very deeply. Christian mission must reject that option for the sake of deeper connections with God, one another, and our neighbors. What is required instead is ongoing learning and discernment as the church discovers—in relationship with its neighbors—places of meaningful connection between God's vision for abundant life in Christ (John 10:10) and what is emerging in the broader culture. Here are some possible touch points.

Local/Global Connections

The twenty-first-century world is globalized and interconnected—via migration, ease of travel, and technology. This brings cross-cultural encounters into their local environment for many Christian communities. Christianity is now a majority-world faith whose areas of greatest growth, strength, and vitality lie in places that have not been captive to the assumptions of Christendom or Western modernity.[11] Moreover, many American congregations have companion relationships with congregations in other cultural contexts around the world. Some host immigrant congregations within their own buildings. There are all sorts of global/local interconnections already present in the neighborhoods and lives of many American churches. What might the Spirit be up to in all this?

There are tremendous opportunities for Christians to learn from one another across cultural lines: how the gospel speaks in different contexts and thus how they can hear it afresh in their own context. Through the intermixing of global cultures on an unprecedented scale, Western Christians have opportunities to encounter the gospel in forms not captive to Enlightenment modernity. Christians from majority-world contexts have opportunities to share their witness as well as being challenged by the gospel in cultural forms different from their own. This kind of exchange must take place in the context of relationships; it requires cultivation and being present to one another over time. The Spirit has brought a lot of energy to congregations engaged in companion partnerships. The question is how these kinds of encounters can go deeper, particularly in connecting to neighbors of different cultures already present in the local.

Seeking Spiritual Meaning and Justice

It would be easy to despair over the number of people who are leaving church in America today, especially younger generations. Established patterns, structures, and assumptions of congregational life are not speaking to huge numbers of them. But these neighbors are genuine and passionate in their search for spiritual meaning and purpose—and in their hunger to participate in creating a more just and peaceful world. The Spirit is alive among these "dones" and "nones," even though they are rejecting traditional forms of church participation and belonging. Rather than adopting a posture of critical judgment, churches would be better served by affirming and joining their yearnings for a better world and their passion for making a difference.

If one's goal of missionary engagement with dones and nones is to get them into the established life of existing congregations so as to sustain those congregations in their present form, that will likely not go very far.

---

11. Lamin O. Sanneh, *Whose Religion Is Christianity? The Gospel beyond the West* (Grand Rapids: Eerdmans, 2003).

However, if the focus of missionary engagement is connecting with what the Spirit is up to in their lives and helping them to know God's vision for human flourishing in the gospel of Jesus, there is much more promise. This requires deep listening to their stories, struggles, and dreams. The church might affirm where God is at work and might invite them into the spiritual depth and wisdom of Christian tradition and practice in the context of community, even if the form of that community may not look much like established congregational life. Such fruitful impulses as the affirmation of diversity, the need for justice, and a willingness to live simply in harmony with the earth might be reframed within the wider perspective of biblical teachings. When secularized ideals of creating a better world run aground on the persistence of human sin, the church may be able to offer a more adequate vision.

Community and Collaboration

Amid the fragmented individualism and fluidity of contemporary American life, there is a deep yearning for connection and community. This is being expressed in new forms, often forms that are outside established institutional structures. Social media and technology are linking people together to cocreate shared spaces of meaning and participation, even if they can also lead to cultural atomization and tribalism. The question of unity amidst diversity is a profound one facing the contemporary United States. There are vital Spirit-led impulses motivating people to find one another, collaborate together, and develop new paths for sharing life.

The church must inhabit these spaces, even as it must also carry forth practices of embodied community life that are in danger of being lost. Christian mission today requires being present to people where they are, which includes whatever forms of connection and community are emerging. At the same time, the church bears the wisdom of centuries of covenant community life, from the biblical witness to Israel and the generative Spirit-led community of the early church, through monasticism and the countless experiments in communal life that have appeared through Christian history. The church must find ways to translate and share this wisdom in a moment when people crave community but no longer inhabit legacy structures that sustain it, take it deeper, and allow it to thrive over time.

The complex challenges of discovering identity, unity, and community in a diverse and fractured America and world present a huge opening for Christians to witness to the work of the Spirit. The Spirit creates patterns of community life in which social and cultural differences are neither negated nor are causes for division. In the community of Christ, the Spirit reconciles people into one body that is both socially heterogeneous and united (Gal. 3:28). As the Spirit continues to diversify the US population, bringing people of every tribe and nation together into this space, the need for an alternative ground for unity and reconciliation beyond secular pluralism, identity politics, and political correctness has grown acute. Christians have a unique and compelling testimony to offer.

Conclusion

Learning to wonder deeply in community about what God might be up to in, among, and beyond us at this moment pushes us into a new posture of patience, vulnerability, and listening. There are powerful cultural forces that distract the church from such a posture. But there are also rich stories and traditions in the church's life that would inform it. A genuinely missionary encounter between the gospel and contemporary American culture will of necessity take many forms, reflecting both the multidimensional character of the gospel and the rich diversity of the US context. The triune God has been faithful in this place over centuries of complicated mission history, even when the American church painfully distorted its witness to the gospel. That faithfulness should free the church to enter with courage into a new era of more fully participating in God's mission.

Ecumenical and Evangelical Mission Conferences of the Twentieth and Twenty-first Centuries

It is helpful to have an understanding of the numerous missionary conferences sponsored by ecumenicals and evangelicals during the twentieth and twenty-first centuries. These conferences represent crucial markers for noting the changes taking place within the missions movement, along with the substantive contributions made toward developing the discipline of missiology and defining mission theology. The attached chart provides a listing of the primary Protestant conferences convened since the beginning of the twentieth century. We provide a brief description of some important events and a definition of key movements.

Edinburgh 1910: The major world missionary conference that built on previous world conferences where the church in the West planned for the completion of the "evangelization of the world in our generation," but which came largely to represent the culmination of the missionary work of the nineteenth century.

IMC: The International Missionary Council was formed in the aftermath of Edinburgh, and was made up of representatives of national councils of mission. It sponsored a missionary conference about every ten years.

Faith and Order: An ecumenical movement growing out of Edinburgh that was formed by the church in the West to consider matters of confession and issues of polity with respect to diverse faith traditions

Life and Work: Another ecumenical movement growing out of Edinburgh that was formed by the church in the West to consider matters of shared ministry and common work among diverse faith traditions.

IFMA: The Interdenominational Foreign Mission Association was formed in 1917 by fundamentalist mission organizations as an alternative to the mission work of mainline churches, especially those they saw as being influenced by modern liberalism. Since the 1960s it has partnered with the EFMA, and it recently changed its name to Cross Global Link.

EFMA: The Evangelical Fellowship of Mission Agencies was formed in 1945 to coordinate mission efforts of the more conservative denominations that had formed the National Association of Evangelicals in 1943. Since the 1960s it has partnered with the IFMA, and it recently changed its name to Mission Exchange.

WCC: The World Council of Churches was organized in 1948 as a result of the joint work of the Faith and Order and Life and Work movements. It has continued to sponsor a major assembly about every five-to-seven years.

CWME: The Commission on World Mission and Evangelism was formed when the IMC merged into the WCC in 1961. It has continued to sponsor a major mission conference about every ten years. It also produced the important document *Mission and Evangelism: An Ecumenical Affirmation* (1982, with a revised update in 2013 published as *Together towards Life: Mission and Evangelism in Changing Landscapes*).

Billy Graham Evangelistic Association: This organization helped shape the reemergence of evangelicalism in the United States after World War II. It sponsored the 1966 evangelical mission conference in Berlin and was a key contributor to the eventual formation of the Lausanne movement.

LCWE: The Lausanne Committee for World Evangelization was formed following the major evangelical mission conference in 1974, which had produced the important Lausanne Covenant. It continues to sponsor many regional mission conferences and host several international conferences under the Lausanne banner at Manila in 1989, which produced the Manila Manifesto, and in Cape Town, South Africa, which produced the Cape Town Commitment.

RCC: The Roman Catholic Church became a major player in the reframing of mission at Vatican II in the early 1960s (see especially the encyclical *Ad Gentes*). The CELAM (*Consejo Episcopal Latinoamericano*) conferences were convened by Latin America bishops in 1955, 1968, and 1979. Pope Paul VI's issuing of *Evangelii Nuntiandi* in 1975 affirmed the role of every Christian in spreading the faith and linked evangelization with concerns for peace, justice, and development. Another CELAM conference in 1992 contributed a progressive view using liberation theology to promote basic ecclesiastical communities and a "preferential option for the poor." More recently (2013), Pope Francis issued *Evangelii Gaudium* ("The Joy of the Gospel"), which defined the church's primary mission of evangelism in the modern world.

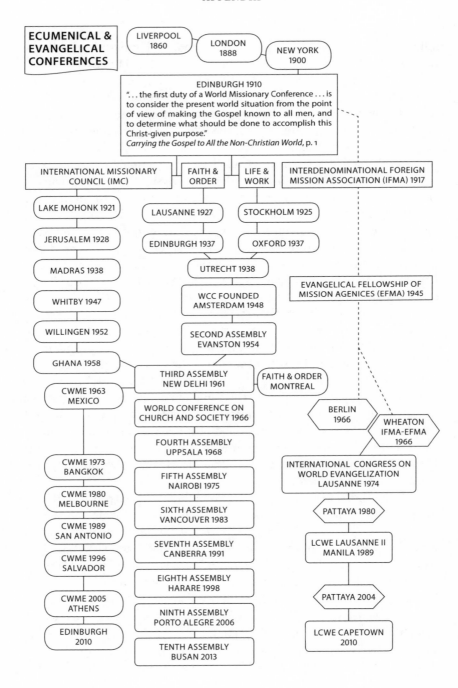

ECUMENICAL & EVANGELICAL CONFERENCES

LIVERPOOL 1860

LONDON 1888

NEW YORK 1900

EDINBURGH 1910
"... the first duty of a World Missionary Conference ... is to consider the present world situation from the point of view of making the Gospel known to all men, and to determine what should be done to accomplish this Christ-given purpose."
Carrying the Gospel to All the Non-Christian World, p. 1

INTERNATIONAL MISSIONARY COUNCIL (IMC)

FAITH & ORDER

LIFE & WORK

INTERDENOMINATIONAL FOREIGN MISSION ASSOCIATION (IFMA) 1917

LAKE MOHONK 1921

LAUSANNE 1927

STOCKHOLM 1925

JERUSALEM 1928

EDINBURGH 1937

OXFORD 1937

MADRAS 1938

UTRECHT 1938

EVANGELICAL FELLOWSHIP OF MISSION AGENICES (EFMA) 1945

WHITBY 1947

WCC FOUNDED AMSTERDAM 1948

WILLINGEN 1952

SECOND ASSEMBLY EVANSTON 1954

GHANA 1958

THIRD ASSEMBLY NEW DELHI 1961

FAITH & ORDER MONTREAL

CWME 1963 MEXICO

WORLD CONFERENCE ON CHURCH AND SOCIETY 1966

BERLIN 1966

WHEATON IFMA-EFMA 1966

FOURTH ASSEMBLY UPPSALA 1968

CWME 1973 BANGKOK

FIFTH ASSEMBLY NAIROBI 1975

INTERNATIONAL CONGRESS ON WORLD EVANGELIZATION LAUSANNE 1974

CWME 1980 MELBOURNE

SIXTH ASSEMBLY VANCOUVER 1983

PATTAYA 1980

CWME 1989 SAN ANTONIO

SEVENTH ASSEMBLY CANBERRA 1991

LCWE LAUSANNE II MANILA 1989

CWME 1996 SALVADOR

EIGHTH ASSEMBLY HARARE 1998

CWME 2005 ATHENS

NINTH ASSEMBLY PORTO ALEGRE 2006

PATTAYA 2004

EDINBURGH 2010

TENTH ASSEMBLY BUSAN 2013

LCWE CAPETOWN 2010

Select Bibliography

Adams, David Wallace. *Education for Extinction: American Indians and the Boarding School Experience, 1875–1928*. Lawrence: University Press of Kansas, 1995.

Adams, James Truslow. *The Epic of America*. 1931; New York: Simon Publications, 2001.

Adeney, Miriam. "Shalom Tourist: Loving Your Neighbor While Using Her." *Missiology: An International Review* 34, no. 4 (2006): 463–76.

Ahlstrom, Sydney E. *A Religious History of the American People*. New Haven: Yale University Press, 1972.

Ammerman, Nancy, et al. *Studying Congregations: A New Handbook*. Nashville: Abingdon, 1998.

Ammerman, Nancy Tatom. *Sacred Stories, Spiritual Tribes: Finding Religion in Everyday Life*. New York: Oxford University Press, 2013.

Anderson, Gerald H., and Thomas F. Stransky. *Liberation Theologies in North America and Europe*. Mission Trends 4. New York: Paulist Press, 1979.

Argyris, Chris. *Knowledge for Action: A Guide to Overcoming Barriers to Organizational Change*. San Francisco: Jossey-Bass, 1993.

Axtell, James. *The Invasion Within: The Contest of Cultures in Colonial North America*. New York: Oxford University Press, 1985.

Barabasi, Albert-Laszlo. *Linked: How Everything Is Connected to Everything Else and What It Means for Business, Science, and Everyday Life*. New York: Plume, 2003.

Barry, John M. *Roger Williams and the Creation of the American Soul: Church, State, and the Birth of Liberty*. New York: Penguin, 2012.

Bass, Diana Butler. *Christianity after Religion: The End of Church and the Birth of a New Spiritual Awakening*. San Francisco: HarperOne, 2012.

———. *Grounded: Finding God in the World*. San Francisco: HarperOne, 2015.

Bass, Dorothy C. *Practicing Our Faith: A Way of Life for a Searching People*. San Francisco: Jossey-Bass, 1997.

Bauman, Zygmunt. *Community: Seeking Safety in an Insecure World*. Malden, MA: Polity Press, 2001.

Bauman, Zygmunt, and Carlo Bordoni. *State of Crisis*. Malden, MA: Polity Press, 2014.

Belcher, Jim. *Deep Church: A Third Way beyond Emerging and Traditional.* Downers Grove, IL: InterVarsity, 2009.

Bellah, Robert N. *The Broken Covenant: American Civil Religion in a Time of Trial.* New York: Seabury, 1975.

Benkler, Yochai. *The Wealth of Networks: How Social Production Transforms Markets and Freedom.* New Haven: Yale University Press, 2006.

Bernstein, Alison R. *American Indians and World War II: Toward a New Era in Indian Affairs.* Norman: University of Oklahoma Press, 1999.

Best, Steven, and Douglas Kellner. *The Postmodern Turn.* New York: The Guilford Press, 1997.

Bevans, Stephen B. *Models of Contextual Theology.* Revised and expanded ed. Maryknoll, NY: Orbis, 2002.

Bevans, Stephen B., and Roger P. Schroeder. *Constants in Context: A Theology of Mission for Today.* Maryknoll, NY: Orbis, 2004.

Beyerhaus, Peter. *Shaken Foundations: Theological Foundations for Mission.* Grand Rapids: Zondervan, 1972.

Bishop, Bill, and Robert G. Cushing, *The Big Sort: Why the Clustering of Like-Minded America Is Tearing Us Apart.* Boston: Houghton Mifflin, 2008.

Blauw, Johannes. *The Missionary Nature of the Church: A Survey of the Biblical Theology of Mission.* New York: McGraw-Hill, 1962.

Bosch, David J. *Transforming Mission: Paradigm Shifts in Theology of Mission.* Maryknoll, NY: Orbis, 1991.

Bottum, Joseph. *An Anxious Age: The Post-Protestant Ethic and the Spirit of America.* New York: Image Books, 2014.

Boylan, Anne M. *Sunday School: The Formation of an American Institution, 1790–1880.* New Haven: Yale University Press, 1990.

Branson, Mark Lau. *Memories, Hopes and Conversations: Appreciative Inquiry and Congregational Change.* 2nd ed. Lanham, MD: Rowman and Littlefield, 2016.

Browning, Dave. *Hybrid Church: The Fusion of Intimacy and Impact.* San Francisco: Jossey-Bass, 2011.

Burtchaell, James Tunstead. *From Synagogue to Church: Public Services and Offices in the Earliest Christian Communities.* New York: Cambridge University Press, 1992.

Bush, Michael. "Calvin and the Reformanda Sayings." In *Calvinus sacrarum literarum interpres: Papers of the International Congress on Calvin Research*, ed. Herman J. Selderhuis. Göttingen: Vandenhoeck und Ruprecht, 2008.

Bustraan, Richard A. *The Jesus People Movement: A Story of Spiritual Revolution among the Hippies.* Eugene, OR: Pickwick Publications, 2014.

Carey, Patrick W., and Earl C. Muller, SJ, eds. *Theological Education in the Catholic Tradition: Contemporary Challenges.* New York: Crossroad, 1997.

Carey, William. *An Enquiry into the Obligations of Christians.* Leicester, UK: Printed by Ann Ireland, 1792.

Castells, Manuel. *The Rise of the Network Society.* 2nd ed. Malden, MA: Blackwell, 2000.

Castro, Emilio, ed. "Mission and Evangelism: An Ecumenical Affirmation." *International Review of Mission* 71, no. 284 (October 1982): 427–51.

Chaves, Mark. *Congregations in America.* Cambridge, MA: Harvard University Press, 2004.

Cherlin, Andrew J. *Labor's Love Lost: The Rise and Fall of the Working-Class Family in America*. New York: Russell Sage Foundation, 2014.

———. *The Marriage-Go-Round: The State of Marriage and the Family in America Today*. New York: Alfred A. Knopf, 2009.

Chester, Tim, and Steve Timmis. *Total Church: A Radical Reshaping around Gospel and Community*. Wheaton, IL: Crossway, 2008.

Clark Hine, Darlene, et al. *African Americans: A Concise History*. Boston: Pearson, 2012.

Cogley, Richard W. *John Eliot's Mission to the Indians before King Philip's War*. Cambridge, MA: Harvard University Press, 1999.

Colby, Sandra, and Jennifer M. Ortman. "Projections of the Size and Composition of the U.S. Population: 2014–2060." Washington, DC: US Census Bureau, 2015.

Cole, Neil. *Church 3.0: Upgrades for the Future of the Church*. San Francisco: Jossey-Bass, 2010.

———. *Organic Church: Growing Faith Where Life Happens*. San Francisco: Jossey-Bass, 2005.

Coleman, Robert. *The Master Plan of Evangelism*. Westwood, NJ: Fleming H. Revell, 1964.

Cormode, Scott. *Making Spiritual Sense: Christian Leaders as Spiritual Interpreters*. Nashville: Abingdon, 2006.

Corrigan, John, and Winthrop S. Hudson. *Religion in America*. 10th ed. Upper Saddle River, NJ: Pearson-Prentice Hall, 2010.

Cox, Stephen. *American Christianity: The Continuing Revolution*. Austin: University of Texas Press, 2014.

Danker, Frederick William. *No Room in the Brotherhood: The Preus-Otten Purge of Missouri*. St. Louis: Clayton Publishing House, 1977.

Dean, Kenda Creasy. *Almost Christian: What the Faith of Our Teenagers Is Telling the American Church*. New York: Oxford University Press, 2010.

Demerath, N. J. "Cultural Victory and Organizational Defeat in the Paradoxical Decline of Liberal Protestantism." *Journal for the Scientific Study of Religion* 34, no. 4 (1995): 458–69.

Dever, Mark. *The Deliberate Church: Building Your Ministry on the Gospel*. Wheaton, IL: Crossway, 2005.

De Zengotita, Thomas. *Mediated: How the Media Shapes Your World and the Way You Live in It*. New York: Bloomsbury, 2005.

Drescher, Elizabeth. *Choosing Our Religion*. New York: Oxford University Press, 2016.

Du Bois, W. E. B. *The Souls of Black Folk*. 1903; Mineola, NY: Dover Publications, 1994.

Dunbar-Ortiz, Roxanne. *An Indigenous Peoples' History of the United States*. Boston: Beacon, 2014.

Dunkelman, Marc J. *The Vanishing Neighbor: The Transformation of American Community*. New York: W. W. Norton, 2014.

Ellis, Richard J. *To the Flag: The Unlikely History of the Pledge of Allegiance*. Lawrence: University Press of Kansas, 2005.

Farley, Edward. *Theologia: The Fragmentation and Unity of Theological Education*. Philadelphia: Fortress, 1983.

Finke, Roger, and Rodney Stark. *The Churching of America, 1776–2005: Winners and Losers in Our Religious Economy*. New Brunswick, NJ: Rutgers University Press, 2005.

Flannery, Austin P., ed. *Documents of Vatican II*. Grand Rapids: Eerdmans, 1975.

Flemming, Dean E. *Recovering the Full Mission of God: A Biblical Perspective on Being, Doing, and Telling*. Downers Grove, IL: IVP Academic, 2013.

Flett, John. *The Witness of God: The Trinity, Missio Dei, Karl Barth, and the Nature of Christian Community*. Grand Rapids: Eerdmans, 2010.

Foley, Michael W., and Dean R. Hoge. *Religion and the New Immigrants: How Faith Communities Form Our Newest Citizens*. New York: Oxford University Press, 2007.

Foster, Mark S. *From Streetcar to Superhighway: American City Planners and Urban Transportation, 1900–1940*. Philadelphia: Temple University Press, 1981.

Frazier, E. Franklin. *The Negro Church in America*. New York: Schocken [Random House], 1974.

Fremon, David K. *The Jim Crow Laws and Racism in the United States*. New York: Enslow, 2014.

Friedan, Betty. *The Feminine Mystique*. New York: Norton, 1963.

Gaddis, John Lewis. *The Cold War: A New History*. New York: Penguin, 2006.

Gerber, David A. *American Immigration: A Very Short Introduction*. New York: Oxford University Press, 2011.

Gibbs, Eddie, and Ryan Bolger, *Emerging Churches: Creating Christian Communities in Postmodern Cultures*. Grand Rapids: Baker, 2006.

Giddens, Anthony. *Modernity and Self-Identity*. Stanford, CA: Stanford University Press, 1991.

———. *The Transformation of Intimacy: Sexuality, Love, and Eroticism in Modern Societies*. Stanford, CA: Stanford University Press, 1992.

Gitlin, Todd. *The Twilight of Common Dreams: Why America Is Wracked by Culture Wars*. New York: Metropolitan Books, 1995.

Gladden, Washington. *Working People and Their Employers*. Boston: Lockwood, Brooks, and Company, 1876.

Goheen, Michael. *Introducing Christian Mission Today*. Downers Grove, IL: IVP Academic, 2014.

Golembiewski, Robert T. *Sensitivity Training and the Laboratory Approach*. Itasca, IL: F. E. Peacock, 1973.

Gorman, Michael J. *Becoming the Gospel: Paul, Participation, and Mission*. Grand Rapids: Eerdmans, 2015.

Grossman, Cathy Lynn. "The Megachurch Boom Rolls on, but Concerns Are Rising Too." *Religion News Service*, December 2, 2015.

Guder, Darrell L., ed. *Missional Church: A Vision for the Sending of the Church in North America*. Grand Rapids: Eerdmans, 1998.

Gunton, Colin E. *The Promise of Trinitarian Theology*. Edinburgh: T. & T. Clark, 1991.

Gusterson, Hugh, and Catherine Besteman, eds. *The Insecure American: How We Got Here and What We Should Do about It*. Berkeley: University of California Press, 2010.

Habermas, Jürgen. *The Theory of Communicative Action*. 2 vols. Boston: Beacon, 1984.

Halberstam, David. *The Fifties*. New York: Villard Books, 1993.

Hanciles, Jehu. *Beyond Christendom: Globalization, African Migration, and the Transformation of the West*. Maryknoll, NY: Orbis, 2008.

Handy, Robert. *A Christian America: Protestant Hopes and Historical Realities.* New York: Oxford University Press, 1971.

Hatch, Nathan O. *The Democratization of American Christianity.* New Haven: Yale University Press, 1989.

Hauerwas, Stanley, and William H. Willimon, *Resident Aliens: Life in the Christian Colony.* Nashville: Abingdon, 1989.

Heifetz, Ronald A., and Martin Linsky, *Leadership on the Line: Staying Alive through the Dangers of Leading.* Boston: Harvard Business School Press, 2002.

Herberg, Will. *Protestant, Catholic, Jew: An Essay in American Religious Sociology.* New York: Doubleday, 1955.

Herring, Hayim. *Tomorrow's Synagogue Today: Creating Vibrant Centers of Jewish Life.* Herndon, VA: The Alban Institute, 2012.

Herring, Hayim, and Terri Martinson Elton, *Leading Congregations and Nonprofits in a Connected World.* Lanham, MD: Rowman and Littlefield, 2016.

Hesselgrave, David J., ed. *Theology and Mission: Papers Given at the Trinity Consultation No. 1.* Grand Rapids: Baker, 1978.

Hirsch, Alan. *The Forgotten Ways: Reactivating the Missional Church.* Grand Rapids: Brazos, 2009.

Hochschild, Arlie Russell. *Strangers in Their Own Land: Anger and Mourning on the American Right.* New York: New Press, 2016.

Hocking, William Ernest, and Laymen's Foreign Missions Inquiry, Commission of Appraisal, eds. *Re-Thinking Missions: A Laymen's Inquiry after One Hundred Years.* New York: Harper, 1932.

Hoekendijk, Johannes Christiaan. *The Church inside Out.* Philadelphia: Westminster, 1966.

Hoge, Dean R. *Division in the Protestant House: The Basic Reasons behind Intra-Church Conflicts.* Philadelphia: Westminster, 1976.

Hoge, Dean R., Benton Johnson, and Donald A. Luidens. *Vanishing Boundaries: The Religion of Mainline Protestant Baby Boomers.* Louisville: Westminster John Knox, 1994.

Hogg, William Richey. "The Teaching of Missiology: Some Reflections on the Historical and Current Scene." *Missiology* 15, no. 4 (1987): 487–506.

Hood, Fred J. "Evolution of the Denomination among the Reformed of the Middle and Southern States, 1780–1840." In *Denominationalism,* edited by Russell E. Richey. Nashville: Abingdon, 1977.

Howe, Daniel Walker. *What Hath God Wrought: The Transformation of America, 1815–1848.* New York: Oxford University Press, 2007.

Howe, Irving, and Kenneth Libo, *How We Lived: A Documentary History of Immigrant Jews in America, 1880–1930.* New York: Putman Publishing Group, 1983.

Hunsberger, George H., and Craig Van Gelder, eds. *The Church between Gospel and Culture: The Emerging Mission in North America.* Grand Rapids: Eerdmans, 1996.

Hunt, Robert. "Public Missiology and Anxious Tribalism." *Missiology* 44, no. 2 (2016): 129–41.

Hunter, James Davison. *To Change the World: The Irony, Tragedy, and Possibility of Christianity in the Late Modern World.* New York: Oxford University Press, 2010.

Hutchison, William R. *Errand to the World: American Protestant Thought and Foreign Missions.* Chicago: University of Chicago Press, 1987.

Irvin, Dale T., and Scott W. Sunquist. *History of the World Christian Movement.* Vol. 1: *Earliest Christianity to 1453.* Maryknoll, NY: Orbis, 2009.

————. *History of the World Christian Movement.* Vol. 2: *Modern Christianity from 1454–1800.* Maryknoll, NY: Orbis, 2012.

Jenkins, Philip. *The Next Christendom: The Coming of Global Christianity.* 3rd ed. New York: Oxford University Press, 2011.

Jones, Robert P. *The End of White Christian America.* New York: Simon and Schuster, 2016.

Kallestad, Walt, et al. *Entrepreneurial Faith: Launching Bold Initiatives to Expand God's Kingdom.* New York: WaterBook Press, 2004.

Kanter, Beth, and Allison H. Fine. *The Networked Nonprofit: Connecting with Social Media to Drive Change.* San Francisco: Jossey-Bass, 2010.

Katongole, Emmanuel, and Chris Rice. *Reconciling All Things: A Christian Vision for Justice, Race, and Healing.* Downers Grove, IL: Intervarsity, 2008.

Kegan, Robert. *In Over Our Heads: The Mental Demands of Modern Life.* Cambridge, MA: Harvard University Press, 1994.

Kelley, Dean M. *Why Conservative Churches Are Growing: A Study in Sociology of Religion.* San Francisco: HarperCollins, 1972.

Kelly, Barbara M. *Expanding the American Dream: Building and Rebuilding Levittown.* Albany: State University of New York Press, 1993.

Kelsey, David H. *To Love God Truly: What's Theological about a Theological School?* Louisville: Westminster John Knox, 1992.

Kidd, Thomas S. *The Great Awakening: The Roots of Evangelical Christianity in Colonial America.* New Haven: Yale University Press, 2009.

Kim, Elijah F. *The Rise of the Church in the Global South: The Decline of Western Christianity and the Rise of Majority World Christianity.* Eugene, OR: Wipf and Stock, 2012.

Kim, Sebastian, and Kirsteen Kim. *Christianity as a World Religion.* New York: Continuum, 2008.

Kraemer, H. *A Theology of the Laity.* Philadelphia: Westminster, 1958.

Kroeger, James. "Papal Mission Wisdom: Five Mission Encyclicals, 1919–1959." In *A Century of Catholic Mission. Roman Catholic Missiology, 1910 to the Present,* edited by Stephen B. Bevans. Regnum Edinburgh Centenary Series. Cornwall, UK: Regnum Books, 2013.

Kwiyani, Harvey C. *Sent Forth: African Missionary Work in the West.* Maryknoll, NY: Orbis, 2014.

LaCugna, Catherine Mowry. *God for Us: The Trinity and Christian Life.* San Francisco: HarperSanFrancisco, 1991.

Latham, Robert O., and World Council of Churches, Commission on World Mission and Evangelism. *God for All Men: The Meeting of the Commission on World Mission and Evangelism of the World Council of Churches at Mexico City, December 8th to 19th, 1963.* London: Edinburgh House, 1964.

Latourette, Kenneth Scott. *A History of the Expansion of Christianity.* 7 vols. New York: Harper and Row, 1937.

Lausanne Committee for World Evangelization and the World Evangelical Fellowship. Lausanne Occasional Paper 21: "Evangelism and Social Responsibility: An Evangelical Commitment," available at: http://www.lausanne.org/all-documents/lop -21.html (accessed July 3, 2016).

Leech, Kenneth. *Youthquake: The Growth of a Counter-Culture through Two Decades.* Totowa, NJ: Littlefield, Adams, 1977.

Lemann, Nicholas. *The Promised Land: The Great Black Migration and How It Changed America.* New York: Vintage, 1992.

Levin, Yuval. *The Fractured Republic: Renewing America's Social Contract in the Age of Individualism.* New York: Basic Books, 2016.

Levine, Bruce. "Conservatism, Nativism, and Slavery: Thomas R. Whitney and the Origins of the Know-Nothing Party." *Journal of American History* 88, no. 2 (2001): 455–88.

Lincoln, C. Eric, and Lawrence H. Mamiya. *The Black Church in the African American Experience.* Durham, NC: Duke University Press, 1990.

Lipka, Michael. "The Most and Least Diverse U.S. Religious Groups." Washington, DC: Pew Research Center, July 27, 2015.

———. "Which U.S. Religious Groups Are Oldest and Youngest?" Washington, DC: Pew Research Center, 2016.

Locke, John. "A Letter Concerning Toleration." In *Locke on Politics, Religion, and Education,* edited by Maurice Cranston. New York: Collier, 1965.

Logan, Bob. *Beyond Church Growth: Action Plans for Developing a Dynamic Church.* Grand Rapids: Revell, 1990.

Luhrmann, T. M. *When God Talks Back: Understanding the American Evangelical Relationship with God.* New York: Alfred A. Knopf, 2012.

Marshman, John Clark. *The Life and Times of Carey, Marshman, and Ward: Embracing the History of the Serampore Mission.* London: Longman, Brown, Green & Roberts, 1859.

Marty, Martin E. *Righteous Empire: The Protestant Experience in America.* New York: Dial Press, 1970.

Matthews, Shailer. *Scientific Management in the Churches.* Chicago: University of Chicago Press, 1912.

May, Mark Arthur, William Adams Brown, and Frank K. Shuttleworth. *The Education of American Ministers.* New York: Institute of Social and Religious Research, 1934.

McGavran, Donald. *Understanding Church Growth.* Rev. ed. Grand Rapids: Eerdmans, 1980.

———. "Will Uppsala Betray the Two Billion?" *Church Growth Bulletin: Institute of Church Growth* 7, no. 6 (July 1971): 149–53.

McKnight, Scot. *Kingdom Conspiracy: Returning to the Radical Mission of the Local Church.* Grand Rapids: Brazos, 2014.

McNeal, Reggie. *Kingdom Come: Why We Must Give Up Our Obsession over Fixing the Church and What We Should Do Instead.* Carol Stream, IL: Tyndale Momentum, 2015.

———. *Missional Renaissance: Changing the Scorecard for the Church.* San Francisco: Jossey-Bass, 2009.

————. *The Present Future: Six Tough Questions for the Church*. San Francisco: Jossey-Bass, 2009.

Mead, Sidney E. "Denominationalism: The Shape of Protestantism in America." In *Denominationalism*, edited by Russell E. Richey. Nashville: Abingdon, 1977.

Mercadante, Linda. *Belief without Borders: Inside the Minds of the Spiritual but Not Religious*. New York: Oxford University Press, 2014.

Miller, Glenn T. *Piety and Intellect: The Aims and Purposes of Ante-Bellum Theological Education*. Atlanta: Scholars Press, 1990.

————. *Piety and Profession: American Protestant Theological Education*. Grand Rapids: Eerdmans, 2007.

Miller, Perry. *Errand into the Wilderness*. Cambridge, MA: Belknap Press, 1956.

Minatrea, Milfred. *Shaped by God's Heart: The Passion and Practices of Missional Churches*. San Francisco: Jossey-Bass, 2004.

Mitchell, Henry H. *Black Church Beginnings: The Long-Hidden Realities of the First Years*. Grand Rapids: Eerdmans, 2004.

Moltmann, Jürgen. *The Church in the Power of the Spirit: A Contribution to Messianic Ecclesiology*. Minneapolis: Fortress, 1993.

————. *The Crucified God: The Cross of Christ as the Foundation and Criticism of Christian Theology*. Minneapolis: Fortress Press, 1993.

————. "Perichoresis: An Old Magic Word for a New Trinitarian Theology." In *Trinity, Community and Power: Mapping Trajectories in Wesleyan Theology*, edited by M. Douglas Meeks. Nashville: Kingswood Books, 2000.

————. *The Trinity and the Kingdom: The Doctrine of God*. Minneapolis: Fortress, 1993.

Moran, Jeffrey P. *The Scopes Trial: A Brief History with Documents*. New York: Bedford/St. Martin's, 2002.

Moreau, A. Scott. *Contextualization in World Missions: Mapping and Assessing Evangelical Models*. Grand Rapids: Kregel Publications, 2012.

Mullin, Robert Bruce, and Russell E. Richey, eds. *Reimagining Denominationalism: Interpretive Essays*. New York: Oxford University Press, 1994.

Murray, Charles A. *American Exceptionalism: An Experiment in History*. Washington, DC: AEI Press, 2013.

————. *Coming Apart: The State of White America, 1960–2010*. New York: Crown Forum, 2012.

Myklebust, Olav Guttorm. *The Study of Missions in Theological Education; an Historical Inquiry into the Place of World Evangelisation in Western Protestant Ministerial Training, with Particular Reference to Alexander Duff's Chair of Evangelistic Theology*. Oslo, Norway: Egede-Instituttet; Hovedkommisjon Land og kirke, 1955.

Nash, Gerald A. *The American West Transformed*. Bloomington: Indiana University Press, 1985.

Neill, Stephen. *A History of Christian Missions*. New York: Penguin, 1964.

Newbigin, Lesslie. "Can the West Be Converted?" *Princeton Seminary Bulletin* 6, no. 1 (1985): 25–37.

————. *Foolishness to the Greeks: The Gospel and Western Culture*. Grand Rapids: Eerdmans, 1986.

————. *The Gospel in a Pluralist Society*. Grand Rapids: Eerdmans, 1989.

———. *The Open Secret: Sketches for a Missionary Theology.* Grand Rapids: Eerdmans, 1976.

———. *The Open Secret: An Introduction to the Theology of Mission.* Rev. ed. Grand Rapids: Eerdmans, 1995.

Niebuhr, H. Richard, Daniel Day Williams, and James Gustafson. *The Advancement of Theological Education.* New York: Harper, 1957.

———. *The Purpose of the Church and Its Ministry: Reflections on the Aims of Theological Education.* New York: Harper and Row, 1956.

Noll, Mark A. *The New Shape of World Christianity: How American Experience Reflects Global Faith.* Downers Grove, IL: IVP Academic, 2009.

———. *The Old World Religion in a New World.* Grand Rapids: Eerdmans, 2002.

Okrent, Daniel. *Last Call: The Rise and Fall of Prohibition.* New York: Scribner, 2011.

Orchard, Ronald K., and World Council of Churches. Commission on World Mission and Evangelism. *Witness in Six Continents; Records of the Meeting of the Commission on World Mission and Evangelism of the World Council of Churches Held in Mexico City, December 8th to 19th, 1963.* London: Published for the Division of World Mission and Evangelism of the World Council of Churches by Edinburgh House Press, 1964.

Packard, Josh, and Ashleigh Hope. *Church Refugees: Sociologists Reveal Why People Are Done with Church but Not with Faith.* Loveland, CO: Group Publishing, 2015.

Padgitt, Doug. *Church Re-Imagined: The Spiritual Formation of People in Communities of Faith.* Grand Rapids: Zondervan, 2005.

Panetta, Roger. *Dutch New York: The Roots of Hudson Valley Culture.* New York: Fordham University Press, 2009.

Parker, Geoffrey, Marshall Van Alstyne, and Sangeet Paul Choudary. *Platform Revolution: How Networked Markets Are Transforming the Economy and How to Make Them Work for You.* New York: W. W. Norton, 2016.

Parker, Michael. *The Kingdom of Character: The Student Volunteer Movement for Foreign Missions (1886–1926).* Lanham, MD: American Society of Missiology and University Press of America, 1998.

Payne, Jervis David. *Missional House Churches: Reaching Our Communities with the Gospel.* Colorado Springs, CO: Paternoster, 2008.

Peterson, Cheryl M. *Who Is the Church? An Ecclesiology for the Twenty-First Century.* Minneapolis: Fortress, 2013.

Pew Research Center. "The American Middle Class Is Losing Ground." Washington, DC: Pew Research Center, December 2015.

———. "Political Polarization in the American Public." Washington, DC: Pew Research Center, June 2014.

———. "The Religious Affiliation of US Immigrants: Majority Christian, Rising Share of Other Faiths." Washington, DC: Pew Research Center, May 17, 2013.

———. "U.S. Becoming Less Religious." Washington, DC: Pew Research Center, November 2015.

Philip, Robert. *Life and Times of the Reverend George Whitefield, M.A.* San Bernardino, CA: Ulan Press, 2012.

Porpora, Douglas. *Landscapes of the Soul: The Loss of Moral Meaning in American Life.* New York: Oxford University Press, 2001.

Priest, Robert, et al. "Researching the Short-Term Mission Movement." *Missiology: An International Review* 34, no. 4 (2006): 431–50.

Putnam, Robert D. *Bowling Alone: The Collapse and Revival of American Community*. New York: Simon and Schuster, 2000.

———. *Our Kids: The American Dream in Crisis*. New York: Simon and Schuster, 2015.

Putnam, Robert D., and David E. Campbell. *American Grace: How Religion Divides and Unites Us*. New York: Simon and Schuster, 2010.

Radner, Ephraim, and Philip Turner. *The Fate of Communion: The Agony of Anglicanism and the Future of a Global Church*. Grand Rapids: Eerdmans, 2006.

Rauschenbusch, Walter. *Christianity and the Social Crisis: The Classic that Woke Up the Church*. 1907; San Francisco: HarperOne, 2008.

Reich, Charles A. *The Greening of America*. New York: Bantam, 1971.

Richey, Russell E. *Denominationalism Illustrated and Explained*. Eugene, OR: Cascade Books, 2013.

———. "Denominations and Denominationalism: An American Morphology." In *Reimagining Denominationalism: Interpretive Essays*, edited by Robert Bruce Mullin and Russell E. Richey. New York: Oxford University Press, 1994.

Richey, Russell E., ed. *Denominationalism*. Nashville: Abingdon, 1977.

Robert, Dana L. *American Women in Mission: A Social History of Their Thought and Practice*. Macon, GA: Mercer University Press, 1997.

Rogers, Carl. *Carl Rogers on Personal Power: Inner Strength and Its Revolutionary Impact*. Philadelphia: Trans-Atlantic Publications, 1978.

Rome, Adam. *The Genius of Earth Day: How a 1970 Teach-In Unexpectedly Made the First Green Generation*. New York: Hill and Wang, 2014.

Roof, Wade Clark, and William McKinney. *American Mainline Religion: Its Changing Shape and Future*. New Brunswick, NJ: Rutgers University Press, 1987.

Roxburgh, Alan J. *Joining God, Remaking Church, Changing the World: The New Shape of the Church in Our Time*. New York: Morehouse Publishing, 2015.

———. *Missional: Joining God in the Neighborhood*. Grand Rapids: Baker, 2011.

———. *Structured for Mission: Renewing the Culture of the Church*. Downers Grove, IL: InterVarsity, 2015.

Roxburgh, Alan J., and Fred Romanuk. *The Missional Leader: Equipping Your Church to Reach a Changing World*. San Francisco: Jossey-Bass, 2006.

Rusaw, Rick, and Eric Swanson. *The Externally Focused Church*. Grand Rapids: Group Publishing, 2004.

Sanneh, Lamin O. *Translating the Message: The Missionary Impact on Culture*. Maryknoll, NY: Orbis, 1989.

———. *Whose Religion Is Christianity? The Gospel beyond the West*. Grand Rapids: Eerdmans, 2003.

Scherer, James A. "Future of Missiology as Academic Discipline in Seminary Education: Attempt at Reinterpretation and Clarification." *Missiology* 13, no. 4 (1985): 445–60.

———. *Gospel, Church, and Kingdom: Comparative Studies in World Mission Theology*. Minneapolis: Augsburg, 1987.

———. "Missiology as a Discipline and What It Includes." *Missiology* 15, no. 4 (1987): 507–22.

Schleiermacher, Friedrich. *On Religion: Speeches to Its Cultured Despisers.* Translated by John Oman. Louisville: Westminster John Knox, 1994.

Schmidlin, Joseph. *Catholic Mission History.* Translated by Matthias Braun. 1919; Techny, IL: Mission Press, 1933.

Schwarz, Christian A. *Natural Church Development: A Guide to Eight Essential Qualities of Healthy Churches.* St. Charles, IL: ChurchSmart Resources, 1996.

Searle, John R. *The Construction of Social Reality.* New York: Free Press, 1997.

Seligman, Adam. *Modernity's Wager: Authority, the Self, and Transcendence.* Princeton: Princeton University Press, 2000.

Shenk, Wilbert R. "Rufus Anderson and Henry Venn: A Special Relationship?" *International Bulletin of Missionary Research* 5, no. 4 (1981): 168–72.

Shenk, Wilbert R. ed. *Exploring Church Growth.* Grand Rapids: Eerdmans, 1983.

Shirky, Clay. *Here Comes Everybody: The Power of Organizing without Organizations.* New York: Penguin, 2008.

Sider, Ronald J., ed. *The Chicago Declaration.* Carol Stream, IL: Creation House, 1974.

Slotkin, Richard. "Nostalgia and Progress: Theodore Roosevelt's Myth of the Frontier." *American Quarterly* 33, no. 5 (1981): 608–37.

Smith, Christian, and Melinda Lundquist Denton. *American Evangelicalism: Embattled and Thriving.* Chicago: University of Chicago Press, 1998.

———. *Soul Searching: The Religious and Spiritual Lives of American Teenagers.* New York: Oxford University Press, 2005.

Smith, Christian, and Patricia Snell. *Souls in Transition: The Religious and Spiritual Lives of Emerging Adults.* New York: Oxford University Press, 2009.

Smith, James K. A. *Desiring the Kingdom: Worship, Worldview, and Cultural Formation.* Grand Rapids: Baker Academic, 2009.

———. *How (Not) to Be Secular: Reading Charles Taylor.* Grand Rapids: Eerdmans, 2014.

Soennichsen, John. *The Chinese Exclusion Act of 1882.* Westport, CT: Greenwood, 2011.

Sparks, Paul, Tim Soerens, and Dwight J. Friesen. *The New Parish: How Neighborhood Churches Are Transforming Mission, Discipleship and Community.* Downers Grove, IL: InterVarsity, 2014.

Steiner, George A. *Strategic Planning: What Every Manager Must Know.* New York: Free Press, 1971.

Sternberg, Robert J. *The Modern Land Grant University.* Lafayette, IN: Purdue University Press, 2014.

Stetzer, Ed. *Planting Missional Churches.* Nashville: Broadman and Holman Academic, 2006.

Surowiecki, James. *The Wisdom of Crowds: Why the Many Are Smarter Than the Few and How Collective Wisdom Shapes Business, Economies, Societies, and Nations.* New York: Doubleday, 2004.

Taylor, Charles. *The Ethics of Authenticity.* Cambridge, MA: Harvard University Press, 1991.

———. *Modern Social Imaginaries.* Durham, NC: Duke University Press, 2003.

———. *A Secular Age.* Cambridge, MA: Belknap Press of Harvard University Press, 2007.

Taylor, Frederick. *The Principles of Scientific Management*. 1911; Mineola, NY: Dover Publications, 1998.

Taylor, Keeanga-Jamahtta. *From #BlackLivesMatter to Black Liberation*. Chicago: Haymarket Books, 2016.

Thiselton, Anthony C. *The Holy Spirit—in Biblical Teaching, through the Centuries, and Today*. Grand Rapids: Eerdmans, 2013.

Thomas, Norman E., ed. *Classic Texts in Mission and World Christianity*. Maryknoll, NY: Orbis, 1995.

Thornton, Russell. *American Indian Holocaust and Survival: A Population History since 1492*. Norman: University of Oklahoma Press, 1990.

Thumma, Scott, and Dave Travis. *Beyond Megachurch Myths: What We Can Learn from America's Largest Churches*. San Francisco: Jossey-Bass, 2007.

Tickle, Phyllis. *The Great Emergence: How Christianity Is Changing and Why*. Grand Rapids: Baker, 2008.

Tinker, George E. *Missionary Conquest: The Gospel and Native American Cultural Genocide*. Minneapolis: Augsburg Fortress, 1993.

Tocqueville, Alexis de. *Democracy in America*. 1835; New York: CreateSpace Independent Publishing Platform, 2014.

Toffler, Alvin. *Future Shock*. New York: Random House, 1970.

———. *Third Wave*. New York: Bantam Books, 1980.

Torrey, R. A., and A. C. Dixon. *The Fundamentals: A Testimony to the Truth*. Grand Rapids: Baker Book House, 1972; reprint.

Troy, Gil. *The Reagan Revolution: A Very Short Introduction*. New York: Oxford University Press, 2009.

Turkle, Sherry. *Alone Together: Why We Expect More from Technology and Less from Each Other*. New York: Basic Books, 2011.

———. *Reclaiming Conversation: The Power of Talk in a Digital Age*. New York: Penguin, 2015.

Turner, Frederick Jackson, and Wilbur R. Jacobs. *The Frontier in American History*. 5th ed. Tucson: University of Arizona Press, 1986.

Tutu, Desmond. *No Future without Forgiveness*. New York: Doubleday, 1999.

Tuveson, Ernest Lee. *Redeemer Nation: The Idea of America's Millennial Role*. Chicago: University of Chicago Press, 1968.

Twomey, Gerald S. *The "Preferential Option for the Poor" in Catholic Social Thought from John XXIII to John Paul II*. Lewiston, NY: Edwin Mellen, 2005.

Van Gelder, Craig. "An Ecclesiastical Geno-Project: Unpacking the DNA of Denominations and Denominationalism." In *The Missional Church and Denominations: Helping Congregations Develop a Missional Identity*, edited by Craig Van Gelder, 12–45. Grand Rapids: Eerdmans, 2008.

———. *The Essence of the Church: A Community Created by the Spirit*. Grand Rapids: Baker, 2000.

———. "Gospel and Our Culture View." In *Evaluating the Church Growth Movement: 5 Views*, edited by Gary L. McIntosh. Grand Rapids: Zondervan, 2004.

———. "How Missiology Can Help Inform the Conversation about the Missional Church in Context." In *The Missional Church in Context: Helping Congregations*

Develop Contextual Ministry, edited by Craig Van Gelder. Grand Rapids: Eerdmans, 2007.

———. "Method in Light of Scripture and in Relation to Hermeneutics." *Journal of Religious Leadership* 3, nos. 1 and 2 (Spring and Fall 2004): 43–73.

———. "Understanding the Church in North America." In *Missional Church: A Vision for the Sending of the Church in North America*, edited by Darrell Guder. Grand Rapids: Eerdmans, 1998.

Van Gelder, Craig, ed. *The Missional Church and Denominations: Helping Congregations Develop a Missional Identity*. Grand Rapids: Eerdmans, 2008.

———. *The Missional Church and Leadership Formation: Helping Congregations Develop Leadership Capacity*. Grand Rapids: Eerdmans, 2009.

———. *The Missional Church in Context: Helping Congregations Develop Contextual Ministry*. Grand Rapids: Eerdmans, 2007.

Van Gelder, Craig, and Dwight Zscheile. *The Missional Church in Perspective: Mapping Trends and Shaping the Conversation*. Grand Rapids: Baker Academic, 2011.

Vespa, Jonathan, Jamie M. Lewis, and Rose M. Kreider. "America's Families and Living Arrangements: 2012." Washington, DC: US Census Bureau (August 2013).

Vicedom, Georg F. *The Mission of God: An Introduction to a Theology of Mission*. Translated by Gilbert A. Thiele and Dennis Hilgendorf. St. Louis: Concordia, 1965.

Volf, Miroslav. *After Our Likeness: The Church as the Image of the Trinity*. Grand Rapids: Eerdmans, 1998.

———. *A Public Faith: How Followers of Christ Should Serve the Common Good*. Grand Rapids: Brazos, 2011.

Wagner, Rachel. *Godwired: Religion, Ritual, and Virtual Reality*. New York: Routledge, 2012.

Wallis, Jim. *Christians, Liberals, and the Fight for America's Future*. Grand Rapids: Brazos, 2013.

Walls, Andrew. *The Missionary Movement in Christian History: Studies in the Transmission of the Faith*. Maryknoll, NY: Orbis, 1996.

Ward, Graham S. *The Politics of Discipleship: Becoming Postmaterial Citizens*. Grand Rapids: Baker Academic, 2009.

Warnock, Raphael G. *The Divided Mind of the Black Church: Theology, Piety, and Public Witness*. New York: New York University Press, 2014.

Weber, Max. *The Theory of Social and Economic Organization*. New York: The Free Press, 1947.

Welker, Michael. *God the Spirit*. Minneapolis: Fortress, 1994.

Wells, Spencer. *The Journey of Man: A Genetic Odyssey*. New York: Random House, 2004.

White, James Emery. *The Rise of the Nones*. Grand Rapids: Baker, 2014.

White, Ronald C., Jr., and C. Howard Hopkins. *The Social Gospel: Religion and Reform in Changing America*. Philadelphia: Temple University Press, 1976.

Whyte, William H., Jr. *The Organization Man*. New York: Simon and Schuster, 1956.

Williams, Daniel K. *God's Own Party: The Making of the Christian Right*. New York: Oxford University Press, reprint edition 2012.

Williams, Rowan. "Traditional and Emerging Church." Address to the General Synod of the Anglican Church. York, UK, July 14, 2003.

Wilson-Hartgrove, Jonathan. *New Monasticism: What It Has to Say to Today's Church*. Grand Rapids: Brazos, 2008.

Winter, Gibson. *The Suburban Captivity of the Churches: An Analysis of Protestant Responsibility in the Expanding Metropolis*. New York: Macmillan, 1962.

Winter, Ralph D. *The Twenty-Five Unbelievable Years, 1945–1969*. Pasadena: William Carey Library, 1970.

Wister, Robert J. "Theological Education in Seminaries." In *Theological Education in the Catholic Tradition*, edited by Patrick W. Carey and Earl C. Muller, SJ. New York: Crossroad, 1997.

Woodard, Colin. *American Nations: A History of the Eleven Rival Regional Cultures of North America*. New York: Penguin, 2011.

Wright, Christopher J. T. *The Mission of God: Unlocking the Bible's Grand Narrative*. Downers Grove, IL: IVP Academic, 2006.

Wuthnow, Robert. *After Heaven: Spirituality in America since the 1950s*. Berkeley: University of California Press, 1998.

———. *After the Baby Boomers: How Twenty- and Thirty-Somethings Are Shaping the Future of American Religion*. Princeton: Princeton University Press, 2007.

———. *American Mythos: Why Our Best Efforts to Be a Better Nation Fall Short*. Princeton: Princeton University Press, 2006.

———. *The Crisis in the Churches: Spiritual Malaise, Fiscal Woe*. New York: Oxford University Press, 1997.

———. *Loose Connections: Joining Together in America's Fragmented Communities*. Cambridge, MA: Harvard University Press, 1998.

———. *The Restructuring of American Religion*. Princeton: Princeton University Press, 1988.

Yoder, John Howard. *The Politics of Jesus*. Grand Rapids: Eerdmans, 1972.

Yong, Amos. *Who Is the Holy Spirit? A Walk with the Apostles*. Brewster, MA: Paraclete Press, 2011.

Yusuf, Shahid. *Development Economics through the Decades: A Critical Look at Thirty Years of the World Development Report*. District of Columbia: World Bank Publications, 2008.

Zabriskie, Stewart C. *Total Ministry: Reclaiming the Ministry of All God's People*. Bethesda, MD: Alban Institute, 1995.

Zizioulas, John D. *Being as Communion: Studies in Personhood and the Church*. Crestwood, NY: St. Vladimir's Seminary Press, 1985.

———. *Communion and Otherness: Further Studies in Personhood and the Church*. New York: T. & T. Clark, 2007.

Zscheile, Dwight. *The Agile Church: Spirit-Led Innovation in an Uncertain Age*. New York: Morehouse Publishing, 2014.

———. "Social Networking and Church Systems." *Word & World* 30, no. 3 (Summer 2010): 249–57.

Index

Titles Published in

THE GOSPEL AND OUR CULTURE SERIES

Lois Y. Barrett et al., *Treasure in Clay Jars: Patterns in Missional Faithfulness* (2004)

James V. Brownson et al., *StormFront: The Good News of God* (2003)

Michael W. Goheen, ed., *Reading the Bible Missionally* (2016)

Michael J. Gorman, *Becoming the Gospel: Paul, Participation, and Mission* (2015)

Darrell L. Guder, *Called to Witness: Doing Missional Theology* (2015)

Darrell L. Guder, *The Continuing Conversion of the Church* (2000)

Darrell L. Guder, ed., *Missional Church: A Vision for the Sending of the Church in North America* (1998)

George R. Hunsberger, *Bearing the Witness of the Spirit: Lesslie Newbigin's Theology of Cultural Plurality* (1998)

George R. Hunsberger, *The Story That Chooses Us: A Tapestry of Missional Vision* (2015)

George R. Hunsberger and Craig Van Gelder, eds., *The Church between Gospel and Culture: The Emerging Mission in North America* (1996)

Stefan Paas, *Church Planting in the Secular West: Learning from the European Experience* (2016)

Craig Van Gelder, ed., *Confident Witness — Changing World: Rediscovering the Gospel in North America* (1999)

Craig Van Gelder and Dwight J. Zscheile, *Participating in God's Mission: A Theological Missiology for the Church in America* (2018)